8 St. Aldate's Oxford
TEL 47262

2/6/1957

My dear BB

I have owed you a long letter for a long time,
— ever since I received yours in Persia. How infinitely
remote in time my visit to Persia now seems ; and yet it
is only ~~just~~ a month since I returned. And how
complacent I feel at having been to some place
unknown to you ! Of course you must go. But if you
go, may I give you one piece of useful practical
advice? Don't go by bus from Baghdad. I did.
In retrospect I wouldn't have missed it for words.
But in prospect ... never, never, never again. It was
a pilgrims' bus : the pilgrims go from Persia to
Iraq, from the land of ~~secret~~ ancient bigotry to the
land of secularism and reason, in order to bury their
dead in the holy cities of the Shi'ites there ; and
having done so, they return by bus, with the
empty coffins and such additional passengers as may
choose to travel with them. The journey takes two
days, and very long days too, from 6.0 a.m. to
midnight. And it was full of incident. There were
violent quarrels between passengers and driver, which I
would like to think were about some abstruse point of
Muslim ~~doctrine~~ theology, but which more probably concerned the

Letters from Oxford

Letters from Oxford

HUGH TREVOR-ROPER
to BERNARD BERENSON

Edited by Richard Davenport-Hines

Weidenfeld & Nicolson
LONDON

First published in Great Britain in 2006
by Weidenfeld & Nicolson

1 3 5 7 9 10 8 6 4 2

A CIP catalogue record for this book is
available from the British Library.

ISBN-13 9 780297 850847
ISBN-10 0 297 85084 9

Typeset by Input Data Services Ltd, Frome
Printed by Butler and Tanner Ltd, Frome and London.

Weidenfeld & Nicolson

The Orion Publishing Group Ltd
Orion House
5 Upper Saint Martin's Lane
London, WC2H 9EA

The Orion Publishing Group's policy is to use papers that
are natural, renewable and recyclable products and made
from wood grown in sustainable forests. The logging and
manufacturing processes are expected to conform to the
environmental regulations of the country of origin.

www.orionbooks.co.uk

Contents

Illustrations

Preface

This book contains letters from Hugh Trevor-Roper (Lord Dacre of Glanton) to two friends in Italy, Bernard Berenson and his companion Nicky Mariano, together with brief extracts from those of their replies that are necessary to make sense of the sequence. Berenson was in his eighties when his correspondence with Trevor-Roper began, and his contribution to their exchanges was increasingly repetitious and uninformative. The bulk of Berenson's letters – begging for Trevor-Roper's news, listing the names of recent visitors, regretting his failing powers – have accordingly been omitted. The originals of Trevor-Roper's letters are held in the Berenson Archive at Villa I Tatti, now the Harvard University Center for Italian Renaissance Studies, Florence, to which admirable institution I make grateful acknowledgment for permission to quote from both sides of the correspondence. The originals of the Berenson and Mariano letters are deposited in the Dacre papers at Christ Church, Oxford. The Beinecke Library at Yale University holds the two letters from Trevor-Roper to Wallace Notestein that are reproduced as an Appendix to this book.

There are omissions and deletions in this published sequence. I have omitted short letters from Trevor-Roper giving travel plans and other humdrum details.[1] I have also deleted the over-elaborate valedictory courtesies in the final paragraphs of Trevor-Roper's letters, as indicated by ellipses in squared brackets [. . .]. (All ellipses that are not in squared brackets occur in the original texts of the letters concerned.) I have also removed – without any textual indication – several libellous passages; while some of these suppressions are regrettable, others, I think, matter not at all. A few words or phrases that, although not actionable, might prove unduly hurtful to the living have also been deleted.

An explanation of my footnoting is needed. Hugh Trevor-Roper delighted in books like Pierre Bayle's *Dictionnaire historique et critique*, with it biographical entries on biblical, classical and historical characters accompanied by a panoply of analytical, argumentative, philosophical and theological footnotes, and he lamented to Berenson, in a letter of May 1951, that the art of footnotes had perished. Conversely, he deprecated collections of letters and diaries – as distinct from histories – with obtrusive or over-elaborate editorial apparatus. For compilers of footnotes in editions of correspondence he would have commended the four watchwords first devised by Anne Olivier Bell, and later invoked by Henry Hardy, when they were preparing their exemplary editions of Virginia Woolf's diaries and Isaiah Berlin's letters: *Accuracy, Relevance, Concision, Interest.* But watch-words tend to oversimplify. If accuracy is a matter of effort, and concision is a matter of skill, relevance and interest require editorial judgement about readers' tastes and needs. Though I have not indulged in Bayle's style of editorial commentary, I have provided more notes than Trevor-Roper, in certain moods, might have judged necessary. To give one example, this book contains copious quotations in Latin, ancient Greek and some modern European languages that he would have disdained to have translated in footnotes, but which must be rendered into English for a 21st-century readership. There are countless allusions to international history, the arts and politics, and many asides about Oxford institutions and personalities, which he might have scorned to have explained but which must be glossed if many readers are not to feel excluded from his world. In biographical footnotes about British men and women, it has been easier to be concise; but in the case of many foreigners – notably refugees from Nazi or communist persecution who found work in Oxford University, but also other indi-viduals who were embroiled in twentieth-century wars – I have chosen to give more extensive details in the hope that what is lost in concision is gained in interest.

The editor of a book of this sort becomes a heavy debtor to many people. My greatest debt is to Blair Worden, executor of the Dacre literary estate, for entrusting me with the task of editing this book and for many agreeable contacts since. Sabina Anrep with the utmost unselfishness has agreed to my publishing letters exchanged between her great-aunt Nicky Mariano and Trevor-Roper: my gratitude to her is profound. I am indebted to the generosity of Professor Alastair Hamilton for permission to quote from the unpublished letters of his father Hamish Hamilton; and to the like gen-erosity of Professor Timothy Sprigge for permission to quote from the unpublished letters of his stepmother Sylvia Sprigge. Xenia Dennen has kindly consented to my use of extracts from the correspondence between Berenson and her mother, Xandra Dacre. Nicolas Barker has allowed me to quote from an unpublished letter of his father Sir Ernest Barker. The Isaiah Berlin Literary Trust has allowed me to quote extracts both from an unpublished letter written by Sir Isaiah Berlin and also from his published writings. Frank Giles, Lord Gilmour of Craigmillar, David Hopkins, Christopher Pemberton and Sir Peter Ramsbotham have also generously consented to the use made of their letters to Trevor-Roper or to myself. Every effort has been made to trace the owners of other copyright material used in this book: I apologise if the rights of any copyright holders have inadvertently been infringed, and the publishers will be pleased to make full acknowledgments in future editions of the book.

Fiorella Superbi and Giovanni Pagliarulo welcomed me to the Archivio Berenson at Villa I Tatti with convivial warmth, and handled my eager demands with immaculate efficiency. It is not conventional civility, but heartfelt gratitude, that makes me say that I will always remember my visit to them with the utmost pleasure. Mrs Judith Curthoys, archivist at Christ Church, Oxford, has responded to my importunities with cheerful patience. The incomparable amenities at the London Library, of which (at the instigation of Logan Pearsall Smith) Trevor-Roper became a lifelong member in 1941, have been indispensable to my work.

Sir Hugh Lloyd-Jones has identified, translated, checked and corrected quotations from Greek and Latin in these letters with patient kindness, and noted infelicities or superfluities in several footnotes: I am indebted to the exacting standards that he has set. My friend Alan Bell read much of the typescript of this book with meticulous care, and offered corrections and improvements, which I have gratefully adopted. I thank Fiona Howard for her scrupulous care in turning Trevor-Roper's holograph letters into a typed text; Xenia Dennen for welcoming me to The Old Rectory at Didcot when her stepfather's papers were still deposited there; Adam Sisman, Trevor-Roper's future biographer, for advice and encouragement; Benjamin Buchan, a most sympathetic, conscientious and attentive editor at Weidenfeld; Jenny Davenport and Christopher Phipps, who helped me to prune over-floriferous annotations, and sanitised the text of errors of taste and fact; my agent Bill Hamilton, of A.M. Heath, for an act of generosity which he would blush to have particularised; Simon Barrow of People in Business for providing photocopying facilities; and Cosmo Davenport-Hines for technical advice.

Many others have helped in the preparation for publication of this collection: Lord Beaumont of Whitley; Mike Bott, archivist of Reading University; Father Ian Brayley, of Campion Hall, Oxford; Ged Clapson of the Jesuit community in Farm Street, London; Patric Dickinson, Richmond Herald; Lady Antonia Fraser; Lord Gage; David Gelber; Lord Gladwyn; Henry Hardy, of Wolfson College, Oxford; David Hopkins; Martin Isepp; Miriam Joseph of Pius XII Memorial Library at St Louis University; Marina Majdalany; Robert Noel, Lancaster Herald; Richard Ollard; Richard Rhodes; Professor Richard Shannon; Lady Spender; Nicholas Tate; and Lady Thomas of Swynnerton. I thank them all.

Everyone but the editor is absolved from responsibility for the final contents of Trevor-Roper's *Letters from Oxford.*

---

[1] Those to Berenson are dated 13 March 1948, 3 February 1949, 25 February 1949, 18 March 1949, 8 April 1949, 27 October 1949, 28 November 1949, 12 January 1950, 28 February 1951, 20 March 1953 and 23 August 1957; and those to Mariano, 16 April 1948, 16 January 1950, 14 July 1953, 23 December 1953, 10 January 1954, 30 December 1954, 27 April 1961, 8 December 1961, 23 March 1962 and 1 May 1965.

Introduction

'There have been memorable moments in my life,' the young historian Hugh Trevor-Roper wrote in 1942, 'moments when I have deliberately turned my back for ever on an old world, or suddenly through a narrow aperture, glimpsed a new, and gone out in search of it. The first was when, at the age of fifteen, in my study at Charterhouse, I discovered Milton's Nativity Ode, and realised the existence of poetry. Another was in the same room, when I was construing Homer. Hitherto my progress had been slow; the forms were unfamiliar, the vocabulary new. Then, quite suddenly, – it was in the 7th Odyssey, the passage describing the Gardens of Alcinous – I found that, at last, I could read it freely and easily and enjoy it. On I read, far past the appointed terminus, till late at night, fascinated; and all my leisure hours for long afterwards were spent in reading Homer, till I knew all the Iliad and Odyssey. In all the variations of my tastes and standards (and very few have lasted intact from my schooldays) I have never wavered in my passion for Homer and Milton.

'And then there was that moment in the summer of 1936, when, walking round the Christ Church Meadow, and pondering on the complicated subtleties of St Augustine's theological system, which I had long tried to take seriously, I suddenly realised the undoubted truth that metaphysics are metaphysical, and having no premises to connect them to this world, need not detain us while we are denizens of it. And at once, like a balloon that has no moorings, I saw the whole metaphysical world rise and vanish out of sight in the upper air, where it rightly belongs; and I have neither seen it, nor felt its absence, since.

'And again, two years later, when the events that preceded the Munich conference brought me in haste to Oxford, and I sat in the Merton Common Room, and Guy Chilver outlined for us all the principles of a sound British foreign policy, explaining, at great length, that in dealing with the problems of Czechoslovakia, we must not allow moral considerations, which are alone valid, to be in the least affected, even to be supported, by strategic considerations, which are inherently immoral, etc., etc.; I listened to these follies with silent contempt and disgust, and I was aware at that moment that another balloon was vanishing for ever into the stratosphere, carrying with it, to their proper home, all those chattering disputants and dogmatists and nebulous left-wing humanitarian dons who, for twenty years, had made the word academic into a synonym for ridiculous.'[1]

Trevor-Roper experienced these epiphanies between the ages of fifteen and twenty-four; and with maturity in the 1940s he underwent the less abrupt but no less decisive process of discipleship. He found, in succession, two inspirational mentors, both of them old men, superbly well-read, brilliantly voluble, prolific letter-writers – and brothers-in-law. They were the Chelsea dilettante Logan Pearsall Smith, whom he first met in 1940; and Bernard Berenson, the art historian, whom he first met in 1947. Trevor-Roper was attracted not only by the suavity, intelligence, vivacity and discriminating values of both men but by their playful naughtiness. Berenson ranked his brother-in-law 'the most irresponsible man I have ever known': Trevor-Roper, talking with reverence of Smith, said with a smile, 'He was a wicked old man; but I like wicked old men.'[2] Berenson, too, was a mischievous old rogue. He first met Mary McCarthy, shortly after reading her story 'Dottie Makes an Honest Woman of Herself' about a woman being fitted with a contraceptive device, waiting for Contessa Anna-Maria Cicogna's launch on the jetty of the Hotel Europa in Venice; he sidled up to her, and whispered, 'Miss McCarthy, have you brought your pessary with you?'[3]

In February 1940, when Trevor-Roper was aged twenty-six, his first book, *Archbishop Laud*, was published by Macmillan. By then he had left his research fellowship at Merton College, Oxford, for war service and, although nominally a lieutenant in a cavalry regiment, was working in the offices of MI5 in Wormwood Scrubs prison as a member of the Radio Security Service, reading and analysing the flood of intercepted German messages. *Archbishop Laud* received rapturous reviews. 'With this life of Laud a new star, of great promise, appears on the horizon,' A.L. Rowse proclaimed in the *New Statesman*. 'Mr Trevor-Roper writes with such vivacity and verve, with such a lively sense of amusement and good judgement both of men and of politics [...] Anyone who wants to know what the best contemporary young historians are thinking – I mean really contemporary and not the eminent holders of professional chairs mooning away in nineteenth-century modes of thought – could do no better than read Mr Trevor-Roper's Introduction to his book. It reads almost like a manifesto. The joke is that though it comes very much to what we Marxists think, it is in fact written by a young Conservative. The explanation is just that this young Conservative is very intelligent.'[4] Trevor-Roper prized rather more the compliments of an Anglican churchman and scholar whom he greatly respected: Herbert Hensley Henson, the former Bishop of Durham, who praised *Archbishop Laud* in the lead review of *The Spectator* of 9 February 1940 as 'detached, discerning ... and brilliantly written.'[5]

These reviews drew the curiosity of Logan Pearsall Smith, who read *Archbishop Laud*, found it scholarly and witty, and invited its author to call. Trevor-Roper arrived dressed in khaki, 'on some mysterious job connected with the war', as Smith wrote, and proved to be such 'a charming, erudite young man' that he had memorised many of Smith's published maxims.[6] As the Blitz rained down on London, he joined the court that Smith held in the house that he shared with his sister Alys Russell in St Leonard's Terrace, Chelsea. (Other wartime courtiers – united by their love of books and gossip – included Robert Gathorne-Hardy, Rose Macaulay, Cyril Connolly, Raymond Mortimer, Robert Trevelyan, Paul Sudley, James Lees-Milne, Dame Una Pope-Hennessy and her sons John and James, and a young American whom Trevor-Roper disliked, Stuart Preston.) In 1941 the Radio Security Service, and Trevor-Roper with it, was transferred to MI6's Counter-Espionage Section based at Arkley in Hertfordshire, and concentrated its efforts on the systematic interception of messages from the German intelligence service, the Abwehr. In May 1943 Trevor-Roper was made head of the Radio Intelligence Section, a new branch of MI6: its three other officers were Charles Stuart, Gilbert Ryle and Stuart Hampshire. He had a free day each week from his duties: in the hunting season he would hitch-hike across southern England in his military uniform, taking rides from brick-lorries or milk-vans, to reach convenient meets of the Bicester & Warden Hill or Whaddon Chase hounds, where his horse would be waiting for him. Often, out of the hunting season, he would call for tea at St Leonard's Terrace or sometimes be taken by Smith for a rationed restaurant lunch at the Ivy. In 1942 Smith made Trevor-Roper the chief heir in his will,[7] which was, however, revoked shortly before his death. Characteristically, Trevor-Roper did not mind forfeiting the money, but was exasperated by his difficulties in obtaining the books that he had been bequeathed under the new will. Smith's greatest gift to his protégé had, anyway, been given in his lifetime: he passed on his literary precepts, which are evident in everything that Trevor-Roper wrote – books, essays, reviews and supremely his private letters – after 1940.

Partly because Trevor-Roper was in Germany, researching *The Last Days of Hitler*, and partly because Smith had suffered a nervous breakdown and was forbidden visitors, the two men seldom met in the nine months before Smith died on 2 March 1946. 'A great section of my life seems to me to have ended with that death. No one else has had such an effect on my personal history. It is ineradicable,' Trevor-Roper wrote *in requiem*. 'What did I learn from him? When I ask myself this question, I do not know how to answer it, for I learnt everything. My whole philosophy seems, now that I consider it retrospectively, to have come from him, and what I would have been without him I cannot envisage, cannot imagine.

'From that day when, walking alone around the Christ Church Meadow, I had resolved to trifle no more among the twigs of matter but to try to understand the root of it, I had, for two years, forsaken all literary and artistic interests. I neglected poetry & prose; cared nothing for music or pictures, read neither Gibbon nor Homer, but only studied, and studied only essential monographs and laborious theses; and in the book that I was myself writing, on Laud, I consciously ignored the temptation of style. I only sought to understand, & to this extent, though I understood imperfectly, it is at least an honest book. But neither humanity nor divinity touched it, & therefore it is also incomplete & a narrow book. I cannot now think why Logan thought so highly of it.

'For it was Logan who afterwards re-interested me, in a time when the war had separated me from desperate academic study, in style & the world of sensation, & enabled me thus to fill in the hard structural pattern of thought I had thus evolved; and how can I express adequate gratitude for such an experience? Who showed me that life is short, and three parts routine, & most of it comedy, & can only be saved from triviality & given significance by some ideal to which all else, or at least much else [...] including humane pleasures and meritorious aims, and especially power and success, must be sacrificed, as by the merchant who sold out to reinvest all in one pearl of great price; and that style is an ideal worthy of this sacrifice. This I learnt from him and believed, & I still believe it, and shall, I hope, continue, like Gibbon, to value reading above the wealth of India. For in his life & conversation, among the tinkle of coronets and the wild extravagant gossip, and the exquisite relish of high life and *la comédie humaine*, of which it was also witness, he illustrated this philosophy to me so vividly that if it has not become mine, at least mine can never be altogether emancipated from its influence.'[8]

Trevor-Roper was a major Oxford figure for half a century: the letters in this book are those of an Oxford don. Yet he was always ambivalent about the university. 'I love Oxford, and I hate it,' he wrote in 1945. 'When I remember it I love it; for memory is a romantic organ, and perhaps I only remember my youthful illusions of the place, – gay company, happy conversations; intellectual interests; walking hounds through the scented fields of Garsington & Cuddesdon early on summer mornings; days of study in the cool & spacious upper reading room of Bodley, or my own high and luminous room in Merton; evenings spent sociably over Stilton cheese & claret in the Christ Church Buttery. But when I visit Oxford, now, in wartime, the sixth year of the war, I hate it; its dreary company of old men, haters of learning & intellectual activity, envious of the absent, fearful of their return. They know they are despised; secretly they despise themselves; but they dare not ask the cause or seek the remedy, for knowledge, to such as those, is as death.'[9]

The hatefulness of Oxford came to seem epitomised by the figure of A.L. Rowse. In 1943, at Rowse's earnest entreaty, Trevor-Roper arranged for him to visit Pearsall Smith in Chelsea. Smith was not impressed. 'Though he is a good historian, I found that he hasn't read any history,' he said afterwards. 'Why, I don't believe he has even read Gibbon.' Trevor-Roper 'realised', as he noted in his diary, 'that of course Logan was right, and I had known Rowse for some years without realising it; for herein Rowse is typical of modern Oxford historians. He lacks the large, European background that the historians of the last century had, that Tawney and Hammond manage still to preserve. There is neither breadth nor depth in him. He is provincial, – a good provincial journalist.'[10] It was the small-town atmosphere of Oxford that Trevor-Roper railed against: he liked Richard Hillary's book, *The Last Enemy*, so he wrote in 1943, for 'representing to me the Oxford I like to believe in, – a gay sceptical tolerant enquiring unshockable world, enjoying experience for its own sake, and unimpressed by proprieties & slogans'.[11] Yet the university, he knew, was crammed with 'old, embittered, repressed, obscurantist figures who must also have their say, and be answered'.[12]

During the war years Trevor-Roper was busy with Intelligence work: he analysed data, compiled reports, kept diaries, but was bursting with creative frustration and felt that he was often working to little purpose. 'I am consciously ambitious,' he had explained in the introspective 'Autopsy' that he wrote at Pearsall Smith's instigation in 1943. 'My outlook is entirely intellectual. Almost everything I choose to do is consciously directed to an intended aim. I am always trying to solve problems [...] My ambition is to solve intellectual problems and present my solutions in satisfying aesthetic form.'[13] Finally, in 1945, Stalin's stubborn denial that Hitler had killed himself in his Berlin bunker on 30 April, the toadying lies of Andrei Vyshinsky, the Soviet commissar for foreign relations, and the connivance of other Communist officials (who pretended to believe that the British were concealing Hitler's mistress Eva Braun) created an exciting opportunity for him to fulfil just such an ambition. Stories were rife that Hitler had escaped by air or submarine to a Baltic island or a Rhineland fortress, was secreted in a Spanish monastery or on a South American ranch, even that he was being harboured by bandits in mountainous Albania. Trevor-Roper, who spent much of the war monitoring the Abwehr's radio traffic, or analysing their intercepts, was instructed to interrogate German intelligence officers with a view to scotching some of these wild tales inspired by Soviet propaganda.

One evening in September 1945 he went drinking with his good friend Dick White, then chief of Counter-Intelligence in the British zone in Germany, afterwards director-general of MI5 and later head of the Secret Intelligence Service, and another MI5 operative, Herbert Hart, sub-sequently Professor of Jurisprudence at Oxford. (In the summer of 1944 Trevor-Roper had been recruited to 'the War Room', a counter-intelligence group preparing for the occupation of a defeated Germany, chaired by White.) 'Over the third bottle of hock', Trevor-Roper recorded, 'I was drawing on this reservoir of conversational raw-material [...] about the last highly charged days in Hitler's Bunker. "But this is most important!" exclaimed Dick, his eyes popping, as they sometimes do, out of universal eagerness of spirit. "No one has yet made any systematic study of the evidence, or even found any evidence, and we are going to have all kinds of difficulty unless something is done. Already the Germans are saying that the old boy's alive, and the journalists are encouraging them, and the Russians are accusing us of concealing Eva Braun".' Trevor-Roper seized White's hint, left within days to interrogate Albert Speer, and then set about the systematic collection and evaluation of evidence about the fate of Hitler and his entourage. 'It was', he recalled, 'a fascinating piece of historical research – a fig for Archbishop Laud; he never led me, or could have led me, on those delightful journeys, motoring through the deciduous golden groves of Schleswig-Holstein, and coming, on an evening, when the sun had just set but the light had not yet gone, and the wild duck were out for their last flight over the darkening waters, to the great Danish castle of Ploen, gazing like a sentinel over those white autumnal lakes. Of the compo-tations and convivia which were a necessary part of my researches it is not necessary to speak; all the same I had deeper and more hilarious bouts over Hitler than ever I had over Laud.'[14]

Trevor-Roper gave a press conference summarising his findings on 1 November 1945, and submitted a report that was circulated in the Cabinet and the Quadripartite Intelligence Committee. Dick White encouraged him to amplify the report, and during the evenings of the spring and summer terms at Oxford in 1946 *The Last Days of Hitler* was written. Objections to its publication were raised by Sir Stewart Menzies, head of the Secret Intelligence Service and Cerberus of official secrets; but White and Harold Caccia of the Foreign Office outwitted him. 'Here is a best seller, if ever there was one', declared Alan Bullock, the future biographer of Hitler, when *The Last Days of Hitler* was published by Macmillan in March 1947.[15] It was a work of rare intellectual and stylistic vitality. Trevor-Roper's character sketches of the Nazi leadership and of Hitler's sordid, cringing entourage had a deadly accuracy. His detective reconstruction of Hitler's last eight days, his accounts of the Führer's ranting and craze for destruction, his evocation of the claustrophobic tension in Hitler's underground lair, all had a palpable impact on his readers.

The commercial success of *The Last Days of Hitler* earned its author a small fortune (Sir Alexander Korda even bought an option on the film rights), but made him the object of envious carping even from ostensible Oxford friends. 'Trevor-Roper is a fearful man', Maurice Bowra wrote to Evelyn Waugh in July 1947, 'short-sighted, with dripping eyes, shows off all the time, sucks up to me, boasts, is far from poor owing to his awful book, on every page of which there is a howler.'[16] Outside Oxford, *The Last Days of Hitler* gained Trevor-Roper a great reputation: he was described in June as the 'young Christ Church don who at the moment has the attention of the whole English-speaking world'.[17] Accordingly David Astor, then foreign editor of the *Observer*, asked him to visit Italy and France as a special correspondent reporting on the communists' electoral strategy of trying to recruit the Mediterranean peasantry to their cause. Pearsall Smith's sister Alys Russell, who regretted that Trevor-Roper had been superseded as her brother's testamentary heir, heard of the projected visit to Italy. 'Do try to see my bro. in law Bernard Berenson, if you can spare the time,' she urged. 'Ring up his Sec. Miss Mariano at I Tatti [. . .] I will tell her to expect a ring from you. BB will love to see you to talk about Logan & books & politics.'[18] Trevor-Roper left England on 10 July, motored to Italy in the elegant grey Bentley that he had bought with his literary royalties, and stayed in Rome from 17 to 27 July: afterwards he spent three weeks of August in France. Both in Rome and in Paris he interviewed British and American diplomats, notably Labour attachés, together with politicians and other observers. As he wrote to a former SIS colleague at the British Embassy in Lisbon: 'I had a most enjoyable time in Italy, where I lived in great opulence and comfort and plenty, and had an interview with Togliatti and a lot of communist bores, and attended the canonisation of a hard-currency saint (a scene of magnificent farce).'[19]

For Trevor-Roper, in retrospect, the most significant event of his time in Italy was not his interviews with communists but his visit, on 30 July, to Bernard Berenson. The old man was not staying at I Tatti, his villa outside Florence (with its long cypress avenue that had been planted at Pearsall

Smith's suggestion), but at Casa al Dono, 'that exquisite mountain retreat at Vallombrosa' (as Trevor-Roper described it)[20] to which he and his companion Nicky Mariano always went to escape the summer heat. He was armed with introductions to Berenson from Alys Russell, who often likened him to her still-adored ex-husband Bertrand Russell: 'Hugh has a reserve or perhaps shyness that it takes time to overcome. But his intellect has a clear and cutting quality like Bertie's.'[21]

Despite the difference in age between the two men (Berenson was eighty-two in July 1947, Trevor-Roper thirty-three), their well-matched interests ensured that this first meeting was a reciprocated delight. Berenson had the spacious, comprehensive European outlook that Trevor-Roper required in historians before he could admire them. The American critic Alfred Kazin, who met him in 1947, pictured him 'at I Tatti as another Voltaire at Ferney, a kind of European intelligence office – yet subtly remote from the pressure of events'.[22] Berenson had created his working life out of 'Seeing and Knowing' (the title of his aesthetic credo published in 1951), and Trevor-Roper's imagination, too, was essentially visual. 'I can't', he confessed, 'understand anything that I can't present to my imagination in a pictorial form; and when I comprehend anything vividly, it's always in the terms of some visual image; which is one reason why I so admire the writers of the Jacobean & Caroline age, with their rich, elaborate fancies, Bacon, and Donne, and Milton, and Sir Thomas Browne.'[23] The spiritual outlook of Trevor-Roper and Berenson was also congruent. 'In religion I am a complete sceptic; but I am not irreligious,' Trevor-Roper had observed in his 'Autopsy' in words that applied to Berenson too. 'I can feel both awe and devotion; the numinosity of Nature is always vivid to me, and devotional poetry I find significant – provided that it deals with direct experience. A world without devotion seems to me arrogant and vulgar, a world without mythology mean and threadbare. But theological doctrine and clerical discipline are both repellent to me: I reject all religious systems and positively hate the arrogance of theological claims on which they are ultimately based, as these seem to me a standing violation of intellectual integrity.'[24] These passionately held views are the source of the jibes against Catholics with which these letters, and Trevor-Roper's essays, are peppered.

Robert Blake, the Oxford political historian and Trevor-Roper's colleague at Christ Church, accompanied him on this first visit to Casa al Dono, but seems to have made little impression on Berenson, nor to have been impressed by him. A certain type of Englishman – wary of singularity or made uneasy by 'airs' – often did not. Blake had, perhaps, a similar reaction to that of James Lees-Milne, who also first visited I Tatti in 1947. 'A tiny man, white-bearded and eighty,' Lees-Milne recorded, 'Berenson is tiresome in that he is very conscious of being the famous art-dictator and sage, surrounded by applauding disciples. This expectancy of deference does not make for ease. And no small talk is allowed [. . .] In stony silence he dismisses a conventional advance as a triviality, which it doubtless is. When he talks he demands attention, and is not the least averse to obsequious confirmation of his utterances [. . .] He conveyed to me the impression of a great man striving to be something which he isn't.'[25]

As to the impression made by Trevor-Roper, if not by Blake, Berenson's diary on the day after their visit may be a guide. 'Why,' he asked, 'do I feel more attracted to the Englishman than to the American of the same abilities, equal achievement and success? It can only be because the Englishman is more of a work of art to be enjoyed as such particularly, whereas the American with rarest exceptions can be admired only. In other words, it is a question of breeding.'[26] Berenson, indeed, had always been susceptible to Oxonians. 'It had been my dream before I went to college at all to go to Oxford, and to spend my life there,' he had written during his first visit to the city. 'I was almost mad with longing for it, and [. . .] cannot get over my surprise at the English, whom I admire beyond measure. Poor Harvard, and its men, it is not fair to compare it and them, especially them to Oxford men. These are all – in as far as I can see – very clever, brilliant, serious even although without too much gravity, and well-taught, just the men whom I admire and even adore.'[27]

The young man who idealised Oxford – he was aged twenty-three when these words were written – was a Jewish refugee from the Russian Pale of Settlement. He had been born in Lithuania in 1865 (when his mother was aged eighteen and his father was only a year older): ten years later his family, fugitives from anti-semitic pogroms, settled in Boston, Massachusetts. There his father worked as a pedlar. In childhood Berenson evinced pro-digious academic gifts: by adolescence he was a confirmed bookworm, who read voraciously through the stock of Boston Public Library; but unlike most adolescents who haunt libraries, he was of striking beauty, with luxuriant auburn hair that compensated for his diminutive stature. 'I made homosexuals' mouths water,' he later claimed.[28] He first enrolled at Boston University, and then in 1884 at Harvard. At Harvard he was much influenced by the philosopher William James, 'from whom', wrote Kenneth Clark, 'he probably derived his determination to approach aesthetics on a psy-chological rather than a mystical basis; and William James's racy style, his love of illuminating philosophical points from popular songs and wisecracks, remained one of the most endearing features of Berenson's conversation'.[29]

Berenson was poor, but his brilliant intellect and intense craving for experience were so conspicuous that a group of rich Bostonians paid for him to go to Europe in 1887. As a youth he intended to become a literary critic or historian of ideas, and thought of translating Sacher-Masoch or Baudelaire into English; but he also knew Walter Pater's *Studies in the History of the Renaissance* almost by heart, and his arduous, extensive European travels during 1888 ignited his interest in the visual arts. Already, by this time, he recognised that family life would be a hindrance for him. 'The idea of a tie with anybody that is not elective is so repugnant to me that I cannot be fair to my own brothers and sisters,' he wrote later. 'They are charming, cultivated people much above the average, but I am always on my guard against claims as a brother.'[30]

He wandered across Europe, suffering many deprivations, but avid for all the sensations of art and nature; and was especially enraptured by the landscape and artistic heritage of Italy. He fixed on Italian painting as his special interest, adopted the new, systematic methods of scholarship developed by the art historian Giovanni Morelli and in 1890 began to write a monograph on Lorenzo Lotto. 'As for Lotto,' he recalled in 1953, 'I went to pilgrimage after pilgrimage, with an almost medieval pilgrim's difficulties, anywhere and everywhere, no matter what season and what weather, to see a picture in a church of remote and difficult access. On the way I got more eager, zestful, got into a state of grace towards the picture I was hoping to see. As I left it I was filled with its image and had the leisure to absorb it, to make it unforgettably my own. After three or four years of living with or for Lotto, I had him in memory as no bringing together of all his output under one roof could have done.'[31] He continued to scour Italian country districts for altarpieces and paintings. In a mood of spiritual and aesthetic elation, he was received into the Catholic Church in 1891 (though he soon lapsed from faith); and later that year he began living with Mary Costelloe, Pearsall Smith's married sister.

In 1893 he gave cautionary advice to a party of rich Americans in Rome on their art purchases, for which he received a fee of $100 – his first dip into the rank waters of art dealers. Four books – *The Venetian Painters of the Renaissance* (1894), *Lorenzo Lotto* (1895), *Florentine Painters of the Renaissance* (1896) and *The Central Italian Painters of the Renaissance* (1897) established his authority as 'the ablest and certainly the most daring of all Morelli's followers', as an essayist on 'The New Art-Criticism' declared in 1896. 'In spite of a style which is often repellent from its apparent affectation, the acuteness of his insight, the zeal and enthusiasm with which he pursues his researches, have already placed this young writer in the foremost rank of living critics.'[32] The three books on Renaissance painters contained lists of paintings, together with an index of churches, museums and galleries, and were published in a cheap, portable format; they thus became indispensable for art tourists in Italy as well as significant contributions to aesthetics. His two-volume *Drawings of the Florentine Painters, classified, criticised and studied as documents in the history and appreciation of Tuscan Art with a copious Catalogue Raisonné* (1903) confirmed his international reputation, and remained his most accomplished work.

Berenson was able to marry the freshly widowed Mary Costelloe in 1900. Both of them had subsequent affairs. Some of his infatuations – with Gladys Deacon (afterwards Duchess of Marlborough), Belle Greene, Clotilde Marghieri and others – were obsessive: 'I honestly don't think in these cases the Object matters much,' Mary wrote.[33] She was a clever, mercenary, wilful, histrionic woman – 'I love opening letters,' she told Kenneth Clark, 'they might contain a cheque'[34] – who tolerated his affairs if they did not disrupt the money-making. 'Bernard, with gaiety of spirit, continues his career of *l'homme susceptible*, but not very seriously, nor with such absorption, as to interfere with his work.'[35] His possessiveness, and need of attention, remain evident in the letters in this book dating from the last dozen years of his life.

In 1900 the Berensons leased a villa, I Tatti, in the hills just behind Ponte a Mensola – then in the countryside and now on the outskirts of Florence. (The hill town of Settignano, a few kilometres away, provided the postal address of I Tatti until the late 1950s, and is consequently used in the Trevor-Roper/Berenson correspondence as a synonym for I Tatti.) Seven years later their landlord, Lord Westbury, who had 'lost his all at Montecarlo',[36] sold them the villa and its surrounding estate of about fifty acres at an overall cost of some £6,000. During the period 1908–11 the Berensons rebuilt the house, and landscaped the grounds, with immaculate effects.[37] These improvements cost a fortune, and were paid from the riches that he had been accumulating since the mid-1890s from the great inaugural phase of American art-collecting. Wall Street financiers and plutocratic industrialists did not trust their own taste or instincts as better-educated European connoisseurs were accustomed to do. J. Pierpont Morgan (whose London house 'looks like a pawnbroker's shop for Croesuses', Berenson reported in 1906; 'I do however like his Van Dyck *Mrs Balbi*, and I love his Fragonard room')[38] typified these tycoons: always suspicious in deals and always in a hurry, they required the pictures they bought from dealers or private collections to be certified as authentic. With some pictures, or some collectors, the certificates counted for more than the art. It was in this business environment, involving huge sums, huge egos and huge opportunities for cheating, that the little American-Lithuanian connoisseur became a redoubtable power. First he became involved in the mid-1890s with P. & D. Colnaghi, the London art dealers, and soon there was an incessant demand for his certification of – in his own rueful words – the 'swagger purchases made by our squillionaires'.[39]

Berenson's admirers blamed marriage for forcing dubious expedients on him. Mary Berenson was condemned by the art historian John Pope-Hennessy, for example, as 'the main propulsion first towards certification and then towards an arrangement whereby a fixed annual income was assured'.[40] Berenson's fees yielded enormous amounts well before he became – spasmodically in 1906–7, concertedly from 1909 – an adviser to a family of art dealers, his 'enemy-friends the Duveens' as he called them, who began by paying him a commission of 10 per cent on their sales of paintings for which he had provided an attribution (he received over $80,000 in commissions from them in 1909). 'I am so afraid it has really happened, that I have become a society-lounger, and money-grubber, and God knows what,' he wrote at this time. 'I do not like it at all, and mean to wrench myself away as soon as possible.'[41] But instead of severing his contacts with the Duveens, he further bound himself to them in a secret contract of 1912 by which he received consultancy fees – not commissions – of 25 per cent on sales of paintings with which he had been involved. In the first year of this arrangement his fees exceeded the then enormous sum of £19,000. A new contract of 1928 established Berenson on an annual retainer of £10,000 plus 10 per cent of those purchases that he had recommended; but these figures were adjusted in several subsequent contracts during the 1930s. Many of his dealings were with the swashbuckling Sir Joseph Duveen (eventually Lord Duveen), who excited his exasperation and mistrust – and whose dying words are said to have been, 'Well, I fooled 'em.'[42] Berenson felt ashamed as the Duveens drew him deeper into the realms of 'Ritzonia and Mammonia',[43] but his wife was exhilarated. 'I like Joe's visits: it's like drinking champagne,' she told him; 'Gin,' he corrected her.[44] Despite his ambivalence about the Duveens, Berenson did not end his arrangements with them until 1937; and eight years later, in 1945, he agreed to act as the expert adviser on Italian Renaissance paintings to the French art dealer Georges Wildenstein, who had opened an art gallery in New York. Berenson received $72,500 for his attributions, notations and confidential opinions in 1946; and from 1947 until his death he was paid $50,000 a year by Wildenstein.

These arrangements have damaged Berenson's reputation unjustly. 'So sad,' said the connoisseur Douglas Cooper as he left I Tatti after a final visit a few months before Berenson's death. 'As a young man he must have had one of the most protean minds of his generation; he was simply too materialistic, too greedy for pomp and circumstance to live up to it. Besides the caterwauling of bereaved acolytes, what will he leave behind? A fine house filled with fine things, a magnificent library, a formidable body of pioneer work, but one that will be forever tainted by dealers' commissions.'[45] Some writers impugn Berenson because his attributions have been questioned, and assume that he misled collectors on Duveen's behalf; but they misunderstand the nature of attributions and they misrepresent Berenson. Attributions are, at best, only expressions of expert opinion framed in the light of current information and after subjective, though carefully trained, scrutiny. Berenson's attributions, for Duveen or any other dealer, could not be of iron-clad infallibility – no one's could – but his certificates were never fraudulent, and indeed he often reached inconvenient decisions. Famously, in 1895, after an exhibition of English-owned Venetian Renaissance art opened in London, he published a pamphlet lambasting spurious attributions that flattered private owners into supposing that they possessed great treasures; and he enjoyed denying slipshod ascriptions that had been made in ignorance or to satisfy family pride. A few years later he visited Alnwick Castle, the seat of the Dukes of Northumberland, which dominates the country town in which Trevor-Roper grew up; and there he found 'Bellinis which are not Bellinis, and Giorgiones [...] which almost disgust me', he reported.[46] Berenson's objectivity was far superior to that of many museum curators, whose catalogues perpetuated manifestly spurious ascriptions of objects in their charge, sometimes from blindness or apathy, but often because they saw their prime duty as the defence of high-prestige attributions.

Regardless of these controversies, Berenson had by the start of the 1920s become 'BB', a celebrated European phenomenon, 'I Tatti's presiding genius',[47] although not every visitor succumbed to his charm or to his ambience. 'The mere fact', Lytton Strachey wrote of his host while staying at I Tatti in 1921, 'that he has accumulated this wealth from having been a New York [sic] gutter-snipe is sufficiently astonishing; but besides that he has a most curious complicated temperament, very sensitive, very clever – even, I believe, with a strain of niceness somewhere or other, but desperately wrong – perhaps suffering from some dreadful complexes – and without a speck of naturalness or ordinary human enjoyment. And this has spread itself all over the house, which is really remarkably depressing [...] with the atmosphere of a crypt.'[48] Lord Lee of Fareham, a musuem trustee who was less preternaturally captious than Strachey, nevertheless felt uneasy after calling at I Tatti in 1930. 'He is a strange being, hypersensitive, cynical, mischievous, malicious, and curiously vindictive towards anyone – whether art critic or private collector – who claims any knowledge of Italian painting or sculpture. The lengths to which he will go, without justification or scruple, to "queer their pitch" would be almost incredible if one had not so often experienced them.'[49]

Berenson was always a keen, anxious political observer, avid for up-to-date news. From the 1920s he mixed with Italian opponents of Mussolini, and in time I Tatti became 'strictly watched by the Fascists', as Count Harry Kessler (a Weimar politician exiled from Nazi Germany) noted in 1936. 'They have thrown a sort of *cordon sanitaire* around him, warning his American compatriots against him, and suggesting he is [...] imbecile.'[50] Despite the anti-semitic legislation imposed on Italy in 1938, despite the declaration of war between Italy and the USA in 1941, and despite other perils, Berenson remained at I Tatti until 1943, when he was forced to seek protection in a villa enjoying diplomatic immunity: it belonged to Marchese Filippo Serlupi Crescenzi, who was the envoy of the tiny republic of San Marino to the Holy See in Rome. There he endured heavy bombardment and other dangers while keeping the diaries and compiling the library notes that were later published as *Rumour and Reflection* and as *One Year's Reading for Fun*.

For many years the atmosphere at I Tatti was strained – Mary Berenson was the source of much conflict and unrest – as well as somehow contrived and over-worldly. After her death in 1945, when Berenson came fully under the relaxed charge of his companion Nicky Mariano, the temper of the household improved: I Tatti became a place of pilgrimage so that, by 1948, Trevor-Roper was envisaging Berenson and Mariano 'animated rather than exhausted by the stream of pilgrims and visitors [...] filing in endless but elegant crocodile from Florence to Settignano'.[51] One inquisitive caller – in 1947 – was Alfred Kazin. 'The Berenson house very beautiful and quietly massed with treasures, but almost too exquisite to walk in,' he noted. 'It is like a private chapel raised to the connoisseur's ideal experience, where every corridor and corner has been worked to make a new altarpiece, and where the smallest detail reveals the mind of a man who has the means to reject all intrusions of mere necessity.' Kazin was ushered round I Tatti by Gertrude Stein's brother Leo, and only later, in Rome, met Berenson, whom he described as a 'delicate little *élégant* with a little white beard, very frail, an old courtier in his beautiful clothes, every inch of him engraved fine into an instrument of aesthetic responsiveness'.[52] More regular visitors included John Pope-Hennessy ('BB was serious and natural and welcoming, and [...] I learnt more than I can describe, not just about Italian paintings but about intellectual standards, too');[53] and Trevor-Roper's friend Frank Giles, *The Times* correspondent in Rome. 'Though close to ninety,' Giles recalled, 'BB had retained all his curiosity, all his appetite for new people to whom he would display his gifts for learned disquisition mixed with outrageous generalisation and a taste for worldly gossip. He could be very nice to the young, provided he liked them.'[54]

In all the disagreements surrounding Berenson's reputation, there is unanimity on one subject: Nicky Mariano. Even James Lees-Milne – to whom Berenson in 1947 seemed 'a vain, blasphemous, tricky Jew' – succumbed to 'Signorina Mariano', a 'sweet woman who relieves tension and makes one happy'.[55] Similarly Harold Nicolson thought 'this pernickety little person', Berenson, 'was fortunate in finding in Nicky Mariano an Egeria of unsurpassable competence and charm, who pampered him something chronic'.[56] Elizabetta ('Nicky') Mariano (1887–1968), the daughter of an Italian father and an aristocratic Baltic mother, was recruited to the staff of I Tatti as librarian in 1919, and rapidly became the mainstay of the household. There developed between her and Berenson an intimacy, trust and love that never faltered. Serene by temperament, selfless and a superefficient organiser, she became indispensable to BB's well-being. His travelling companion in the inter-war years, she accompanied him to Marchese Serlupi's wartime refuge and in the post-war years became (in John Pope-Hennessy's words) 'the angelic architect of his apotheosis'.[57] As the hostess at I Tatti she was tactful, attentive and generous: 'one of the most delightful women ever to draw breath,' thought her guest Frank Giles.[58] 'Even the most casual visitor to I Tatti must have been captivated by her unequalled sweetness and gaiety,' Kenneth Clark insisted. 'She was interested in everyone and everything – people, places, pictures and books. She was prodigiously well read; anyone who knows Berenson's *One Year's Reading for Fun*, and realizes that every book referred to was read aloud to him by Miss Mariano, will get an idea of what she must have got through over the years. She also had an astonishing memory for places, on which Mr Berenson frequently relied. But these intellectual endowments were forgotten in one's admiration for her human qualities. Coping with the endless stream of pilgrims to I Tatti needed special gifts. She saw the funny side of the many preposterous visitors who forced their way in, but on the whole she was amazingly tolerant, and as the door closed on the most excruciating bores, would murmur "dear people".'[59] Berenson did not marry Mariano (as his wife urged as she lay dying), perhaps because, under Italian laws of inheritance, this might have jeopardised his bequest of I Tatti and its library, supported by a rich endowment, to Harvard University. Yet she made his last years as near perfect as possible.

If Berenson's vices – vanity foremost – were conspicuous, he had many disarming virtues too. His finest characteristics, which became ever more touching in extreme old age, were his loathing of wasted time and his eagerness for new discoveries, perceptions and experience. 'I am getting on,' he wrote in 1924, 'and a frightful yearning for knowledge has seized me, and I begin to fear that I shall not live long enough to get even to the threshold.'[60] He lived another thirty-five years, and this heroic yearning and glorious receptivity persisted almost to the end. Berenson was, after all, the man who, in his eighty-seventh year, read J.D. Salinger's novel of adolescent rebellion, *Catcher in the Rye* (1951), and after an initial revulsion, ultimately decided that it was, in places, 'delicious'.[61] His outlook became calmer with age, and his conversation gentler, though he raged with frustration against the encroaching torpor that was cruelly curbing his activities and reducing him to mental impotence. As he complained to Trevor-Roper in 1954, for every hour that he spent studying his collection of photographs of Italian paintings or meeting visitors, 'I have to waste more than as much time resting in the dark, dozing, sleeping.' As a result he had 'no time at all for reading, & scarcely any for writing'.[62]

Trevor-Roper paid some dozen visits to Berenson – mainly at I Tatti, where he first stayed on 20–23 March 1948.[63] 'The conversation and the intellectual vivacity and the library and the cypress-walk and that wonderful numinous ilex-grove never cease to excite me at I Tatti and at the same time to make me feel at home,' he declared in 1950.[64] The two men talked through lunch, talked during their afternoon walks in the grounds or surrounding hills (for both men were inveterate country walkers) and talked during the evenings. A typical visit in 1951 was recorded by Berenson: 'he & I talk English history all [the] time, & gossip about politics & politicians of the day. He is fabulously well-informed, but I have as yet discovered no inside of his own.' Two days later Berenson continued his assessment of Trevor-Roper: 'passionate & obstinate, but for ideas only [...] Very donnish, & often wearing a look of suffering superiority as he forbearingly listens to an interlocutor.'[65] Thirty years later Trevor-Roper recalled his visits in a letter to Berenson's biographer Meryle Secrest. 'The whole atmosphere of the house appealed to me. I felt it was a sophisticated, civilized world where the conversation was on an intellectual level. We didn't talk about paintings very much as [...] he didn't want to be thought of as "BB the picture man". He wanted to be thought of as Goethe in old age. He wasn't, quite.'[66]

Both men adored erudite, dazzling talk. 'Conversation,' Berenson declared, 'the give and take of talk, has been from my earliest years and remains the crowning joy of my life.' He particularly relished people – like Trevor-Roper – who 'give themselves to others only in talking'.[67] His own talk was luxurious, flamboyant, playful, near mesmerising. 'He spoke English', Alfred Kazin reported, 'with such purity and beauty of diction, blandly delivering himself of words, one by one, that he might have been putting freshly cracked walnuts into my hand.'[68] Berenson's table-talk in his nineties entranced Alan Pryce-Jones, editor of the *Times Literary Supplement*. 'As his mind also darted with breathless rapidity from one aspect of a subject to another, the thread of talk unwound after this fashion. He might begin speaking of Kleist, then move on to the merits of Kleist's *Penthesilea*. This brought him to Othmar Schoeck's opera on the theme. Had I been to the first performance in Zurich, in 1921, wasn't it? – No – he did not greatly care for music but he was playing up to his guest – passing briefly over Schoeck's settings of Lenau and Mörike, he skipped to the influence of Swiss scenery on the Swiss imagination, paused to reflect on the pleasurable horror inspired by the Alps in relation to romantic poetry, and by the very different horror which excited the mind of Fuseli – not that Fuseli was any good, of course; switched to John Martin's somewhat superior madness; paused again to wonder if any mad poet were the equal of Hölderlin; and finally returned to Kleist as an atypical suicide.'[69]

Trevor-Roper's lust for reading was as pronounced as Berenson's, although their literary preferences were not identical. Trevor-Roper seldom read novels, whereas Berenson was very up-to-date in his fiction reading, and even became a mentor to the young science-fiction writer Ray Bradbury after inviting him to I Tatti. If Berenson in old age had little time for poets, Trevor-Roper found rich fulfulment in the poetry of the early modern period. In all, though, books were their nourishment and their most valued possession. 'Any historical work regarding any people, any period, any movement in religion or in thought, any anthropological or ethnological publication, the more detailed the better,' wrote Berenson: 'Information, interpretation, reflection are what I am after.'[70]

This overmastering appetite for information meant that Berenson was inquisitive, vicariously excited and almost voyeuristic about the emotional lives of his favourites: 'I revel in the family history of friends.'[71] Yet Trevor-Roper was always taciturn on such matters. His father – a physician absorbed in his work and addicted to the Turf – was aloof, silent and unresponsive; and his mother (the daughter of a Belfast linen family) was cold, rigid, humourless, intensely disapproving and class-conscious. 'Ours was a grim household without warmth, or affection, or encouragement, or interest,' he recalled in old age.[72] As a result he read avidly so as to escape, in imagination at least, from the narrow confines of his parents' world; and he preferred his life at boarding-school to his life at home. His emotions were set in childhood: he was solitary, tense and reticent with a pent-up accumulation of aggression.

Berenson, in the early years of his friendship with Trevor-Roper, was disappointed by the younger man's lack of emotional self-revelation, which had so thoroughly frustrated Pearsall Smith before him. (Trevor-Roper had unwisely joked to Smith that he had once had advances made to him by a French North African soldier outside the papal palace at Avignon: Smith thereafter teased Trevor-Roper with claims that he was soliciting tales of sexual indiscretions in Oxford, and his camp, prying questions on this theme led Trevor-Roper to leave his eightieth birthday party in irritation.) Actually Trevor-Roper had been candid with Smith about the only feelings that mattered to him much. 'Sometimes I suffer from deep depression, feeling intellectually helpless, doomed to ineffectiveness, and oppressed by a sense of utter solitude,' he had told Smith in 1942. 'I crave for affection and consolation, but am afraid to solicit it, and so emphasise my isolation.'[73]

When the right circumstances arrived, Trevor-Roper was ready to take his host and hostess at I Tatti into his most precious trust. Berenson and Mariano – it is the crucial fact that explains the developing intimacy of the letters in this book – were wonderfully generous in 'aiding and abetting' the clandestine early phase of Trevor-Roper's passionate love affair with his future wife.[74] This developed during the early summer of 1953 with Lady Alexandra Howard-Johnston, the unhappily married sister of his friend Dawyck Haig (and daughter of Field Marshal Haig, commander-in-chief of British troops in the First World War). The couple met when they could, and spent nights together in country hotels outside Oxford. On 12 July they both went to Paris – she staying at 14 rue Vaneau, and he nearby at Hôtel Sevres-Vaneau. They met friends there – the historians John Nef and Fernand Braudel, the diplomat Patrick Reilly, Nancy Mitford, Kitty and Frank Giles – and then went south to Italy. So successful was their time at I Tatti that five months later they returned there together. Berenson and Nicky Mariano were, as these letters show, entirely in their confidence at a fraught and critical time.

Xandra Howard-Johnston was – to Trevor-Roper – the most important of the English visitors whom he introduced to I Tatti; but his other introductions were numerous. In 1949, for example, two Christ Church undergraduates, David Hopkins and Donald Allchin, went for tea. 'The precise time of our afternoon visit had to fit BB's sleeping pattern,' Hopkins recalled. 'The day was beautiful and sunny and from where we sat on a settee we could see a very beautiful garden all around. Nicky made us very welcome and put us at our ease.' Berenson, when he appeared, initiated an intense discussion on teetotalism and the evils of Prohibition. 'The intensity was akin to the grilling I received from the Chairman of the Civil Service Selection Board a couple of years later,' Hopkins recalled.[75] Senior members

of the university were welcomed at I Tatti on Trevor-Roper's recommendation too: in 1951, for example, his close friend and Christ Church
colleague, Dimitri Obolensky (later Professor of Russian and Balkan
History at Oxford), and Constantine Trypanis, the Professor of Byzantine
and Modern Greek (afterwards Greek Minister of Culture and Science),
joined the pilgrim route from Ponte a Mensola.

But most effectively of all, Trevor-Roper in 1950 inveigled a somewhat
apprehensive Isaiah Berlin into visiting I Tatti, and a deep rapport
developed between Berlin and his host. 'Berenson', so Berlin wrote in
1961, 'possessed a very powerful intellectual personality, and when he was
interested in a subject or a visitor (he was infinitely sensitive to nuances
both of persons and ideas – about works of art I cannot speak), his
conversation was sharp and arresting. His views were original and first-
hand, and the ratio of thought to words was uncommonly high, so that
one's own mind was made to race. My first impression was that of a
polished, mannered and highly self-conscious aesthete; but presently I
became aware that I was in the presence of a man of extraordinary
breadth and precision of knowledge, of acute ironical and deeply civilised
intelligence, but above all of a man who possessed the unique vitality
and distinction (if not the creative gifts) of a man of genius.' Berenson
was one of the finest conversationalists whom Berlin ever encountered:
'the only persons in my experience in whose talk ideas and images
mingled with a similar "life-enhancing" effect were Pasternak, Keynes
and Freud.'[76]

Berenson loved correspondence with distant friends, craved their intimate confidences, hugged to himself privileged information; and he enjoyed
political news and social data more than art-world chatter. He had long
correspondence (published partly or entirely) with Americans such as
Isabella Stewart Gardner, Edith Wharton and Henry Coster.[77] He treasured
letters from a Swedish connoisseur, Axel Boethius. He savoured the gossip
sent by the London hostess Sybil Colefax; and after her death in 1950, he
encouraged the London letters of the publisher Hamish Hamilton. And so,
in July 1947, he extracted from Trevor-Roper a promise to write, though he
cannot have known that his new English friend was to prove the greatest
letter-writer of his generation, a letter-writer whose irony, grace and knowledge make him the twentieth-century equivalent of Madame de Sévigné
or Horace Walpole. As the diplomat Peter Ramsbotham had recently
written from Hamburg: 'Your letters are a source of very real pleasure; they
regale me in moments of deep depression in this city of misery, self-pity
and frustration. If you have written many such letters to other friends, I
look forward to the time when we can each assemble our possessions and

publish a collection of "belles lettres" to codify your wit and embalm the fragrance and charm of your literary style."[78]

The Last Days of Hitler was Trevor-Roper's first post-war masterpiece. His second post-war masterpiece was his correspondence – of which his letters to Berenson are a crucial part of the early corpus, as their recipient recognised. 'Hugh is a good talker, a fine historian, but above all a superb letter-writer,' Berenson decided.[79] Similarly the American historian Wallace Notestein – the recipient of two Trevor-Roper letters that are printed as an Appendix to this book – told Berenson that Trevor-Roper 'was not a historian [so much as] a great letter-writer'.[80] His correspondence became voluminous, incessant and inveterate. It consumed the time in which he would otherwise have written books: his letters to Berenson often refer to books that he began but never finished, and books that he visualised but never began. Trevor-Roper's copious correspondence with his contemporaries was more than an ingrained habit, more than a pretext to avoid less congenial work, more indeed than just a correspondence. It was his subtle and intricate history of late twentieth-century folly; his emulative tribute to two books that he adulated, written by two historians whom he venerated, Gibbon's *Memoirs* and Clarendon's *Life* in his *History*; and his ultimate masterpiece of sustained, perfectly poised irony.

For the *mentalité* expressed in Trevor-Roper's letters was, supremely, ironic. His irony was mordant, entrenched, rational; and consummate in its execution. It had been fostered and polished by Pearsall Smith, but it was more than mere Loganite affectation. Trevor-Roper loved a fight – these letters describe him in combat with figures as diverse as his wife's nautical ex-husband, Arnold Toynbee, Communist renegades and philistine town-planners – and for him irony was the weapon of reason and intellect. The range of his correspondents – fox-hunting men, statesmen, spies, raffish noblemen, librarians, war criminals, publishers, fashionable ladies, political hacks, country neighbours, and professors across many continents – was formidable. His international outlook, the extent of his travels in the Americas, Africa and Europe, and his passionate sense of European cultural traditions – an ardour that ignored frontiers and nationalism – are manifest throughout his letters to Berenson, as they are in his letters to other friends and in his travel writing for the *Sunday Times* and other newspapers. The diversity of his human interests, the cosmopolitanism of his mind, were indispensable to his letter-writing, for he was intent on producing (at what level of consciousness one cannot know) a history of his times to rank with those of his professional forebears Clarendon and Gibbon.

Berenson, in contrast, was a profuse but not a great letter-writer: 'I have no *jolie plume*,' he declared; 'I am no *epistolier*'.[81] His style of letter-writing was as idiosyncratic as his conversation: he darted from one subject to another, often in the same paragraph, if not consecutive sentences, and wrote in an idiom that was uniquely his own. Accordingly, his letters have been omitted, pruned and paraphrased in this book: they are too allusive, elliptical and abbreviated to be worth printing in their entirety; occasionally they are too full of his slang and quirky coinages to be easily comprehended; and when he was tired and ill, they contain little more than his reiterated pleading for news.

During the course of this correspondence Trevor-Roper becomes a prominent Oxford figure, a sought-after contributor to the London weekly newspapers (paid by both the *Sunday Times* and *New Statesman* at their highest rates), and pre-eminent among English historians. 'The most intelligent man in Oxford,' said John Russell, the art critic who had supplanted Trevor-Roper as Pearsall Smith's testamentary heir, when recommending him to an undergraduate going up to Christ Church in 1950.[82] He could be an attentive, considerate and even protective tutor to favoured pupils. 'He was very scathing in public but a very kindly person in his private life,' according to David Hopkins, one of several Christ Church undergraduates whom he sent to call at I Tatti. When Hopkins, who came from a Nonconformist, teetotal family, hesitated to accept Trevor-Roper's invitation to a drinks party, he was not only assured that it would be acceptable to drink orange juice throughout the evening, but on the night his host also confined himself to orange juice – to the amazement of other guests such as John Wheeler-Bennett.[83]

Another Christ Church undergraduate who visited I Tatti with an introduction from Trevor-Roper was Nicolas Tate. At the first interview, in 1951, Trevor-Roper had seemed to Tate 'astonishingly young and, with his near pebble glasses and slightly stooping, almost collapsible bearing not at all the sort of person I imagined "sleuthing" any buckshee Nazi'. Tate, from his first term at the House, was sent by Trevor-Roper on expeditions to exceptional country churches, and later was driven by him – perilously, in the dashing Bentley – to see places that combined historic political associations with objects of rare beauty: the St John family's house and church at Lydiard Tregoze, for example, or Lord Spencer's collection at Althorp. Together they visited marvellous churches and many houses not yet open to the public; 'Hugh seemed to know everyone,' and was welcomed almost everywhere, Tate thought. 'Gradually I got to know Hugh not only as a bottomless mine of historical information but also as a viciously witty raconteur.' He regarded Trevor-Roper's influence on him as 'a truly wonderful gift'.[84]

Senior members of the university, and scholars from overseas, were equally impressed by his achievements and influence. 'Mr Trevor-Roper is by so far the most outstanding historian of the post-Namier generation,' his Oxford colleague Max Beloff judged in 1956.[85] Christopher Hill, a Marxist scholar whose historical differences with Trevor-Roper were irreconcilable, nevertheless conceded his opponent's pre-eminence by the 1950s. 'If Professor Trevor-Roper did not exist, it would be necessary to invent him,' Hill averred in 1957. 'His clear-cut, brilliantly argued, convincing and wrong hypotheses about seventeenth-century English history [...] have set a whole generation of researchers at work [...] Trevor-Roper has provoked, bullied, goaded and stimulated his generation of historians.'[86] Noel Annan, a Cambridge historian, reckoned Trevor-Roper 'the most eloquent, sophisticated and assured historian of Our Age [who] never wrote an inelegant sentence or an incoherent argument'.[87]

Trevor-Roper's visits to Paris were prized by Fernand Braudel and other leaders of the *Annales* school in the 1950s: he was the foremost advocate in England of their interdisciplinary methodology which drew on literature, economics, sociology, the visual arts, music, language and religion to create *l'histoire totale*. In the United States, magazine editors and book publishers were eager to have Trevor-Roper's work. 'He's a brillant person and a writer of the first rank as well as being an outstanding scholar,' Cass Canfield of Harper Row in New York declared in 1954.[88] When, four years later, Canfield's firm published a volume of Trevor-Roper's essays entitled *Men and Events*, the American response was at times rapturous. 'What a versatile and brilliant man he is!' Wallace Notestein enthused to Canfield. 'What a wide view of history he has! He is possibly the most brilliant mind in the English historical world. Few men write so well.'[89] To another American academic he seemed, in 1958, 'the spokesman of a post-war generation which has re-instated the traditional British emphasis on hard-headed [...] empiricism'.[90]

Trevor-Roper and Berenson shared an intense curiosity in the political behaviour of humankind: political concerns permeate their correspondence. Trevor-Roper was writing from a country that was shocked, exhausted and impoverished by the recent war, and yet still seemed stable, decent and enviable. 'England seemed to him', Isaiah Berlin wrote of Trevor-Roper's Austrian friend Raimund von Hofmannsthal, who settled in London after the war, 'the embodiment of a quiet, honourable, humane existence, above all of a civilisation singularly free from violence, hysteria, meanness and vulgarity.'[91] That is how England seemed to Berenson, and (often enough) to Trevor-Roper. The two men were united in their rationalism: they both felt their working lives were devoted to the exercise of

Reason, and despised people who betrayed their fine intellects in mysticism or mystification. Their high valuation of intellectual integrity meant that they loathed demands for spiritual obedience or intellectual submission from either totalitarian governments or church hierarchies. Trevor-Roper was revolted by the irrationality, violence and triumphant stupidity of the Nazi and Soviet leadership; he detested the bigotry and ignorance of cardinals and popes, and referred to the Vatican's Index of Prohibited Books as 'that incomparable roll of genius'.[92] Berenson, as Trevor-Roper and Alys Russell agreed in 1948, was 'obsessed' about Soviet infiltration of post-war Europe, and scorned the papacy; he denounced the Vatican to Trevor-Roper (alluding to a hill in Rome) as 'the Kremlin on the Gianicolo'.[93]

There was toughness, too, about both men: they valued physical fortitude as well as intellectual vitality. Admittedly, Berenson deplored his own failures of moral courage, and ensured that he was coddled and indulged by the arrangements at I Tatti. Yet his self-discipline in his working life, his perseverance in old age, his insatiable curiosity and zest for living even as his infirmities worsened – these set a wonderful example. Trevor-Roper was to display similar hardihood when old age and (like Berenson) near-blindness engulfed him. In turn, Berenson admired his friend's uncompromising intellectual courage. He recognised, too, and relished Trevor-Roper's vitality, courage and endurance; the younger man was a fearless rider to hounds until, as described in these letters, he broke his back in the hunting field; he exercised a pack of hounds twice a week before breakfast until the early 1950s; and he took pleasure during the visits to France and Spain also mentioned in these letters in sleeping out of doors in the fields.

Two other English habitués of I Tatti – the journalist Sylvia Sprigge and the publisher Hamish Hamilton – recur through the pages that follow. They are mentioned, and their letters to Berenson or to Trevor-Roper are quoted so often, that they should be introduced to readers in more detail than footnotes allow.

Sylvia Sprigge was born in 1903 and was killed in a motoring accident in 1966. A graduate of St Hilda's College, Oxford, she was Rome correspondent of the *Manchester Guardian* from 1928 to 1933 and again from 1945 until 1953. At the suggestion of Louis MacNeice, Trevor-Roper had sought her out in Rome while acting as the *Observer*'s special correspondent in July 1947, when she gave him useful introductions. The dinner he gave in her honour on 25 October 1949 (to which he invited Isaiah Berlin, Robert Blake, A.J.P. Taylor and Enid Starkie) was the first of a series of annual parties that he held for her in Oxford. She was an eager, affectionate, zestful woman who in the early years of these letters was one of the most frequent guests at I Tatti: 'very jolly, a little aggressive physically, and yet engaging in her "Backfisch" [teenage girl's] sense of fun and sometimes very interesting on the subjects she really knows about', as Nicky Mariano described her to Trevor-Roper in 1952.[94]

Berenson responded to her warm admiration with the rash suggestion that they might jointly publish a selection of their correspondence as a sort of commentary on Italian life; this was the germ of her regrettable decision to write his biography. As early as 1956 Berenson was recording his misgivings in his diary: 'Sylvia Sprigge, daughter of a Scotch Saunders, Berlin correspondent of London *Times*, and grand-daughter of Jewish Berlin banker named Hainauer, is a gifted journalist who had a remarkable understanding while many years in Rome of Italian politics and politicians, BUT by nature a slum-dweller with a strong distaste for traditional classes, passionate defender of the "Welfare State" at it most levelling and utterly unrestricted. By what hidden ways she has hypnotised herself into making the centre of her present life writing MY life I can't imagine. I have always from earliest awareness felt little but aversion to the populace, the mob, the crowd, the mass as such. She knows all that, or at least I have made it very plain to her. I care ultimately for nothing but *Bildung* – Culture, and states of society that promote it – hitherto "aristocratic" societies. So what can she understand of me if she sympathizes so little with ideals and aversions I have cherished and felt since childhood? I wonder what sort of Horatio Alger "ragged Dick" story she will make of it, and how repellent to me!'[95] Sprigge's biography appeared in 1960 six months after his death. Trevor-Roper felt it showed 'the irrelevant curiosity of a gossip writer'.[96]

Hamish Hamilton (born in Indianapolis in 1900, but brought up in Scotland) and his Italian wife Yvonne were introduced to the I Tatti circle by the American judge, Learned Hand, who was their close friend, as he was Berenson's. Their first visit in June 1947 was a month before Trevor-Roper's with Robert Blake, and from early in 1951 'Jamie' Hamilton and 'BB' maintained an intensive correspondence. Hamilton was the survivor of a sometimes unpleasant childhood: highly self-conscious and self-critical, he adulated his wife and doted on his son. His manners were reserved, even brooding, for his underlying feelings could be uncomfortably strong. He had deep, sometimes overwhelming emotional responses to music, and was a loving friend to the singer Kathleen Ferrier during her battle against cancer.

A busy, ambitious commercial publisher, Hamilton made several attempts to recruit Trevor-Roper to his list of authors. He was inexhaustible in extending the already broad range of his social contacts, and in London society of the 1950s he cut a conspicuous figure, though his spruce appearance was at odds with his almost dour manner. Yvonne Hamilton gave a glittering dinner party at their home in St John's Wood once a week, and was the earliest London hostess to serve Italian dishes, including pasta, to her guests. The Hamiltons' visits to I Tatti were frequent and welcome. 'Hamish and his wife to lunch and tea,' Berenson noted in 1954. 'She dressed all but gossamer, appetizing peep of breasts, still slender body, supple, youthful, but face and throat beginning to show wear. Hamish quiet, something of a sportsman, somewhat intellectual, a publisher keen on his job, but not aggressively protruding it, *très regardant* I suspect, genuinely affectionate. She bubbling, fizzling, bird-like chatter, cascades of silver laughter [...] He uxuriously in love, her slave, she keeps him up to all hours of the night, and worse obliges him (as he will not be separated) to spend a good chunk of the summer with her family by the sea.'[97]

Hamilton's letters from London gave Berenson occasional glimpses of Trevor-Roper's English life. In 1951, for example, he reported on two sightings: the first, on 21 November, at the National Book League, where Trevor-Roper spoke on 'History in Our Time'. 'Hugh is such a good talker that it was a surprise to find ourselves eyeing our watches and praying for the end.' A few days later Lord Rothermere, proprietor of the *Daily Mail*, and his wife (subsequently Mrs Ian Fleming), threw a party after the première of Noel Coward's play *Relative Values* for 'about 100 people of diverse talents, artistic and social, drinking unlimited champagne. Hugh found himself, to his dismay, next to Princess Margaret, but acquitted himself well by giving a caricature sketch of Cyril Connolly (who had had a hypnotic effect on the Princess) and encouraging her to be indiscreet about her experiences in Christ Church. He was then supplanted by Noël Coward and rejoined the commoners. [...] Diana Cooper was there, and Maugham and everyone else you can think of.'[98] Or again, in July 1953: 'We spent the weekend with the Buccleuchs at Boughton, in glorious weather. It is certainly the most beautiful house I have ever stayed in; and the Duke of Alba, a fellow-guest who knows most of the stately homes of Europe, says he has never seen its equal for furniture. New treasures come to light all the time in the extensive attics, so that every year has new surprises. Hugh Trevor-Roper was there, and we found ourselves wondering if one so young and gifted ought to spend *quite* so much time hating people. He has hardly a charitable word for anyone, and seems to relish the discomfiture even of those he is supposed to like. A strange mixture, and rather a frightening one. He is always most pleasant to us, but I wouldn't bank highly on his loyalty. This particular weekend saw him at his worst, for amongst the company was a certain Kenneth Rae (sometimes known as "Violet") who has a maddening voice and manner, but is otherwise innocuous. Hugh hadn't spoken to him for years, and was bent on leaving this record unbroken with, to us, hilarious results. The Menuhins were also there.'[99]

Trevor-Roper valued his excursions into high society. As these letters show, it was not unusual to find him being entertained by the Buccleuchs or other ducal couples. 'Socially I am a snob,' he had written in his 'Autopsy'. 'I like the world of grace and leisure, and the opulence necessary to maintain it. But in fact, though I always look for it there first, I seldom find it in its traditional haunts, and recognise that the upper-classes more often betray than cultivate their natural opportunities. I am continually disgusted by the triviality and vulgarity of the great world, and bored by its lack of education.'[100]

It was for this reason that he so prized his friendship with Berenson, and felt undying gratitude and admiration for the older man. Percy Lubbock – another playful, serene old man whom Trevor-Roper used to visit in Italy – believed that true friends were the people who put a fine edge on one's mind.[101] Berenson, by this standard, was the best of friends to Trevor-Roper. He inspired Trevor-Roper's rules of life and formed his interests quite as much as Pearsall Smith had done: 'I first got interested', Trevor-Roper recalled in 1968, in 'the symbolism of the Renaissance and [...] the new science of the 17th century' – subjects about which he was to write so richly – 'by reading (on the recommendation of Bernard Berenson) a German book by Moritz Carrière.'[102] It was Berenson who encouraged Trevor-Roper to read the works of Jacob Burckhardt, then 'regarded only as a historian of art' but (as Trevor-Roper urged in 1955) 'one of the profoundest of historians'. Burckhardt intensified Trevor-Roper's loathing of historical determinism, and fostered his belief that the history of art and literature are more expressive of the history of ideas than any amount of metaphysics: 'history which ignores art or literature is jejune history, just as society without art or literature is a jejune society, and, conversely, art and literature which are studied in detachment from history are only half understood.' In Trevor-Roper's summary of what he learnt from Burckhardt, 'if man is the agent, not the mere dead matter of history, then his historical character must be revealed in his work, not in the neuter systems of which he is said to be the victim. In other words, human art, being the last expression of man's ideas at any time, is more valuable to the historian than abstract philosophical theories.'[103] This, too, must be counted as a lesson that Trevor-Roper learnt from Berenson.

The younger man's devotion was steadfast. The letters in this book, which brought so much pleasure to I Tatti, are Trevor-Roper's repayment for the intellectual vitality, for the wonderful generosity of ideas and for the sumptuous hospitality that he enjoyed each time that he visited the aesthete-historian. If Trevor-Roper in his lifetime never published the great book that his friends expected from him, these posthumously published letters, with their coruscating descriptions of European social, intellectual and political life after the shock of a world war, are a partial substitute.

Trevor-Roper, who teased or mocked so many of his contemporaries, and for whom several warm friendships chilled with time, never ceased to extol the amplitude of Berenson's intellect, the originality of his ideas or the depth of his perceptions. Always he was vigilant in Berenson's defence; and he never shied from causing social discomfort by his championing of Berenson. Once, in the early 1970s, the historian Richard Shannon lunched with him at the Savile Club, where they met Harold Acton, whose recently published *More Memoirs of an Aesthete* contain many admiring references to Berenson but no mention of the retainer paid for so long by Duveen. Shannon, who thought Berenson's *Sketch for a Self-Portrait* as carefully sanitised as Acton's memoirs, made some tart comment about BB's probity and the suppression of discreditable facts. Trevor-Roper brought him up sharply – no doubt with that decisive gesture of his left hand, held up like a policeman's on traffic duty, with which he customarily halted, and then dismissed, foolish opinions. 'I won't,' he rapped out, 'have you speaking ill of BB: he was a very great man.'[104]

Richard Davenport-Hines

[1] Dacre diaries, 1942; ff. 20–1. The classicist Guy Chilver (1910–1982), whom T-R elsewhere characterised as 'a fool', had been a Fellow of the Queen's College, Oxford, since 1934.
[2] Sir John Pope-Hennessy, *On Artists and Art Historians* (1994), p. 262; information from Blair Worden, 17 August 2005.
[3] Carol Gelderman, *Mary McCarthy* (1989), pp. 193–4; Frances Kiernan, *Seeing Mary Plain* (2000) p. 399; Quentin Crewe, *Well, I Forget the Rest* (1991), p.91.
[4] A.L. Rowse, 'The Puritan Revolution', *New Statesman*, 9 March 1940, pp. 318–9.
[5] Cf. Herbert Hensley Henson, *Retrospect of an Unimportant Life*, III (1950), pp. 78–9.
[6] Robert Gathorne-Hardy, *Recollections of Logan Pearsall Smith* (1949), pp. 170, 174.
[7] Logan Pearsall Smith to Trevor-Roper, 2 October 1942 and 14 January 1943, Dacre papers.
[8] Dacre diaries, 1946; ff. 363–4.
[9] Dacre diaries, 1945; f. 288.
[10] Dacre diaries, 1943; f. 181.
[11] Dacre diaries, 1943; f. 224.
[12] Dacre diaries, 1944; f. 256.
[13] Trevor-Roper, 'Autopsy' [1943], Dacre papers.
[14] Dacre diaries [1945–6]; ff. 338–9.
[15] Alan Bullock, 'A Theme for Gibbon', *Spectator*, 21 March 1947, p. 306.

[16] Martin Stannard, *Evelyn Waugh: No Abiding City*, II (1992), p. 197.

[17] James Brodrick, 'Jesuits and Nazis', *The Tablet*, 21 June 1947, p. 316.

[18] Alys Russell to Hugh Trevor-Roper, 3 July 1947, Dacre papers.

[19] Trevor-Roper to George Pinney, 7 November 1947, Dacre papers.

[20] Trevor-Roper to Berenson, 7 May 1949, Archivio Berenson.

[21] Alys Russell to Berenson, 23 March 1948, Archivio Berenson.

[22] Alfred Kazin, 'From an Italian Journal', *Partisan Review*, XV (May 1948), p. 315.

[23] Dacre diaries, 1942; f. 141.

[24] Trevor-Roper, 'Autopsy'.

[25] James Lees-Milne, *Caves of Ice* (1983), pp. 190–1.

[26] Berenson diary, 1 August 1947, Archivio Berenson.

[27] Rollin Hadley (ed.), *The Letters of Bernard Berenson and Isabella Stewart Gardner 1887–1924* (1987), pp. 13–14. (Hereafter referred to as Gardner.)

[28] Ernest Samuels, *Bernard Berenson: The Making of a Connoisseur* (1979), p. 63.

[29] Kenneth Clark, *Another Part of the Wood* (1974), p. 134.

[30] Dario Biocca (ed.), *A Matter of Passion: Letters of Bernard Berenson and Clotilde Marghieri* (1989), p. 55. (Hereafter referred to as Marghieri.)

[31] Bernard Berenson, *The Passionate Sightseer* (1960), p. 44.

[32] 'The New Art-Criticism', *Quarterly Review*, 184 (1896), p. 456.

[33] Gardner, p. 483.

[34] Clark, *Another Part of the Wood*, p. 139.

[35] Gardner, p. 503.

[36] Gardner, p. 416.

[37] Charles Quest-Ritson, *The English Garden Abroad* (1992), pp. 126–8.

[38] Gardner, p. 388.

[39] Gardner, p. 444.

[40] Pope-Hennessy, *Artists and Art Historians*, pp. 264–5.

[41] Gardner, p. 451.

[42] Samuel Behrman, *Duveen* (1972), p. 213.

[43] Gardner, p. 458.

[44] Clark, *Another Part of the Wood*, p. 144.

[45] John Richardson, *The Sorcerer's Apprentice* (1999), p. 268.

[46] Gardner, p. 148.

[47] Viscountess D'Abernon to Berenson, 31 December 1953, Archivio Berenson.

[48] Paul Levy (ed.), *The Letters of Lytton Strachey* (2005), p. 488; cf. Cyril Connolly, *A Romantic Friendship* (1975), p. 287.

[49] Alan Clark (ed.), *A Good Innings* (1974), p. 299.

[50] Count Harry Kessler, *Berlin in Lights* (1971), p. 479.

[51] Trevor-Roper to Berenson, 4 June 1948, Archivio Berenson.

[52] Kazin, 'From an Italian Journal', pp. 313, 315.

[53] Pope-Hennessy, *Artists and Art Historians*, p. 263.

[54] Frank Giles, *Sundry Times* (1986), p. 98.

[55] Lees-Milne, *Caves of Ice*, pp. 191, 193.

[56] Harold Nicolson, 'The Berenson Story', *Observer*, 27 March 1960, p. 22.

[57] Sir John Pope-Hennessy, *Learning to Look* (1991), p. 150.

[58] Giles, *Sundry Times*, p. 99.

[59] Sir Kenneth Clark, 'Miss Nicky Mariano', *The Times*, 14 June 1968, 10e; cf. John Julius Norwich (ed.), *The Duff Cooper Diaries 1915–51* (2005), p. 481.

[60] Gardner, p. 665.
[61] Berenson to Hamish Hamilton, 1 and 9 February 1952, Archivio Berenson.
[62] Berenson to Trevor-Roper, 25 June 1954.
[63] The dates of T-R's other visits were: 4–6 April 1948; 24–9 September 1948; 28 December 1949 to 4 January 1950; 24–30 September 1950; 10–17 April 1951; 13–26 December 1951; 23–5 July 1953; 9–16 December 1953; 29 December 1953 to 2 January 1954; 10–13 December 1955; 21–8 October 1956; and 23–9 March 1958.
[64] Trevor-Roper to Berenson, 12 January 1950, Archivio Berenson.
[65] Berenson to Hamish Hamilton, 17 and 19 December 1951, Archivio Berenson.
[66] Meryle Secrest, *Being Bernard Berenson* (1980), p. 373.
[67] Marghieri, p. 2.
[68] Kazin, 'From an Italian Journal', p. 315.
[69] Alan Pryce-Jones, *The Bonus of Laughter* (1987), pp. 205–6.
[70] Bernard Berenson, *Sketch for a Self Portrait* (1949), p. 43.
[71] Berenson to Hamish Hamilton, 25 November 1951, Archivio Berenson.
[72] Autobiographical notes in the Dacre papers.
[73] Trevor-Roper, 'Autopsy', Dacre papers.
[74] Hamish Hamilton to Berenson, 17 March 1954, Archivio Berenson.
[75] David Hopkins to Richard Davenport-Hines, 11 April 2005.
[76] 'Isaiah Berlin and Meyer Schapiro: An Exchange', *The Brooklyn Rail*, September 2004, p. 14. I am grateful to Dr Henry Hardy for providing this reference.
[77] R.W.B. Lewis and N. Lewis (eds.), *The Letters of Edith Wharton* (1988).
[78] Peter Ramsbotham to Trevor-Roper, 8 February 1947, Dacre papers.
[79] Berenson to Hamilton, 1 March 1952, Archivio Berenson.
[80] Berenson diary, 13 September 1954, Archivio Berenson.
[81] Marghieri, p. 211; Giles Constable (ed.), *The Letters between Bernard Berenson and Charles Henry Coster* (1993), p. 268.
[82] Richard Rhodes to Richard Davenport-Hines, 18 September 2005.
[83] David Hopkins to Richard Davenport-Hines, 11 April 2005.
[84] Nicolas Tate to Richard Davenport-Hines, 3 October 2005.
[85] *Twentieth Century*, 160 (August 1956), pp. 175–6.
[86] Christopher Hill, 'Among the Amalekites', *Spectator*, 25 October 1957, pp. 551–2.
[87] Noel Annan, *Our Age* (1990), p. 271.
[88] Cass Canfield to A.D. Peters, 8 October 1954, Harry Ransom Humanities Research Center, University of Texas at Austin.
[89] Cass Canfield to Trevor-Roper, 26 March 1958, Harry Ransom Humanities Research Center.
[90] George Lichtheim, 'Philosophy of History', *Commentary*, XXV (May 1958), pp. 448, 451.
[91] Isaiah Berlin, 'Raimund von Hofmannsthal', *The Times*, 26 April 1974, 20f.
[92] Hugh Trevor-Roper, 'The Triumph of Evolution', *Commentary*, XXVIII (September 1959), p. 266.
[93] Alys Russell to Trevor-Roper, 29 April 1948; Berenson to Trevor-Roper, 28 August 1956; both in Dacre papers.
[94] Nicky Mariano to Trevor-Roper, 21 January 1952, Dacre papers.
[95] Berenson diary, 3 March 1956, Archivio Berenson.
[96] Trevor-Roper, 'Schapiro on Berenson', *Encounter*, XVI (April 1961), p. 63.
[97] Berenson diary, 7 August 1954, Archivio Berenson.
[98] Hamish Hamilton to Berenson, 3 December 1951, Archivio Berenson; Mark Amory (ed.), *The Letters of Ann Fleming* (1985), pp. 101–2.

[99] Hamish Hamilton to Berenson, 8 July 1953, Archivio Berenson.

[100] Trevor-Roper, 'Autopsy'.

[101] J.A. Gere and Logan Pearsall Smith, *Bensoniana and Cornishiana* (1999), p. 17.

[102] Trevor-Roper to Gerald Brenan, 11 March 1968, Harry Ransom Humanities Reserach Center.

[103] Hugh Trevor-Roper, *Historical Essays* (1957), pp. 273, 277; Trevor-Roper, *Princes and Artists* (1976), p. 7.

[104] Professor Richard Shannon to Richard Davenport-Hines, conversation of 21 October 2004, letter of 1 July 2005; Blair Worden, 'Remembrance of Hugh Dacre', *Peterhouse Annual Record 2002/2003*, pp. 201–2.

1947

29 August 1947   20, Bondgate Without, Alnwick, Northumberland[1]

Dear Mr Berenson

I have just returned to England, and have sent you the things which I promised, – *Archbishop Laud*,[2] Dulles' book on the German Opposition,[3] & my article from *Polemic*.[4] I am not now very enthusiastic about my *Laud*. I think it is full of crudities of this kind or that, and that the matter is not sufficiently adapted to form; so I send it with some reluctance. But I have not repented of any of the conclusions; & I mustn't slang it too much since it was the means of my introduction to Logan, & if I have learnt anything about style since then, it has been from him.[5] Not, of course, that this is my only debt. He was a very good friend to me, & a great influence at that time, & since I can recollect nothing else of him in my personal relations with him, I find it impossible to take part in the rather unedifying controversies which have since been aroused about him; preferring (romantically perhaps) to believe rather in a final lapse of judgment than in a premeditated perversity.[6]

As a corrective, or rather a supplement, to the book, I have sent you also an article on Laud which I wrote in 1945.[7] A mixture of fear & vanity has prompted this addition.

I had a hateful time in Paris, which was hot and desolate & frustrating, as is (I find) nearly all travel, which is to me a penance rewarded by incidents. In France, Albi and Chantilly and Rousseau's retreat at

---

[1] The house of the writer's parents, Dr Bertie Trevor-Roper (1885–1978) and Kathleen Trevor-Roper (1885–1964).
[2] T-R's first book, published in 1940: see Introduction (pp. xiv–xv).
[3] *Germany's Underground* (1947) by Allen Dulles (1893–1969), Director of the Central Intelligence Agency 1953–61, unravelled the wartime conspiracies against Hitler: T-R reviewed it in *The Listener* of 10 July 1947.
[4] T-R's 'The German Opposition, 1937–1944' in *Polemic*, no. 8 (1947), pp. 2–14, is a review essay centred on Fabian von Schlabrendorff's 'scholarly and self-critical' memoirs, *Offiziere gegen Hitler* (Zurich, 1946).
[5] Logan Pearsall Smith (1865–1946), a Philadelphia Quaker who became an English man-of-letters.
[6] During his final months Pearsall Smith was even more 'selfish, capricious and malicious' than usual (BB diary, 19 September 1949). Shortly before his death he replaced a will benefiting Alys Russell, Robert Gathorne-Hardy and T-R with a new will, bequeathing the bulk of his property to John Russell (b. 1919), then a *Sunday Times* book reviewer and afterwards chief art critic of the *New York Times*.
[7] 'Archbishop Laud', *History*, XXIX (September 1945), pp. 181–90.

Ermenonville were such incidents; in Italy, the Villa d'Este, Bernini's Rome (I don't care twopence for those rubbishy remains of antiquity, & have a genuine sympathy for the cultivated Barberini who made such better use of them),[8] the Certosa di Pavia,[9] and my visit to Vallombrosa which I shall always remember with pleasure, & which I shall hope one day to repeat, if we are ever allowed to travel again, and are not, like the Russians, to be immured for ever in the intellectual autarky of the sterling area.[10]

As for my studies of communism, – I think I have learnt a great deal about it, but I haven't written them yet. I am particularly grateful to you for your observation about the compromising attitude of the Italians compared to the theological attitude of the French. I had not thought of this before; but once you had mentioned it, the evidence of it became overwhelming. I have not yet seen Mrs Russell,[11] or indeed anyone; but I shall see her when I return south, & I know she will be glad to hear news of you. Meanwhile, if I can be of any help to you in England in getting books or anything else, I should be very glad to do so. It would remind me, if I needed any reminder, of that delightful pilgrimage to your oracular mountain cave. [...]

PS. The Jesuits still furiously rumble in dark, & hitherto unknown, organs issuing from Dublin and the less rational quarters of Liverpool. The noise of their anathemas reaches me not unpleasantly through the Press-cutting Agencies.[12]

---

[8] The Barberini family, which included Pope Urban VII, employed Giovanni Bernini (1598–1680) as architect of the Barberini palace and library in Rome, and commissioned him to sculpt the triton fountain in Piazza Barberini. Supposedly at Bernini's prompting, the Barberini tore out the ancient bronze girders of the Pantheon to make cannons for one of Rome's defensive forts.
[9] The first stone of the Carthusian monastery of Certosa di Pavia was laid in 1396; architecturally it is probably the most magnificent monastery in existence.
[10] On 27 August 1947, to protect the British government's dollar resources, Hugh Dalton, Chancellor of the Exchequer in the Labour government, reduced the amount of cash that could be taken on journeys outside the sterling area to £35; and announced that, with effect from 1 October, no currency would be available for travel outside the area without the approval of the Exchange Control authorities.
[11] Alys Russell (1867–1951), sister of Logan Pearsall Smith and Mary Berenson, had divorced Bertrand Russell in 1921. Social reformer, temperance worker and campaigner for women's suffrage.
[12] Jesuits protested against the references to Joseph Goebbels in the first edition of *The Last Days of Hitler*. 'The prize-pupil of a Jesuit seminary, he retained to the end the distinctive character of his education: he could always prove what he wanted [...] As the Jesuit persuades his penitent that all is well, that he has not really sinned at all, and that the obstacles to belief are really much less formidable than they appear, so Goebbels persuaded the Germans that their defeats were really victories [...] As the Jesuits created a system of education aimed at preventing knowledge, so Goebbels created a system of propaganda, ironically styled "public enlightenment", which successfully persuaded a people to believe that black was white.'

Berenson replied on 7 September that he was 'eager' to read Trevor-Roper's reports in the Observer *on Communist political infiltration in France and Italy. The austerities of post-war Britain were a deterrent to visiting London again, but he hoped that 'the Daltonic severities' would not endure and that Trevor-Roper could soon visit I Tatti.*

25 October 1947   Christ Church, Oxford

Dear BB

Thank you very much for your letter, which brought me a great deal of pleasure. Having got my car back to England, and written my newspaper articles,[1] I can now regard my visit to Italy as closed, or at least as reduced to the raw material of possible boasts: for I still boast about it a good deal. I boasted to Alys Russell, who was very glad to hear you are well & active – she now tells me that you have been sweeping over the exhibitions of Italy, as you threatened to do: a journey which I envy you, as I shall always envy those who can live in that elegant country. I do not intend to let Dalton or anyone else prevent me from returning when I want. That is arranged. Life without travel is inconceivable to me.

At present I am preoccupied with other matters: particularly two crises which have broken out almost simultaneously to enliven the tedium of university routine. The first comes from your transatlantic home, where the American jesuits, not content with the mere verbal protests of the timorous Fr Brodrick,[2] are taking economic action, and are even now besieging the headquarters of my publishers in Fifth Avenue, New York. They have declared, through the mouth of Fr Patrick Holloran SJ, president of St Louis University,[3] that unless the passage in my book which ascribes intellectual illiberalism to their Society is suppressed, expunged, and recanted, they will ban the purchase in all their schools, universities & other institutions of all books, on whatever subject, which happen to be published by Messrs Macmillan. This ultimatum has caused consternation in Fifth Avenue, and cables from the beleaguered redoubt anxiously ask permission to surrender. But from the fanatical *Führerbunker* in Oxford a stream of

---

[1] T-R incorporated BB's remarks about the Italian and French dispositions to compromise and to dogmatise in his two articles, 'Communism in Europe', *Observer*, 14 September 1947, p. 4, and 'Communism in France', 21 September 1947, p. 4.
[2] Father James Brodrick (1891–1973), an Irishman, was a member of the Jesuit community in Farm Street, London, and wrote numerous histories of the Society of Jesus and its members. He had reviewed *The Last Days of Hitler* in *The Tablet* of 21 June 1947.
[3] Father Patrick Holloran (1906–69), President of St Louis University (1943–8), a private university in Missouri founded by Jesuit fathers in 1818.

inflexible cables orders them to hold out for ever. What will be the end of it I don't know, but while it lasts, I find that it raises my morale hugely.

This is the American crisis. But since, as is well known, the world is now divided into equal & opposite blocs which respond exactly to every mutual move, it is quite impossible for an American crisis to happen unaccompanied by an equal and opposite crisis in Eastern Europe. A crisis has therefore engaged my attention in Bulgaria, where the Bulgarian militia has swooped on the (pirated) Bulgarian edition of *The Last Days of Hitler* and confiscated every unsold copy, – much to the relief of my legitimate Bulgarian publisher, who is thus saved a good deal of trouble. The explanation of this incivility has been obligingly given by the Bulgarian authorities, who have explained that the book was found to be politically offensive, being 'too objective.' For instance, they say, 'Hitler is often referred to simply as "Hitler" without the necessary epithets "fascist scum" and "monster" ...' These reactions in the remote, incomprehensible Balkans I also find exhilarating.

After this you will not expect that my articles on Italian (or any other) Communism have been uncritical panegyrics. In fact I agree with you both about communism and the *Risorgimento*; and am even contemplating delivering a course of lectures here to dispose of some popular myths about the latter movement.

Alys Russell, as you may have heard, has plunged into the air, and a fortnight ago gave an admirable talk on Walt Whitman.[4] I think she enjoyed writing it, and it was very well received: a lot of it of course was based on Logan's *Unforgotten Years*, but she wrote it and delivered it with great sense & balance, and seems very pleased at having conquered a new world at 80.

If I come to Italy again, as I hope to do, I hope I may visit you again; but in any case I shall always remember my visit to Vallombrosa as a memorable incident. My plans at present are uncertain. I may spend Xmas in Prague; but I'm afraid my name may not smell too sweetly in Slavonic nostrils at the moment, so I can be sure of nothing. [...]

From Rome, on 1 November, Berenson responded enthusiastically to Trevor-Roper's priest-baiting. 'I congratulate you on standing out ag. the threat of the Jesuits. It is becoming more & more difficult to say anything about them or Holy Church (let alone anything ag. them) that American or even Engl. publishers will dare to print.'

---

[4] Her broadcast was published as 'Walt Whitman in his Old Age' in *The Listener* (9 October 1947), p. 616.

1948

22 January 1948   Christ Church, Oxford

Dear BB

I am ashamed that I haven't replied to your last letter, sent from Rome, or thanked you for sending me a copy of Ilse von Hassell's letter,[1] or even taken notice of your kind suggestion that I should visit you in Italy in the winter. Are these faults of omission pardonable? I hope so, for I'm afraid I often commit them. At times I find the mere administrative burden of keeping alive so heavy that all personal business, all the duties of civility, are neglected, and I take refuge in apathy & escapism. The end of last term was such a period of congestion, & when it was past I fled to Prague, to look, before the curtain fell, on that famous baroque city, the Cisalpine Rome. I am glad I went: I was not disappointed. Politically I found it most interesting – I don't think I need have hurried, for I don't think the curtain (that non-existent abstraction) will fall yet, or soon – and the city is fascinating: it reminded me more of Dublin than Rome, the great palaces and buildings of a foreign aristocracy gradually crowded out by the shoddy hutches of a peasantry come to town. And I was driven there by Kenneth Clark's son,[2] who provided me with company & tolerated my whims with universal compliancy. But I ought to have answered your invitation to Italy. May I invite myself at some later time, – perhaps in the spring, if I don't have to go to America in a desperate effort to regulate my hopelessly irregular economic affairs, or am not imprisoned in Oxford in the deadly routine of my college office? For this double burden weighs oppressively upon me at present, making me sometimes wonder whether the leisure for scholarship will ever again be attainable. The twentieth century, I find, is a fascinating century to live in and to study – when, since the 5th century, was Europe so interesting and mutable to observe? – but the leisure for study can seldom have been more difficult to attain!

---

[1] Ilse von Tirpitz, daughter of Admiral Alfred von Tirpitz, creator of the German battle fleet, had in 1911 married Ulrich von Hassell (1881–1944), who was dismissed as Ambassador in Rome in 1938 for his opposition to Nazi foreign policy, arrested after the July Plot and killed by the Gestapo. Hassell's diaries were published as *Vom andern Deutschland 1938–1944* (Zurich, 1946) and as *The Other Germany* (London, 1948). T-R judged them as 'more moving, more restrained and more careful of fact' than most German books about the war (*Foreign Affairs*, XXXI (1953), p. 227).
[2] Alan Clark (1928–1999) was the elder son of Sir Kenneth Clark, who had worked for BB at I Tatti in 1925–7. In 1948 he was a Christ Church pupil of T-R's heading towards a third-class degree. He wrote several works of military history before election to Parliament as a Conservative in 1974.

You very kindly ask me to send you some articles. Alas, I have written nothing to send, except an article on 1848 which I will send as soon as it is published; and perhaps I shall write, when I have a few moments to spare, something on Czechoslovakia. Or would you care for these two products of my Latin visits? They were better than the *Observer* articles, I think, although time, in my opinion, has already caught up on the *New York Times* article.[3] The foundation of Cominform seems to me to be an admission that the 'majority policy' has failed in the west, & that the Communists are reverting, there at least, to the policy of 'an incurable minority'.[4] Only in Czechoslovakia do they still cling to conditions & legality; & that is one reason why I was so eager to visit it. Only one; for really I am, or pretend to be, a seventeenth century historian, & Bohemia to me is the Bohemia of Wallenstein[5] and Comenius,[6] of Wenzel Hollar[7] & the White Mountain,[8] of aristocratic Italian palaces and baroque jesuit churches. Only the chance of war projected my studies into this our own complicated but, on acquaintance, fascinating century.

If you have time to write, I hope I may hear from you, and hear that life in Tuscany is still leisured, and that the mutinous *mezzadri*[9] are quiescent, and that you are well, and Sylvia Sprigge[10] and Max Majnoni.[11] If you should be visited by Sylvia, please tell her that her wishes are commands to me, and that I am trying to arrange that Sforza[12] is honoured as she wishes at the summer Encaenia. [...]

---

[3] T-R's article 'The Politburo Tries a New Tack' (*New York Times Magazine*, 19 October 1947, pp. 7, 63–5, 67), was based on the premise: 'European Communists no longer preach violent revolution; they aim at legitimate power as the leading party of a "democratic" coalition. They no longer rely on an urban proletariat alone; they have sought and won the peasant vote.'
[4] Cominform was established in October 1947 as the propaganda agency representing the Communist parties of the Soviet Union, Poland, Czechoslovakia, Hungary, Yugoslavia, Romania, Bulgaria, France and Italy: it was disbanded in 1956.
[5] Albrecht von Wallenstein (1583–1634), a brilliant military commander in the Thirty Years' War.
[6] Johann Comenius (1592–1670), philosopher, theologian and last bishop of the Moravian Church.
[7] Wenceslaus Hollar (1607–1677), etcher, was born in Prague, but entered the Earl of Arundel's household in 1637.
[8] As a result of the Battle of the White Mountain (1620), the first major battle of the Thirty Years' War, Bohemian autonomy was lost for 299 years and Hapsburg absolutism established in its place.
[9] 'In central Italy the majority of peasants are sharecropping farmers or "mezzadri", who deliver usually one-half of their crops to the landlord in lieu of rent, and let the landlord pay the taxes and supply the capital equipment, seed, fertilisers, repairs and farm machinery.' (T-R, 'Politburo Tries A New Tack', p. 64.) The Italian Communists were promising to alter the system of *mezzadro* to the advantage of the *mezzadri*.
[10] On Sylvia Sprigge see Introduction (pp. xxxv–xxxvi).
[11] T-R had lunched in Rome on 26 July with Marchese Massimiliano ('Max') Majnoni d'Intignano (1894–1957), a distinguished mountaineer, banker and society figure.
[12] Count Carlo Sforza (1873–1952) was Italian Ambassador in Paris at the time of the Fascists' March on Rome 1922, but refused to cooperate with Mussolini and was forced into exile in 1928. Minister of Foreign Affairs 1947–51.

On 28 January, Berenson commended the proposal that Oxford University should award an honorary degree to Sforza, 'the one Italian who is aware of what is going on in the world, the only one who is free from chauvinism, nationalism & all the other symptoms of inferiority complexes that relatively recent statehoods suffer from'. He asked about Trevor-Roper's travelling companion, Alan Clark: 'Is he more like his father or more like Jane; or like neither but a combination of both?' But the bulk of his letter was a response to Trevor-Roper's recent article on the Politburo published in the New York Times *of 19 October 1947:*

'You are extraordinarily right in pointing out that the Sovietists have adopted the Fascist methods of promising all things to all men. Here the bait has been swallowed by peasants, workmen & even artisans, & small shop-keepers – those slop-pails of propaganda. More distressing is the fact that my own intellectual acquaintances, with almost no exceptions, are Sovietic "fellow-travellers", as impenetrable or impermeable to evidence as if they were Stalinist officials. [...] they go on assuring me the Sovietists will not win the coming election. [...] Then most Stal[inists] believe that even if they do [win control in the election], it would be an Italian, human affair of compromises & exchange of good fellowship. So did my Viennese friends a few months before the Anschluss *speak of Nazism if it came to Austria.'*

29 February 1948   **Christ Church, Oxford**

Dear BB

I am taking advantage of a comfortable minor illness to write letters, and to acknowledge yours of 28 January, which I greatly enjoyed. You ask in it for a report on Alan Clark. I will try to give you one.

I don't feel I know his family well enough to answer your question about family resemblances, but when I ask myself the same question, I reply that he takes after his mother. He is an attractive character, and although I took him at first with some misgivings – for it is always rather risky to choose a travelling-companion – he turned out an excellent colleague, co-operative, tolerant & not too deferential. But he isn't a serious intellectual character. Though he likes intellectual company he will never make an intellectual effort, & suffers (in my opinion) from always – in consequence of his family background – having had it too cheaply. The clink of intellectual and aesthetic currency has always sounded easily in his ears, and he has effortlessly spent the small-change of it as if he had earned it. He never will earn any, nor wants to, nor will realise that it must be personally earned; but he is a pleasant companion and drove me well to Prague and back, & I should be quite happy to take him again.

It now seems to me that I was right after all to go there, even in midwinter, lest the curtain should fall and it should prove too late by the spring.[1] Really the spinelessness of the liberal forces in Europe is disgusting. They can win elections but simply don't bother to resist *coups d'état,* however obvious the technique, however often & identically it has been repeated.[2] I visited Masaryk in Prague.[3] He was alleged to be ill, but I think it was an illness of convenience, for he seemed in excellent form when I found him, lying in bed in a vast and luxurious apartment of the Czernin Palace. He was writing private letters in violet ink, and reading Gogol's *Dead Souls,* and the elaborate canon of the bells of the Capuchin Loreto drifted in through the curtains, and he made elaborate jokes in brisk brogue, and all the time he was leaving the foreign policy of Czechoslovakia to his communist under-secretary. And now he and Beneš[4] – *magni nominis umbrae*[5] – still survive in the new government which they could (as it seemed to me) so easily have prevented. Are they really any different from the Neuraths[6] and the Weizsäckers[7] and the Schwerin von Krosigks?[8]

I suppose Togliatti[9] is now taking courage from the example, & since Cominform in Europe and currency restrictions in England threaten continually to diminish the area of possible travel, I am determined to visit

[1] T-R reported on his visit to Prague (30 December 1947 to 8 January 1948) in 'Policies in Prague', *Observer,* 22 February 1948, p. 4.

[2] After Soviet Russian troops occupied Prague in May 1945 there was a long struggle for political control between the Communist party and other non-revolutionary socialist and democratic parties. On 25 February 1948 the Communists staged a successful *coup d'état,* and imposed a single-party constitution which prevailed until the Velvet Revolution of 1989.

[3] On 7 January 1948 T-R called on Jan Masaryk (1886–1948), Czechoslovakian Minister of Foreign Affairs. Masaryk reluctantly remained in office after the Communists' seizure of power but was found dead on 10 March 1948, having thrown himself – or more probably having been defenestrated – from his window at the ministry in Prague.

[4] BB, who had met Edvard Beneš (1884–1948), Czechoslovakia's future President, during the Paris peace conference, commented on the Communist *coup d'état*: 'Beneš whose heart thrilled with rapture, with fellow-feeling and sympathy for everything Russian (as he told me in Paris in 1919) can now study in detail what the breath and paw of the Bear is like' (diary, 29 February 1948).

[5] 'Shadows of a great name'. Lucan, *Pharsalia,* I, 135.

[6] Baron Constantin von Neurath (1873–1956), German Ambassador in London 1930–32 and Foreign Minister 1932–8, failed in his efforts to restrain Hitler.

[7] The posthumous *Memoirs* of Ernst von Weizsäcker (1882–1951), the chief civil servant in the German Foreign Office from 1938 to 1943, were contemptuously reviewed by T-R in 'The Silent Opposition', *Commentary,* XIII (January 1952), pp. 97–8.

[8] Johann Schwerin von Krosigk (1887–1977) served as Minister of Finance 1932–45 and as Minister of Foreign Affairs for three weeks after Hitler's suicide.

[9] Palmiro Togliatti (1893–1964) founded the Italian Communist party together with Antonio Gramsci in 1921. He lived in Moscow for many years before serving as Comintern's chief in Spain during the civil war there. Returning to Italy from Moscow in 1944, he held posts in successive coalition governments until 1947 and was leader of the Italian Communist party until his death. T-R, who had interviewed Togliatti, judged him 'a very able man, perhaps the ablest Communist in Western Europe' (*Observer,* 14 September 1947).

Italy again this spring, & to spend three weeks there from about 16 March to about 6 April. [...] If I could visit you first, I should have the advantage of your advice about my further movements; but I shall leave you to say which if any time suits you. I hope at any rate that it will be possible to see you for a short time.

I hear from Alys Russell that Bob Gathorne-Hardy has been to see you with his MS, – about which I have secret but probably quite unfounded doubts, which you will perhaps now be able finally to quieten.[10] I don't know why I should entertain them, especially since Alys apparently has no reservations about the book; but I cannot quite forget the way in which (in my opinion) judgements were unbalanced by Logan's last vagaries. Perhaps that disequilibrium has now been restored. Anyway you will be able to tell me, if you have seen the document, which I haven't. So I shall wait for your verdict if I see you, as I hope I shall. [...]

A further letter of 13 March from Trevor-Roper was mainly devoted to travel plans, but contained one paragraph of recantation:

I take back my harsh words about poor old Jan Masaryk. Those charitable Tractarians said of archbishop Cranmer, that most sympathetic character, that they knew no good of him except that he burnt well; and I feel of Masaryk that if in a testing crisis he showed a weakness that cannot objectively be justified or politically condoned, at least his remorse and death humanise his errors. He was a sunshine character who failed in a position to which he had not sought to climb – for his name had pushed him thither – and in a test to which his character was quite unfit so suddenly to be subjected.

Trevor-Roper stayed at I Tatti from 4 to 6 April after visiting Sicily. Berenson noted in his diary on 5 April: 'The Temples of Girgenti [Agrigento] he thought "vulgar" – the last word I'd apply to them. Selinunte left him indifferent, but Segesta enraptupted him. Why? Perhaps because unfinished it is so schematic, so legible.'

---

[10] Hon. Robert Gathorne-Hardy (1902–1973), bibliographer, botanist and secretary-companion to Pearsall Smith, discussed the manuscript of his *Recollections of Logan Pearsall Smith* with BB at this time.

16 April 1948   20, Bondgate Without, Alnwick, Northumberland

Dear BB

Before going back to the long polar night of an Oxford term, when the pen shall never be used except to sign leave-of-absence forms, I am writing this overdue letter to thank you for your kindness & hospitality when I was in Italy. I am not in the least disconcerted by having been ill in Sicily: I look back to nothing but a recollection of pleasure. I Tatti was delightful; and even in Sicily I had the benefit of your directions, & think rather of Monreale and Segesta and Selinunte than of that interlude in a darkened & stifling closet in Palermo. As for Segesta – I would exchange all Sicily for it. Out of sight of the sad, slow, sickly, glutinous old Mediterranean sea, which interferes with so many otherwise beautiful places in your latitudes, and set in those pastoral solitudes which I so pursue, – what Lucretius calls *loca pastorum deserta atque otia dia*[1] – I thought it (in the pagan sense) divine. It was as if the Greeks had built a temple in Ireland, or in the Cheviot hills.[2] But I suspect I am uttering the syllables of some monstrous heresy, & ought to remember that Sicily was the original home of the palinode.[3]

I have stopped in Oxford before coming north, and told Parker's to send you a copy of Semmier's diary, if it is still available.[4] I sha'n't know till I return whether they have been able to get it, but I hope so. If not, I shall get you the German edition when it comes out. I am sure you will find it interesting, &, above all, what I know is an important recommendation to you, – short. But for this essential condition I would sing the praises of another book which fails to fulfil it. I brought here a large number of heavy books on my proper subject, none of which I have read, because I suddenly noticed in a bookshop two volumes by that great historian, the Vichy Minister of Education, Jérôme Carcopino, on Cicero's letters.[5] I have been unable to stop reading them. They are like Purcell's *Life of Manning*.[6] You

---

[1] 'Through the deserted haunts of shepherds, and the divine places of their rest.' Lucretius, *De rerum natura*, 5, 1387.
[2] The Cheviot Hills extend some thirty five miles along the frontier between England and Scotland, running from Redesdale in Northumberland to the Jed valley in Roxburghshire.
[3] An ode or song in which the author recants what has been said in a former poem.
[4] Parker's bookshop was in Broad Street, Oxford. Rudolf Semmler (b. 1913), who had served on the personal staff of Josef Goebbels, Reichminister of Enlightenment and Propaganda (1933–45), wrote *Goebbels, Der man achter Hitler* – published in London as *Goebbels, The Man Next to Hitler* (1947).
[5] Jérôme Carcopino (1881–1970), French historian, museum director and educational administrator, had in 1947 published *Les Secrets de la Correspondance de Cicéron*.
[6] BB's confirmation service as a Catholic had been performed by Cardinal Henry Manning, Archbishop of Westminster, in 1891. T-R was given Edmund Purcell's biography of Manning by Pearsall Smith in 1943, and noted after reading it: 'A wonderful book. The footnotes are Gibbonian

cannot believe how odious Cicero is demonstrated, on his own evidence, to have been. At one time I nearly stopped reading, through nausea at his character, but the inexorable genius of curiosity led me on to the technical evidence whereby Carcopino proves that the letters were edited by the prudent Atticus as propaganda for Octavian against the memory and political friends of Cicero. I suppose you are familiar with the works of Carcopino. You once said that we know too little of Caesar. Carcopino has written a book on him, which I haven't read: but it must be good. But I mustn't try to persuade you to read *Les Secrets de la Correspondance de Cicéron*, because it is too long!

Your other commissions haven't been forgotten and will be fulfilled; but here, in these subarctic regions, I feel too far away from the world. North of the Tyne no one has heard of Katkov[7] & it would be useless to ask after him. But I enjoy here the advantage of seeing a second spring in one year. The first was at I Tatti, where now, I suppose, your stream has become dry & silent, while here the trees are only just in flower, & I am reluctant to leave Northumberland, & its fishful streams, for the treadmill-life & enervating air of Oxford. But in this at least it is more like I Tatti – it has more books and better conversation!

I hope you are keeping well, and that your elections will go well.[8] How dull the walls of Florence & Rome will be after Sunday, when there are no more posters and *graffiti* to enliven these, & Monsignor Cippico[9] will have become as obsolete as Cambyses.[10] But I put my trust in those consolatory prophets who assure me that no descending curtain will prevent me from paying you another visit some time; and I hope that in the interim I shall continue to hear from you whenever you have time to write and

---

[...] He obviously disliked Manning, but the subtlety with which he infects an official, laudatory, documented, & complete biography with little drops of fatal poison is delicious; and devastating to Manning.'

[7] George Katkov (1903–1985) fled Russia in 1921 for Prague, and Czechoslovakia for England in 1938. He was a research lecturer in philosophy at Oxford, 1947–50, joined St Anthony's College, Oxford in 1953 as a Russian historian, and was an erudite, witty and exuberant university lecturer on Soviet institutions and economics, 1959–71.

[8] The first Italian general election under the post-monarchical constitution was held on 18–19 April 1948: the Christian Democrats secured 307 seats as against 182 seats won by the Popular Front of communists and socialists.

[9] Monsignor Edoardo Prettner-Cippico (1905–1983), an official of the Vatican secretariat who was defrocked in September 1947 for fraud and illicit currency dealings. His case was revived for electoral purposes by the Italian communists in March and April 1948. Cippico, who had been in the pay of the US Office of Strategic Studies (the forerunner of the CIA), was later reinstated in the Vatican. Twenty years later he purloined confidential Vatican documents on Germany and sold their contents to the Soviet Union.

[10] T-R had recently re-read Herodotus' account of Cambyses II, King of Persia (d. 521 BC), conqueror of Egypt.

illuminate our now parochial life with news from your intellectual cosmopolis. [...]

On 16 April, from Alnwick, Trevor-Roper also sent a letter of thanks to his hostess at I Tatti. 'I suppose you will have a house full, and conversation buzzes furiously about the Elections, and you must be far better informed about goings-on in the world of wit and fashion in England than I can possibly be in these remote northern solitudes, where no-one meets anyone except at point-to-point meetings, or talks about anything there except horses. But tomorrow I shall be in London & hope to see Alys Russell, who will be glad to hear of you all; & then I go to that famous medieval prison at Oxford (I really like it very much, if only I was allowed to do my own work instead of other people's!).'

Berenson replied from Siena ('this most fascinatingly preserved of medieval towns') on 2 May that he had already ordered Carcopino's book on Cicero's correspondence: 'I knew the author well when he was presiding [over] the "Ercola de Roma". Rather pompous but a real scholar.' He was relieved by the outcome of the Italian elections. 'The results show that when thoroughly roused the great majority of Italians are as conservative politically as (whether they know it or not) they are patriarchal socially. The dangers of infiltration, of rat-like gnawing, of worming on the part of the Soviet-minded is still great.' He and Nicky Mariano were returning next day to I Tatti: 'Lady Colefax may be there before us.'

4 June 1948   Christ Church, Oxford

Dear BB

    I suppose you are back at I Tatti, and Lady Colefax has been & gone, and the echo of her fashionable conversation is still audible after her, as the rustle of her coming preceded her; so it is no good my attempting to send you any news from the world, – she will have given you all.[1] But you asked me to send you anything I wrote, so I am sending a few items, and also to answer some questions, which I can now answer; so perhaps these communications will justify a letter.

    You asked about Katkov. Katkov is alive and flourishing and advancing the study of philosophy in Oxford, where some fugitive scholars still sometimes stop in their flight from Central Europe to America. You asked about the Bowes Museum at Barnard Castle. That is also still flourishing; in fact

---

[1] Sibyl Colefax (1874–1950), the most genuinely warm-hearted of the inter-war London hostesses, first met BB when she was eighteen, and became his beloved friend. Her letters to him were a privileged source of the latest confidential news.

a few days ago I was sent a notice of a pamphlet about it, just published by its new Curator. I will try to get you a copy so that you may be entirely reassured on this point, – although a taste for Durham seems to me a strange, exotic taste for one who lives in Florence. The inhabitants of Durham have sometimes developed a taste for Italy – there was a 15th century bishop of Durham who had humanist tastes and had sat at the feet of (I think) Guarino in Ferrara;[2] but the reverse taste is perhaps even more rare and refined. You also asked about the cleaning of the Christ Church pictures. They are done by Buttery. An annual grant is made from Corporate Funds for general maintenance of the pictures, & this includes cleaning.

The articles I send are rather miscellaneous, – one on Goebbels, which was published in the *New York Times Magazine* when the diaries were released (you will see that it contains gobbets from Semmler, which, I agree, is a better book than Goebbels);[3] one on 1848, done originally for the Central Office of Information to publish in foreign languages, – hence its compressed style – & then in English in the *Cornhill*;[4] one on Cromwell in the *New Statesman*, which I'm afraid has made the virtuous Marxists very angry & Sir Ernest Barker very pained[5] (but in a book published in 1937 he *did* praise Cromwell as an English Hitler; perhaps it is malicious of me to remember these things. He has 'reprinted' the essay in a new book just out, but has silently omitted that unfortunate comparison from the reprint);[6] and a review of a book on *Munich* which I send you in the hope that I may interest you in the book; it is, in my opinion, fascinating.[7] I don't know if you know its author, John Wheeler-Bennett.[8] He is an interesting man. He

---

[2] Guarino da Verona (1370–1460), Professor of Greek at Ferrara, revived the study of the Greek classics in Italy. John Shirwood (d. 1493), Bishop of Durham, was among the earliest Englishmen to learn Greek; he collected Greek manuscripts and printed works of classical Roman authors, subsidised Greek exiles in England and wrote polished Latin prose.

[3] 'His Diary Explodes the Goebbels Myth', *New York Times Magazine*, 14 March 1948.

[4] '1848', *Cornhill Magazine*, vol. 163, (spring 1948), no.964, pp. 109–17.

[5] While reviewing *The Writings and Speeches of Oliver Cromwell* (*New Statesman*, 29 May 1948, p. 440) T-R declared that historians must adjudicate 'between the Nazis (and Professor Ernest Barker) praising him as an English Hitler and the Marxists denouncing him as the creature of monopoly capitalism'. This led to protests from Christopher Hill (1912–2003), a Marxist historian of the sixteenth and seventeenth centuries at Balliol College, Oxford, and from Sir Ernest Barker (1874–1960), Professor of Political Science at Cambridge, 1928–39.

[6] Barker's essay 'Oliver Cromwell and the English People' had originally been delivered as a lecture at Hamburg in 1936, and in its final version was reprinted in *Traditions of Civility* (1948). As he explained to T-R, 'I was trying hard to tell a Nazi audience that they were wrong – utterly wrong – in their view of Cromwell. Indeed I was trying to do the opposite of praising Cromwell as an English Hitler' (letter of 29 May 1948).

[7] T-R's review of John Wheeler-Bennett's *Munich: The Prologue to Tragedy* was published as 'Munich, its Lessons Ten Years Later' in *New York Times*, 8 August 1948.

[8] (Sir) John Wheeler-Bennett (1902–1975) lived during the 1920s and 1930s in Germany, where he developed a lifelong fascination with the country's junkers, generals, diplomats and politicians.

went to Germany when a young man, having (I think) refused to go into the family business, & being rich & fashionable soon got to know everyone in Berlin, & being serious & scholarly was well placed to study the politics of Germany from the centre & on the spot. He wrote a good life of Hindenburg & a good book on the Treaty of Brest-Litovsk,[9] & is now in charge of German documents captured in this war, together with an American colleague R.J. Sontag.[10] *Hindenburg* & *Brest Litovsk* are too long for you (you see I now prescribe your books by length, with complete confidence), but the operative part of *Munich*, – i.e. the history of events from the annexation of Austria in March 1938 to Munich in October 1938 – is less than 200 pages & is (in my opinion) fascinating: but fascinating (for an Englishman) with a morbid fascination, which you, as an American, need not share – though as a European I think you would. Would you care to have this book? I should be delighted to send it to you if you would. [...]

In his reply from Venice on 14 June, Berenson looked forward to receiving a copy of Wheeler-Bennett's study of the Munich crisis, and urged Trevor-Roper to write a full-length biography of Cromwell. 'Did you ever,' he continued, 'read a skit by a scoundrel of genius (almost) who calls himself Curzio Malaparte on Lenin. It is called "Le Bonhomme Lénine".'

12 July 1948   Christ Church, Oxford

My dear BB

Many thanks for your letter. I hope you have got through all your 'operations' in Florence successfully & I suppose you have now withdrawn like some devout anchorite to the higher, clearer, holier and more meta-physical air of Vallombrosa. I wish I could visit you there, but am going back to the Arctic this summer, – to Lapland & Finland, I hope, after a brief rest in Ireland with your engaging *bon-viveur* friend Henry McIlhenny, who stopped with me here on his way from the Eternal City to its most

---

He was attached to the British prosecuting team at the Nuremburg trials of war criminals, and British editor-in-chief of captured German Foreign Ministry archives.
[9] *Hindenburg: The Wooden Titan* (1936) was Wheeler-Bennett's authoritative analysis of German chauvinism and the collapse of the Weimar republic. *Brest Litovsk: The Forgotten Peace* (1938) described the German-Soviet treaties whereby Russia renounced control over Estonia, Latvia and Lithuania in 1918.
[10] Raymond Sontag (1897–1972), a historian at the University of California at Berkeley specialising in German diplomacy after the fall of Bismarck, was US editor-in-chief of *Documents of German Foreign Policy 1918–1945*, 1946–9.

forlorn and forgotten dependency.[1] I have no doubt you will have plenty of visitors even on your remote hilltop.

I haven't read *le Bonhomme Lénine*, but I know a little about Curzio Malaparte, & I enclose a review of his recent book *Kaputt* which I published a year ago.[2] I was surprised to find that the ingenious publisher had contrived to discover in this review one sentence which he could quote as a tribute of praise on the dust-cover! Can you discover it?

My time at present is being consumed by elaborate legal manoeuvres in order to escape libel actions from outraged Germans who are discovering that losing a war has at least this advantage, that the victory of liberalism enables them to sue their victors. The situation is rather farcical, but very time-wasting. You once flattered me by saying that what you liked in my book was the judgments: 'when a man is a cad, you say he is a cad'. I am now finding the disadvantages of this alleged virtue. There may be less money in seventeenth century than in 20th century history, but there is also less danger –

> Periculosae plenum opus aleae
> Tractas, et incedis per ignes
> Suppositos cineri doloso![3]

I think I shall go back to Oliver Cromwell now, safe behind the legal maxim that is is impossible to libel the dead!

Have you read Ciano's *L'Europa verso la Catastrofe* which has been published by Mondadori?[4] I am reading it and find some of the documents fascinating. On pages 249–278 there is a most interesting report from Grandi in London on his meeting with Chamberlain & Eden.[5] If you haven't

---

[1] The theocratic political constitution imposed on Ireland in 1937 by Eamon de Valera had made the country a forlorn dependency of the Vatican, T-R felt. Henry McIlhenny (1910–1986), Philadelphia art collector and philanthropist, owned Glenveagh Castle in County Donegal. He visited T-R in Oxford for a weekend in June 1948: T-R stayed with him at Glenveagh, 16 to 27 July 1948.

[2] Kurt Suckert (1898–1957), newspaper editor and war correspondent, joined the Italian Fascist party in 1922 and wrote under the pseudonym of Curzio Malaparte. T-R's review of *Kaputt* (1944) characterised him as 'an ex-Fascist playboy' and 'cosmopolitan snob' who wrote with 'some of the qualities of brilliance'.

[3] 'You are performing a task full of dangerous hazards, and you are walking through fires hidden beneath treacherous ashes.' Horace, *Odes* 2, I, 6–8.

[4] Galeazzo Ciano (1903–1944) had been Mussolini's son-in-law and Foreign Minister. The English translation of his diaries was entitled *Ciano's Diplomatic Papers* (1948).

[5] Describing secret contacts between the Prime Minister, Neville Chamberlain, and Count Dino Grandi, Italian Ambassador in London, as well as the conversations held in Rome by his sister-in-law Ivy Chamberlain with Ciano and Mussolini.

read this, do – I am sure it would interest you. It may also interest you to know that the English translation will omit the references to Sir Joseph Ball, because Ball has threatened a libel action if they are included.[6] Of course it is all bluff – no action would lie & the facts can be proved true – but the bluff has worked with the pusillanimous publisher. I intend to review the book & sha'n't notice that these passages have been omitted from the English text – I shall assume that they are in & mention them. I don't consider that historical facts should be suppressed by such man-oeuvres.

I saw Alys Russell in London last week. She is well, & I surprised her subscribing virtuously to the dwindling Socialist Cause, so I suppose I may say she is politically active too.

I hope the excommunication of Tito has given you as much pleasure as it has given me![7] [...]

Berenson's reply from Casa al Dono on 28 July discussed Malaparte – 'the D'Annunzio of the Fascist regime, & by so much the less gifted & more shoddy' – and asked that Trevor-Roper, while in Finland, buy him a catalogue of the Helsinki picture gallery and photographs of any Italian paintings in its collection.

5 August 1948   Christ Church, Oxford

Dear BB

Many thanks for you letter – alas, unless some miracle occurs (and although the Age of Miracles is alleged by some to have returned, I doubt if any will be operated in my favour), I shall never be in Helsinki, & therefore shall be unable to send you details of the Italian pictures there, as I should certainly and most gladly have done had not an unexpected last-minute incident made my journey impossible. I regret it greatly: I hate spending August in Oxford, where everything is shut and the climate invariably makes me ill, but all movement requires such preparation, especially in this congested month, that to repair broken plans suddenly is quite impossible. Almost I am persuaded to revisit Italy, the one country where I feel so much at home that I do not mind travelling in it alone. But the heat is too great; my eyes at this season turn magnetically towards the Pole.

---

[6] Sir Joseph Ball (1885–1961) was recruited in 1927 from MI5 to become the Conservative party's Director of Publicity and expert in political espionage. He acted as Chamberlain's secret intermediary with Grandi.
[7] On 28 June 1948 Cominform denounced Marshal Tito for ideological heresies, and launched a campaign of denunciation and economic boycott of Yugoslavia.

I haven't read Malaparte's *Technique du Coup d'Etat* but I have heard of it.[1] I have been told that it is really a plagiarism, all taken from a book by either Lenin or Trotsky, I forget which (one does mix up these communists so; and yet at least in the first twenty years of them there were *some* divergences and differences and heresies among them: for I can't believe that Tito's sin of 'grandeeism' is really an intellectual heresy).

Yes, I really do mean to write about the Cromwellian interlude. It is a subject that fascinates me, as you seem to have deduced from my review (or perhaps I bored you with enthusiasm on that topic at I Tatti); but I should like to do it well, and there is so much still to be done, and I feel so ignorant, and time is so short and leisure so scarce (that is the worst thing: the others can be overcome) that I am sometimes assailed with doubts about it.

At present I am assailed by much more positive and formidable and palpable and insistent and inexorable things than mere doubts – by Scotch professors. A cloud of them, as of locusts, has settled upon us, and fretted every green thing. Since the centre of Scotch life shifted, by some disastrous natural cataclysm comparable with the development of the Dustbowl in your transatlantic home, from the clear, dry, sceptical, eighteenth century city of Edinburgh to the morose, metaphysical, fuliginous air of Glasgow, you cannot conceive what a disastrous change has come over Scotch professors. (I say you cannot conceive it, for I am sure you have managed to avoid them: they hate art, and letters, and music, and never go to Italy; indeed, a Scotch undergraduate of Balliol, a contemporary of mine, refused a classical award that was pressed upon him on the grounds that it would only finance him to go to Italy and Greece, while he preferred Aberdeen.) Well anyway, there are no more Boswells, no more Humes among them now, and they have a curious pleasure in hearing their own voices answering endless unasked questions, with infinite promptitude, on matters of totally uninteresting fact. I suppose as a historian I ought to be interested in facts, but I'm afraid they bore me: I much prefer ideas, or even mere gossip, to being told how many towns called Bradford there are in America or what was the first occasion on which hospital-ships were used ... but they have bored me all evening; why should I bore you?

Do you ever see a German paper *Die Gegenwart*? I think it might interest you, so I am sending you a few copies. It is run by the staff of the former *Frankfurter Zeitung*, and is edited in Saig-über-Titisee in Baden and published in Freiburg im-Breisgau under the intellectually liberal *régime* of the

---

[1] Mussolini condemned Malaparte to internal exile after its publication in 1931. Sylvia Sprigge translated the English edition of 1938.

administratively corrupt French. Sometimes it has good things in it, and anyway it is the only thing of its kind in Germany now, so perhaps it has some interest if only for that reason.

I hope the heat of the sun comes to you strained and filtered to a gentle temperature through the beech-leaves of Vallombrosa. (I forget if they are beech-leaves, I only remember that they are deciduous, and therefore to be praised above all the olives and cypresses of Italy); and I look forward to seeing your *Estetica*,[2] whenever it shall come. [...]

Berenson replied on 4 September that Nicky was reading Wheeler-Bennett's Munich *aloud to him: 'God knows how horrified I was by events that lead up to it, & to what extent I made myself obnoxious to friends (including Walter Lippmann) by the way I bayed ag. Chamberlain & Co. But this book makes their policy even worse than I realised at the time. And are we repeating it? A bad symptom is the Pacifist meeting at Breslau. It was unquestionably got up by Sovietist fellow-travellers and geese. When a government promotes pacifism abroad it is preparing for war. Germany promoted it as an* Export Bier *before World War One, & captured many sentimentalists & humanitarians in Engl. & USA – Is Namier's bk. on what led up to Munich worth my reading? – Thanks for 'Die Gegenwart' wh. I find most praiseworthy. I am subscribing for it. – The K. Clarks are staying at I Tatti & came up a day or two ago. K. talks of his eldest son as an utter Philistine of whom he yet is proud & expectant.'*

18 September 1948   **Christ Church, Oxford**

Dear BB

I was very glad to hear from you and to hear that you are working at the English translation of your essay, which I look forward to reading. I haven't been away from these islands all this summer, much to my regret. This means that I have done a lot of work, but I have also been unwell, & I now wish I could get away for a short time before next term, but I fear it won't be possible. As for your question, Yes, I think you would enjoy Namier's *Diplomatic Prelude*; it is very good indeed; I don't think you would find it too long; and it is better than Wheeler-Bennett both in structure & style. And I think you would particularly appreciate its excellence. Namier is in

---

[2] *Estetica, Etica e Storia nelle arti della rappresentazione visiva* was published in Milan in 1948. Mario Praz's translation was published in New York in the same year as *Aesthetics and History in the Visual Arts*, and in London in 1950 as *Aesthetics and History*.

my opinion the best living English historian.[1] He is something of a historian's historian, with a wonderful technical virtuosity, and he is one of those rare historians who never write on one subject without illuminating a whole range of subjects outside their immediate scope. If you would like to read it, and haven't got it, let me know & I will of course have it sent to you. I enclose two articles I have written recently, one being on *Munich*; you will see how indebted I am to Wheeler-Bennett.[2] It has got me into some trouble already from the chamberlainites of whom, it seems, there are still a few left. But I rather like a little trouble, so long as it remains only a little; & I got into much more at the time of Munich, when I had to leave a country-house I was staying owing to the ill reception of my views on the subject!

I have had a good deal of amusement out of the Breslau conference, which doesn't seem to have been a success at all from the point of view of its sponsors.[3] I have had one Marxist account, which was very dispirited, and one from A.J.P. Taylor, who was responsible for spoiling it.[4] I don't think he will ever get a free ticket beyond the Iron Curtain again.

I am fascinated by the internal struggle in Palestine. It is just like the development of revolutionary politics in Cromwell's time, – the mystical fanatics on the left struggling against the realist revolutionaries on the right after the initial military victory. I suppose I ought to go there and see it happening; but as I have been condemned to death by the Stern gang (I don't know why) I think I sha'n't take any risks, especially after the fate of the unfortunate Count Bernadotte.[5] Instead I am going to America this winter. No doubt I shall find just as *strange* human material to study in that vast, unexplored, terrifying, exotic continent of yours.

---

[1] (Sir) Lewis Namier (1888–1960), Professor of Modern History at Manchester University, 1931–53, had lately published *Diplomatic Prelude 1938–1939* (1948). BB wrote (29 October 1953): 'How easy and warm the atmosphere between born Jews like Isaiah Berlin, Lewis Namier, myself, Bela Horowitz, when we drop the mask of being goyim and return to Yiddish reminiscences and Yiddish stories and witticisms. After all, it has been an effort (no matter how unaware) to act as if one were a mere Englishman or Frenchman or American, and it is something like homecoming and reposing to return to "Mother's cooking".' (Berenson, *Sunset and Twilight* (1963), p. 223.) Berlin, however, explicitly denied the accuracy of this passage to T-R.
[2] 'Munich, Its Lessons Ten Years Later', *New York Times*, 8 August 1948.
[3] The Cultural Congress for Peace, held at Wroclaw [Breslau] in Poland in August and September 1948, was a Soviet-managed propaganda stunt against American capitalist imperialism.
[4] The response by A.J.P. Taylor (1906–1990), Fellow and tutor in history at Magdalen College, Oxford, since 1938, to a hectoring speech by Alexander Fadeyev, head of the Soviet Writers' Union, ruined the congress's semblance of unity.
[5] Among other acts of terrorism, the Stern Gang assassinated Lord Moyne (British Minister Resident in the Middle East), attacked Sir Harold Macmichael (High Commissioner for Palestine), bombed the King David Hotel in Jerusalem and on 17 September 1948 murdered Count Folke Bernadotte (1895–1948), a grandson of King Oscar II of Sweden and United Nations mediator between the Arabs and Jews in Palestine.

I am very sorry about Bernadotte. I never met him, but of course I came across his activities in Germany, where he showed himself extraordinarily efficient in negotiation, & saved a great number of lives from concentration camps as well as indirectly securing local surrenders in Norway & Denmark. I have had a certain amount of correspondence with him, which has increased my respect both for his efficiency and for his fundamental assumption that an aristocracy must earn its keep, – an assumption not, on the whole, shared by the Italian aristocracy, I think. In his last letter, sent just before he went to Palestine, he told me that he was going to Nuremberg to give evidence for Schellenberg: 'I have the opinion, that now seems to be rather old-fashioned, that if a man has helped me when I had great difficulties, I want to help him when he is in trouble, even if that *might* be criticised by other people.' This seems to me a most attractive characteristic. When I think of Bernadotte I think of the similar attitude of Sarpedon in the Iliad, book, 12,

$$\text{Γλαῦκε, τίη δὴ νῶϊ τετιμήμεσθα μάλιστα ...}^{6}$$

I had meant to see him in Sweden this summer, but it is obviously rash to speculate on the success of any plans that one may prepare at present.

Have you read Winston's memoirs – the first volume, I mean, which alone is yet published?[7] I have just finished it. I began it rather wearily, for one begins to think one knows all about a man who has filled so much of the world for so long; but really it is a wonderful work, majestic in its scope & completely olympian in its judgments. His vitality is really extraordinary. I hope he will last long enough to finish it down to 1945 and not waste his time in English politics in which, at the moment, he is no good!

In my few leisure moments I am working hard on Cromwell. I hope to have at least a short preliminary article to send you some time. But I hope you won't wait for that before writing, as it might be a long time in coming! [...]

PS. I had a visit from Luisa Vertova a month ago.[8] She was just in time as I was leaving Oxford for Northumberland that afternoon; but I was able to show her the pictures here & was very glad to see her, as I always will be glad to see anyone from I Tatti.

Have you read Osbert Sitwell's trilogy? I have enjoyed it enormously.[9]

---

[6] 'Glaucus, why is it that we two are specially honoured?' Homer, *Iliad*, XII, 310.
[7] *The Gathering Storm* (1948).
[8] Luisa Vertova (b. 1920), the eager and lively daughter of a Florentine professor, worked at I Tatti from 1945 until her marriage in 1955 to the art historian Benedict Nicolson.
[9] Sir Osbert Sitwell (1892–1969), poet and novelist, had published so far three volumes of autobiography. Pearsall Smith had introduced T-R to Sitwell.

Berenson's reply on 25 September took up the topic of Count Bernadotte's assassination. 'No people reaches statehood except through blood & filth & terror. If you read such remarks about Poland & the Warsaw Ghetto as appeared in [...] penultimate 'Spectator' you understand why all of those fr. Zentral Europe want Palestine, no matter on what terms. And now that the Jew is ready to dig the soil, fight & die, nothing will stop him – unfortunately & unhappily. On the other hand he may establish a power there that Engl. may regret having embittered as she has in Ireland. As for the Arab I understand how he fascinates sedentary-based Brit. officials & how amenable compared with the vulgar, violent, obstreperous Israelites, but politically he never (in our historical horizon) can have other than nuisance value.'

There was no prompt reply from Oxford, and BB wrote again on 27 October from Zurich. He had met two people of special interest in Switzerland: Ilse von Hassell – 'I had not seen her since her husband's execution and she had a great deal to say about what led up to it, & how she said it!' – and 'an old friend, a big industrialist', who had gossiped about a Swiss painter-dealer named Montag who had 'somehow got to be very thick with Winston [Churchill], and as the story goes taught him how to paint, & some individuals boast that the better ones & most of those exhibited as Winston's were largely if not wholly his, Montag's'. Montag had remained in Paris during the German occupation, 'and behaved fairly well saving Jewish lives & collections from the jaws of Wuotan. [...] It was he who organised Winston's visit to Switzerland & had him treated so sumptuously, & sent off with cartloads of gifts. It was done by making all the blacklist people contribute. For this they got invitations to banquets in Winston's honour, after which nobody dared trouble them.' It was also Montag who had arranged for Time-Life Incorporated to finance Churchill's recent painting holiday in Marrakesh, so Berenson had been told.

8 November 1948   Christ Church, Oxford

Dear BB

I am ashamed that you should have written to me before I had written to thank you for so kindly & so hospitably (and so suddenly) welcoming me in Italy – I was waiting for something to send you, & it has been very late in coming – and even now I'm afraid this is only an interim letter. I enclose a short historical sketch which might interest you, but I have no answers yet to your questions. The fact is that I am rather isolated, being confined to my rooms with a broken spine, the result of a hunting accident a week ago. My horse fell suddenly & rolled on me crushing a couple of vertebrae – not badly, but I have emerged from hospital encased from neck to rump in a dull, solid, heavy, resounding cage of imperishable plaster, from which I shall not emerge for at least three months. This must be my excuse for the weak, partial and fragmentary answers which I shall now try to give to your questions.

First Montag.[1] I have asked Lord Cherwell about him, & Cherwell says that M. is an exhibitionist who amuses or amused Winston & persuaded him that he (Montag) knew about pictures.[2] There is no truth in the story that Montag shared the triumphal drive through Paris, or painted any of Winston's pictures: this is just part of the exhibitionism. Cherwell says that Montag has now gone too far & has fallen out of favour: he turned up uninvited at Aix-en-Provence and tried to force some unwanted Rumanian on to Winston. Of course one must remember that in a sense Cherwell & Montag are both competitive members of Winston's court, so no doubt they would belittle each other, but Cherwell is by far the grandest member in the court – in fact the Grand Vizier – so he *ought* to feel it unnecessary to damn Montag on those grounds. Still, as Logan said, 'I rather like singing for my supper; what grates on my ears is the song of the other singers'; so I can't be sure. But I don't think it can be true that Montag fixed Winston's holiday in Morocco – Winston's dealings with *Time* & *Life* were handled by the Berrys,[3] & he uses official agents & lawyers who are well known. It seems to me that Montag must be a rogue who has got a foothold in the court & wants to pretend that the whole thing is managed by him. However, I will investigate further, as Cherwell is obviously a dubious source & I have much better ones once I am able to get about & consult them. [...]

The article I enclose was written for the magazine of my old school (Charterhouse) – hence the somewhat elementary form and lack of scholarly apparatus![4] I am interested in millionaires whose economic activities – either in getting or spending – shed real light on periods of historical change, & I think Thomas Sutton is one of those.[5] I have for some time

---

[1] The painter Charles Montag (1880–1956) had first met Churchill in 1920. During the inter-war years they corresponded about and met to discuss painting, and resumed contact after the war. Montag had visited Churchill in Marrakesh in January 1948.

[2] Frederick Lindemann, Viscount Cherwell (1886–1957), physicist and expert in weaponry, was Professor of Experimental Philosophy at Oxford 1919–56 and a Student of Christ Church 1921–57. He was Churchill's confidant, scientific adviser and political ally. T-R contributed a profile of 'Churchill's "Prof"' to *New York Times Magazine* of 24 May 1949.

[3] William Berry, 1st Viscount Camrose (1879–1954), co-proprietor and editor-in-chief of the *Daily Telegraph*, arranged the transfer of Churchill's house, Chartwell, to the National Trust and negotiated the sale of the world rights of the ex-prime minister's war memoirs for an enormous sum.

[4] 'Thomas Sutton', *The Carthusian*, October 1948, pp. 2–8.

[5] Sir Thomas Sutton (1532–1611) amassed a fortune through land acquisitions and money-lending. His will established the London Charterhouse, containing almshouses and a school at which, on a later site at Godalming, T-R was educated. As a schoolboy T-R saw Sutton represented in the Charterhouse Masque dressed as an Elizabethan seadog surrounded by small boys pulling imaginary nautical ropes. T-R never completed his biography of Sutton but when he was old, ill

contemplated a little work consisting of accounts of the lives of four such figures, who in different ways can illustrate the social & economic changes of the 16th–17th century in England. I should like to do John Dudley Duke of Northumberland,[6] Thomas Sutton, Sir Thomas Bodley,[7] and Richard Boyle 1st Earl of Cork.[8] Between them they illustrate almost the whole range of social & economic opportunity and aims. Anyway, here is a brief résumé of my work on Sutton! [...]

11 December 1948   Christ Church, Oxford

Dear BB

I have now emerged from the horrors of the term, but am still, & shall be for another two months, in the horrors of my plaster cage: but at least I can divert my mind from the treadmill of routine which is the more hateful of the two prisons, & write a few letters. I hope you are all well, and that life at I Tatti is as olympian as it always seems to me to be among its books & pictures, terraces & cypresses. Do visitors still descend ceaselessly upon you, to envy you that felicity, even in the dead season of winter, or are you travelling again around Italy & Switzerland? In my present state of immobility any movement seems to me travel, & I have had to cancel my visit to America, with which I was going to fill in the December void. Nor have I been able (for discomfort inhibits the fastidious mind) to write anything. But I have at least, & at last, succeeded in exposing the documentary malpractices of Sir Joseph Ball, who, by threatening legal action, succeeded in persuading the English publishers to falsify the translation of *The Ciano Papers* & conceal his part in the policy of appeasement. My first attempt failed. I reviewed the Italian text in the *Economist*, whose editor took fright and cut out the references to Ball.[1] He said it was on legal advice, but I suspect it was for another reason. (The *Economist* is paid £300 a time for publishing Company Reports, & Ball is a director of 11 companies.) But now I have had the whole thing exposed on three successive days, in the *New Statesman*, the *Evening Standard*, & the *Observer*. It would make

---

and nearly blind, he devoted months to re-reading his notes for the book and writing a condensed summary of Sutton's career for the *Oxford Dictionary of National Biography*, 53 (2004), pp. 406–10.

[6] John Dudley, Duke of Northumberland (1504–1553), Lord Protector during Edward VI's reign, was a businessman–politician rather than a traditional territorial magnate.

[7] Sir Thomas Bodley (1545–1613), diplomat and re-founder of the Oxford university library.

[8] Richard Boyle, 1st Earl of Cork (1566–1643), went to Ireland as a ruthless young adventurer, amassed immense landed wealth there and was appointed Lord High Treasurer of Ireland.

[1] 'Ciano's Papers', *Economist*, 13 November 1948, pp. 791–2.

me feel quite sorry for the victim if I could forget the facts![2]

In my last letter I mentioned Lord Cherwell's reply to your question about Montag. Since then I have seen Bill Deakin, a friend & contemporary of mine who helped Winston with his *Marlborough*, was with Tito in the war, & is now helping Winston with his *Memoirs*.[3] He is, I think, more objective & therefore more reliable than Cherwell, & is a very close friend of Winston's, accompanying him on most of his travels. He tells me that there is 'an element of truth' in the claim that Montag fixed Winston's journey to Switzerland (Montag is a director of *Crédit Suisse*), but no truth at all in any claim that he fixed anything else. Montag has advised Winston in the technique of painting, but no more.

Alys Russell is in splendid form, broadcasting like mad, and getting excited over her fan-mail; Bob Gathorne-Hardy's book, which I await with apprehension, is expected shortly from the Press; & in general the world here is in motion. I'm sure yours is moving even faster. How is your *Seeing & Knowing*? Remember I am expecting a copy & hope I may expect a letter with it, giving me news from your Italian Paradise. I look forward eagerly to both.

May I take this opportunity to introduce a friend whom you are almost certain to meet shortly? Dawyck Haig, the present Earl Haig (son of the controversial Field-Marshal),[4] is going to be a guest of Derek Hill[5] at your *villino*[6] very soon, & I expect you will meet him. He is a painter, – how good I don't know. He began under the influence of a rather fashionable social-climbing Frenchman, Paul Maze,[7] and then was a regular soldier in

---

[2] Ball was not, however, named for fear of libel action. The *New Statesman*, 4 December 1948, p. 477, referred to 'a private and personal messenger' between Chamberlain and Grandi, adding, 'it would be interesting to know who this was.'

[3] (Sir) William Deakin (1913–2005), a Fellow and tutor of Wadham College, Oxford, 1936–49, became the first Warden of St Anthony's College, Oxford, 1950–68.

[4] George Alexander Eugene Douglas Haig, 2nd Earl Haig (b. 1918) was always known as Dawyck (pronounced Doik): his courtesy title until his father's death in 1928 had been Viscount Dawick. A friend of the painter Victor Pasmore, and Pasmore's pupil at the Camberwell School of Arts in the 1940s; his sister Alexandra subsequently married T-R.

[5] Derek Hill (1916–2000), portrait and landscape painter, spent five winters from 1948 living in a guesthouse at I Tatti. He said of BB: 'I was completely devoted to him and to Nicky Mariano [...] They became my family [...] It was a serious place, there was quiet and work and reading but mealtimes could be dazzling with arguments in every European language taking place [...] His talk could be an education, a life in itself; certainly it brought me into a life I'd never known [...] By the time I knew him his instinct, his judgement for painting was still very fine but somehow he'd moved on, out of art and into life.' Grey Gowrie, *Derek Hill* (1987), p. 104.

[6] A small but elegant villa.

[7] T-R had met Paul Maze (1887–1979) in Dawyck Haig's undergraduate rooms at Christ Church. Maze's paintings of such fashionable sporting fixtures as the racing at Goodwood, the rowing in Henley and the yachting at Cowes contributed to T-R's sense that he was a social-climber.

the Scots Guards (I think),[8] & was captured & imprisoned in Italy. After the war he was influenced by Lawrence Gowing,[9] whom I think you may have met, & whom anyway you will know of since he shares Alys' house in London. He is rather an attractive character: has intellectual interests without intellectual stamina, & has both the limitations and the qualities of sensitivity, made conscious by experiences in the war. I think you might like him. [...]

---

[8] Lord Haig was an officer in the Royal Scots Greys, not the Scots Guards.
[9] The painter (Sir) Lawrence Gowing (1918–1991) taught at the Camberwell School of Arts, and established his reputation as an art historian with a book on Vermeer. His portrait of T-R hangs at Peterhouse, Cambridge.

1949

An exchange of letters in February 1949 about arrangements for a photograph of a supposed second Caravaggio at Christ Church has not been reproduced.

Two hasty notes from Trevor-Roper – the first written on 18 March a few hours before he flew to the USA, and the second dated 8 April from Washington, DC – are also omitted. 'I find everyone extremely serious-minded in pursuit of extremely high-minded but somewhat abstract objects,' he declared in the second message.

Berenson (who had not visited the USA since 1921) wrote on 11 April seeking Trevor-Roper's American impressions. He asked whether Trevor-Roper had yet glanced at Robert Sherwood's The White House Papers of Harry L. Hopkins, *'a poor affair as interpretation but overflowing with interesting information'.*

7 May 1949   Christ Church, Oxford

Dear BB

Thank you very much for your letter, & for Kordt's *Wahn u. Wirklichkeit,* which I am reading with interest – but rather critically; I think he is unreliable in his use of sources and doesn't distinguish between opinion and verifiable fact, so I feel very distrustful of some of his statements when they are unverified from other sources.[1] The Hopkins book I have read, and think it excellent – that is, in the matter which it reveals. It seems to me to explain a great deal of Roosevelt's diplomatic failure. Hopkins clearly had no political understanding. He made the Churchill–Roosevelt personal alliance, which was a success, since basically we & you had similar aims and therefore Hopkins' lack of political sense didn't matter; but as between the West & Russia the difference of aims and principles was huge, & Hopkins, being blind to this, made a disastrously personal alliance between Roosevelt & Stalin. The personal relations between Roosevelt & Churchill illustrated a real alliance of interests; the personal relations between Roosevelt & Stalin concealed a real opposition of interests. Hopkins, a mere

---

[1] Erich Kordt (1903–1969), German diplomat, was *chef de cabinet* to the Nazi Foreign Minister, Joachim von Ribbentrop – despite a well-attested antipathy to his superior – until December 1940. He assisted the British War Crimes Executive at Nuremberg: 'a reliable if not a very impressive figure' (Patrick Dean to David Scott-Fox, 25 March 1946, PRO FO 371/57648). Kordt's *Wahn und Wirklichkeit: die aussenpolitik des dritten reiches* (Stuttgart, 1947) [Delusion and Reality: the Foreign Policy of the Third Reich] was necessarily written without reference to crucial sources, and has an understandable personal bias.

personal contact-man, unfamiliar with real politics, never saw this. *Hinc illae lacrimae.*[2] At least this is my interpretation!

Have you read Eliz. Wiskemann's *Rome–Berlin Axis*?[3] It is very competent & scholarly, Namier *manqué*. She can't write, which is a pity, for it is a good subject. I enclose a review I wrote of it. I would enclose the book too, but I don't think it's really your book. It lacks distinction, & diplomatic history without distinction, be it never so competent & accurate, is rather dull!

You ask me why I went to America. Well, I had never been there, and America matters in politics, & I am interested in politics, and I had never been there, and it was to my economic advantage to make such an expensive journey now, when I am relatively rich, rather than later when I shall not be so. Between these various motives I went. I didn't expect to enjoy it; but I did enjoy it. That is, I didn't enjoy it as I enjoy Italy, which I enjoy more every time I visit it: I enjoyed it for the opposite reason, because it was new and strange. And, *very strange*! I still feel inarticulate about it, as one who has returned from the Moon; and in some ways depressed. Their standard of education is really very saddening! Harvard depressed me a great deal, & New York I found rather too hard; but I greatly enjoyed Washington, & met some really delightful people there, including your friends Johnnie Walker[4] & Walter Lippmann.[5] I hope I may come to Italy some time this summer or autumn, & by then I will have had time to sort out my emotions & experiences about that remote incomprehensible continent, & shall convey them to you. At present I hardly dare to try! [. . .]

22 May 1949   Christ Church, Oxford

Dear BB
    Our letters have become crossed through that long transatlantic delay,

---

[2] 'From this come these tears.' Terence, *Andria*, I, i, 99.
[3] *The Rome–Berlin Axis* (1949) by Elizabeth Wiskemann (1899–1971) was a definitive account of Mussolini's relations with Hitler. She had lived in Germany for five years, and published many acute reports on National Socialism in the British press, until her expulsion by the Gestapo in 1936. Afterwards she became Rome correspondent of *The Economist*. She and T-R met regularly in the late 1940s; he reviewed *The Rome–Berlin Axis* in *The Listener*, 5 May 1949, p. 771.
[4] John Walker (1906–1995), heir to a Pittsburgh iron and steel fortune, went out to I Tatti from Harvard in 1930 and become a devoted pupil of BB's. He was appointed as (the first) chief curator of the National Gallery in Washington DC (1939–56) and as (the second) director of the gallery (1956–69).
[5] Walter Lippmann (1889–1974) was the most influential American newspaper columnist then writing on international relations. BB first met him in Paris in 1919, and they maintained lifelong contact.

so I am writing you another, partly out of a desire to write, partly to ask something of you. One of my pupils is going to Italy and I wonder if you would be so kind as to let him call on you? His name is David Hopkins & he is quite the best pupil I have at present.[1] He is very young & very enthusiastic and has a very clear mind and is an engaging character. He hasn't had many opportunities of moving in the world (his father is a wholesale grocer in Worthing & he was at school at Worthing before coming to Christ Church with an exhibition), but his intellectual purity, which I find very attractive, makes him at ease anywhere. I know you are visited by rather too many friends of friends, & of course you will have fled from such visits to Vallombrosa when he is in Florence (which will be for about ten days from 7 July), or possibly even to Zurich, so please tell me if you would rather not be visited then. On the other hand, if you should be able to see him, he is a young man whom I think you would like, and it would certainly be a great pleasure for him.

Two posthumously published essays by Keynes have just come out, and the reception given to them (I have not seen them myself) shows – together with other evidence – a disconcerting growth of obscurantism in Cambridge (England).[2] It is ironical that whereas forty years ago the metaphysical darkness of Oxford was dispelled by a growing pinpoint of light in Cambridge, Oxford is now defending the Cambridge rationalists against new and desperate bigotries in their original home. The new prophet of darkness is apparently a man called Oakeshott,[3] who is alleged to advance his appeals to unreason with great brilliance; which however, having met him, I doubt; and now their professor of history (a very undistinguished historian called Butterfield)[4] has published a series of lectures of darkest

---

[1] David Hopkins (b. 1930) joined the War Office in 1953, and held posts in the Ministry of Defence, Home Office and United Kingdom Delegation to NATO. 'May I send a friend to you?' T-R wrote at this time to Sylvia Sprigge in Rome. 'He is David Hopkins, a pupil of mine, very able, very enthusiastic, a pure scholar with the emphasis on the purity, the limpid purity of the intellect. Do you like intellectual purity? It is the quality I admire most, I think, in the world.'

[2] Two essays by John Maynard Keynes (1883–1946), entitled 'Dr Melchior: a defeated enemy' and 'My Early Beliefs', were posthumously published in May 1949 under the title *Two Memoirs*. In the second essay – a discussion of the impact of G.E. Moore's *Principia Ethica* on Edwardian Cambridge – Keynes suggested that rationality might impoverish rather than enrich human nature. Keynes, who stayed at I Tatti in 1906, 1911 and 1920, judged BB 'rather a bad man'.

[3] Michael Oakeshott (1901–1990), editor of the *Cambridge Journal* 1947–54 and Professor of Political Science at the London School of Economics 1951–69, collected his essays on the destructive consequences of using reason as the exclusive basis of political action in *Rationalism in Politics* (1962).

[4] Six lectures by Sir Herbert Butterfield (1900–1979), Professor of Modern History at Cambridge 1944–63 and Regius Professor of History 1963–8, were published in *The Listener* between 7 April and 12 May 1949, and later collected in his book *Christianity and History* (1949). They concluded with the injunction: 'Hold to Christ, and for the rest be uncommitted.'

mysticism – Toynbee[5] is an angel of lucidity by comparison – which has evoked a chorus of rapture from those melancholy fenlands. All Cambridge undergraduates are alleged to prostrate themselves abjectly before these gloomy prophets; but I can find no trace of any such doctrines having been received in Oxford yet, and am watching the north-eastern skies apprehensively, like a locust-officer in the Sudan, anxiously apprehending the first casual detachments of the approaching pestiferous swarm.

Of course, the alleged irrationalism of Cambridge, alarming though it may seem here, is nothing compared to some of the phenomena I observed in your transatlantic continent; but of those I would rather speak than write! [...]

15 July 1949   20 Bondgate Without, Alnwick

Dear BB

You very kindly sent me your *Sketch for a Self Portrait*,[1] and for some time it lay on my table, with other tempting volumes; but with the end of term I turned to it. I have read it in Wales and in Cumberland and in Northumberland, where I now am, and had it been a little longer (as I wish it had been) I would still be reading it, and would take it with me tomorrow to the remote, sub-arctic northern shore of Iceland; and then, as Dr Johnson, hearing (though falsely) that he was read on the banks of the Wolga, evinced a 'noble love of fame', so you might boast of being read on the banks of the river Vatnsdalsá.[2] I am sorry that the interest & brevity of the book have deprived you of this boast. Really I was delighted with it: I found so many things in it with which to agree (& to find agreements in one's minority opinions is one of the great pleasures of reading), & some

---

[5] Arnold Toynbee (1889–1975), Director of Studies at the Royal Institute of International Affairs 1925–55, compiled *A Study of History* (12 volumes, 1934–61) purporting to show the cycles of growth and decline that characterised civilisations and urging the creation of a new universal religion to save the West from decay. BB had written to Alys Russell (23 October 1947) expressing contempt for 'Toynbee's ocean-stream of so-called history. It is romance, philosophical, theological, propagandist, anything you like but not history. To Toynbee's kind of stuff I greatly prefer Dumas' *Trois Mousquetaires* or better Sir Walter Scott's Scotch romances. But every generation seems to need its nonsense.'

[1] *Sketch for a Self-Portrait* – originally written as the introduction to BB's war diaries – was published in 1949 by Constable in London and in Milan (in Arturo Loria's translation) as *Abbozzo per un Autoritratto*. 'A reader may be tempted to dismiss the whole book as charlatanry. The temptation is to be resisted. The book is the meditative self-examination of a scholarly and civilised mind. What Mr Berenson says about his quest of the absolute [...] is said wisely, learnedly and with tranquil sincerity.' Charles Morgan, 'Mr Berenson's Looking Glass', *Spectator*, 8 July 1949, p. 52.

[2] The Vatnsdalsá river in north-west Iceland was renowned for its salmon fishing and beauty.

even with which to disagree. The phobia of idleness, the sense of Time's
wingèd chariot hurrying near, the conviction that rationality and 'good'
values are in fact abnormal in history, & yet the invincible refusal to accept
ultimately the consequences of this conviction – how well I feel I know &
share these emotions! How I agree that adolescent-mindedness – the
capacity for curiosity – is a perpetual essential of civilisation! But I can't
agree that expertise, the careful perfection of a precise technique, was a
mistake. I don't believe that it can be *exchanged* for general appreciation. I
submit that one's general appreciation is only made possible, in its most
acute form, by such severe testing in a narrow, experimental field – without
necessary regard to the nature of that narrower field. The study (for
instance) of Greek or mathematics seems to me to derive half its value from
these general consequences; & though one may afterwards regret that time
was spent on expertise, narrowly, yet could one in fact have dispensed
with it as a necessary intellectual discipline in acquiring the capacity for
intellectual appreciation? These anyway are some of the thoughts that your
book has suggested to me; but also I admired something else in it: your
images. How delightful to read metaphors that really suggest the phenomenon which verbally they recall! I enjoyed them all, and one particularly, both because it expresses a sentiment I share and refers to it by a
metaphor which pleases me, I shall quote in my next course of lectures on
politics & history: I refer to that magisterial sentence on page 100 ending
'. . . and woe to him who tries to lead them by means of intelligible speech
instead of brutish sounds & the skilful use of the lasso'.[3] And to think that
I had never even heard of Burckhardt's *History of Greek Civilisation*.[4] I must
get it at once; but alas, it will be too late to take with me to Iceland. Thither
I must take whatever I can find here in Northumberland, – & I am still
desperately searching for the ideal book, portable but full, sustaining but
not too dry, varied but consistent, to carry with me across those laborious
lava-humps. [. . .]

---

[3] 'As for men in the lump, the mass, they are about as rational as a drove of oxen or a stampede of
buffaloes, and woe to him who tries to lead them by means of intelligible speech instead of
brutish sounds and the skilful use of the lasso.'
[4] T-R wrote of Jacob Burckhardt (1818–1897), author of *The Age of Constantine* and of *The
Civilisation of the Renaissance*, in *Historical Essays*, pp. 273–8.

28 September 1949   Christ Church, Oxford

Dear BB

I was very sorry to hear that you have had such a poor summer,[1] and from Alys that you will not now be able to go to Paris next month; but I hope you will get your visit to Naples or some other less ambitious journey. I wish I had been able to come & see you in Italy instead of being misled by a foolish infatuation to go to Iceland again – a totally disastrous visit: for I found nothing but sleet and mist and cold, and a steadfast north wind blowing incessantly from the Pole up my river on the north coast of that remote inhospitable island. Before long I got ill with the endless cold and wet & the exhaustion of long hours fishing with a pony in such weather, & was in bed with the same complication which laid me low in Palermo; only there is a difference between being ill in the Albergo delle Palme in Palermo & being ill in a primitive farmhouse on the edge of the desert in Iceland. I got home ultimately, after a dreadful journey of 300 miles to Reykjavik, & a still more dreadful journey, through four days of terrible storms, to Glasgow, resolved never again, by any subtle persuasion or mad whimsy, to be tempted north of Berwick-on-Tweed, the last frontier-post of civilisation! I have been recovering from Iceland ever since my return & would have come to Italy except that I didn't feel capable of further travel, even southwards!

It was very kind of you to entertain my pupils Hopkins & Allchin,[2] who were delighted with it, & sent me such *verbatim* transcripts of the conversation that I almost feel I was there too. [...]

Alys is in splendid form & very pleased with the new book of her mother's letters which she wants me to review 'as an expert on Quakers'![3]

---

[1] Sylvia Sprigge had written on 23 September: 'BB is only just recuperating from a bad summer in which walks at Vallombrosa were reduced to a bare few steps & a lot of rather grim post-mortem arrangements had to be made with visiting lawyers and art pundits from Harvard. Nicky bore up wonderfully and pulled him through.'
[2] Donald Allchin (b. 1930), then at Christ Church, took holy orders, became Librarian of Pusey House, Oxford, 1960–69, and Warden of the Community of the Sisters of the Love of God in Oxford, 1967–94.
[3] T-R had reviewed *George Fox's Book of Miracles* edited by Henry Cadbury, and Isabel Ross's *Margaret Fell, Mother of Quakerism* in the *New Statesman* of 26 February and 13 August 1949, so it was reasonable to credit him with expertise. Alys Russell was delighted by T-R's review ('Unorthodox Apostle', *Observer*, 16 October 1949) of Hannah Whitall Smith's correspondence, *A Religious Rebel* (1949).

1950

Trevor-Roper wrote briefly on 5 February. 'I have just emerged from a week in bed owing to the intolerable Oxford climate & am getting busy again, & the mind dwells nostalgically on Italy, where I hope you are all well on that incomparable hillside. Owing to illness I haven't yet delivered my broadcast on Logan, & anyway I am having infinite *trouble with that obscurantist body the BBC who want to change it in a hundred minute particulars. I have obliged them in fifty, but as a point of principle am holding out on the other fifty; so at present there is deadlock!' This letter crossed with one from Berenson written on 7 February, promising to send the newly published American edition of his* Aesthetics and History, *and offering to send the Italian edition of his war diaries 'if you read that* favella *[speech] with enough ease'. Berenson wrote again on 14 February with gossip about his sister-in-law and her ex-husband Bertrand Russell: 'Have you seen Alys & heard her jubilation over her reconciliation with Bertie? I am glad she has lived to enjoy it.'*

12 March 1950   Christ Church, Oxford

Dear BB

Many thanks for your letter, and for *Aesthetics and History*, which I have been reading with the greatest interest & enjoyment. How enviably you traverse those widely separate centuries! The book has been very well received in England & I am so glad it is properly welcomed after all these delays. And of course I shall be delighted to read your war diary, in Italian or English – preferably in English;[1] but I can read Italian easily (only I would miss the *nuances* of style) & would rather read it in Italian than wait over-long for it!

My broadcast on Logan has caused some indignation in the opposite camp, I'm afraid. The sky is still black and thunderous over Stanford Dingley:[2] Gathorne-Hardy & his friend Kyrle Leng,[3] whom I have never

---

[1] *Echi e Riflessioni: Diario 1941–44* was published by Mondadori of Milan in 1950; and as *Rumour and Reflection, 1941–1944* by Constable in London in 1952.
[2] Robert Gathorne-Hardy lived at Stanford Dingley in Berkshire. His letters of 24 February and 1 March 1950 are pained and sorrowful rather than angry. In his BBC broadcast T-R had said that Gathorne-Hardy's *Recollections of Logan Pearsall Smith* would 'be valued by all Loganists' for providing 'so much of the wonderful letters and Table Talk of the Sage of Chelsea'. Although this 'record of a friendship that ended in disaster' was 'eloquent, sensitive, well-written', in his later chapters 'Mr Gathorne-Hardy accumulates detail not, as earlier, to illustrate a character, but to protest against it; and therefore the detail which had formerly – even when trivial, even when hostile – been interesting and suggestive, now becomes distasteful, repetitive and boring.'

met, have both bombarded me with angry letters, & Alys, from Chelsea, has added a brisk fusillade. I am very sorry to have upset her. But in fact, though it has all been very troublesome, I don't feel really repentant. It would have been much easier to have kept out of the whole affair, but it seemed to me that that was what most of Logan's friends were doing, & I think it would have been rather cowardly if (having gained as much as I did from him) I had done the same. Anyway I hope the indignation will gradually subside, so that I can visit Alys again. I haven't seen her for some time now, so I don't know about the reconciliation with Bertie that you speak of.

What news can I tell you? The election – what a splendid election! it was like an infinitely long steeplechase reported by commentators at every fence when we listened-in to the results! – is now old & stale.[4] But I am gradually learning more about history. A long time ago I used to think that great political crises were always in fact the illustration of some deep and important economic struggle. What a naïve view! I wonder if anyone holds it now – except possibly a few Marxist reactionaries grown obstinate in their inveterate illusions. If so, they ought to have been cured by recent events – by the case of Seretse Khama,[5] at present splitting the precarious British government, and the case of King Leopold, which looks like doing the same for the Belgian Government.[6]

I suppose it is now spring at I Tatti, which must be delightful. I wish I could visit you there again, – but I always wish this. At present I am mechanically examining applicants who want to come to Christ Church; & when that is over I must lock myself up & really get on with that slim volume which I am writing on that dull old Elizabethan millionaire Thomas Sutton.

I believe you may find yourself visited by a compatriot of yours, Professor

---

[3] Kyrle Leng (1900–1958) and Gathorne-Hardy shared rooms as Oxford undergraduates and lived together for thirty-seven years. His family owned the *Sheffield Daily Telegraph*.
[4] At the British general election on 23 February 1950, Labour won 315 seats, the Conservatives 298, the Liberals 9 and the Irish Nationalists 2.
[5] (Sir) Seretse Khama (1921–1980), chief of the Bamangwhato tribe, married a while Englishwoman in 1948. Settler politicians in southern Africa objected that white supremacy was jeopardised by this miscegenation, and the Labour government in London excluded Khama from the chieftainship in March 1950. Prime Minister of Bechuanaland 1965; President of independent Botswana 1966.
[6] King Leopold III of the Belgians (1901–1983) surrendered unconditionally, against his Cabinet's wishes, to the German invaders in 1940, and was detained as a semi-prisoner. His post-war return to Belgium was opposed by the Left, but a referendum in 1950 upheld his restoration by a narrow majority. In July he regained his kingdom but, confronted by continuing unrest, subsequently abdicated.

Notestein.[7] Do you already know him? He is the greatest authority in the world on the English parliament in the early seventeenth century, & has revolutionised historical knowledge of that subject as completely, in that period, as J.E. Neale & Namier in their periods.[8] He has edited seven stout volumes of parliamentary diaries and written one slim, slim, inconceivably slim volume – a mere lecture – on *The Winning of the Initiative by the House of Commons* which has done more to reinterpret a historical subject than any comparable number of pages in the English language.[9] The French language, of course, is different. French historians, in their little *Annales*, are thoroughly accustomed to achieving such revolutions.[10] But they are a race apart. [...]

Berenson wrote from I Tatti on 18 March, asking whether Notestein's lecture 'The Winning of the Initiative by the House of Commons' was easily procurable: 'I ask because N's visit here has been announced by various common friends.'

25 March 1950   Christ Church, Oxford

Dear BB

I have sent you a copy of Notestein's British Academy Lecture on *The Winning of the Initiative by the House of Commons* – a bad title: it should be *The Losing of the Initiative by the Crown*, for this process it describes, the other it does not; but it is a very good lecture. Notestein's great work is his seven volume edition of Parliamentary diaries for 1621, of which he discovered a great number: he is a great hunter of diaries, & I suspect his interests have narrowed rather than widened with time. Though his lecture was a revelation, he has in general, I think, seemed to lack the capacity to use antiquarian exactitude in the service of historical generalisation – a gift which seems to me the real test of a historian, or at least of a historian's historian. Namier has this gift (though his last book – a series of reprinted

---

[7] Two of T-R's letters to Wallace Notestein (1878–1969), Professor of English History at Yale University 1928–47, are reproduced as an appendix to this book. Notestein first visited I Tatti on 15 April 1950. His wife Ada Comstock (1876–1973), whom he had married after her retirement as President of Radcliffe College in 1943, was a close friend of Berenson's sister Senda Abbott (1868–1954), the pioneer physical educator who introduced basketball as a team sport for women and popularised Swedish gymnastics in the USA.

[8] Sir John Neale (1890–1975) was a historian of Elizabethan England. Namier established his reputation with *The Structure of Politics at the Accession of George III* (1929).

[9] This was originally the Raleigh Lecture delivered to the British Academy in 1924.

[10] Marc Bloch and Lucien Febvre had founded the journal *Annales d'histoire économique et sociale* (from 1946 entitled *Annales: economies, sociétés, civilisations*) in 1929. See T-R's essay 'Fernand Braudel, the *Annales*, and the Mediterranean', *Journal of Modern History*, 44 (1972), pp. 468–79.

reviews – is disappointing).[1] & Pirenne had it,[2] & of course Tawney:[3] but not, I think, Notestein.

I Tatti must be delightful now. I wish I could visit you there again. But I am buried in administrative work & for such time as I can get away I must go home to Northumberland, where my father has succeeded in turning himself over in a motor accident, the day after returning from the Riviera, & breaking a collar-bone. But will you, if it should be convenient to you, see a friend of mine who is going to Florence? He was a pupil of mine, called Christopher Pemberton, who lives in Suffolk & was at Eton & Christ Church & is fond of painting and I think you would find him an attractive character.[4] Anyway I have taken the liberty of telling him to telephone you when in Florence, but I have warned him that you are beset by visitors, American consuls, passing *cognoscenti*, etc., and might not be able to face an addition to their number; so don't think I have committed you.

There has been a great deal of indecent puffing of Rommel here, & a book by an English brigadier (a journalist I think) has sold 100,000 copies.[5] All the hack military-commentators have been reverberating its notes in the press, so I dare say some of their echoes have been audible even at Settignano. I am sending you here a little counterblast I have published just to preserve the equilibrium of the world, thus endangered.[6] [...]

Berenson wrote on 23 April reporting the Notesteins' visit: 'she impressed me as a magnificent person, & he as a great dear. I happened to say something about the hypnotising danger of research, & she almost jumped up with approval.'

[1] T-R's review of Namier's *Europe in Decay: A Study in Disintegration 1936–1940* in *The Listener*, 30 March 1950, p. 573, contains a phrase that illuminates T-R's own preference for writing essays rather than finishing books: 'these essays reveal, as more sustained historical writing, if it is written by an artist, seldom does, the unceasing critical vigilance of a scholar at work.'
[2] Henri Pirenne (1862–1935) wrote a monumental history of Belgium and many works of medieval economic history.
[3] Richard Tawney (1880–1962), Professor of Economic History at the London School of Economics 1931–49, author of *Religion and the Rise of Capitalism* (1926), also a Christian Socialist.
[4] The painter Christopher Pemberton (b. 1923), at this time teaching art at Bryanston School, afterwards joined the staff at Camberwell School of Art. His proposed trip to Italy was postponed, but when he and the biographer Richard Ollard visited I Tatti a year later, BB told them that T-R was 'the great hope of all his young friends' (Pemberton to T-R, 7 July 1951).
[5] Brigadier Desmond Young (1892–1966) was captured by Erwin Rommel's forces in North Africa in 1942 and spent eighteen months as a prisoner-of-war. The camaraderie of desert warfare prompted him to write *Rommel: The Desert Fox* (1950) in which he admitted his liking for German generals. The book was such a commercial success that it was converted into a Hollywood film, *The Desert Fox* (1951): Young retreated with the profits to live on the Isle of Sark.
[6] 'Why Should We Idolise Rommel?' *Picture Post*, 18 March 1950, pp. 25–7.

21 May 1950   Christ Church, Oxford

Dear BB

Has summer arrived at I Tatti? Snow and sleet & cold have been our portion, & for a fortnight I have been in bed with influenza (I rashly got up, thinking I was better, & lectured: *hinc illae lacrimae*),[1] and I think enviously of that exquisite retreat of yours, with its cypress-walks & ilex grove, & hope you are well there & enjoying a more delightful climate. I'm afraid Christopher Pemberton, who was going to visit you, never left England, falling ill just before he was due to leave, so you will not have seen him after all. I am glad to think you are getting to Paris after all: I remember you were prevented last year; I hope you will have an enjoyable visit this time. I am probably going to Berlin for a few days at the end of June, so I may find a chance of stopping in Paris &, if so, shall hope to see you there & find you well. I don't think I shall visit Italy this summer, what with all those pilgrims,[2] & I should like to see you all again if you are going to be nearer to this northern (at present much too northern) latitude.

Some time ago you asked me about Kenneth de Courcy's so-called Intelligence Survey,[3] about which Prince Paul had spoken.[4] I haven't seen it for a long time, but prejudices wear off very slowly & I am still very prejudiced against it. It is very pretentious, and I don't know how it is financed – for I don't think it can pay its way on the scale on which it advertises itself; but I *suspect* it has (or at least had) political support from

---

[1] 'From this come these tears' (Terence).

[2] 1950 was the twenty-second Holy Year – the first having been in 1300. It drew some three million Catholic pilgrims to Rome (one-third of them non-Italian). Extra lodgings were erected in the city, and townships of tents arose on its outskirts.

[3] Kenneth de Courcy, self-styled Duc de Grantmesnil (1909–1999), had a German mother and an Anglo-Irish father (whose head, he claimed, was blown off by an exploding magic lantern). He was co-founder of the right-wing Imperial Policy Group, touring central Europe and the Balkans on its behalf in the 1930s; a British Secret Service informant; and an insalubrious appeaser. From 1938 until 1976 he published an *Intelligence Digest*, which at its peak had 200,000 subscribers (mainly Mid-West American businessmen), and circulated Red Scares concocted either by reactionary informants in central Europe or in his own angry imagination. Convicted in 1963 for fraud, perjury and forgery relating to a Rhodesian land company, he claimed to have been framed by the KGB. After his release in 1969, he became an excitable and confiding correspondent of T-R's, who was intrigued by his self-glorifying fantasies and amused by his name-dropping. The T-Rs had a grim holiday in Umbria with de Courcy in August 1982.

[4] Prince Paul of Yugoslavia (1893–1976) read modern history at Christ Church, and was thereafter a cultivated, Anglophile *grand seigneur* in his outlook. He became Regent of Yugoslavia in 1934 following the assassination of his cousin King Alexander. The British made him a Knight of the Garter in 1939 but, after the crisis that ended his regency in 1941, interned him in Kenya. During the post-war period he lived at Pratolino, near Florence. BB's meeting with the Prince at St Moritz, when the latter was a boy, led to an enduring friendship.

those industrial circles which supported appeasement in 1938. It then (with its usual pretentious phraseology) called itself the *Imperial Policy Group*, and produced a very pompous news-sheet; but in 1940 it discredited itself, and changed its name. The discredit was connected with its policy on the collapse of France: for it produced a very grave, sagacious *de-haut-en-bas* number explaining that to anyone who knew as much of the facts as the Imperial Policy Group, it was clear that Pétain was right & that the prudent course of England would be to do the same.[5] After this, the Imperial Policy Group was quiet for a time, explaining that the bombing and general dislocation of war was really too much for it, and pleading for indulgence & sympathy from its supporters (though every other newspaper had the same problems & none of them went out of circulation even for a day). I forget how long it lay low; but since the end of the war it has continued, as portentous and omniscient as ever, & still run by Kenneth de Courcy. Of course it may be quite different now, but I am sceptical of conversions & haven't given it another trial, charm it never so sweetly!

Owing to my illness I haven't been about much, but I shall hope to see both d'Entrèves[6] & Notestein & get some news about you. I agree, Notestein is a bit desiccated by research: but research must be done! I feel that it's only on the basis of research done & standards thereby acquired that one *can* confidently live among the humanities. Unfortunately Notestein has got embogged in the first stage & so has never really entered the second! [...]

On 15 June, Berenson wrote from Paris, which he was visiting for the first time in fourteen years. He and Nicky Mariano had 'been haunting museums, & exhibitions, & [had] seen a very few old friends who have survived the storms. Not a word about politics.'

28 July 1950   Christ Church, Oxford

Dear BB

I am ashamed that I haven't written to you for so long. I hope you are all well, and enjoyed being in Paris, and that Unesco no longer makes

---

[5] Philippe Pétain (1856–1951), Marshal of France, called for a ceasefire after the collapse of French military resistance to the Nazi invasion in 1940, and negotiated the division of France into a German controlled zone and the so-called *zone libre*.
[6] Count Alexander d'Entrèves (1902–1985), one of the young anti-Fascist intellectuals who congregated at I Tatti during Mussolini's ascendancy, had perplexed BB during a recent visit there. Professor of Italian and Fellow of Magdalen College, Oxford 1946–57 and Professor of Political Theory at the University of Turin 1958–72.

Florence impossible for you. I suppose you are at Vallombrosa, among those delightful beech-trees, above the heat and haze of the plain, like Epicurus' gods. How delicious it must be! I have been in Oxford incessantly, slowly – with infinite slowness – writing a book of infinite pedantic exactitude on a character of infinite dullness; but I must rehabilitate myself with the learned world after writing a best-seller! Consequently I haven't been abroad except for four days in Berlin for a so-called 'Kongress für Kulturelle Freiheit',[1] where I misbehaved. That is, aided by my English colleague A.J. Ayer – a Christ Church philosopher who, 14 years ago, at the age of 24, demolished the entire metaphysical world with a small octavo volume[2] – I led a resistance movement against the organisers of the Congress, which in fact was a totally illiberal demonstration dominated by professional ex-communist *boulevardiers* like Arthur Koestler[3] & Franz Borkenau,[4] confident in the support of German ex-Nazis in the audience. We were very unpopular, especially as we won in the end – largely because Silone deserted to us at the end.[5] No more aeroplanes, I'm afraid, will be sent to fetch us, in luxury, to international congresses: at least of that kind. But I enjoyed the fight![6] On the way back I got off at Amsterdam to cool the blood before returning to England. I had never seen Amsterdam. What

---

[1] The Congress of Cultural Freedom held in West Berlin in June 1950 (with indirect CIA funding) was intended to channel funds to anti–Communist periodicals such as *Encounter* in England and *Der Monat* in Germany.

[2] (Sir) Alfred Jules ('Freddie') Ayer (1910–1989), a philosopher at Christ Church 1932–44 and Grote Professor of the Philosophy of Mind and Logic at London University since 1946, had visited BB at I Tatti three years earlier. T-R read his first book *Language, Truth and Logic* on its publication in 1936, and was attracted by its austere language and repudiation of metaphysics. In 1959 Ayer returned to Oxford as Wykeham Professor of Logic and Fellow of New College.

[3] Arthur Koestler (1905–1983) was an occasional visitor to I Tatti: 'He stimulates me like strong drink' (BB to Hamish Hamilton, 12 July 1951). The bitterness of Koestler's adherents at the interventions by Ayer and T-R is shown in Sydney Hook's memoir *Out of Step* (1987), pp. 434, 438, 440–3, and in David Cesarani, *Arthur Koestler* (1998), pp. 357–64.

[4] Franz Borkenau (1900–1957) was the son of an Austrian civil servant and reared as a Catholic. His discovery of his Jewish ancestry shocked him into becoming a Communist; but he later repudiated the party and wrote *The Spanish Cockpit* (1937), a searing account of the civil war. At the Congress he made a provocative speech hailing America's atomic supremacy. 'Pouring out his German sentences with hysterical speed and gestures, he screamed that he was a convert from Communism and proud of it; that past guilt must be atoned for; that the ex-Communists alone understood Communism and the means of resisting it; and that it must be destroyed at once by uncompromising frontal attack. And yet terrible though it was, this fanatical speech was less frightening than the hysterical German applause that greeted it' (T-R, 'Ex-Communist v. Communist', *Manchester Guardian*, 10 July 1950).

[5] Ignazio Silone (1900–1978), novelist and founder member of the Italian Communist party in 1921, was later expelled from the party, and exiled by the Fascists. His visits to I Tatti disappointed BB.

[6] T-R published two accounts of the Congress: 'Ex-Communist v. Communist', in the *Manchester Guardian* 10 July 1950, p. 4; and 'The Berlin Congress', *The Economist*, 15 July 1950, p. 118.

a beautiful city it is, – a cool northern Venice; & how delightful after Berlin. I don't think anything will ever make me enjoy being in Germany! Interesting politically, yes; enjoyable, no. Give me the Latin world, or the Atlantic world; but beyond the *Limes* a Cimmerian darkness seems to me still to prevail, a sort of twilight heralding the total blackness ever further east.[7]

I am going north for the latter part of August and then back to Oxford for September; but I hope to get abroad towards the end of September. If so, may I come to see you for a day or two, if that is convenient for you, at Vallombrosa? Will you be there? And could I bring Isaiah Berlin, whom you said that you would like to see? He is going to be at Aulla, not far from Spezia, until about 20 August, & I told him that if I came out about that date, and if it should be convenient to you, I would pick him up & bring him to introduce him to you; so perhaps you will let me know if that should happen to suit you.[8] It may not prove possible for me to come to Italy; but I hope it will. There is nothing that I would enjoy more.

I have read no books – only dry & dusty 16th century leases and records of debt and bills and docquets of inconceivable philistinism. What a price one pays to write history! But I hope to get back to literature soon, once I have proved myself capable of pure Teutonic pulverisation!

Incidentally I have just brought out a new edition of my book on *The Last Days of Hitler*, with a new preface. The preface is about fifty pages, & since I hope that this is not too long to bore you – at least in length – I am sending you a copy. But the Arabian Nights are far better! I wish I could hear Nicky reading from them again!

PS. Alan Pryce-Jones, editor of the *Times Literary Supplement*,[9] is credibly reported to have been converted to Rome, & certainly attended the dinner given by all the converts, under the presidency of Frank Pakenham,[10] to

---

[7] The Limes Germanicus, the ancient frontier between German and Roman provinces stretching from the Danube to the Rhine.

[8] (Sir) Isaiah Berlin (1909–1997), then a Fellow of New College, was at this time the liveliest of T-R's Oxford friends and allies. He was elected to the chair of social and political philosophy in 1957. He wrote from Aulla to T-R on 6 September, explaining that for complex reasons he might be unable to join the visit to Vallombrosa: 'also I suffer from acute nerves about meeting Mr B: I conceive a large company & brilliant general chit chat & nothing discomposes me more. I only really like tête-à-têtes, and not because as you will, I fear, be quick to suggest, because then I can chat away myself: No! No! [...] So if you are writing, paint me to the Vallombrosiani in dark colours as feckless and confused: but still ardently panting to see them.'

[9] Alan Pryce-Jones (1908–2000), editor of *The Times Literary Supplement* 1948–59, converted to Catholicism during 1950.

[10] Francis Pakenham, 1st Baron Pakenham (1905–2001), later 7th Earl of Longford, a Christ Church don and Labour politician, had converted to Catholicism in 1940.

Father D'Arcy – a pure jesuit charlatan – who (so long as they are rich or fashionable) converts them all.[11] So there is another good paper on the way downhill!

'I look forward to seeing you here,' Berenson wrote from Vallombrosa on 11 August, '& at last the hitherto unapproachable Isaiah Berlin. Everybody except me seemed to be on intimate terms with him.' Trevor-Roper reached Casa al Dono on 24 September, and stayed until the 29th. There he met, among others, the veteran Italian statesman Vittorio Orlando, the poet Natalie Barney and Lord Killanin, later President of the International Olympic Committee. During this visit Berenson reflected in his diary (25 September): 'I have but a tangential relation to my younger friends; I know very little about their love affairs, their commitments, etc. After all, they do not think of me as one of themselves, they are not on terms of complete intimacy and trust with me. I dare say they frequent me because I can lodge and feed them in Italy, because they can boast of having stayed with me, and perhaps because they do enjoy my company. I hope so.'

Two days later, on 27 September, he made another diary entry. 'V.E. Orlando, more smartly dressed than I had ever seen him, talked before, during and after lunch, altogether more than two hours, without stopping, what about did not matter. He retains la trombone de la sonorité, and le sens (in his case) n'est qu'un parasite. So it did not matter that he repeated himself, lapping our minds to sleep like waves that slip under and inward as they die on the beach. I dozed off again and again. He is more than five years my senior. May I be saved from the stage he has reached, babbling and jabbering, as he enjoyed impressing (so he thought) Kenneth Clark and Trevor-Roper. How I should hate to discover (as I certainly should) that I was making a senile spectacle of myself.'

17 October 1950   Christ Church, Oxford

Dear BB

I write, rather belatedly I'm afraid, to thank you for so kindly receiving me at Vallombrosa, and for sending me to that Phaeacian peninsula at Lerici, and to send you, as I promised, the obituary notices of Sybil Colefax

---

[11] Martin D'Arcy (1888–1976), ordained as a Jesuit priest in 1921, had his heyday of social and spiritual influence as Master of Campion Hall, Oxford 1932–45. As a young man T-R often dined at Campion Hall, and drank spirits late into the night, with D'Arcy. He believed that Pakenham, after being received into the Catholic Church, promised D'Arcy to try to convert three Christ Church men: Ayer, Lord Birkenhead and himself.

from *The Times*.[1] I promised also, & have not in fact forgotten my promise, and hope to implement it, to send you my undelivered speech at Berlin; and the otherwise unpardonable delay in my correspondence is due to my attempts to recover from Peter Quennell the text of this document.[2] But he is like Baal: he is away on a journey, or peradventure he sleepeth; at all events, like Baal, he pays no attention to prayers. But I hope that ultimately I shall recover it, & then of course you shall have it.

I greatly enjoyed seeing you all at Vallombrosa – it is the most certain form of physical and mental refreshment to visit you, as everyone agrees. Isaiah Berlin enjoyed his visit immensely also, and when I hear him describing it I feel a complacent self-satisfaction at my share in bringing about that meeting. I also greatly enjoyed seeing Percy Lubbock.[3] He is a charming host and entertained me with antique courtesy on his timeless promontory, where the sun shone every day and I discovered books in the Library that I had not known before. I understand that he too had been visited from Aulla; but the Warden of Wadham had boomed out of existence all conversation but his own ...[4]

I hope you are enjoying Rome and not being exhausted by admiring pilgrims. Your rival the Pope (at least I suppose he can claim to rival you this year) is said to find their ceaseless arrival somewhat wearing; but perhaps you have got more used to it.[5] I am sure Nicky, like some cardinalatial chamberlain, will be controlling the audiences with selective skill. But if, among your pilgrims, you should find Frank Giles, to whom I wrote, I hope you will both see and like him and his wife. He is a man of sense and discrimination, and (an indispensable quality) a good deal of gaiety.[6]

---

[1] Lady Colefax had died, after a long struggle against cancer, on 22 September. In an undated letter to T-R, sent shortly before her death, she had written, 'Delighted to hear that you are going to BB with Isaiah. Do warn Isaiah to speak slowly, because BB is deaf and it will be an agony for him if he doesn't hear what's being said.' Previously, in June, BB had travelled for a final meeting with her at Duff and Diana Cooper's house outside Paris, and recorded in his diary: 'she would talk in such a clipped, mumbling way that neither Diana nor I understood half she was saying' (Berenson, *Sunset and Twilight*, p. 182).
[2] (Sir) Peter Quennell (1905–1994), editor of *Cornhill Magazine* 1944–51, decided against publishing T-R's paper (entitled 'Truth, Liberalism and Authority') written for the Congress for Cultural Freedom. It analysed the antagonism of Christian and Marxist ideologues to intellectual freedom.
[3] T-R stayed from 30 September until 4 October with the English man-of-letters Percy Lubbock (1879–1965) at Gli Scafari, his villa on a high coastal promontory outside Lerici.
[4] (Sir) Maurice Bowra (1898–1971), the extrovert Warden of Wadham College, Oxford, 1938–70, was the university's Professor of Poetry 1946–51. He and Berlin had journeyed from Aulla to visit Lubbock at Lerici. Neither Bowra nor BB enjoyed their few encounters.
[5] Pius XII – formerly Cardinal Eugenio Pacelli (1876–1958) – had been elected Pope in 1939.
[6] Frank Giles (b. 1919), husband of Lady Katharine Sackville (b. 1926), had lately been appointed chief correspondent of *The Times* in Rome. He was subsequently Paris correspondent of *The Times* 1953–60; and Foreign Editor (1961–77) and Editor (1981–3) of the *Sunday Times*. In the early 1980s both he and T-R were directors of Times Newspapers Ltd, and were implicated together in

I have sent you a copy of Moyzisch's book, *Operation Cicero*.[7] I don't think you will find it too long, although it won't add much to what I have said; but it may amuse you. Note the judicious reticence with which Moyzisch conceals the fact that he was a member of Himmler's organisation! [...]

18 November 1950   Christ Church, Oxford

Dear BB

I heard from Frank Giles (who was delighted – really delighted – to meet you: it was very kind of you to see him in Rome) that you were ill while you were there.[1] I hope you are better, & that it was nothing, and that you are now back at I Tatti; and there, though you have so much to read, nevertheless (responding, as always, to flattery) I am sending you this letter to enclose the speech which I made to deliver at Berlin, but which I did not deliver, but which you nevertheless ask me to send you, and which I have now at last contrived to recover from Peter Quennell. Whether I would have improved or even further damaged my reputation by delivering it, I don't know – probably I should have done myself no more good than I did without it. Even as it is, I understand, I am now described throughout the *haut monde* and the *beau monde* of London (insofar as it knows of me and can be reached by Mrs Arthur Koestler, *née* Paget)[2] as a well-known member of the Communist Party. But this doesn't really disconcert me very much. There is a certain amount of Senator-McCarthyism not only in Washington and Berlin (its natural haunts) but even in London. It hasn't yet reached Oxford – except possibly in the persons of a few Dominican priests – but no doubt it will.

But there is one thing in all this matter which perplexes me. Why do Quakers most easily of conscientious people become communist? Alger

the fiasco of the forged Hitler diaries.

[7] Ludwig Moyzisch, a Viennese who joined the Nazi party in 1932, was an attaché at the German Embassy in Turkey during the war years. His best-seller *Operation Cicero* (1950) told the story of an Albanian, Eleyesa Bazua ('Cicero'), employed as a valet in the British Embassy in Ankara. During 1943–4 Bazua filched keys from the pockets of the Ambassador, Sir Hughe Knatchbull-Hugessen, and provided the Germans with photographic copies of secret documents. He was paid for his espionage mainly in sterling banknotes forged by inmates of Romanian prisons. BB wrote on 20 October that he and Nicky had read *Operation Cicero* 'with bated breath'.

[1] Frank Giles had written on 8 November, thanking T-R for 'having been the link between us & BB. We saw him several times when he was in Rome and of course each time was better than the last. A conversation with him is as if one was being injected with the distilled essence of European wisdom: yet he remains completely un-pedant and un-prig.'

[2] Mamaine Paget (1916–1954), a cousin of the Marquess of Anglesey, had married Arthur Koestler, and thus bridged several social sets. A visitor to I Tatti and correspondent of BB's.

Hiss, I am told, was a Quaker;[3] John Peet is a Quaker;[4] the American whose name I have forgotten but who has gone off to Russia is a Quaker. The Quakers of the 17th century interest me beyond all other sects, and this problem I cannot solve. Can you, who have been far more intimately connected with them? Would Logan have suddenly slipped off to Russia like Professor Pontecorvo?[5] I suppose Logan was capable of doing anything! On the other hand the Jehovah Witnesses seem to have an equally bad time under Nazism & communism.

I would have written to you before, but have been ill with the approach of winter. I take these seasonal visitations for granted now, & require no sympathy; but they stop up the pen. However, if you still get the *New Statesman* – politically a very drab paper – you will see that I have not been altogether costive, and can still be, on some subjects, as malicious as ever.[6]

My dear BB, you cannot believe how much I enjoyed staying with you in the autumn. I hope I may come again. And how delightful it was to find that, at Vallombrosa, I like Kenneth Clark much more than I thought I did anywhere else![7] [...]

PS. Have you any influence with Lady Berkeley?[8] All the muniments at Berkeley Castle are inaccessible to scholars unless she orders the turning of a golden key. I have a friend who is precisely such a scholar & has worked on all the Berkeley records in Gloucester but cannot complete his work unless the golden key, on orders from Assisi, is turned. Is she amenable to

---

[3] Alger Hiss (1904–1996) had married a Quaker, but was not a hereditary member of the sect. Secretary General of the United Nations on its formation, and afterwards Director of the Office of Special Political Affairs, he was denounced in 1948 as a Communist, who had supplied secrets to Soviet Russia. He was convicted of perjury in 1950 and imprisoned.

[4] John Peet (1916–1988), chief correspondent of Reuter's news agency in West Berlin, defected to the Soviet sector of Berlin on 12 June 1950. He remained in East Berlin until his death.

[5] Bruno Pontecorvo (1913–1993), a Jewish Italian physicist who went into exile when the Fascist campaign against the Jews began in 1938. He became a British subject in 1948, joined the newly formed Atomic Energy Research Establishment at Harwell; but disappeared into the Soviet Union, 1–2 September 1950, although his disappearance was not reported until 21 October.

[6] T-R's review of G.G. Coulton's *The Last Days of Medieval Monasticism* – reprinted in *Historical Essays* as 'The Twilight of the Monks' – celebrated the collapse of monasticism in England.

[7] BB's former pupil Sir Kenneth Clark (1903–1983), later Lord Clark, director of the National Gallery 1933–46, Slade Professor of Fine Art at Oxford 1945–50, chairman of the Arts Council of Great Britain 1953–60 and chairman of the Independent Television Authority 1954–7. He and T-R had first met in the socially competitive mini-court that surrounded Logan Pearsall Smith.

[8] Mary ('Molly') Lowell (1884–1975) of Boston had married in 1924 Randal, 8th and last Earl of Berkeley (1865–1942), a world expert on osmosis and the only man at that time to be simultaneously a Fellow of the Royal Society and Master of Foxhounds. In 1955 BB spent his ninetieth birthday as her guest in her home, the former pilgrims' hostel of San Lorenzo, which commanded superb views over Assisi.

the voice of academic persuasion, or is her heart of stone?[9] Scholars, I hear, have sighed outside those unyielding portcullises for generations, – ever since John Smyth of Nibley, in the 17th century, compiled his *Lives of the Berkeleys*;[10] but perhaps the dark history of the famous Berkeley Scandal of the last century frightens those who might otherwise unbolt those protective castle-gates.[11]

Berenson replied on 26 November, praising Frank and Kitty Giles as 'just the kind of young people I do enjoy'. Having read Trevor-Roper's paper for the Congress on Cultural Freedom, he railed against the way that Stalinists were courting public opinion. 'Nowadays the most screwed-up, most unscrupulous, most inhuman totalitarians feel bound to lay claim to humanity, to liberty, to tolerance, although as we know at the cost of every perversion of our vocabulary.'

---

[9] Namier also asked BB to intercede with the owners of Berkeley Castle, and the archives finally became accessible in 1956.

[10] John Smyth (1567–1641), lawyer, MP and man of business to the Berkeley family, spent forty years delving in the muniments of Berkeley Castle: his *Lives of the Berkeleys* is replete with fascinating, exact and delightful information.

[11] Mary Cole (1767–1844), daughter of a Gloucestershire butcher, underwent a bogus marriage in 1785 with Frederick Augustus, 5th Earl of Berkeley, and had seven illegitimate children before their legal marriage in 1796. She then had a further six legitimate children. This caused great complications among her descendants, including several hearings before the Committee of Privileges of the House of Lords between 1811 and 1891.

1951

6 January 1951   Bemersyde, Melrose, Roxburghshire[1]

My dear BB

Before returning to Oxford, where an iron curtain descends upon me, inhibiting correspondence and cutting me off from the outer world, I must write to elicit another letter from you and hear, I hope, that all are well at I Tatti. How I envy you your mild Florentine winter sitting, as I do, among great frozen icebergs in the ultimate north: i.e in Scotland, a country unknown to art or literature, but possible now known to you by more recent history, – for I suppose that the great crisis caused by The Rape of the Stone has been reported even in Italy, and certainly at that great cosmopolitan clearing-house of world intelligence, Settignano.[2] The capture of the Ark by the Philistines, the rape of the Sabine women, the triumphant acquisition by the barbarian crusades of the True Cross – these historic pilferings have now (according to some enthusiasts) been eclipsed by the achievements of those Scots nationalists who filched the coronation stone from Westminster Abbey on Xmas Day. Living at present an isolated Englishman in a Scots house I have had opportunities to observe native reactions, and have concluded that (as Marx sagaciously noted) these vary according to class-differences. The upper classes (as always) prefer the *status quo ante*.[3] After all, if such things are to be allowed, where will they stop? Are not the halls and castles of the Scots aristocracy stuffed with relics and *objets d'art* dubiously conveyed thither from distant origins far more recently than the 13th century? If everyone is going to claim his own, there will be scenes like the competition for disputed limbs and organs in the great day of the Resurrection of the Flesh ... The lower classes, on the other hand, are intensely nationalistic: they regard the Stone as some trophy won by Scotland in an international football match against the consistent

---

[1] T-R had spent Christmas of 1950 with his parents at Alnwick, and was Dawyck Haig's guest at Bemersyde from 30 December to 7 January.
[2] The Stone of Scone, on which Scottish monarchs were crowned until King Edward I of England ordered its removal to Westminster Abbey in 1296, was stolen by Scottish Nationalists on 25 December 1950. Subsequently it was returned to London, but in 1996 it was installed at Edinburgh Castle by John Major's government in an unsuccessful ploy to revive the Conservative party's popularity in Scotland.
[3] T-R had lunched at Floors Castle with the Duke and Duchess of Roxburghe on 31 December, and at Bowhill on 3 January with the Duke and Duchess of Buccleuch.

prizewinner of the last six centuries. In this house, during the rudimentary festivities of Hogmanay, the Stone being indiscreetly mentioned, the chef sprang on to a table and, waving a rolling-pin of Scots pine, denounced the memory of Edward I so roundly that I have been apprehending a poisoned mince-pie ever since. However, I have opportunities for showing rival English nationalism if required; for there is, on the edge of these grounds, a statue, gigantic in size, hideous in aspect, monstrous in proportion, of William Wallace, erected by the Earl of Buchan during the 19th century Scottish *Risorgimento* (if you can conceive of such a movement).[4] It looks south, defiantly, towards England, from a cliff above the Tweed; and I please myself by devising the obscene mutilations or taunting *graffiti* (e.g. 'Remember Flodden') which I might inflict upon it, as a Parthian gesture, before crossing the river to safety. Such is the competitive character of nationalism. I used to think that historical events always had deep economic causes: I now believe that pure farce covers a far greater field of history, and that Gibbon is a more reliable guide to that subject than Marx. I am sure that Italian history confirms my theory – I hope you will assure me that it does.

I wish I could come to Italy again. I begin to wonder if I shall ever leave England for the next two years. I have just had imposed upon me a new administrative task, and must, for that period, manage the affairs of my college.[5] However, I am determined to spite the serious-minded and to show that a college can be administered as well from abroad as from home, and if my ambitious plans of devolution succeed, I hope to see you in the spring. I have a terrible conscience which preys upon me, incessantly reminding me that I have never been to Greece; and who knows how long it will be possible to go there? So I am trying to persuade Dawyck Haig to accompany me there this spring. In that case I should come to Italy and hope to spend a few days with you, if that should be possible, and then fly to Athens from Rome. But I shall know later whether this is to be possible: I hope it is. Meanwhile I hope you are all well. Do write and tell me what is happening in Italy & I Tatti. What are you reading? Everyone here is reading Boswell's Diary – would you like it?[6] I haven't yet read it so can't

---

[4] David Erskine, 11th Earl of Buchan (1742–1829) is depicted in Sir Walter Scott's *Journals* as 'a prince of Bores'. In 1814 he erected near Dryburgh a sandstone statue seven metres high representing the Scottish warrior William Wallace.

[5] T-R had been appointed Censor of Christ Church: 'the office of Censor,' he noted, 'has no equivalent in any other college: an ancient and somewhat mysterious office, undefined in the statutes of the college, but central to its operation.' (*Independent*, 10 August 1991.)

[6] The recent publication of *Boswell's London Journal* had delighted London reviewers, but BB was less impressed by it (diary, 25 September 1951).

give a verdict. Don't read A.L. Rowse on *Elizabethan England*, – he is a scholar-toady.[7] I have been writing a preface to an interesting book by a Pole, Z. Stypulkowski,[8] which you might find interesting – I mean the book, not the preface. It is to be called *Invitation to Moscow* & will be published this spring. The author is I suppose the only man who has been tried in one of the great public 'Purge' trials in Moscow and has been able to escape and given an account of the methods by which the famous confessions are obtained. It is really a remarkable story. Otherwise I am now writing only in the *New Statesman* in order to build up a *corpus* of historical essays to publish ultimately as a consecutive book.[9] But I should like to hear what *you* have found interesting. [...]

Berenson replied on 16 January, enclosing an article clipped from the latest issue of Figaro Littéraire *describing Himmler's final months and mentioning Trevor-Roper. 'You advise me not to read Rowse yet your review would have tempted me to!!'*

18 February 1951   Christ Church, Oxford

My dear BB

Many thanks for your letter and for the article in *le Figaro Littéraire*, which is particularly interesting to me: there is an immense secret history behind the whole question of Himmler and the Jewish Agency, with ramifications in Sweden, Finland and Holland, furious international controversies, bitter polemic and large interests at stake. I have been aware of it for some time – it provides the explanation of the fact that Countess Bernadotte[1] (as I believe) hired an English hack in Stockholm to write a savage attack on me, and it has caused governments and royal families in Sweden and Holland to take sides in the great struggle over the reputation

---

[7] (Alfred) Leslie Rowse (1903–1997), Fellow of All Souls 1925–74. T-R's review of Rowse's *The England of Elizabeth* (*New Statesman*, 13 January 1951) praised the book as 'by far the best and most scholarly account of Elizabethan society' and as 'a real portrait of an age, vivid but exact, tumultuously expressed but scrupulously excogitated'. However Rowse's prose was 'sometimes arch, sometimes angular, sometimes shrill', and T-R was repelled by his 'arrogance', 'hatred of intellectuals', 'contempt for the lower classes' and 'his worship of Philistine high spirits, his romantic admiration of the English, the successful, the upper classes'.
[8] Zbigniew Stypulkowski (1904–1979), a Polish lawyer and former National-Democratic member of the Sejm, was one of sixteen Polish leaders who in 1945 were invited to lunch with the Soviet Marshal Zhukov, kidnapped, and taken to the Lubianka prison in Moscow, where they were interrogated until all but Stypulkowski confessed to crimes that they had not committed. Stypulkowski learnt Russian in prison, defended himself at trial and received a virtual acquittal.
[9] Selected reviews from the *New Statesman* and other periodicals were published by Macmillan as T-R's *Historical Essays* in 1957.
[1] Estelle Manville (1904–1984), of Pleasantville, New York state, had married the Count in 1928.

of Himmler's Estonian masseur . . .[2] Have I ever told you this secret history?
If not – & if it interests you – I will, if I may, at I Tatti. For this letter is also
to ask you whether I may come & spend part of the vacation with you in
the spring, probably about the 16th of March. My plans are not fixed, but
if you can have me, I should of course be delighted. I have just recovered
from a week in bed with my recurrent complaint, and I should like nothing
better than another visit to see you and enjoy your company. So do let me
know if I may do that.

  You said that you had sent your booklet on Caravaggio, but I haven't had
it. Do let me see it. As an empiricist, hostile to all abstract terms, I tremble
at the word baroque applied – as I think it was first applied by Burckhardt –
to whole ages, and I should read your remarks on that subject, I know, with
delight. There are some excellent observations on 'the Baroque Age' in that
monumental work of French historical scholarship, Fernand Braudel's *La
Méditerranée* ... an immense book, 1,100 pages (not for you, I fear, with
your Alexandrian doctrine *Μέγα βιβλίον μέγα κακόν*),[3] but one which
seems to me the greatest work on the 16th century produced in my memory.[4]
But in general I am coming to the view that only the French can write
history: Marc Bloch[5] and his disciples have made all other historians seem
trivial: we are nowhere, and the Germans, who are still in the buried
geological age of frothblowing nationalism or virtuous pedantry, are, if
there is anywhere beyond nowhere, there. I believe the French achieve their
results by slave-labour, as the Pyramids were built; but so, after all, was
civilisation.

---

[2] Felix Kersten (1898–1960), Estonian by birth, fought in Finland's war of liberation from Russia
and became a fashionable Berlin physician and masseur. After being recommended to Prince
Hendrik, the consort of Queen Wilhelmina of the Netherlands, he became a member of the
Dutch royal household, but was visiting Berlin when the Germans invaded the Netherlands in
1940. Trapped there, he became personal physician to Himmler, 'that terrible, impersonal,
inhuman, but naïve, mystical, credulous tyrant of the New Order', as T-R called him. Himmler
depended heavily upon Kersten, who interceded on behalf of prisoners detained in German
camps. The World Jewish Congress credited Kersten with the rescue of 60,000 Jews, and the
Dutch government nominated him for the Nobel Peace Prize in 1952.
[3] 'A great book is a great plague': a remark from the grammatical works of Callīmǎchus, head of
the Alexandria library.
[4] Fernand Braudel (1902–1985) went to teach in Algiers in 1924 and became so intrigued by the
Mediterranean that he began to research its geography, ecology, agriculture, demography, trade,
beliefs and politics to create *l'histoire totale*. During five years spent in a German camp at Lübeck
he wrote from memory the 700 pages of his doctoral dissertation, which was published in 1949
as *La Méditerranée et le monde méditerranean à l'époque de Philippe II*.
[5] Pirenne's pupil Marc Bloch (1886–1944) was appointed to the chair of medieval history at the
newly opened University of Strasbourg in 1919 and to the chair of economic history at the
Sorbonne in 1937. His monograph, *Les rois thaumaturgues* (1924), a study of eight centuries of
belief in the miraculous cure of scrofula by kings, was crucial in launching the history of
mentalités. Bloch joined the Resistance, was tortured by the Gestapo and shot in a meadow with

But there is one English book that I have just read with pleasure, by a rather spiky Northumbrian neighbour of mine, Steven Runciman[6] (son of that disastrous Northern shipping magnate who, in 1938, went to Prague for Neville Chamberlain to diddle Hitler). It is volume I of a history of the Crusades. I have written a review of it for the *New Statesman*.[7] When you read the review, tell me if you feel that you would like to read the book & I will send it. But you must anyway send me your essay on Caravaggio – I will hold you to that!

I was very sorry to read about Alys's death, which I hadn't had any reason to expect. I hadn't seen her for some time – I don't think that she really forgave me for not approving of Gathorne-Hardy's book – but she had seemed well and sprightly then, – indeed in a kind of *euphoria* through falling in love with Bertie Russell again; which is no doubt exhausting too.[8] [...]

PS. Isaiah Berlin tells me that he had hoped to be in Italy but all his plans are broken by the inability of the Foreign Office to fit in with his Palestinian time-table; but I hope he will pause there on his way back.

Berenson replied on 23 February, welcoming Trevor-Roper's proposed visit. 'Please tell Isaiah Berlin that I should be grieved if he failed to come. His visit last Sept. was the kind of sip that does not suffice to tell you just what you are tasting. As for Runciman [...] it seems that he avoids I Tatti.' He had been scanning Heinrich von Srbik's recently published historiography Geist und Geschichte vom Deutschen Humanismus bis zur Gegenwart, *which he judged 'enough to drive one to drink'.*

Trevor-Roper replied on 27 February, giving his travel plans to Greece. 'I have been ill and haven't had a chance to see Isaiah Berlin, but I will give him your message without fail,' he added. 'I don't believe in Srbik. I don't think the Germans

---

twenty-seven other prisoners.
[6] Although the Runciman family's seat was in Northumberland, (Sir) Steven(son) Runciman (1903–2000) lived mainly at this time on the Isle of Eigg off the west coast of Scotland.
[7] T-R's review of Runciman's *History of the Crusades* (*New Statesman*, 3 March 1951) declared: 'A great movement, disconcerting three cosmopolitan civilisations, and leaving its evidence in Slavonic and Arabic, Syriac and Armenian records, is obviously beyond the scope of those narrow medievalists who crouch, in devout but rigid and uncommunicative postures, before their national repositories. But Mr Steven Runciman is a scholar who can study such sources, and – what is almost as rare – an historian who can use, a writer who can express, their evidence. His learning is deep, his presentation clear, his style firm and graceful. He has the gift of occasional irony.'
[8] Alys Russell died on 21 January aged eighty-three. In 1950, after meeting her ex-husband for the first time in thirty-nine years, she convinced herself that they might resume life together. Her diary for 1 January 1951 read: 'Bertie doesn't telephone nor come, & I feel dreadfully sad. From 3 to 4 every day after my nap I have a fit of the blues, & cry & long so much to see him that I can hardly bear it.'

know what history is now: they haven't done for years, – since about 1900. But I
expect this is a generalisation which, like all other generalisations, is no sooner
uttered than regretted. I begin to regret it already.'

On his return journey from Greece, Trevor-Roper spent the week beginning 10
April at I Tatti, and sent his hostess the following letter of thanks (knowing that she
would immediately read it aloud to Berenson).

25 April 1951   Christ Church, Oxford

My dear Nicky

When I come to I Tatti, from the material discomforts of the Peloponnese (when shall I forget Megalopolis or the excoriating bed-rock of the poetic river Alpheus?), or look back at it from the remorseless administrative treadmill of Oxford which at present, sustained like a camel in the desert by the lingering aftertaste of that remote oasis, I am energetically treading, – but all my metaphors are getting mixed and the syntax of my sentence is out of hand – at all events you make it the most delightful spot and I am infinitely grateful to you all: there is no place where I so enjoy the leisure I find there and feel myself so happily at home ...

And yet did I not behave outrageously? I recollect yielding suddenly to a gust of English nationalism (an emotion I utterly reprehend), denouncing the Welsh, or at least the Black Welsh (the distinction is important, and desperate social solecisms can be committed by those who disregard it), the nation of King Arthur and the Holy Grail and those exquisite Metaphysical Poets Herbert and Vaughan and Traherne,[1] – but the nation also (for I feel a black dionysiac passion overcoming me) of Lloyd George[2] and that disreputable demagogue Aneurin Bevan,[3] now (O ecstasy!) cast into outer darkness, and Lord Trefgarne, *alias* Mr Garro Jones MP,[4] whose private finances will shortly, it is supposed, provide an interesting scandal,

---

[1] George Herbert (1593–1633), Henry Vaughan (1621/2–1695) and Thomas Traherne (1637–1674).
[2] David Lloyd George, 1st Earl Lloyd George of Dwyfor (1863–1945), radical orator and Prime Minister 1916–22.
[3] Aneurin Bevan (1897–1960) oversaw the implementation of the National Health Service as Minister of Health in 1945–51. He was appointed Minister of Labour in January 1951, but resigned on 21 April in protest at proposals to introduce certain health charges. He was admired for his principles by many socialists but considered a trouble-maker by other Labour colleagues.
[4] George Garro Jones, 1st Baron Trefgarne (1894–1960), businessman and former MP (originally Liberal, then Labour), had resigned as chairman of the Colonial Development Corporation in September 1950. It was revealed in March 1951 that the Corporation had suffered immense losses. Shunned by his former colleagues, he left the Labour party in 1952.

and Mr Emrys Hughes MP,[5] and ... But I must stop (if I can): you see how overmastering these passions can be. Do you entertain them, in respect perhaps of the Estonians or the Letts, who I suppose are a sort of Welsh of the Baltic shores?

I am sorry that while at I Tatti I did not calm this passion by sublimating it, as the psychologists say. It can be sublimated by reading, as a sort of purgative incantation, the splendid character-sketch of Lloyd George by Maynard Keynes. Do you know this heroic essay, which for sheer irresponsible gaiety and brilliant euphoria out-logans Logan, even at Logan's best? I ought to have read it to BB. But if, at I Tatti, it is unknown, then you must read it. It was expurgated from *The Economic Consequences of the Peace* at the instigation of Asquith; but afterwards Keynes regretted his weak compliance and printed it in his *Essays in Biography*. Do read it, and I will be there in spirit, listening to those golden periods of highest farce and most exquisite malice. If only he were alive to do the same to Nye Bevan! Then my spirit would be entirely purged and I would never denounce even the Black Welsh again.

Now I must convey a message from Isaiah Berlin. He is infinitely sorry that he could not pause on his way home to see you; but his family were at Nice and could not, without grave offence, have been left unvisited. But I hope, and he hopes, that he will visit you on his next move; and I hope (but he seems to regard this as an absurd and quixotic hope) that he will visit you in a new capacity, as Warden of All Souls: a distinguished office which, I think, would be splendidly embodied in him. But alas, everything in Oxford depends on votes, so that the exquisite pleasure of mortifying the majority is, by definition, unattainable. However, I know he wants to revisit you and I have assured him that he will be welcome *even* as Warden of All Souls.

I, of course, unless suddenly forbidden in consequence of some outrageous act, intend to revisit you as soon as I can and express by reappearance the gratitude I feel for your delightful hospitality.

Keep well; give my love to all; and tell BB that he will be receiving a letter from me in two days. [...]

---

[5] Emrys Hughes (1894–1969), socialist editor, rabble-rouser and incorrigibly rebellious Labour MP.

4 May 1951   Christ Church, Oxford

My dear BB

I write belatedly – but I do everything belatedly, I'm afraid – to thank you for the kindness which I never fail to meet, and the pleasure I never fail to experience, at I Tatti. I enjoyed my visit – as of course I always do – enormously: and I am glad I came after not before my visit to Greece; – partly, of course, because this enabled me so loudly and long to boast of my adventures and experiences there (which I am still doing); partly because after the comfort of I Tatti I would have instantly succumbed to the rigours of Megalopolis (I regard these two places as symbolising the opposite poles of experience). Even as it is I have succumbed, though not seriously, to the rigours of Oxford: but that is perhaps my own fault, for exercising a pack of hounds early on a May morning in a snowstorm. This is a mistake, and I advise against it. I regard it as my duty to exercise the creatures twice a week in the summer (Prof. Seznec will have informed you, if I have not, that the duties of Oxford dons are sometimes strange and unpredictable), and I do it before breakfast to avoid the heat of the day.[1] Unfortunately the day, in England, is also an unpredictable experience.

What report can I make to you now? There are, I think, since the glorious resignation of Aneurin Bevan and the return of the Stone,[2] each to its own appropriate place, one to Wales, – where may he long remain, preaching nonconformity to the barbarian inhabitants –, the other to Westminster Abbey, no great controversies presently raging; and in the universal dullness of life thus created we intellectuals have to resort, as an escape for *tedium vitae*, to reading; for of course, as Seznec (that disastrous betrayer of all our well-kept humbugs) has no doubt revealed – as I am sure d'Entrèves never has – reading, at Oxford, is the last desperate resort of those who have, for the time being, no opportunity of talking, electioneering, dining out, or intriguing. In case you are in like case, I have sent you a book: it is a book which I mentioned to you, by a Pole, and for which I have written a preface.[3] The first part of it is, I think, dull, and the whole is written without any distinction; but I think that, if you read it, you may find it interesting. At

---

[1] Jean Seznec (1905–1983), a spruce, alert and eloquent Breton, had been befriended by BB during his five years' teaching at the French Institute in Florence 1934–9. An art historian as well as a literary scholar, *La survivance des dieux antiques* (1940) was published in English translation as *The Survival of the Pagan Gods: Mythological Tradition in Renaissance Humanism and Art* (1953). Marshal Foch Professor of French Literature at Oxford and Fellow of All Souls 1950–72.
[2] The Stone of Scone: see T-R's letter of 6 January 1951.
[3] Zbigniew Stypulkowski's *Invitation to Moscow*: see T-R's letter of 6 January 1951.

least I did, for I know of no other case of a man who has emerged from a Russian treason trial since the technique was perfected. (Theoretically, of course, Radek should now be at large: for his ten years' sentence has elapsed; but I doubt if we shall hear of him.)[4] Anyway, if you read it, let me know what you think of it: I should be interested to hear your views on it. At any rate it has one virtue which I know you appreciate (it is the only trace of Alexandrianism I have so far noticed in your otherwise classic character): it is *short*. I, unlike you, prefer my books to be long (though this may be a sign of laziness: it spares one the mental effort of repeated choice); and I am now re-reading, for the nth time, that greatest of all historians, as I continually find myself declaring, – Gibbon. What a splendid writer he is! If only historians could write like him now! How has the art of footnotes altogether perished and the gift of irony disappeared! I took a volume of Gibbon to Greece and read it on Mount Hymettus and the island of Crete; I read it furtively even at I Tatti, where 40,000 other volumes clamoured insistently around me to be read; and I cannot stop reading him even now. And then there is that other great historian Clarendon, whom I have just read from beginning to end, a million words;[5] and Doughty's *Arabia Deserta*[6] ... but I know I must not reiterate these ancient sentiments to you. *Μέγα βιβλίον μέγα κακόν*[7] you will briefly reply; so I have sent you Stypulkowski.

I had a visit the other day from another distinguished Pole, L.B. Namier. Did you read his article on Herbert von Dirksen in the *Times Literary Supplement* last week? It seemed to me excellent.[8] Of course he can be excellent – is indeed, in my opinion, the greatest living historian writing in English. But don't let him visit you. Flee rather to the utmost extremities

---

[4] Karl Sobelsohn (1885–1939), a Russian revolutionary known as Radek, was arrested during a Stalinist purge in 1937, condemned to ten years' imprisonment and afterwards, as T-R surmised, murdered.

[5] Edward Hyde, 1st Earl of Clarendon (1609–1674), Lord Chancellor of England, wrote *The True Historical Narrative of the Rebellion and Civil Wars in England* after his impeachment and exile in 1667.

[6] Charles Doughty (1843–1926), author of *Travels in Arabia Deserta* (1888). T-R had written to Pearsall Smith (16 September 1944): 'I have lost the taste for travel-books since I read that great heraldic monster among them, Doughty's *Arabia Deserta*, which extinguishes all the others, making them seem thin and trite.' BB likened Doughty's prose to Meredith's when he read *Arabia Deserta* in 1908.

[7] 'A great book is a great plague' (Callĭmáchus).

[8] Herbert von Dirksen (1882–1955). German Ambassador in Moscow 1928–33, Tokyo 1933–8 and London 1938–9. Namier's review of Dirksen's *Moskau, Tokio, London* in the *TLS* of 20 April pictured Dirksen as 'a highly egocentric, ambitious, bitter and yet pliant man, who adjusted himself to situations in a cold, resentful manner', and his book as 'unimportant reminiscences [...] seasoned with howlers'.

of Italy to cower, until the danger is over, in some protective juniper bush or inaccessible mountain cave. He is also, without doubt, the greatest living bore. And for that distinction the competition, I'm afraid, is even hotter!

6 July 1951   Christ Church, Oxford

My dear BB

I must apologise for my long silence, or at least explain it. As Sir Walter Scott observed, when explaining the sudden intermission of Lord Ravensworth's vast building programme, 'elections have intervened';[1] and indeed, as you doubtless know, Oxford and Cambridge are now the only places where elections are still conducted in the old 18th century manner: with that elaborate attention to the individual weaknesses, cupidities, ambitions etc. of a small and personally manipulated electorate. This term there have been three elections: consequently all research, teaching, administration have been suspended, and such social life as has been allowed to continue has been solely governed by the design to win over, by appropriate attentions, that elusive abstraction: the Floating Vote. But I shall descend from the general to the particular.

Of the election in University College, from which your distinguished compatriot Professor Goodhart has emerged triumphant in apostolic if indirect succession to the alleged founder of that institution, King Alfred, there is little to say.[2] Contrary to all Oxford tradition, the Election (which like all Oxford Elections, was officially secret) was also *almost* secret in fact. This was partly, of course, because no one is much interested in what goes on in University College, so the usual system of espionage has never been developed. The college is a sort of Oxford Tibet, with primitive inhabitants, strange superstitions, and few economic attractions for colonising powers. Consequently the election was enveloped in that secrecy which customarily shrouds (it is said) the election in Lhasa of a Dalai Lama. Quite opposite, of course, was the election of a Warden of All Souls. That should rather be compared with a Presidential Election in America. Every process of it was accompanied, illustrated, promoted, or obstructed by radio-broadcast, appeals, propaganda, television, ticker-

[1] Thomas Liddell, 1st Baron Ravensworth (1775–1855), spent his coal-mine revenues on rebuilding Ravensworth Castle, which was being demolished at the time of T-R's letter. Sir Walter Scott's *Journal* noted (5 October 1827) that the castle was 'but half built; elections have come between'.
[2] Arthur Goodhart (1891–1978), a Yale-educated American, was Professor of Jurisprudence at Oxford 1931–51 and Master of University College 1951–63.

tapes, and utterances of oracular ambiguity by highly paid commentators. I am therefore enabled to give you, I hope, as full an account even as your friend Seznec, who – having never before tasted the exhilarating experience of a college election – has been quite intoxicated by the experience and has seldom interrupted the sparkling Latin flow of his excited commentary. Some repressing drops of this rapidly bubbling stream may perhaps have been carried even to Italy; but I nevertheless intend to supplement them.

You must understand that there is in this university, as in all institutions (see the Bible, *passim*) a Party of Light (to which the writer belongs) and a Party of Darkness (consisting of those who hold different views). Our party of Light regards a University as a place of Learning and Pleasure, to be controlled by us; their party of Darkness regards it as a place of administrative efficiency and Dullness, to be controlled by them. These two parties are nearly always locked in apparently insoluble deadlock; which however is ultimately solved by the existence, at a far lower level, of a third party, conveniently described as the Jellies, or party of compromise. Whereas the Parties of Light and Darkness are distinguished by the enlightenment or blackness of their views, the Jellies – or perhaps I should say Jellyfish – are distinguished by their complete absence of any views. They float now this way, now that, as the tide ebbs or flows, sucked helplessly into the wake of ships passing now this way now that, sometimes stranded on the beach by the advancing tide, and left there to dissolve in the sun, sometimes carried by the receding tide, quavering, into the strange and terrifying currents of the uncomprehended Ocean. In spite of their general helplessness the Jellies have, however, two important qualities: first, though sometimes submerged, they never sink; secondly, though unable to control the direction of their movements, some of them can, if touched, sting. In periods of violent storm (naturalists observe) these Jellies appear in large numbers around our otherwise placid academic coasts; and the result of their intervention in our elections (I must now return from metaphor to the world of plain fact) is almost always the same: a compromise candidate is discovered who, in the exhaustion of both parties, is found acceptable by all. This compromise candidate always has certain important negative qualities whereby he secures this general assent. First, he appeals to the Party of Light by being thoroughly inefficient at administration; secondly he appeals to the Party of Darkness by showing no interest in either Learning or Pleasure. Thus, although nobody positively wants him, each party prefers him to the candidate of the other, and he is elected. This, in brief, is the analysis of all Oxford Elections. I now return to the two particular elections which have interrupted all work for the last two months: the election of a Warden of All Souls and the election of a Professor of History.[3]

Of course the late Warden of All Souls had hardly been buried, and the black hatchment had hardly been hung out, like a somewhat tipsy pub-sign, over the college gate, before the preparations and speculations about the succession had begun. There are in All Souls 51 voting Fellows, and a candidate, to be elected Warden, must obtain at least 26 votes at the formal meeting; but before this formal meeting there are preliminary meetings at which those candidates who are thought to be worth running are selected by a straw vote. Our candidate was, of course, Isaiah Berlin. Theirs was, of course, a professional administrator. At the first straw vote they obtained a majority for their candidate, Sir Edward Bridges,[4] head of the civil service, Isaiah being second; but Bridges declined the offer, and from this moment the battle can be said to have begun.

The most determined advocate of Darkness in All Souls – A.L. Rowse – happened, at this crucial juncture, to be in California, and ever since airplanes were invented he has loudly declared that his neuroses would never allow him to travel in such a vessel; but when the fate of Darkness in Oxford hung thus precariously in the balance, he at once disinterestedly jettisoned his long and carefully sustained neuroses and appeared within a few days in the surprised cloisters of All Souls. For a week every alcove hummed; then, at the next meeting of the Fellows, when a new straw vote was taken in consequence of the retreat of Bridges, 26 Fellows, with apparent unanimity, supported the proposal of Rowse of a hitherto quite unknown figure: Sir Eric Beckett. Such support, if repeated at the official meeting, would infallibly bring Beckett in. The question which everybody naturally asked (including some of those who had already voted for him) was, Who is Sir Eric Beckett?[5]

Deep research has been devoted to this problem. So far the only clear facts which have emerged are that Sir Eric Beckett is (thanks to an airplane-crash which killed his superior) legal adviser to the Foreign Office; that he

---

[3]The sudden death on 25 April of Benedict Sumner (1893–1951), Warden of All Souls, caused intense machinations until the election of his successor on 10 June. The diplomatic historian Sir Llewellyn Woodward (1890–1971) had become the first holder of the chair in modern history at Oxford in 1947, but in 1951 moved to a chair at Princeton.

[4]Sir Edward Bridges (1892–1969), later 1st Baron Bridges, Fellow of All Souls 1920–27 and 1954–68, Permanent Secretary of the Treasury and Head of the Civil Service 1945–56, was one of the most powerful men in Britain. He declined the Wardenship when he realised that his election would be contested by Berlin's supporters.

[5]Sir Eric Beckett (1896–1966) was a dry, painstaking, etiolated man who had been a Fellow of All Souls 1921–8. He became Legal Adviser at the Foreign Office in 1945 after the loss of an aircraft carrying Sir William Malkin back from the San Francisco Conference.

was once struck in the face by Douglas Jay who, though himself a well-behaved Wykehamist, was outraged beyond endurance by his pro-Franco views,[6] and that he has twice been in a lunatic asylum.

Conceive, if you can, the crescendo of buzzing in the alcoves, the feverish motion from staircase to staircase in these normally somnolent quadrangles, the sudden attentiveness towards young voters of hitherto aloof elderly peers, the carefully timed indiscretions and skilfully calculated chance meetings by which, in the next fortnight, each party sought desperately to detach from the other its floating voters; and having conceived it, transport yourself in imagination to the official meeting at which whoever obtained 26 votes would thereby become Warden of the College. The first proposal was made by Rowse who, as sub-warden, controlled the machinery of debate. He proposed Sir Eric Beckett; and thereupon the carefully oiled mechanism of election began those calculated revolutions which would slide the candidate effortlessly into place. Began – but did not complete them. Suddenly strange creaks issued from parts of the equipment, as if saboteurs had secretly inserted sand in some essential aperture. The great engine groaned suddenly to a standstill, and certain small but important cogs, rods or pistons had not moved – with disastrous consequences: the candidate was not in place. In spite of his earlier absolute majority, he had now only got 23 votes; and 23 votes are not enough.

At once the Party of Light advanced to try their hand at the machine. Their candidate in turn was placed on the springboard: Isaiah Berlin; and the Party foremen wound enthusiastically with the recalcitrant handles. But once again certain essential springs failed to respond, and the candidate could not be carried forward into the Warden's lodgings. He had only obtained 21 votes, and 21 votes are not enough either.

And now began a famous scene which will long be remembered in Oxford history and quoted in the manuals of our constitutional procedure. Each party in despair began to put up candidate after candidate in the hope of breaking the deadlock, and every advocate of Light, and every advocate of Darkness, in turn submitted to the test in the hope of detaching either three votes in one direction or five in the other in order to achieve a majority. Scenes of indescribable confusion followed. Twice did Isaiah withdraw his candidature amid applause from his adversaries; twice was he dragged back by his supporters. Now one hand, now another, grasped the handle of the obstinate machine, but failed to turn it. The issue was always the same. Whoever stood against Isaiah infallibly obtained 23 votes – the voting

---

[6] Douglas Jay (1907–1996), an economist, had been a Fellow of All Souls 1930–7. Elected as a Labour MP in 1946, he eventually became a Cabinet Minister and life peer.

strength of embattled Darkness; whoever stood against Beckett as infallibly obtained 21 votes – the voting strength of mobilised Light. There was total deadlock. What was to be done?

At this point the watchers on the academic cliffs began to espy, out at sea, the familiar phenomenon of the storm: great shoals of Jellies drifting slowly towards the shore; and within the conclave, by a natural consequence of this news, the cry for a compromise candidate began to be heard. The question was, who could that compromise candidate be? You will have observed that the full toll of voters was 51, but also that the united voting strength of the two parties amounts only to 44; and whereas we can account for one of the omissions by the fact that the candidate of the moment was always out of the room at the time of the voting, and for a second by the fact that one voter – Professor Wheare – overcome by the strain of the conclave, had been carried out on a stretcher,[7] there are still other abstainers to be accounted for. Naturally it was among these abstainers that a compromise candidate would be sought. Who among them was the most appropriate candidate?

Sir Hubert Henderson, Drummond Professor of Political Economy,[8] is a respectable elderly gentleman who is generally known in Oxford for one reason only: in 1949 he made, before the largest meeting of Convocation ever remembered in Oxford, the most boring speech that has ever been heard in that assembly. Had there been any votes to lose on that occasion, it is universally agreed that Henderson's speech would indubitably have lost them all. (In fact his speech made no difference at all: everyone came to that meeting with his mind so firmly made up that no oratory, however plausible, could have altered it: for we were voting an increase in our own salaries). When the first straw vote for the Wardenship of All Souls was taken, Sir Hubert Henderson had only obtained one vote; and it was perhaps this fact which (by rendering the whole issue academic to him) had caused him to sleep, and thereby to abstain, throughout the long struggle of parties. At all events, when the deadlock within the college walls was complete, and the swish of Jellies in the tide had suddenly become audible, the double fact that nobody seemed to want Sir Hubert Henderson and that Sir Hubert Henderson did not seem to want anyone, naturally made him the man of the hour. And thus it was that suddenly, at the crucial moment, when Sir Hubert Henderson was placed in the machine, the handle at last turned

---

[7] (Sir) Kenneth Wheare (1907–1979) was elected to the Gladstone chair of government and public administration with a Fellowship at All Souls in 1944. Rector of Exeter College, Oxford, 1956–72.
[8] Sir Hubert Henderson (1890–1952), Fellow of All Souls since 1934 and Drummond Professor of Political Economy since 1945.

effortlessly in its socket, the wheels revolved, the rods and cams, ratchets and pinions all slid with lubricated ease on their intended courses, and the candidate was at last, by 36 votes, carried effortlessly forward into the Warden's Lodgings of All Souls.

It only remains to add that Sir Hubert Henderson, overcome by the excitement of election, has retired to hospital with a heart-attack; so a spare hatchment has been commissioned and discreet preparations are already, but I hope wrongly, being made for a resumption of the struggle.[9]

My dear BB, I had meant to touch but briefly on the All Souls election, which concerned your friend Isaiah Berlin, in order thereafter to describe at greater length the even more protracted election – for it lasted more than two months – to the Chair of History, which concerned me; but I have already written too much, and perhaps on more personal matters it is more prudent to be brief. Suffice it then that this election too ran true to form. For two months there was total deadlock between those who insisted that they would interpose their dead bodies between that candidate and that chair. (The objection is that I *write* history; and that, they say, should *never* be done: it has certainly never been done by them.) Then, at the usual moment, the Jellies advanced; and the leisure that I had hoped to achieve for study and writing has been awarded instead to a last-minute candidate whose historical studies, confined to one branch of the State Papers during the reign of Elizabeth, have so far yielded, in 25 years, two slender articles.[10] I am sure they are exact and competent articles; but since the author of them touches nothing that he does not desiccate, I cannot find anyone who has read them. However, I must not make any uncivil comment on this election, so I will only say that the standards of Oxford professors of history have been maintained. We have now four such professors, and the total output of original work by all four together amounts to five articles.

Now the pen begins to falter in my hand, and I have written about myself and about Oxford and asked nothing about you. How are you all? Did Ischia cure you? Your letter from Venice has just reached me: I am enviously delighted to imagine your travels: I wish I could join you on your cool Olympian hill-top. If I can, I will. [...]

---

[9] Henderson was elected Warden on 10 June but suffered another coronary thrombosis on 20 June during the Encaenia ceremonies. After a long absence, he resigned the wardenship in January 1952 and died on 22 February.

[10] Bruce Wernham (1906–1999), Fellow of Worcester College, held the chair of modern history at Oxford 1951–72. He published his first book – on Tudor diplomacy – at the age of sixty.

25 September 1951   Christ Church, Oxford

My dear BB

My first emotion on writing to you is to excuse, or seek to excuse, my long silence; my second, by way of excuse (but a weak excuse) to add that indirectly, if not directly, I have been in regular contact: such is the social and intellectual bloodstream which is circulated through the Western World by the central organism of I Tatti. My latest reports come from the Hamish Hamiltons; my latest news will perhaps be brought to you, if you see them, by the Notesteins. But I am sorry that you have been so troubled with illness. I hope you are better. As a fellow-sufferer from the same kind of complaint, I send you (from my own bed to which it has again sent me) my condolences & my hopes that the dry air of Ischia or the clear air of Vallombrosa has by now cured you of that most uncomfortable of complaints. Considering (as I often do) the relative insignificance of the pleasures of smell compared with all the others, I could dispense altogether with the nose if I could dispense also with its inconveniences!

Now what news can I give you in exchange for the news which I hope to elicit from your great intellectual cosmopolis? I have been to Spain, a country which (the shame of this omission had in the end become intolerable to me) I had never previously visited: and my visit, partial though it was, and indeed had to be, has *almost* – but not quite – seduced my affections away from Italy. Fortunately, even if it had, there are personal friendships which would even then lead me back to Italy, and which, at Xmas, I hope will again do so. But the Prado is a wonderful gallery. The Uffizi (dare I say it?) deadens me. The infinite orderly development of the Italian masters, *maestro di* this after *maestro di* that painting Madonna after Madonna, St Jerome after St Jerome – their very beauty becomes, after a time, tedious to my quickly satisfied senses, and like a sudden claustrophobe I cry out for more space and fewer pictures – that is one reason that makes me love the Frick gallery in New York, – there are so *few* pictures! – But in the Prado I find an altogether different spectacle: three great giants – Velásquez, Goya, El Greco – rising, clear, obvious & different, like the Eildon Hills[1] (but I must not expect you to recognise such parochial images) above the flat plain strewn with the rubbish of Murillo, Ribera, Zurbarán ... Perhaps I shock you by these statements? But I am sure you also have relished, and still do, the pleasures of heresy! Otherwise the things that most impressed me in Spain were the baroque church of Sta Maria de la

_____

[1] Three conical volcanic hills standing outside the town of Melrose in Roxburghshire.

Huerta, which I lit upon quite accidentally, near Medinacelí, – as perfect as
Ottobeuren or St Florian – and the cathedral at Léon, and the wonderful
high, endless, golden emptiness of the Castilian plateau: everything was
golden – golden stubble fields, and, in the villages, golden heaps of corn
being winnowed, and lanes golden with blown chaff, and the air impregnated with a golden dust from the process of it. The most obvious differences from Italy seemed to me two: first the emptiness over that vast, high
plain compared with the crowded termite-villages in the creases and clefts
of the Italian mountains; secondly the interesting fact that whereas in Italy
I have been into hundreds of churches and never found a service going on
in any of them, in Spain I never seemed to enter any church anywhere
without finding a thin white line of dry bald heads, studding, like a row of
beads, the carved stalls of the *coro*, and a strange nasal mumbling arising
therefrom, like the rhythmical noise, as I imagine it, of endless prayer-
wheels in a Tibetan lamasery. You see I was fascinated altogether by that
extraordinary, incongruous, accidental, isolated appendage to Europe. How
did it ever get there?

I went to Portugal too – at least the north of it. I didn't like it. The
slovenliness of the people compared with the ancient *gravitas* of even the
poorest Spanish peasant! And then the English colony in Oporto with their
splendid Georgain headquarters – but oh what bores! But the university of
Coimbra is wonderful, – that exquisite Renaissance quadrangle suddenly
poised like a Greek acropolis high above the city: that is worth all the rest
of Portugal that I saw.

Now of course I am back working: already read, read, read and scribble,
scribble. I am not scribbling much – not much for immediate publication,
that is: an article in *Commentary*[2] – one or two in the *New Statesman*; but
I think you see these papers. (*Commentary* incidentally seems to me to
contain some excellent things – though I can't put up with all the virtuous
Jewish stuff – e.g. a very good article on Keynes & another on the Alger
Hiss case.)[3] But I am working hard in the Record Office & writing silently
away at that infinitely dull book which, I fondly hope, *may* rehabilitate me
in the learned world after my unforgivable lapse into the shocking crime
of *success!*

---

[2] 'Is Hitler Really Dead?', *Commentary*, XI (February 1951), pp. 120–30.
[3] *Commentary* had been founded in 1945 as a monthly magazine for American Jewry. Elliot Cohen,
who was its editor until 1960, sought to nurture Jewish pride and cultural integrity without
rejecting such modern trends of thought as psychoanalysis. T-R is referring to John Kenneth
Galbraith, 'Will "Managed Capitalism" Pull Us Through?', *Commentary*, XII (August 1951),
pp. 126–31, and Leslie Fiedler, 'Hiss, Chambers and the Age of Innocence', *Commentary*, XII
(August 1951), pp. 109–19.

Have you found any interesting books recently? I read, as I travelled across Spain, *Hitler's Tischgespräche* which I found interesting.[4] The old wretch was of course a terrible bore, & the vulgarity of his mind is dreadful; but the fashionable view that he was a pure charlatan, only accidentally placed in a position of absolute power, seems to me not only wrong but, by its almost inevitable political consequences, disastrous. Who ever, from nothing, acquired absolute power, & kept it, by accident? His *Tischgespräche* – taken from the stenographic record at his private dinner-table during the year of greatest confidence, 1941–1942 – correct that view. I contemplate (if I can find the time) writing something on *The Mind of Hitler*, to correct those opposite errors: the error of the moment, that he was a mere Jew-baiter & charlatan, & the error of tomorrow (& yesterday) that he really could have solved the crisis of our century. But I think only an article. That mind was too coarse, too hard, too insensitive to fill a book (it filled one – *Mein Kampf*, – & what a book!); and anyway such a book might (*horresco referens*)[5] succeed!

Otherwise I am reading at last that great work, Bataillon's *Erasme en Espagne*.[6] Do you in fact know that great school of historians who, as it seems to me, have suddenly freshened the whole science (or art: one must avoid begging the question in this famous controversy!) of history: Henri Pirenne, Marc Bloch & his disciples: Lucien Febvre,[7] Fernand Braudel, etc? There are some Italians among them too – Gino Luzzatto,[8] Robert Lopez (a Genoese Jew now, I think, in America),[9] and, above all Carlo M. Cipolla, at Pavia.[10] Do you know anything about him? He interests me greatly. But of course there are no Germans, nor ever – I fear – will be. German historiography is sunk in obsolete nationalistic ruts. But perhaps some

---

[4] T-R was later paid £300 by George Weidenfeld to write the prefatory essay 'The Mind of Adolf Hitler' for the English translation of *Hitler's Tabletalk, 1941–44* (1953).

[5] 'I shudder as I recall it' (Virgil, *Aeneid*).

[6] Marcel Bataillon, *Erasme et l'Espagne: recherches sur l'histoire spirituelle du XVI siècle* (1937).

[7] Lucien Febvre (1878–1956), Professor of Modern History at Strasbourg, where his teaching drew on literature, economics, sociology, the visual arts, music, language and religion.

[8] Gino Luzzatto (1878–1964), historian of Italian medieval economic history.

[9] Roberto Sabatino-Lopez (1910–1986) left Italy because of racial persecution and had a long career in the history department at Yale (where he was known as Robert S. Lopez). He wrote, among other works, *Medieval Trade in the Mediterranean World* (1955) and contributed an essay, 'Dante, Salvation and the Layman', to *History and Imagination: Essays in Honour of H.R. Trevor-Roper* (1981).

[10] Carlo Cipolla (1922–2000) was a medieval and Renaissance historian who divided his time between Pavia and the University of California at Berkeley. Author of major works of economic and monetary history, pioneering studies in demography and disease, *Guns and Sails in the Early Phase of European Expansion 1400–1700* (1965) and *Clocks and Culture 1300–1700* (1967).

Austrian, some Swiss, some German Jew may ultimately supply an exception. [...]

23 November 1951   **Christ Church, Oxford**

My dear BB

Unanswered letters accumulate on my desk – including (I'm afraid) unanswered letters from you and from Nicky; I neither read nor write, but spin, like a top vertiginous though apparently immobile, and with a futile buzzing noise, in a vortex of administration. I am eager to escape from it. Would you receive me if I came, with my pen and paper, and a few disconnected and disorderly ideas in my head, prepared to transfer them thence on to the paper, in December? If that were convenient to you, of course it would be delightful for me, and I would invite myself to arrive about 13th December, and I should hope to find you all well, and know I should find I Tatti, as always, more intellectually stimulating than any of these much publicised centres of learning. Do let me know how you are and where you have been and whom you have seen and whether I shall see you.

Your friend Arturo Loria, about whom Nicky wrote to me, is in England; but alas, I have not seen him.[1] I wrote to him, but apparently he had already paid a secret, fleeting visit to Oxford, too short for social purposes; and I cannot go to London, immobilised, like the Baron von Holstein,[2] in my administrative cabinet. I am sorry I missed him. But who is Lord Charnwood, who apparently (according to my college porter) visited me yesterday, and finding me away left a verbal message of his visit accompanied by 'Mr Bernard Berenson'?[3] Are you really in England? Or is it, as seems more probable, one of those *lapsus linguae* such as caused me recently

---

[1] Arturo Loria (1900–1957), poet, essayist and raconteur.
[2] Friedrich von Holstein (1837–1909) seldom left his office in the Foreign Ministry in Berlin, never attended balls or banquets, and denounced an active social life as inimical to success or efficiency.
[3] John Benson, 2nd Baron Charnwood (1901–1955) had been an idle, difficult undergraduate who left Oxford without a degree. He then trained in mechanical engineering, and became chief engineer of the company that manufactured the Aston-Martin sports car. In 1939 he set sail from Cornwall to circumnavigate the globe, and had reached Peru when war was declared. After being recalled for military service and wounded in action, he joined the Coast and Anti-Aircraft Artillery Experimental Establishment, where he became so fascinated by his experimental work on range-finders that after the war he qualified at Northampton Polytechnic as an ophthalmic optician. Thereafter he undertook much brilliant research on space perception, and won prizes for his work on physiological optics and binocular vision. He knew T-R's younger brother, Patrick Trevor-Roper (1916–2004), a distinguished ophthalmic surgeon.

to be announced, in an English house, by a French servant, as 'Monsieur Talleyrand'?

From the general account which I give of my life in Oxford, you will not expect much information from me; but I can tell you that I am entirely converted to your view about anonymous reviewing. As you may have seen, I have been engaged in a brisk attack on the *Times Literary Supplement*, whose editor timidly expurgated from my letter (thus leaving the bleeding rump of the sentence scandalously ill-constructed) my dry phrase about the advantages of oracular anonymity.[4] This is the second time this year that that pontifical paper, which, as you know, is secretly controlled by bigoted Roman Catholics, has adopted this technique of informing the world in advance that all controversy has long ago been definitely settled to the satisfaction of their claims. I intend to give them no peace, and to render the life of the editor burdensome until the system is changed. But alas! I fear that the directors would sooner change the editor!

I am sorry you missed the Notesteins, whom I greatly like; but his summer visits to England and Italy are always fugitive and unpredictable, and he is presumably now back at Yale, lecturing to unheeding but obediently scribbling multitudes; while at Harvard, to our temporary loss, Isaiah Berlin is now doing the same, – only there, I am sure, only those students who have taken the precaution of previously learning shorthand can scribble fast enough to keep up with *his* oratory. No wonder, since that fountain of bubbling information, that once played all over Oxford from its *settecento* bason in All Souls, has now dried up – or rather, like the ancient river Alpheus, has travelled under the sea to break out in a remote continent – that I have so little to say! [...]

'I hasten to assure you the Dec. 13 will suit us,' Berenson replied on 28 November. 'I look forward to hearing more about Berlin & the all-conquering & devouring Bowra, & other great & good men.' Trevor-Roper stayed at I Tatti for a fortnight from 13 to 26 December 1951, then visited Siena, and returned for two nights at the end of the month. This visit marked a deepening of the intimacy between Trevor-Roper, Berenson and Mariano. 'Hugh', Berenson wrote to Hamish Hamilton on 27 December, 'grew more & more human as his visit went on, & at last I got the feeling that he was beginning perhaps to think of me & treat me as a contemporary, & not as a dodo by accident surviving from a remote past.' Henceforth Trevor-Roper was

---

[4]T-R's letter 'Treason and Plot' (*TLS*, 16 November 1951) challenged the reviewer of Hugh Ross Williamson's *The Gunpowder Plot* for reviving the suggestion of an earlier Jesuit historian that Thomas Winter's confession was a forgery. T-R suspected that the anonymous reviewer – John Carswell (b. 1918), historian and civil servant – was a Catholic apologist.

steadfast in his affection for Nicky Mariano; with her, most unusually, he felt able to be almost unguarded. This trust survived even her indiscreet handling of his letter of 14 January 1952.

1952

14 January 1952   Savile Club, 69 Brook St., W1

My dear Nicky

I ought of course to have written long ago (but I have an excuse – see below) to thank you for having me on my long visit to I Tatti, which I greatly enjoyed, as I always do. There is nowhere that I enjoy more – or indeed learn more at! When I examine with myself the additions made to my knowledge in the last few weeks, I find myself staggered by their extent: the beliefs of the Baha'i (if I have remembered even their name aright, let alone their doctrines), the operations of *streghe* and *stregoni*,[1] and the infinite complexities of Florentine society which (I'm afraid) never stay properly arranged in my head long enough to prevent me from making the same social errors, misrecognitions and misnomenclatures (which I anyway always commit everywhere) on my next visit. From here I look back to life in your mist-enshrouded islet of civilisation as to another world across a great barrier of intervening oblivion; because (I must now admit) on the way back, in the train, at about Genoa to be precise, I was suddenly struck down by that repeated and therefore boring complaint to which I periodically surrender. By the time I reached London I was in a somewhat decayed condition, and never got any further. In fact I retired to bed there for a week. So in the end I never attended that Servants' Party to which, in an excess of erratic conscientiousness, I was hastening, and to my nicely calculated time-table of administration, learning, and swimming (with somewhat spasmodic, feeble gestures) in the now slightly overcrowded and not very well drained social pool, has been totally disconcerted. However, these blows of fate have at last forced me to make a decision, and I am now going obediently, next week, like a pig to the shambles, on to the operating table which I have, for the last few years, largely avoided. I understand that bits will be removed; but out of an Oriental fatalism I am not very curious about the details. I am assured it will not take long. The undergraduates must look after themselves (under my liberal *régime* – admittedly interrupted now & then by arbitrary acts of tyranny – they have to do that anyway); and who knows? I may emerge cured.

In consequence of this sad tale of inactivity I can give you very little news

─────────────

[1] Witches and wizards.

from the social and intellectual world of England which I have hardly
seen. Only Frank Pakenham (who discovers everything by a kind of Irish
leprechaun-telegraph) discovered my recondite bed in London & came
with a series of highly improbable accounts of politics under the new
régime. Winston, he assures me, is more erratic, more arbitrary, more
nepotistical than ever, in his cabinet-making: he makes his cabinets on
purely 18th century principles of titbits for peers who have become bored
with country life; there is a general apprehension that the next job will go
to the Duke of Marlborough (an illiberal, illiterate dolt); and even Frank
Pakenham (who sets a pretty high standard in inconsistency) was surprised
when he, as Labour First Lord of the Admiralty, was asked to suggest a
good conservative peer (it had to be a peer – Winston is all for peers *pour
épater les bourgeois*) who would do as a permanent under-secretary under
a rival government.[2] My only other news comes from the medical world,
which has swirled around me, as it has seemed to me, with a choice noise
of tinkling tongs and sizzling forceps, to the exclusion of all other noises,
since my return. In the rare intervals of specialised polysyllables I have
gathered that the King will die and that he will have been killed (don't leave
this letter lying about, as what I am about to say is legally actionable) by
Sir John Weir,[3] his domestic surgeon: a brassy Scot (as a general rule I can
do without the Scots) who refused to pay any attention to the first symptoms
and carried the King off to Balmoral, to be out of the reach of his rivals,
where he undertook to cure him with a diet of herbs. I am further told that
it was only a counter-manoeuvre by the household (who fetched in the
local doctor while Sir John Weir was out shooting with Dukes in a loud-
checked suit) which led to the King being diagnosed at all. Hence the sudden
rush to London and belated operation which he has so far miraculously
survived. However Sir John Weir is said to be a great favourite of royal old
ladies – this too is a speciality of the Scots nation: compare the career of
that famous old Caledonian curmudgeon, John Brown the ghilly,[4] with
Queen Victoria. When Queen Mary was told that the King must have an
operation which he was unlikely to survive, all she said was, 'What a blow
for Sir John.'

    As you know, I am a stickler for exact evidence; so I should add that all

---

[2] Churchill had kissed hands as Prime Minister on 26 October 1951: six of the sixteen members of
his Cabinet were peers. His cousin the 10th Duke of Marlborough (1897–1972) was not appointed
to government office.
[3] Sir John Weir (1879–1971), physician at the London Homeopathic Hospital and royal favourite.
King George VI died at Sandringham on 6 February.
[4] John Brown (1826–1883) was a plain-spoken, heavy-drinking and uneducated Scottish servant
who achieved excessive influence over Queen Victoria.

the above comes from the hospital (it is my brother's hospital) from which the operation was carried out, and to which afterwards the royal lung was devoutly carried, wrapped up in *The Times* newspaper (it is remarkable what a variety of uses that excellent paper serves), in a taxicab.

Otherwise, what can I tell you? How can I tell you anything when I live like a hermit and the entire *beau monde* & *haut monde* streams through the hospitable doors of I Tatti? But of course there is one character, I now remember, who will never (according to Kitty Giles) turn up at your door because of his infinite frailty: one who, like Leonardo's *Last Supper*, cannot be moved lest he should finally and altogether disintegrate: Eddie Sackville-West.[5] Well, I have seen a little of him & heard a good deal about him, since my return, and I can assure you that he is famous for his gigantic physical strength. Of course the façade of tremulous frailty is kept up; but I am assured that when a grand piano was delivered at Crichel which nobody else could lift (and Raymond Mortimer refused even to try to lift) Eddie – who wanted it – sauntered quietly out of the house, looking like a pale, recessive ghost, or – with his dark glasses which give an added impression of invalidity – like one of those excessively delicate white monkeys (or are they lemms?) which, in the Zoo, always sadly pine away and die – and, without a word, picked it up and carried it in. I am also assured that when a new and expensive architectural feature of plate-glass and wrought-iron was built on the house at Crichel to keep the south wind off Eddy, lest he should wilt beneath its breath and perish (in fact it was a total failure: it only served to canalise and accentuate the wind, which now whistles up it, as through a Tube-station, with tempestuous force), the navvies who brought the plate-glass on a lorry were quite unable to lift it, and all had to be lifted and carried by the Herculean figure of Eddie ... So tell this to Kitty next time she tries to solicit sympathy for her so fragile cousin! But of course at Crichel they all have to pay lip-service to the myth, because only Eddie, with his gentle, aristocratic charm, can keep the servants from leaving daily!

Now all this is gossip; and you know that I (like Logan) 'hate gossip'. Give me the Good, the True, and the Beautiful. I admit I am not very strong on the Good, and the Beautiful of course I leave as the undisputed empire of BB; but I am a fanatic for the True. So tomorrow, I shall leave this wicked city and go to Oxford in pursuit of it (until I must return for the snipping).

---

[5] Edward Sackville-West, 5th Baron Sackville (1901–1965), author and music-lover, shared a house at Long Crichel in Dorset with several bachelor friends including Raymond Mortimer and Patrick Trevor-Roper, who commemorated him in 'Against the Crowd', *Spectator*, 29 October 1988, pp. 38–9.

There I shall perhaps acquire a staider, more respectable character; thence, having thus improved myself, I shall write a more decorous letter than this, impregnated with virtuous sentiments and full of exact, factual, carefully weighted statements, to BB. Meanwhile accept, incongruously inter-mingled with these casual fragments of reprehensible gossip, my thanks – I am infinitely grateful to you all – for having & keeping and feeding & tolerating and listening to and instructing & entertaining your devoted guest.

Trevor-Roper's letter of 14 January elicited replies from Sylvia Sprigge, who was visiting I Tatti, as well as from Nicky Mariano. 'I have just had to read your gay letter aloud to the assembled company – Lina Waterfield, Derek [Hill], Patrick Lindsay, & the residents,' Sprigge wrote on 18 January before giving news of the house-party. 'There is a strange, agreeable, & yet icy and elegant reader in the library called Mostyn Owen – Rosamond Lehmann's cavalier servente he is – and Derek has painted a little picture of BB in bed, with Nicky reading to him [...] BB is, as always, in the throes of what he calls generically "new love affairs", the latest with Hamish Hamilton who has taken to writing to him twice & sometimes thrice a week. To my suspicious mind this has a whiff of "for future publication" – but that, maybe, is ungenerous of me. I haven't been privileged yet to hear any of the letters, but have been promised one soon. One wd need to hear it, to know. BB misses Sybil [Colefax]'s illegible gay scrawls & HH wants to make good the loss: but BB says his total unawareness of current political affairs is another loss.'

Nicky Mariano wrote on 21 January: 'I need hardly tell you that your letter enchanted and amused us for you know that I am a great admirer of your epistolatory style. We read it again with Lina, Sylvia and Derek as audience and they too were delighted. I felt like sending it on to the Giles, but then did not feel like doing it without your permission.'

28 January 1952   Westminster Hospital, London SW1

My dear BB

I am now emerging into rationality and consciousness again, having had my operation a week ago in the well-appointed hospital in which I now more or less comfortably recline; and my mind, or what is left of it, goes back over intervening wastes of time to the most enjoyable period which I spent at I Tatti. It was very kind of you to have me again: as you know, I always enjoy visiting you; & I was glad to find you looking so well. I hope you remain so, and that your cauterisation has been as effective as I hope that my operation may prove to be. I am even grateful to the fog which, by reducing the temptation to outside activities, enabled me to concentrate on your splendid library and discover, as I had never done before, its wonderful completeness.

As for this operation – the removal of the *septum* or dividing cartilage of the nose – there is something absurd about it, for I have already had it done once, in 1940, in order to cure the same trouble; and theoretically it is as impossible to have it twice as to have the appendix removed twice: once it is out, it is no longer there to take out again. However, it now appears that my first operation was very inadequately done, & a large part of the thing was left behind, which, capsizing through the maladjustment of stresses occasioned by the removal of the rest, quickly formed a far greater obstruction than the part which had been removed. My tidy mind is outraged by such absurdity, especially as the operation, though not serious, is extremely miserable & uncomfortable in its immediate consequences; however, the whole thing is now removed, & I hope to be up in a few days, and possibly even to find myself, in due course, cured of what the Apostle, in a crude metaphor, has described as 'a thorn in the flesh'.

On recovering from the anaesthetic, almost the first thing which was laid before me was Nicky's letter, which I read with great pleasure, until suddenly, my uncertain eye lit on a most alarming passage. Can it be that she really contemplated sending it on to third persons, & – what is even more disconcerting – to *journalists*, a notoriously garrulous and irresponsible class of people! In my weakened state I was almost carried off by a blood-clot on the brain at the mere thought of such a disaster. Next time I visit you, as I hope I may, I must give Nicky a short course on that fascinating subject, *the Law of Defamation*. Why, in the famous 'Talking Mongoose Case', in about 1932, a man secured damages of £1,500 – or was it £400? – merely because someone had said at a lunch-party that he had believed in a talking mongoose in the Isle of Man![1] That was mere slander, being oral; my letter, being written, would have been, if published (and, legally, to send it to the Gileses is publication), libel, which is far worse. I shudder to think of the sum which Sir John Weir might have claimed if the Gileses, at a fashionable Roman party, had indiscreetly

---

[1] In 1932 a sheep-farmer named James Irving reported that a talking mongoose had taken up residence in his farmhouse on the Isle of Man. The mongoose liked to be called Gef, and could sing the Manx national anthem, speak Flemish and chant Hebrew prayers – though not, it was emphasised, talk in Yiddish. These wonders were described by Harry Price and Richard Lambert in *The Haunting of Cashen's Gap* (1935). Subsequently, in 1936, Lambert, who was editor of *The Listener*, sued Sir Cecil Levita for suggesting that he believed in the talking mongoose and tapping his forehead to indicate that Lambert was mad. Lambert was awarded damages of £7,500 for the slander.

repeated it, or, worse still, casually dropped the letter, as one so often does, in a public *gabinetto*[2] ... As soon as I am in circulation again I must clearly take out an insurance-policy against actions for defamation brought or to be brought against me in consequence of my irrepressible epistolary indiscretion.

Now what new indiscretions can I offer you? Well, you may remember that last summer there was an election at All Souls about which, if I remember aright, I sent you a brief account, describing in turn the well-known customary stages of what, in Oxford, has now become as stylised a process as a Greek drama: the formation of parties; the irresoluble deadlock; the sudden, spontaneous, gradual but irresistible coagulation of the Jellies; and the resultant compromise candidature. On that occasion the compromise candidate was Sir Hubert Henderson. Now, after a brief reign of a few months, Henderson, who has had three strokes, has resigned, and so, once again, the whole battle is to be fought out from the beginning. Already the exhausted parties of Light & Darkness are re-forming their shattered ranks; improbable candidates are grooming themselves for the competition and, by sudden attentions, seeking to reconcile long-alienated votes; already Lord Simon[3] has begun that protracted process of sedulously stroking his nose in simulated meditation before urging the claims of his disreputable nominee, A.L. Rowse; already, in America, Sir Oliver Franks,[4] shortly to be relieved of his post as British Ambassador in Washington, is uttering those preliminary refusals which will precede his ultimate apparently reluctant willingness to stand. Cut off as I am from the world I can only report such safely deducible general certainties as these; the particular details must wait till I am again in touch with particular things. Then, if the election is on the same heroic scale as before, I will send you an account of it; as also of all those other events in the great world with which at present, owing to my isolation both from visitors (whom, with few exceptions, I keep ruthlessly at bay) and newspapers (which, owing to some breakdown in the hospital administration, fail to arrive), I am, alas, unable to season what must therefore remain an undiluted letter of thanks for your never-failing, ever-appreciated hospitality. [...]

---

[2] Lavatory.
[3] The barrister-politician John Simon, 1st Viscount Simon (1873–1954), was the senior Fellow of All Souls, having been elected in 1897, and had been High Steward of the university since 1948.
[4] Sir Oliver Franks (1905–1992), later Lord Franks, was Provost of Queen's College, Oxford, before his appointment in 1948 as British Ambassador to the USA. T-R's part in defeating his candidature for the Chancellorship of Oxford University in 1960 is described in the appendix to this book.

From I Tatti, on 16 March, Berenson wrote 'begging' for a letter 'full of news & your plans'. He felt 'more or less of a wreck, almost cleaned out of sweat & marrow & brain by a flu'.

23 March 1952   Christ Church, Oxford

My dear BB

I was delighted to hear from you, but very sorry indeed to learn that you have been ill with 'flu; I hope you are now better, and that the arrival of spring in your delightful garden (and the arrival of not too many guests in your delightful house) will perfect the cure. I feel sure that it will (if anything can persuade you to ration your hospitality): I can think of nothing more refreshing than that paradisical garden when the streams are running in the spring, – how I wish I could even now be revisiting it! And yet Nature, green as she seems (as Carlyle says – that dreadful but eloquent old German nationalist), rests everywhere on dread foundations; and now, when I think even of I Tatti (to me the most perfect, most exquisite expression of a philosopher's home), I cannot help also thinking of Nicky's story of the *stregone*,[1] which is indelibly imprinted in my mind, as a reminder – useful I suppose to a historian in the (sometimes) rarefied world of an Oxford college – of the irrational basis of civilisation. Not that this reduces for me its fascination – indeed it increases it – and I hope I may soon find an opportunity, with your permission, to revisit it. Meanwhile, alas, I am imprisoned in Oxford by a succession of tiresome duties. I had meant to revisit Spain, where there are a number of interesting historical problems for me to pursue; but between my own illness and other more disconcerting events (the death of the King, being our Visitor,[2] and the illness of the Dean[3] – the Head of the College, whose deputy I am, who had a stroke in Ceylon while I was in hospital in London, – have both given me a good deal of trouble), I have found my work greatly increased, and cannot at present leave Oxford; although I intend to spend a few days with friends in Holland over Easter to secure some reprieve from the nuisance of

---

[1] Sorcerer.
[2] The cathedral and college of Christ Church had been founded in 1546 by Henry VIII, 'the greatest patron of learning that ever sat on the English throne', as T-R had described him in a booklet of 1950. Christ Church's highest officer, its 'Visitor', is always the reigning sovereign.
[3] John Lowe (1899–1960) had been Dean of Christ Church since 1939. When, in 1948, the university's Vice-Chancellor while drunk fell to his death from a train, Lowe had been catapulted at two days' notice into the Vice-Chancellorship. After three years of office, with its crushing burden of committee-work, he left for a strenuous tour of universities in Pakistan, India and Ceylon, overstrained himself and suffered a stroke in Colombo.

administration. But I hope you will continue to write to me when you find the time & give me news, and good news, of yourself & Nicky & all at I Tatti.

Meanwhile, what news can I give you? There is a young man who, I think, will be brought to visit you by Derek Hill, if you will see him. He is called Desmond Guinness,[4] a son of Lord Moyne; and since all Ireland, that lunatic country, drinks unrestrainably of the liquor which they so lucratively brew, the family is far from poor. Desmond has gone to Florence to learn Italian, but in fact, as I have assured him, will learn none in that Anglo-Saxon city, but (being, I fear, of a weak and pliable character) will be carried off by a series of titled Florentine flibbertigibbets, – unless, of course, you give him some firm advice; which he will accept from you, as being a long if distantly revered oracle, more readily than from me. He is quite an attractive character – removed, at an early age, from Eton to Gordonstoun, a bogus Eton founded by a German *émigré* called Kurt Hahn (who tried to copy Eton, but of course got it all wrong) on the uttermost, extreme, uninhabitable sub-arctic fringe of barbarian Scotland.[5] However, we must not hold that against him; so I hope that, if he visits you, you will order him firmly (as I less persuasively have already done) to live as a hermit in a cheap *pensione* in an unfashionable part of Florence, and to take an example from that admirable young man (if I have correctly judged his character), against whom I was, I fear, at first prejudiced, but whom I came to like, & whom I wish I had got to know better, William Mostyn-Owen, who seemed to me to have that rare and admirable virtue – I admire it the more as I become more conscious of its rarity – resistance to social pressure.[6] But perhaps I have misjudged either him or the Cosmos? Have I?

As for myself, I believe that my health has been greatly improved by the operation which I had in January. It will be some months before this is demonstrable; but at present, although I have had a little trouble since, I am obstinately convinced, on straws of evidence cemented together by faith, of its ultimate efficacy; so my morale is high. I only wish that, if yours

---

[4] Hon. Desmond Guinness (b. 1931), founder in 1958 of the Irish Georgian Society.

[5] Kurt Hahn (1886–1974), a Berliner who had been an undergraduate at Christ Church, ran a co-educational boarding school on the shores of Lake Constance until 1933 when, as a Jew, he was arrested by the Nazis. In 1934 he founded Gordonstoun School on the Scottish coast.

[6] William Mostyn-Owen (b. 1929) was educated at Eton and Magdalene College, Cambridge. At the age of eighteen he inherited the Woodhouse estate, near Oswestry in Shropshire, and Aberuchill Castle in Perthshire. After being introduced to BB by Rosamond Lehmann, he worked in the library at I Tatti, where among other tasks he compiled a bibliography of BB's writings which was published in 1955.

is low, I could communicate some of it to you. But that, I am sure, is really unnecessary. Doubtless dozens of voluminous correspondents keep you still in touch with every gyration of the world. Indeed, it is from you that I learn most of my English news. How would the news of Jamie Hamilton, Freya Stark,[7] Rosamond Lehmann,[8] and all those luminous London *literati* ever reach my hermitage by the sluggish waters of the Isis, were it not for that ever-perceptive, constantly-manned, smoothly serviced relaying-station by the brighter, more reflective waters of the Arno? May I have more regular bulletins, so that when I move (as I still sometimes timorously do) in the great world of letters & society, I may be properly briefed for such dangerous excursions, and not make – as, alas, I too often make – those unfortunate social *gaffes* to which hermits have, in all ages, been disastrously prone? [...]

'Two months minus two days have slipped by since I received one of your incomparable epistles,' Berenson wrote on 10 May. 'I have not replied because there is so little to tell you.' He was leaving in a few days for Naples: 'Ischia is unfortunately fast being Audenized, then Bowrafied, & there will be no island left for simple, sensuous sybarites like me.'

14 June 1952   Christ Church, Oxford

My dear BB

I have become – or perhaps I always was – a very bad correspondent. Please ascribe it not to the blindly scattered poppy of oblivion but merely to the exacting treadmill of administration, from which however I shall shortly and gladly be emancipated. I was delighted to hear from you, and to hear that you are so active. As to Lorenzo Lotto's *Christ at Emmaus*,[1] the cleaning is not yet complete, but I am assured that it is most successful, and I have arranged that you shall have a photograph as soon as it is: I hope it will not be long delayed. Isepp is delighted to hear of your interest in it.[2]

---

[7] Freya Stark (1893–1993), mountaineer, traveller and author, was a welcome visitor to I Tatti and a diligent correspondent of BB's. T-R first met her among Lord Salisbury's guests at Hatfield in July 1951.
[8] Rosamond Lehmann (1901–1990), a fashionable novelist and regular visitor to I Tatti.
[1] Lorenzo Lotto (c.1480–1556), whose paintings BB had studied intensely in the 1890s.
[2] Sebastian Isepp (1884–1954) was an avant-garde painter until 1925, when he joined Vienna's Kunsthistorische Museum and dedicated himself to restoring Old Masters with consummate skill and infinite compassion. After the Anschluss in 1938 he settled in England, where in 1940 he was interned until Kenneth Clark obtained his release; he became a British subject in 1947. A man of gentle, unworldly charm, he cleaned Lotto's *Christ at Emmaeus* for Christ Church 'with wonderful results' (BB to T-R, 15 May 1952).

What news can I give you? Almost none. I have seen no one, not even
Jamie Hamilton, who writes that he has all kinds of Italian news for me
since visiting you, but as he waits to see me and I have been buried here for
two months I have not yet had it. I went abroad for a fortnight at Easter, to
Belgium & Holland, to stay with friends there: two countries which, being
so near, I hardly knew before. How delightful Belgium is if one knows (or
has friends who know) where to look! Antwerp & Brussels – which I
had ignorantly & superficially seen before – are full of such unsuspected
treasures, and I have a passion to return to Antwerp now. The black-and-
white, marble & jet Renaissance tombs & altars, chapels and *baldacchini* in
the churches – do they exist anywhere else? – fascinated me: and so also
does everything to do with that splendid *virtuoso* who dominates both the
city of Antwerp and the period of European history in which I am most
interested – or at least an important part of it – Sir Peter Paul Rubens! You
see I am working still on the subject to which (as far as my own instruction
is concerned) I so profitably and comfortably applied myself in your wonderful library at I Tatti: the new courts of the Spanish era, and the art-
market that they so powerfully set in motion. I am most grateful to you for
those opportunities, and I wish I could recover them for a while. May I
question you still further on this subject? Is there, for instance, any book
on the Habsburg collection at the Hradschin in Prague, under Rudolf II,[3]
comparable with those admirable works which I found in your library,
Berogni's *Tiziano en el Prado* and Luzio's *La Galleria dei Gonzaga*? Is there
anything on the collecting activity of Cardinal Richelieu and Cardinal
Mazarin, or Queen Christina of Sweden?[4] The subject, as a whole, seems to
me of great importance, and the specialists of the Warburg Institute,
however valuably they have established the detail, have not seen it as a
historical phenomenon. I wish I could be at I Tatti, with direct access to
the oracle of that numinous shrine, instead of being thus obliged, like the
Kings of Lydia, to send *questionnaires* from a distance! But you, I suppose,
are anyway not there, but in Ischia or Vallombrosa or some other marine
or mountain retreat, whither I can hardly pursue you ...

Will you be there in July or August? I plan – since I cannot anyway work
here in August (one is gradually turned out of college by the silent, tactful,

[3] Rudolf II (1552–1612), Holy Roman Emperor, was the most avid art collector of his age.
[4] Cardinal de Richelieu (1585–1642), Louis XIII's chief minister, filled his palaces in Paris and at
Rueil with artistic treasures. Cardinal Mazarin (1602–1661) succeeded him as chief minister.
Christina, Queen of Sweden (1626–1689), amassed a sumptuous collection of paintings, sculp-
tures, books and manuscripts in her palace in Rome. BB felt she 'had finer taste than any other
person of her time' (Rollin Hadley (ed.), *The Letters of Bernhard Berenson and Isabella Stewart
Gardner 1887–1924* (1987), p. 232).

unremitting pressure of servants' holidays, and without access to libraries
historians – unlike novelists – cannot work) – to go to a spot hitherto
culpably unvisited by me: Constantinople. The plan is vague, but I shall
probably motor to Venice & go by boat to Athens (what shall I read on that
boat?) and then by car, via Meteora and Thermopylae and Salonika &
Mount Athos to Constantinople. What shall I do, what read, what study,
whom seek out in that fabulous imperial city? And when I return, in mid
August, shall I find you in Italy, or will you have gone on your summer
tour to Paris or Zurich? I may have with me on my way back to Italy one
of the most intelligent of my historical pupils, a cultivated but hardworking
Italianate Etonian, whom I would like to send to call on you if you were
there and could receive him. He will anyway be in Italy all September, since
(in the intervals of my exacting historical discipline) he has so perfected
his knowledge of Italian that the University has given him a special scholarship to go there. His name is Richard Rhodes, & I think you would like
him & I know he would like to call on you if you are discoverable.[5] (My
other emissary to you, in the spring, Desmond Guinness, never called
on you, although he was in Florence, because – owing to some postal
eccentricity – my letter telling him to do so never reached him, and he
lacked the courage – so formidable is your fame – to dispense with such
positive orders.) But if you are free to receive Rhodes I would be glad to
make him the bearer sometime of my never-failing good wishes to you and
Nicky & Luisa and the whole *casa Berenson*.

What else can I tell you? I have not written much, – partly because I have
been so preoccupied with other work, partly because I am accumulating
matter for books, not articles; and I think you see both the *Sunday Times*
(where I anyway don't value my articles) and the *New Statesman* (where –
though I detest the politics of the paper – I do). I have been having some
fun there with the Jesuits, indeed with the same Fr Brodrick who once
attacked me in *The Tablet*.[6] When his letter was published, I (presumably

---

[5] Richard Rhodes (b. 1929), who had previously taken evocative photographs for his brother
Anthony's book *A Sabine Journey: To Rome in Holy Year*, was Heath Harrison travel scholar of
1952. A classical pianist (taught by Artur Schnabel) and composer, he married Leopold Stokowski's
daughter. Author of a satirical novel, a barrister in Lord Hailsham's chambers, and an international
lawyer in Paris and Geneva.
[6] T-R's glowing review (*New Statesman*, 17 May 1952; *Historical Essays*, pp. 119–24) of C.R. Boxer's
The Christian Century in Japan included this aside: 'the newest, most militant, most devoted, and
yet most flexible of religious orders, founded indeed by a Spanish bigot, but quickly transferred
to more skilful Italian management, the observant Jesuits, in every country, studied the rules of
politics and deduced the terms of success.' In the issue of 31 May, Brodrick deplored T-R's remarks
as 'disingenuous', 'illiberal' and 'erroneous'; but T-R's retort, 'Jesuits in Japan' (7 June), was
unyielding.

by some magical cause) was taken ill & had to go to bed. At once, a Jesuit came to visit me. I thought that perhaps he had come to finish me off, or to convert me while in that weakened state; but in fact he had come to angle for an invitation to a party which he had heard that I was giving (the Oxford Jesuits are the most absurd snobs: they live in Christ Church, angling for society, and give champagne-breakfasts to the aristocratic undergraduates, however heretical!). I didn't ask him, and, the magic failing, I recovered. Now that my letter has been published Fr Brodrick has been taken ill, so I conclude that God is pretty impartial in the controversy! Actually the Jesuits here have suffered a double blow, because they have recently undergone the most serious reverse that is known to their theology: a social failure. Their star-performer (a slow, pudding-like, complaisant priest called Fr Wingfield Digby)[7] has been totally eclipsed by a charming, elegant, well-born, rich, handsome and intellectual Dominican from Belgium, Fr Dominic de Grunne,[8] before whom all social doors have flown irresistibly open and without whom no party in the *beau* or *haut monde* is judged complete; while Fr Wingfield Digby now receives no invitations at all and is altogether excluded from the fashionable feasts of this cultured city. It is very mortifying for them, and they feel the bitter shafts of social ridicule piercing even through their triple covering of holiness, spiritual pride, and black soutane!

But now I see that I am getting (as I so easily do) malicious. I must stop at once, before I exhibit the worst side of my character. [...]

On 11 July Berenson sent Trevor-Roper a list of books that should be read before going to Istanbul.

24 July 1952   [Corfu]

My dear BB

Many thanks for your letter and its bibliographical advice for Constantinople. I am now on my way there, and am at this moment immobilised

[7] John Wingfield Digby (1909–1984), ordained as a Jesuit priest in 1944, was a tutor in modern history at Campion Hall, Oxford 1948–52. Afterwards a member of the Jesuit community in Mount Street, Mayfair (where he ran a successful enquiry centre); he left the Society of Jesus in 1971, and married.
[8] T-R had been introduced in 1948 by Isaiah Berlin to Count Dominic de Grunne (b. 1913), pantomath, wit and traveller, then a Benedictine priest at the Abbaye de Maredsous in Belgium. De Grunne became a junior member of Wadham College, Oxford in 1952, and joined the staff of the Royal College of Art in 1968 (teaching poetry, philosophy, and African, Polynesian and Chinese art).

in the harbour of Corfu – I am going *via* Athens, and, if my plans hold, *via* Mount Athos as well. If I come back by Italy, I shall certainly travel *via* Vallombrosa in order to see you, & will not interrupt the Kress foundation and will give you as much notice as I can.[1]

You may have a call from a friend of mine, Sir Keith Joseph, & his wife.[2] I think Isaiah has already written about him to Nicky. I hope it may be possible for you to see them. He is a mercantile Jewish baronet. His father was Lord Mayor of London – hence the baronetcy – (and incidentally was famous for the stinginess of his City feasts), & Keith, having been an alderman at 29, would inevitably, by the routine of that ancient institution, have been the youngest Lord Mayor of London in history; but illness determined him to abandon all civic activities. He is a lawyer, a Fellow of All Souls, very civilised, somewhat *bien-pensant*, and virtuously & self-consciously Jewish (so is his wife, Helen, *née* – I think – Guggenheim, and as rich as he is: they were married in a synagogue with immense Hebrew formalism and equally immense quantities of champagne). They are both gay and cultivated people & I think you will like them if you have an opportunity of seeing them.

I came here via Germany, where I paused to make a few investigations at Munich. Have you read Hitler's *Tischgespräche* – which I think is of great historical importance? But perhaps you have no interest in that coarse & unmethodical though powerful mind. Anyway there is now another instalment coming out in France, called *Libres Propos sur la Guerre et la Paix*, and an immense legal case is blowing up in consequence. For who holds the copyright in Hitler's Table-Talk: Hitler (who uttered it) or Bormann[3] (who had it recorded), or Dr Picker (the shorthand-typist who took it down)?[4] The *Tischgespräche* were published by Dr Picker and the Athenäum Verlag of Stuttgart; but the entire original texts (as distinct from Dr Picker's personal copies) have somehow been acquired by an enterprising Swiss

---

[1] The Samuel H. Kress Foundation had been endowed by an American millionaire collector (a pre-war visitor to I Tatti) to foster European art history and conservation. In 1951 it undertook to subsidise publication of the illustrated edition of BB's *Italian Painters of the Renaissance*.

[2] Sir Keith Joseph (1918–1994), later Lord Joseph of Portsoken, had married, in 1951, Hellen Guggenheimer (not Guggenheim) of New York. First elected as a Conservative MP in 1956, he was a crucial influence in the Thatcher cabinets between 1979 and 1986.

[3] Martin Bormann (1900–1945?) joined the Nazi party in 1925, succeeded Rudolf Hess as the omnipotent Party Chancellor in 1941 and consolidated his power as Hitler's personal secretary from 1943.

[4] Henry Picker, the stenographer who noted and typed up Hitler's musings, later amassed a collection of Hitler relics. His edition of Hitler's table-talk, *Tischgespräche im Führerhauptquartier, 1941–42* (1951), was less reliable than the texts inherited by Martin Bormann's widow Gerda, which were acquired by a Lausanne banker, François Genoud.

ex-Nazi called François Genoud who has translated them for the French edition, published by Flammarion and serialised in *France Soir*.[5] Now Dr Picker & the Athenäum Verlag have filed an action against Genoud, Flammarion and *France Soir* for breach of copyright. The ingenious Genoud has however fortified himself with documents appointing him literary executor of *both* Hitler *and* Bormann! So there should be an enjoyable *cause célèbre*, which is to be tried by the same judge who tried the Kravchenko case.[6] Meanwhile the British Foreign Office have been ringing me up in some perplexity because Eugen Dollmann (former SS grandee in Italy) has offered to obtain for them valuable original MSS from Hitler's office.[7] I suspect – though it is mere surmise – that Genoud's title is really bad & that he is trying to off-load the documents before the trial exposes him! However, I am looking forward to the case!

I long to hear about Apulia. Professor Dawkins, of whom you may know (an amusing old modern Greek scholar, biographer – under the name Richard McGillivray – of Norman Douglas, and participator of his tastes – I mean his intellectual tastes), has often spoken of it to me – he goes there unearthing Greek survivals – and I would like to visit Lecce & many other places mentioned by him.[8] Now, I hope, I shall have a vicarious report from you. Did you go to the hexagonal – or is it octagonal – castle of Frederick II *Stupor Mundi*? But I expect you have been there dozens of times, & long ago. Incidentally did you read the *TLS* on Norman Douglas? I thought it

---

[5] François Genoud (1914–1996) hero-worshipped Hitler from the day that he shook the Führer's hand in 1932. He worked as German agent in Switzerland during the war, funded post-war neo-Nazi groups, and donated money for the legal defence of Adolf Eichmann and Klaus Barbie. After the fall of the Third Reich, Genoud cultivated the families of Hitler's henchmen, bought any documents they would sell and came to control the literary estates of Goebbels and Bormann. A supporter of the Popular Front for the Liberation of Palestine, who was suspected of involvement in aircraft hijackings, he joined Exit, the suicide society, and, a few days after telephoning T-R in genial mood, poisoned himself before a group of invited onlookers.

[6] Victor Kravchenko (1905–1966), a member of the Soviet Purchasing Commission who defected to the USA in 1944, published a hard-hitting account of Stalinist Russia, *I Choose Freedom* (1946). Its sales were promoted by Cold War propagandists. In 1949, amid much publicity, Kravchenko sued the French Communist weekly *Les Lettres Françaises* which had denounced him as a traitor and liar. He fell into obscurity and eventually shot himself.

[7] Eugen Dollmann graduated from the University of Munich in 1926, and moved to Rome. A handsome, cultivated man-of-the-world, he impressed BB by speaking of the smartest society ladies by their pet names. He joined the National Socialist party in 1934, and acted as the SS's wartime representative throughout Italy, as its liaison officer with Mussolini and as Hitler's Italian interpreter. During the final stages of the war he collaborated with the Allies; after post-war interrogation, he was recruited as a paid informant of the American Office of Strategic Studies, and earmarked as an anti-Communist agent in Germany. Afterwards he opened the Hotel Dollmann Splendide in Munich.

[8] Richard McGillivray Dawkins (1871–1955) held the Bywater and Sotheby chair of Byzantine and modern Greek at Oxford 1920–39. His book on Norman Douglas was published in 1933.

somewhat elliptical, but very interesting. It was by his nephew – or great-
nephew? – Constantine Fitzgibbon.[9]

The ship moves; my ink begins to run out; I will write again. [. . .]

30 August 1952   Christ Church, Oxford

My dear BB

Alas, I could not do it. Your delightful summer eyrie must remain for a
while unvisited by me. Hitler's executor in Lausanne, Himmler's masseur
in the Hague, – these are the people among whom my life must now and
then be spent, being, as I am, the prisoner (though the well-rewarded
prisoner) of a casual, fortuitous, and not altogether enjoyable expertise.
Still, I learn something about the world from these strange inhabitants of
it (see the enclosed note, which might entertain you, about the true facts
concerning Count Bernadotte, now at last established by me. It is a copy of
a prospectus which I sent to a paper: I don't think it will inspire them to
want the full story!). Incidentally, is Jamie Hamilton still with you? If so,
tell him that I have a project to sell him when he is back in a buying and a
speculative mood!

As for my travels, have you been to Mount Athos? If so, all that I say will
be redundant. If not, don't go! What potions have I drunk of Sirens' tears
in those gigantic but squalid palaces, filled with dirty monks and other
vermin! But no, for Sirens' tears have at least (I presume) a taste, a salty
tang perhaps and explosive after-effects: on Mount Athos I was *starved*,
and that in spite of holily and hypocritically spending two hours – starting
at 6 a.m. – at their dreary liturgy in order to qualify to see their treasures
(which, instead of rare MSS and exquisite craftsmanship, consisted of the
forefinger of St John the Baptist and the bashed-in skull of St Jehosophat).
However, I have survived, and, as Homer philosophically observes, one can
bear everything afterwards. Only I wish that instead of resting after that
dismal experience in the generously offered but somewhat knobbly bed of
a Turkish private soldier in the dreary wilds of Thrace, I had been able to
re-compose my disordered intellectual equipment in the comfort and
civility of *Casa al Dono*!

Now to revert to more serious matters. Our Lorenzo Lotto is at last
cleaned, and a photograph of it should be in your hands within a week at

---

[9] Constantine FitzGibbon (1919–1983), Comte Lee-Dillon in France, novelist and historian, was
prosecuted for a drunken bout of incest with his sister in 1954. His 'Portrait of Norman Douglas',
the lead article in the *TLS* of 4 July 1952, reviewed an essay on Capri; his biography of Douglas
appeared in 1953.

the latest. Byam Shaw has been, as your compatriots would put it, alerted;[1] liaison is established; and although Isepp has swept off *incommunicado* to the Continent, I hope that no slip can now occur. Please tell me if all does not go well, and the prong shall be applied to the dilatory buttock, wherever it is to be found. Incidentally, on the subject of cleaning, can you tell me the low-down (as Logan would say) on Dr de Wild, a famous Dutch picture-cleaner and snob, well known in the great houses of England, whom I met when I was staying with one of his clients, customers or patrons (which is the right word?) in Holland?[2] A smooth but resilient man whom, I feel, I am likely to meet again in his swift cannonading bounces to and fro on the social billiard-table. Do tell me something!

I wasn't much in Turkey, I was mostly in Greece (I missed your friend Freya Stark – unfortunately, for I had enjoyed our only meeting – by a day in Athens); but I enjoyed Constantinople and was most grateful for your bibliography. In Kaufmann's, that excellent bookshop, I found almost all the works of Diehl.[3] How good, how readable they are! But I am not becoming a Byzantinist. *Ne sutor supra crepidam*:[4] I am preparing a little aluminised bombshell on the English 17th century, and then, when it has been placed under the hieratic throne of the most respected of our professors, I shall retire in haste, to avoid the explosion, to the timeless, cultivated security (if the right of asylum is still granted to me) of I Tatti. [...]

PS. I have a malicious story to tell you about Cecil Sprigge but I am reserving it for my visit![5]

[The following was attached to this letter.]

The Bernadotte Myth

Since 1945 there has been a great campaign in Sweden to build up the late

---

[1] John James ('Jim') Byam Shaw (1903–1992), the drawings specialist and a director of the Colnaghi gallery 1937–68, maintained a keen interest in the art collection of his old college, Christ Church, and later catalogued its paintings and drawings.
[2] T-R had met Martin de Wild (1899-1969), picture conservator at the The Hague, at Ophemert Castle, the Dutch seat of his friend Aeneas Mackay, 13th Baron Reay (1905–1963).
[3] Charles Diehl (1859–1944), Byzantine historian.
[4] 'Let the cobbler stick to his last' (Pliny the Elder).
[5] Cecil Sprigge (1896–1959), a pre-war foreign correspondent and City editor of the *Manchester Guardian*, was Reuter's correspondent in Italy 1943–6. Sylvia Sprigge was his second wife. T-R cherished 'the image of Sprigge, with his monocle and mannerisms and dryly expressed but real learning' (letter of 24 December 1959).

Count Bernadotte as 'the Prince of Peace' who by his diplomacy ended the war and rescued some 20,000 prisoners from Nazi Concentration Camps. This campaign is connected with internal Swedish politics, i.e. the politics of the 'Neutral' party who claim that Sweden served humanity better by neutrality than it could have done by belligerency. It was begun by Bernadotte himself who published two books towards it (one has the significant title *Instead of Arms*) and indulged in heavy private propaganda, especially in England and USA. It has been continued in inspired articles, commissioned biographies, etc., largely emanating from Countess Bernadotte (the daughter of H.E. Manville, an asbestos-king); and has been largely successful. In fact it is both dishonest and untrue.

The negotiations which ensured the rescue of the 19,500 prisoners were almost exclusively the work of Felix Kersten, Himmler's doctor, who had concerted the plan with the Swedish Foreign Minister, Gunther,[6] long before Bernadotte appeared. When Bernadotte arrived in Germany, it was simply as an official of the Red Cross sent to arrange the details of transport according to the plans already made between Kersten and Gunther. Further, when it came to implementing these plans, Bernadotte explicitly *refused* to save any Jews, telling Himmler that he shared his racial views. He also refused to take French and Dutch prisoners. In all this he was overruled by Kersten and disowned by Gunther, and Himmler in fact promised to Kersten and to the representative of the World Jewish Organisation (with whom he had a secret interview!) that he would release the Jews, Frenchmen and Dutchmen as well as the Scandinavians to whom Bernadotte had sought to confine the operation.

In order to obtain the credit for the whole operation, Bernadotte made an alliance with Himmler's head of intelligence, Schellenberg.[7] Schellenberg was afraid of condemnation as a war-criminal for the major part that he had played in the Venlo incident (the kidnapping of Stevens and Best).[8] Bernadotte promised to protect Schellenberg in Sweden if Schellenberg

---

[6] Christian Gunther (1886–1966), a career diplomat who wrote poetry and novels, was appointed Swedish Foreign Minister on the outbreak of war in 1939 and implemented Sweden's wartime policy of strict neutrality. He was Swedish envoy to Italy 1946–50.
[7] Walter Schellenberg (1910–1952), who trained as a lawyer, was in charge of counter-intelligence inside and outside Germany 1939–41. He was chief of foreign intelligence from 1941 until the collapse of the Third Reich, and preened himself as Himmler's *éminence grise*. T-R reviewed *The Schellenberg Memoirs* in *Sunday Times* of 18 November 1956.
[8] Major Richard Stevens (1893–1967), an Indian army officer who had recently been appointed head of Secret Intelligent Service operations in the Netherlands, and his chief field agent, Sigismund Payne Best (1885–1978), were lured to the village of Venlo on the Dutch-German border in November 1939, and kidnapped by commandos led by Schellenberg. The two Englishmen were subjected to a show-trial and sent to Sachsenhausen concentration camp.

undertook to ascribe the rescue-work to Bernadotte. Although Bernadotte was unable to save Schellenberg from arrest when Schellenberg, as arranged, fled to Sweden, this bargain was nevertheless kept, being to the interest of both parties. Bernadotte went to great lengths to give public testimonials to Schellenberg. Schellenberg in turn ascribed the rescue-work to negotiations between himself and Bernadotte.

For this plan it was necessary of course to silence Kersten. Bernadotte achieved this partly by threats, sing his own position as a member of the Swedish roayl house, and exploiting the fact that Kersten practises in Stockholm and is therefore vulnerable. Further Kersten knows no English and therefore could not control Bernadotte's propaganda in England and America; and it was easy to denounce Kersten as Himmler's doctor. In Bernadotte's book Kersten is never even named, and before its publication Bernadotte threatened Kersten with harm in Sweden if Kersten made any protest.

These facts are well-known to several people in Germany, the World Jewish Organisation, and Holland. The Germans, being mainly members of Himmler's organisation, keep pretty quiet; the Jews – after the murder of Bernadotte by Jewish extremists – dare not criticise him; but in Holland there have been reactions. (Kersten lives part of the year in Holland and is doctor to the Dutch royal family, and he saved great numbers of Dutchmen in the war.) Finally, last year, a Dutch Royal Commission was set up under a distinguished historian, Prof. Posthumus.[9] The report of this commission has been kept secret (presumably because of its damaging revelations about Bernadotte. I know that it does damage Bernadotte from personal conversations which I have had with Prof. Posthumus); but the result of it was that Kersten was made a Chevalier of the Order of Orange-Nassau and has now been recommended by the Dutch Government for the Nobel Peace Prize.

Of all the foregoing facts I am certain. They are based on documents in the Dutch Royal Institute of War Documentation, on affidavits from Germans and Swedes who were involved, on Himmler's papers, and on evidence possessed by the World Jewish Organisation. I cannot publish the whole story, since I cannot produce some of the documents which prove it and since I must avoid causing difficulties to Kersten in Sweden; but I can safely give an account which will be (a) proof against legal action, (b) capable of substantiation, (c) sufficient to prick the Bernadotte bubble.

---

[9] Nicolaas Posthumus (1880-1960), an economic historian, was Director of the Netherlands State Institute for War Documentation and edited *The Netherlands during the German Occupation* (1946).

'Am suspicious of all restorers, except Isepp,' Berenson replied on 9 September. 'You should tell your friends that under no circumstances must they entrust an Italian (or even English) picture to this de Wild. He can be relied on for Flemish, Dutch or German paintings.'

9 December 1952   Christ Church, Oxford

My dear BB

My conscience twitches me when I think of my long epistolary silence, which I now, and herewith, at last break. Of course it is not lack of interest or curiosity that inspires it: is not my curiosity daily satisfied by the reports which, whether I write or not, daily stream into England from Italy of your least movements? Have I not heard how you have been keeping court in Rome, how you attended, *en maître*, K. Clark's lecture, escorted (or is this detail perhaps a later scholiastic gloss?) by a fashionable coloured singer?[1] With the Gileses, the Hamiltons, & Sylvia I do not lack sources: but they, after all, are but tributary streams, of uncertain property: sometimes there are bubbles of air in their water, or a taste of salt, or even the casual deposits of irrelevant passing creatures: if I want the pure, undiluted, essential living water of truth, art, social gossip, etc., I must of course touch with this wand, my pen, the authentic living rock itself, *rupes Berensoniana,*[2] and cause it, as I hope this elaborate trope may now cause it, to spout freely again. For alas, only thus can I at present keep in touch with you: from this fog-bound isle I cannot yet visit you; indeed, after Christmas, I am going, I fear, not to the Elysian groves of Italy but (strange freakish behaviour, you will say) to the North Pole. Or rather, in that direction. Why? you naturally ask. Did I not, three years ago, solemnly vow, after my last return from Iceland, never again to venture north of Berwick-on-Tweed, that last outpost, as it then seemed to me, of attenuated civilisation in the barbarous northern wastes? Well, I can only say that I have now recovered from that temporary phobia, and since it may well be that if I do not go to Sweden now I never shall – for soon the *Atlantic Monthly* will reach those desolate shores and then, no doubt, all social doors in Stockholm will be shut against me: already indeed, with that inner ear which poets often mention but which otologists, I believe, have not yet professionally located, I seem to hear the

---

[1] Katherine Dunham (b. 1910) studied anthropology at the University of Chicago, then undertook intensive research into black dance and ethnic choreography in the United States and Caribbean, and toured the world with the Katherine Dunham Dance Company. She first visited I Tatti in 1950. BB enjoyed her beauty, grace, character and performances: she dedicated her memoirs of her girlhood, *A Touch of Innocence* (1959), to him.
[2] 'The rock of Berenson'.

premonitory squeaking of their hinges – I have decided to go now. What shall I do there? There is no wine, I believe, in that benighted land, and doubtless sleet and snow eternally descend upon it. My heart sinks at the thought of it. However, I must go: like Aeneas (only his mission was to Italy) I have a mission: I am determined – such is my love of truth (or perhaps of controversy) to infuriate the Swedes by officially proposing Dr Felix Kersten, Himmler's masseur, for the Nobel Peace Prize next year. You will (I hope) read all about this in due course, as I have already darkly hinted, in the *Atlantic Monthly*.[3]

Meanwhile what of you? Please send me some news of all of you. Don't read Namier – his fugitive essays, detailed and accurate and of exquisite pedantic virtuosity though they are, are not worthy of your leisure.[4] Use it rather to write long communicative letters to your friends describing life in Italy, and especially at I Tatti. Have you been listening to Isaiah Berlin's famous broadcasts which have so convulsed the intellectual *beau-monde* of England that they have even been the subject of the first leader in that grave organ of opinion, *The Times*?[5] Alas, they are not, apparently, to be published – and anyway, the delivery was part of their brilliance: a wonderful *tour de force*, Isaiah at his best, on *Freedom and its Betrayal*, the political thinkers who, in the period 1789–1830, buried the 18th century.

When did I last write to you? What did I last tell you? Did I tell you of my eremitical life among the monks of Mount Athos; of the battles in which I am now involved (I love battles!) about Hitler's inheritance; of the new series of *Propyläengeschichte*[6] which Isaiah and I are starting, on lines which, I think and hope, would appeal to you? (Whenever I write anything, I ask myself, will it appeal to BB? This is a great stimulant!) Since you have sometimes kindly asked about my work, you will find an article by me in the next number of *Foreign Affairs*,[7] and I have written a short historical

---

[3] T-R's article, 'Kersten, Himmler and Count Bernadotte' (*Atlantic Monthly*, 191 (February 1953), pp. 43–5), described Kersten's successes in saving Jews and others from Nazi captivity, reported Bernadotte's opposition to the transfer of Jewish prisoners to Sweden and urged that Bernadotte had initiated 'a deliberate campaign' of misrepresentation about the rescue of prisoners from German concentration camps during the final stages of the war. T-R asked: 'What were Bernadotte's motives in thus suppressing all credit but his own? His own work was perfectly reputable: why did he think it necessary so busily and [...] so unscrupulously to inflate its significance? Possibly it was personal vanity; perhaps Swedish politics.'

[4] T-R reviewed Namier's *In the Nazi Era* together with Alan Bullock's *Hitler* in *Sunday Times* of 9 November 1952.

[5] *The Times*, 6 December 1952.

[6] Historical introductions. Henry Hardy suggests that this refers to a Weidenfeld series, 'The Library of Ideas', which Berlin was instrumental in launching.

[7] T-R, 'The Germans Reappraise the War', *Foreign Affairs*, XXXI (January 1953), pp. 225–37, surveys books about Nazi Germany that had been published in the previous seven years.

opusculum which will be published in May – but perhaps it is too detailed for you – on the rise of the gentry in 16th century England; and from now on, I hope, there will be more, because on Xmas Day I cease, at last, to be an administrator and become again, if I may claim that title, a scholar. *O frabjous day, Calloo! Callay!* as my late colleague Lewis Carroll observed. If, in this letter, you detect any trace of apparent inebriety, ascribe it not to the intoxication of drink but rather of impending liberty, – a draught which, according to many sage philosophers, is much more heady and dangerous even than the Irish *poteen* or that hideous schnapps which, with a sinking heart and stomach, I apprehend must be my only refreshment in Sweden.

But what of you? What of Nicky? How do you like your new *Phaidon* edition which has been so huge a success here – the whole printing, as you no doubt know, sold absolutely out in a week?[8] I hope you are pleased with it. And have you numerous visitors, filing devoutly before your well-appointed shrine? I saw your admirable friend Judge Learned Hand[9] at Jamie Hamilton's great rout (as Boswell would have called it ...) in the summer – you know that the mantle of Sybil Colefax has fallen on the Hamiltons? – has he been to see you? or the Notesteins, those other peripatetic worshippers at your shrine? Do write and tell me everything that has happened during my reprehensible, indeed unforgivable months of silence, before I sail, on 27 December, from this already frozen island to the even more frozen North. [...]

Nicky Mariano wrote to enlist Trevor-Roper's help in obtaining the loan for a forthcoming exhibition in Italy of a painting The Virgin and Child and Three Angels, *owned by Christ Church. Berenson in 1926 had attributed it to Luca Signorelli (c.1450–1523).*

29 December 1952   [on board SS *Saga* outward bound from Millwall docks]

My dear Nicky,

Yes, of course I will do all I can to get the Signorelli to Italy. Your letter arrived, unfortunately, just after the end of term, so the decision cannot be taken before the first Governing Body meeting of next term, which will be

---

[8] Phaidon's lavishly illustrated new edition of BB's *Italian Painters of the Renaissance* indeed sold out in a week. John Pope-Hennessy's (anonymous) *TLS* review extolled it as 'studded with vivid phrases evoking a specific visual experience', 'incomparably the best introduction in any language to any school of painting' and 'a vindication of absolute standards in art criticism'.

[9] Learned Hand (1872–1961), an influential American jurist and congenial visitor to I Tatti, whom T-R had met in Washington in 1949.

on January 28th. But I will then make an eloquent speech and hope to convert the floating vote (that elusive but decisive electoral factor) in favour of sending the picture.

I am now on the high seas (if my script is somewhat tremulous, ascribe it to their height) on the way to Sweden. It was very kind of BB to write to the King and to send me that letter to him: I will write to him at length after my visit, and give a full account of everything.[1] I hope the King doesn't regard the late Count Bernadotte as an inseparable member of the royal family, for I'm afraid he is going to be exposed very shortly; but I hope I shall be able to navigate these social Narrows!

Now what news can I tell you? I have been quiescent for a while, leaving the controversies that seem inseparable from the cloistered academic life to whirl, for a time, round my colleague Robert Blake, whom you may remember (he came to Vallombrosa the first time I visited you).[2] He has just published the diaries of the late Field-Marshal Haig,[3] and by leaving in the passages which Duff Cooper,[4] in his biography of Haig, had left out, has caused a convulsive storm in France so violent that Xandra, the FM's daughter, whose husband is a naval officer *en poste* in France, no longer gets those lavish favours formerly pressed by Parisian dressmakers on *la fille du maréchal*, and her husband, after a tirade from the French admiral at Fontainebleau to whose staff he had just been appointed, has felt obliged to send in his resignation to the First Sea Lord![5] The crux of the matter is that Haig's decisions in 1917 were based on the fact that all the French generals – especially Pétain – assured him that the *morale* of the French army was broken and that only a British offensive could prevent a total French collapse. Naturally the French are not anxious for this fact to be known now; but none of us expected so violent a reaction as has in fact ensued. We all thought that the second world war had rendered the first a somewhat academic matter – foolishly forgetting that of course the French,

---

[1] BB had provided T-R with a letter of introduction to King Gustaf V of Sweden (1882–1972), a regular visitor to I Tatti.
[2] Robert Blake (1916–2003), later Lord Blake, historian, Student and tutor in politics at Christ Church 1947–68 and Provost of The Queen's College 1968–87. He and T-R were close collaborators in college and university politics at this time.
[3] Douglas Haig, 1st Earl Haig (1861–1928), commander-in-chief of British forces in France 1915–19, was promoted to Field Marshal in 1917 and given the Bemersyde estate by a grateful Empire in 1921.
[4] Duff Cooper, 1st Viscount Norwich (1890–1954), Secretary of State for War 1935–8 and British Ambassador in Paris 1944–7, had written Haig's official biography.
[5] Clarence Howard-Johnston (1903–1996) joined HMS *Repulse* as a midshipman in 1921. He was Director of Studies at the Naval War College in Athens 1938–40, Naval Attaché at the British Embassy in Paris 1947–53, and promoted to the rank of rear admiral. He had married first, in 1928, Esmé FitzGibbon, and, after their divorce in 1940, Lady Alexandra Haig (1907–1997) in 1941.

having taken no very serious part in the second, take a different view of their relative importance; also that the French generals of the first war, being now in retirement, have nothing else to do except to rage furiously together in their clubs. This they are now doing to some tune – indeed Marshal Juin[6] has been made a member of the French Academy – all the other candidates withdrawing in his favour – solely for having denounced Robert's book as a forgery (for the Field-Marshal, being a gentleman, *could* not have said such things!). The most disreputable behaviour has been that of Duff Cooper, who, consulted by Robert, urged him to publish all – it was different, he explained, in the 1930s, when he had written, for then it would only have played into the hands of the pro-German appeasers if he had published criticisms of the French army, but now it would do positive good to show up Pétain as a defeatist, etc. etc. . . . When Robert's book came out, Duff praised it in the English Press. But then he went back to France and found that, in consequence of having praised the book, three challenges to duels were awaiting him at his house at Chantilly, and the entire com-mittee of the French Travellers' Club (of which he is president) called on him asking him to resign. Whereupon, in the most abject manner, he judged it prudent to execute a brisk *volte-face*, and published a statement in *Figaro* saying that he deplored the inopportune publication of documents which ought to have been permanently suppressed! Robert Blake's rage against this pusillanimous behaviour is rendered the more acute because he is a Norfolk man, and all Norfolk men, I have discovered, now turn purple and tremble when Duff Cooper is even mentioned. For some obscure local reason unintelligible to those who have not been born among the turnips and partridges of those inaccessible fens, they violently resent Duff's presumption in taking the title of Viscount Norwich. Indeed, if they mention him by that name they invariably place it between emphatic quotation-marks to illustrate their otherwise inexpressible indignation. Dawyck Haig tells me that the only member of his own family who has not denounced the publication is an aunt who lives in Wales,[7] and whose reason for praising it is simply that it has given such mortal offence to her neighbours the Lloyd Georges!

Well, by the time I next write to I Tatti I expect it will be I, not my colleagues, who will be struggling in a desperate quagmire of controversy, so I must not seem too openly to be at present enjoying their difficulties.

---

[6] Alphonse Juin (1888–1967), Commander-in-Chief of Allied Land Forces in Central Europe, had received his field marshal's baton in 1952 and was elected to the Académie Française in 1953.
[7] Hon. Violet Vivian (1879–1962), daughter of 3rd Baron Vivian, British Ambassador in Rome, twin sister of Xandra's mother and maid-of-honour to Xandra's godmother Queen Alexandra.

Meanwhile I hope you are having a more peaceful life (unless, like me, you secretly rather *enjoy* the battle and the breeze). How is everyone? What new books are being written? Who is with you? Who is visiting you? I hope myself to visit you, if I may, in the spring: meanwhile all keep well and distribute my love among the *circolo I Tatti*. [...]

1953

Nicky Mariano's reply from I Tatti on 7 January 1953 bubbled with gratitude that 'the fancy took you to write to me while navigating on the northern seas' because Trevor-Roper's letter had brightened her convalescence after an unpleasant infection. 'We are all very impatient to hear what developed out of your Stockholm visit and how you got on with the King and Queen.'

18 January 1953   Christ Church, Oxford

My dear Nicky,

I was sorry to hear of your illness, and I do hope you are completely recovered. I don't think illness is ever 'interesting', though of course con-valescence is delicious: I hope yours was exquisitely prolonged. What books did you read in it? Doubtless *The Thousand-&-One Nights*, or perhaps *Glanvill on Witches*[1] (you know I associate you, by some automatic reflex process, with these two subjects – indeed I still dine out on your *stregone*); or have you discovered some new great work, opening a new window on the world? I live in hopes of such experiences, but how rarely I discover them! However, I have now discovered one, which I am going to reveal in my next letter (which is going to follow this one by a very narrow margin of time) to BB, – a golden book which has fascinated me for the last two days causing me totally to abandon pupils, scholarship, administration, almost food and drink ... But this I am reserving for BB. You ask for an account of my visit to Sweden. Prepare, and I shall give it.

Imagine (if in the delicious mild Mediterranean ease of I Tatti, sur-rounded by your shapely cypresses and gentle ilex-groves, you can bend the mind to so distant a thought), imagine a vast gothic wilderness all hidden, except for a few dismally protruding pine-trees, beneath a firm, uniform, disinfectant crust of frozen snow. For some five hours a day a somewhat reluctant, diffused luminosity renders these disagreeable features visible; then Night mercifully withdraws them for the remaining nineteen hours from human sight. Superimpose upon this desolate natural crust a population as gloomy as their climate, feeding heavily on sandwiches and

---

[1] Joseph Glanvill (1636–1680), Anglican clergyman and natural philosopher, sought to refute atheism by collecting evidence of supernatural phenomena. *A Philosophical Endeavour towards the Defence of the Being of Witches and Apparitions* (1666) was his earliest book on this subject.

ardent spirits, and organised on the dispiriting principles of the welfare state; a population who only occasionally vary the organised tedium of their lives by bouts of convulsive lunacy, of Strindbergian neurosis, of Swedenborgian hallucination; imagine – but no, for perhaps in your Baltic past you have actually been to Sweden and know perfectly well that this won't do. So let me simply say that I greatly enjoyed my visit; that I did everything I intended to do; visited the places that I went to see, studied in the libraries where I meant to study, and returned enlightened to Oxford which I find (at least indoors) *very* much colder.

The King was extremely kind to me for the sake of his friends at I Tatti, to whom he commanded me to send all manner of good wishes, which I hereby do. Whether he was equally pleased to see me for my own sake is a question which I hesitate to ask myself: it depends, no doubt, on his real views about his cousin Folke Bernadotte whom, as I have perhaps too darkly hinted, I am soon to expose – not indeed in his true colours, but at least in some faint shadowy approximation to them. (The truth, I am afraid, is much blacker than I have said: I have only said the minimum necessary to rehabilitate his victim, Felix Kersten.) However, since BB had so kindly written to him, I called after his return from the funeral, in Copenhagen, of the Danish Queen Mother, and he took me to Drottningholm² and showed me everything there, and told me all about Queen Christina's pictures – the Swedish subject I am most interested in – and arranged my visits to the Museum for me, and saw to it that all my needs were so admirably supplied that the research of a week could be expeditiously done in a day; and sent me on my way loaded with messages of goodwill to you and BB. He had obviously *greatly* enjoyed his stay at I Tatti – as indeed who does not. I told the King, as seemed only fair, that I had written an article which might not be welcome in Sweden, and its nature: behind his perfect diplomatic civility I think I detected evidence that he was not altogether surprised at the facts, though not very pleased that they should be revealed – I'm afraid his Bernadotte relatives seldom achieve creditable limelight. The Queen was not there, so I didn't see her.

I also visited the victimised masseur, Himmler's masseur, Felix Kersten, whom I am now proposing for the Nobel Peace Prize. He showed me some fascinating documents – which incidentally showed one reason why certain Swedes at least are determined to discredit him: for he knows far too much for their convenience about their approaches to Germany in the days of German triumph. For instance, Otto Bonnier, the head of the great

---

² A royal residence on an island in Lake Mälar on the outskirts of Stockholm.

Stockholm publishing house, and himself a Jew, twice offered secretly to sell his business to the Nazis, to give them organs of propaganda in Sweden, and once to name all Jews in Swedish public life in return for exemption and a safe permit to Portugal for himself and his family in the event of a German occupation.[3] Kersten prudently keeps copies of all his papers in Holland ...

Now I must stop. A few small germinative mustard-seeds of news and gossip I must withhold and keep for BB. Tell him I shall write in a few days to thank him for his very kind letter of introduction; and after you have disseminated to the household the royal messages of affection of which I am the slender, obedient automatic funnel, then, at a decent interval, as befits my status, please distribute also, to that most well-beloved and hospitable of households, my own.

5 February 1953   Christ Church, Oxford

My dear BB

I have owed you a letter for a long time and now I am going to write it. How are you? How is everyone at I Tatti? What are you doing, whom seeing, what reading? Have you, for instance, any news of Isaiah Berlin? He is believed to be in All Souls, only a few yards from me; but he is so elusive that I have now firmly decided that the only possible means of discovering anything about him is to consult the great intellectual postal exchange at Settignano. It is true, Isaiah moved Heaven and Earth, and in the end the Postmaster-General, Kitty Giles' father, Lord De La Warr,[1] in order to have a telephone installed in his rooms in All Souls, so that his friends might be able to communicate with him; but he then defeated the whole purpose of the operation by having a highly complicated machine attached to the telephone to prevent it ever ringing, as he finds that the noise disturbs his social meditations! And if this is my ignorance of life even here in these umbratile cloisters, think how profound it must be of events in the greater world, of which I depend for news upon you! I hope I may elicit from you a reply to keep me up to date in these matters.

---

[3] Karl-Otto Bonnier (1856–1941) headed the family firm of Albert Bonnier's Forlag from 1900 until 1938; it celebrated its centenary with conspicuous splendour in 1937. During the 1930s Swedish racists accused him of masterminding a Jewish conspiracy in Sweden. The Bonniers, who had borne the surname of Hirschel until the early nineteenth century, were the paramount power in Swedish book-publishing, and had an unequalled influence on their national literature. They owned *Dagens Nyheter*, the largest circulation daily newspaper in wartime Sweden.
[1] Herbrand ('Buck') Sackville, 9th Earl De La Warr (1900–1976), Postmaster-General in Churchill's peacetime administration, was in charge of nationalised telephone services.

Meanwhile let me thank you for so kindly writing to the King of Sweden. As I explained to Nicky, this entailed certain social complexities; but I hope that at any rate your credit is not involved in the incidental consequences of my researches![2] The King was extremely civil to me for your sake and very anxious to have news of you: he had clearly very greatly enjoyed his stay at I Tatti; but indeed, who does not enjoy staying at that delightful, intellectual, and not *too* eremitical hermitage!

I am sending you, separately, an article I have written in *Foreign Affairs*, since you so kindly say that you like reading my occasional works. The style has (in my opinion) been barbarised by the editor, Hamilton Fish Armstrong, on principles of syntax hitherto unknown to me; but I hope it remains nevertheless, at least in its main lines, intelligible. It is about German books on Nazism written since the war, and the shift in contemporary Germany opinion which, in my opinion, they betray. I have also been reading a little! At last I am free from the administrative duties which are the curse of the English university system, and hope to return to full-time historical work. May I name these two admirable works from which I have recently derived such pleasure? One is a new anthology called *Letters of Jews through the Ages*, from the Old Testament to the Emancipation, edited by Franz Kobler, published by a new Jewish firm, the East & West Library. Do you know it? You know so much about the subject that perhaps it would contain nothing new to you; but to me it has been a revelation: some of the medieval letters are quite fascinating; & it is very well and learnedly edited. My other *trouvaille* is very different. Do you know Pieter Geyl?[3] He is a Dutch historian, and in my opinion one of the best of living historians, indeed in a class by himself, or perhaps a class which he shares with Namier, Braudel, and one or two others. He has written a history of Holland 1550–1672 which revolutionised that subject, and then, during this

---

[2] T-R's researches into Himmler's relations with Bernadotte. On the same day that T-R wrote this letter, Sir Roger Stevens, British Ambassador in Stockholm, sent a despatch to London deploring the 'sensation' caused in Sweden by T-R's article 'Kersten, Himmler and Count Bernadotte': 'it is somewhat unfortunate that he should have used his powers of historical detection, not only to do honour, perhaps justifiably, to Dr Kersten, but also to blacken the memory of Count Berna-dotte. By so doing he has caused needless pain to many Swedes and in particular to members of the Swedish Royal Family, who have mentioned the subject to me with evident distress.' (Despatch 32, 5 February 1953, PRO FO 371/106616). Richard Faber of the Foreign Office minuted on this despatch (12 February): 'Mr Trevor-Roper's bent as a historian is as a "de-bunker". I do not think he would ever allow his work to be much affected by other people's feelings; and [...] I am sure it would be quite useless for us to try to get him in any way to recant.'

[3] Pieter Geyl (1887–1966), was the first holder of a chair in Dutch history and institutions at London University 1919–35, and Professor of Modern History at the University of Utrecht 1936–58. After the Nazi invasion of the Netherlands in 1940, he was incarcerated in Buchenwald and other camps.

war, he was arrested by the Germans and while in prison wrote a book *Napoleon, For and Against,* being an analysis of the attitude of historians to Napoleon. Well, he has recently been in America & has there delivered a series of lectures now published by Smith College, which he has sent me. I think they are really excellent – on Ranke, Macaulay, the Dutch historians, the French biographers of Talleyrand, and Toynbee. The essays on Ranke & Toynbee – but indeed all the essays – would, I think, delight you. And (for I know that you share the view of Callimachus on the general desirability of *brevity* in authors) it is also a short book. Have you got this little book? It is called *From Ranke to Toynbee.*[4] If not, would you like me to send you a copy? I should be delighted to do so if you think that I have correctly judged your interest!

As for other news, – if, through your infinitely complex, infinitely centralised, infinitely extended Settignano grape-vine you should perchance hear that I have been converted to the Church of Rome, don't believe it: I am as Protestant as ever; but I am taking a leaf out of your book and making, in Oxford, a spectacular appearance, suitably accompanied by gilded peeresses (if one is doing the thing at all, one should do it properly), at the RC chaplaincy in order to hear Fr Dominic de Grunne preaching on that counter-reformation *seicento* topic 'Death'. But this, of course, is purely a social occasion and the rumours which will no doubt wildly fly are *not to be believed*!

For do you know Fr de Grunne? Surely his reputation has by now reached Settignano? Padre Pio, I assure you, is *nothing* to him![5] But if I am to tell you the cyclical story of this great spiritual conquest, perhaps I should begin at the beginning, with the sad case of the eclipse of Fr Wingfield Digby SJ – perhaps I should even go further, plunging into the dark Backward and Abysm of Time, to the days of Fr Martin D'Arcy SJ, that spiritual *conquistador* of our time who, in as many months, netted four peers, two cabinet-ministers, one fashionable novelist, a chain-store-millionaire, and a brace of musical-comedy actresses. But no; it will be enough, I think, if I go back to my old pupil Fr Wingfield Digby.

Yes, my old pupil; for how, without my patient hoeing and watering, would that bucolic mind ever (I proudly say) have attained, as it did, to a second class degree? However, a second class degree in the Roman Catholic

---

[4] T-R reviewed a later edition of Geyl's Smith lectures, entitled *Debates with Historians*, in *Sunday Times* of 21 August 1955.
[5] Francesco Forgione (1887–1968), a Capuchin priest known as Padre Pio, received the gift of stigmata while praying in 1918, and remained bleeding for half a century. Also reputedly able to bilocate and levitate, his miracles drew hordes of pilgrims in his lifetime. He was made a saint in 2002.

Church in England is an intellectual peak not often scaled, and it launched Fr Wingfield Digby as the great intellectual figure of the Oxford Jesuits, who, from their elegant citadel at Campion Hall (built by Lutyens, on a foundation-stone ceremonially laid by a converted Earl),[6] cast their dry-flies over the noses of the Oxford *beau-monde*. Was not Fr Wingfield Digby a scholar, a man of the world, with an aristocratic surname and the suave manners of a professional *abbé*? Did he not appear readily – perhaps even a little *too* readily – at every elegant Oxford party? Did he not entertain the most aristocratic, the most elegant, the most intellectual, and the most frivolous undergraduates to champagne breakfast-parties in the Mitre Hotel? Yes, he did all these things, and tinkled (as Logan would say) coronets often in his conversation. Then, quite suddenly, there came unobtrusively over from Belgium le R.P. (Comte) Dominique de Grunne, OSB, modestly to study English literature in the university of Oxford, with one or two discreet letters of introduction in the folds of his exquisitely tailored *soutane*; and all was over with Fr Wingfield Digby.

Alas, one must admit that the undergraduate society of Oxford is very similar to the society of Mayfair. Like fashionable but feather-headed peer-esses, they take up, and they cast down, their intellectual idols in sudden, tribal unison, not delicately, nor furtively, nor one by one, but furiously, unanimously, competitively, each terrified lest he should be – or seem – the last to have detected the jewel in the ore, or the paste in the jewel. For a year or so Fr Wingfield Digby had reigned supreme; then suddenly all agreed that he was totally bogus. Fr de Grunne was so obviously the real, handsome, intellectual, social, aristocratic *abbé*; how could Fr Wingfield Digby be anything but a fake? Suddenly, Fr Wingfield Digby received no more invitations and Fr de Grunne delighted private audiences in cultivated *salons* by his delightful imitations of a cardinal confessing a lady of fashion. In Campion Hall there was a wailing and a gnashing of priestly teeth; the Benedictines had triumphed; and Fr Wingfield Digby (since social decline is a far greater offence in his order than mere theological error) has been sent off to a suburban dormitory town in Surrey, where there are no countesses and no intellectuals and no champagne and no elegant parties, there to expiate his grave misdemeanour whereby his whole order has so grievously suffered in repute.

So you see, Fr de Grunne is now the rage. He is very discreet, and, being not nearly so easy to get to parties (except of course the *most* fashionable),

---

[6] The foundation stone on Lutyens' buildings for Campion Hall was laid on 24 November 1934 by Archbishop Alban Goodier SJ and the eighteen-year-old Earl of Oxford and Asquith. The college was opened on 26 June 1936 by the Duke of Alba and Berwick.

is thereby the more desirable as a guest. How maddening of poor Sybil Colefax not to be alive to get him along to Lord North Street! But *the* great social occasion will undoubtedly be his impending sermon on 'Death'. My devout sponsors insist that we must get there at least an hour before the service begins to be sure of a seat ... The whole affair, I'm afraid, delights me: it is like Dr Donne at St Paul's or a scene from *le Rouge et le Noir*.[7] But at all events, it has no religious significance whatever, so don't let any of your numerous fashionable visitors (who will all, I have no doubt, have heard of Fr de Grunne) beguile you into supposing that it has!

My dear BB, I have exhausted myself by this ascent into the high realms of religious fervour; now (I hope) it is your turn to send me some news from Italy. You know how I long to hear from you & about you all. Best wishes to everyone in your terrestrial paradise. [...]

PS. I forgot to say that I am very sorry that I have failed to persuade the Governing Body to agree to send the 'school of Piero della Francesca' *or* Signorelli *Madonna* for the forthcoming Signorelli exhibition. Everyone was most anxious that it should go if at all possible, especially since you had yourself asked, but K.T. Parker of the Ashmolean[8] was positive that the panel on which it is painted is too delicate to risk such a journey. We had a long discussion, but I couldn't argue against the experts on such a subject, and so I'm afraid we had to decide against sending it. Nothing else except fear of damage for this reason would have interfered with the fulfilment of this, or I think any other, request from you.

A short message from Trevor-Roper, dated 20 March, is omitted. It announced that he was leaving for Spain in search of 'some ballast for my historical studies', and promised a letter 'from Madrid or Seville'.

'The visitors at I Tatti', Sylvia Sprigge reported to Trevor-Roper on 8 April, 'are more numerous than ever. Elizabeth Bowen, Raymond Mortimer (who retired with an operation gone wrong, poor chap), your I.Berlin – & all the world. Even an oil tycoon of immense wealth called Paul Gatty [sic] called & stayed & was rung up from 4 continents during every meal. It gave one a view of the hell real wealth can bring.'

Shortly afterwards Raymond Mortimer, who had been a friend of Trevor-Roper's since their wartime meetings at Pearsall Smith's house, reviewed Hitler's Table-Talk *somewhat recklessly in the* Sunday Times *of 26 April; Trevor-Roper's riposte, an*

[7] Stendhal's novel *Le Rouge et le noir* (1830) describes the adventurous career of Julien Sorel, a provincial seminarian who becomes briefly the darling of fashionable Parisians.
[8] (Sir) Karl Parker (1895–1992), Keeper of the Ashmolean Museum in Oxford 1945–62.

article entitled 'Hitler, Mr Mortimer and Universal Suffrage', appeared on 10 May;
Mortimer tried to justify his views in a letter printed a week later. This well-
mannered disagreement, which did not ruffle the friendship between the two men,
was mentioned in Berenson's letter of 2 June, written while he was touring Sicily.
He began, though, with a reproach:

'Your short note of many weeks ago promised a long letter fr. Madrid and Seville.
It has not reached me. You must be back now. I greatly enjoyed yr introductory essay
to Hitler's Table-Talk, *& followed the controversy it aroused. Of course Raymond*
does not know German, [or] Germany as the Germans. Without such knowledge, &
besides without much historic or political sense, what can the like of him understand
about Hitler!'

17 June 1953   Christ Church, Oxford

My dear BB

Of course you are right: I have behaved outrageously: and to think that
I even now have in front of me the first three pages of an unfinished letter
to you, dated 2nd May, which even then began with expressions of shame
and contrition at my epistolary dilatoriness! That letter, or rather fragment,
seems to have got sanded up, like the river Oxus, in the middle of a long
commentary on the *cause célèbre* of the Duke & Duchess of Roxburghe,[1]
which evidently I found too tedious to finish (you see, I hope, how reluctantly I struggle through these tales of English high-life). I shall not risk
embogment in such aristocratic morasses again. But first, – since my letter
will now only just reach you in time for that occasion – may I wish you the
best of wishes on what (if my calculations are correct) should be your 88th
birthday? I hope – indeed, from your letter, I deduce – that you are well
and enjoying your Sicilian excursion: an excursion which I both admire
and envy – I myself only know the other end of Sicily, I mean the western
end, and even there I spent most of the time in bed in the Albergo della
Palme in Palermo; how I should like to visit Enna, & Syracuse, and the
slopes of Etna! Meanwhile, since my return from Spain, I have been working
in Oxford, hearing news of you from Sylvia, from Henry McIlhenny, from
Isaiah, from the Haddingtons[2] – and how glad I am that it is always such
good news – but also, I implausibly repeat, *working*. At *what* am I working?
Well, I have produced a slim *opusculum* on the Gentry which I have sent

---

[1] See T-R's letter of 22 September 1953.
[2] George Baillie-Hamilton, 12th Earl of Haddington (1894–1986), had married Sarah Cook of
Montreal in 1923. T-R and his future wife Xandra Howard-Johnston often visited their houses
Mellerstain, in Berwickshire, and Tyninghame in East Lothian.

you and which is causing some (to me) pleasurable commotion in the academic mutual-admiration society of the London School of Economics;[3] and I have launched *Hitler's Table-Talk,* of which you have observed the reactions (Leonard Woolf[4] was, I fear, furious: but I suspect that his real motive was a thirst for revenge on me for my review, in the *Sunday Times,* of the laudatory biography of his fellow Bloomsbury-socialist Harold Laski);[5] and I am now preparing a booklet which I hope (but perhaps it is too much to hope) may cause a paralytic stroke to my old enemy Evelyn Waugh,[6] *viz*: a study of the Roman Catholic Revival in 19th century England, which I hope to have ready for the press this summer.[7] I have offered to dedicate this last little work to my colleague Frank Pakenham,[8] and he, rather to my surprise, is all agog to be the dedicatee, being convinced that it is a manifest sign of my impending conversion. So pure and naïve is his conviction on this point that I am almost ashamed now of my offer, and hardly dare show him the text. And finally, I have applied for a year's leave of absence from my duties here in order to devote myself, from 1st January 1954, to the composition of a major work: a book on the rule of Robert Cecil in England, from 1590 to 1612, which (I believe) may explain a hitherto unexplained set of problems in English history.[9] My essay on the gentry is, in part, a sample or prefiguration of this work; but of course only in very small part: it is intended to clear away the cobwebs of controversy so as to make the path plain for a narrative history.

---

[3] T-R's 'The Gentry 1540–1640' was published as a supplement of the *Economic History Review* in 1953.

[4] Leonard Woolf (1880–1969), founder of the Hogarth Press and socialist intellectual, wrote prolifically on colonialism, capitalism and international affairs.

[5] Harold Laski (1893–1950) held the chair in political science at the London School of Economics and was chairman of the Labour party in 1945–6. T-R's review of Kingsley Martin's *Harold Laski* (*Sunday Times,* 18 January 1953) commented: 'There is something tragic in the endless, boring pontifications of this once brilliant man whose rigidity left him, in the end, far behind many of his less gifted but less arrogant colleagues.' The long, affectionate correspondence between Laski and Oliver Wendell Holmes, edited by Mark Howe and published in two volumes as *The Holmes–Laski Letters,* was sent to T-R by the *Sunday Times* for review in 1954. T-R's scornful demonstration that Laski was a compulsive liar, sustained by self-glorifying fantasies in which he changed the destinies of governments, proved too daunting to be published.

[6] Evelyn Waugh (1903–1966), novelist and Catholic convert. His letter headed 'The Last Days of Hitler', *The Tablet,* 28 June 1947, was the opening shot of his recurrent acrimonious public exchanges with T-R.

[7] T-R signed, but then cancelled, a contract for this book to be published by Weidenfeld. Although later included in an Oxford University Press catalogue of forthcoming books, it was never published.

[8] In 1952, at the instigation of Robert Blake, Lord Pakenham, a former Student and tutor at Christ Church, had (after an interval as a government minister) resumed his Studentship and became a part-time tutor in politics at the college.

[9] This was not written.

So you see I am not – or at least do not feel myself to be – entirely inactive. And then there are always a few battles to keep the blood circulating. My great battle in Sweden has been going pretty well and has led to a Riksdag debate and a commission of inquiry and a most enjoyable attack on the present Foreign Minister of Sweden, Östen Undén,[10] who had issued an official *communiqué* denouncing me but has since been exposed in the Press as having been personally involved in some of the (in my opinion) shady courses which I had sought to reveal. I do not know whether my two little articles on General Franco will get me into trouble.[11] I had thought them very inoffensive; and was therefore rather disconcerted to be told by no less than four candid friends that they presumed I did not intend to revisit Spain for a while. In fact I do of course so presume: how can a historian of the 16th & 17th century do otherwise? – but perhaps, if one wants both to write and to travel round Europe, one is best advised to write only about the 16th and 17th, not about the 20th century!

And now, with a sudden pang of conscious egotism, I realise that I have written nearly four pages exclusively about myself. What about you? How is Nicky, how Alda,[12] how Luisa? What is going on in the Villa Berensoniana? Who is studying in the Library, what visitors have caused the terrace to hum with cosmopolitan gossip? Do send me news of you all, how you fare, what you are doing, what is happening all around you. And will you perhaps, if occasion serves, receive a pupil of mine who will be staying for a fortnight in Fiesole next month? He is very young – about 19 and duly deferential, but has civilised (and various) tastes and would, I know, properly appreciate such an opportunity. His name is Nicolas Tate.[13] The family, being hereditary sugar-kings, contrive even in these iron days to maintain a certain standard of life; but they have also some claim to a higher (also hereditary) distinction, since the young man's great-grandfather founded the Tate Gallery, and he himself (apart from being master of the beagles) has an interest in art and architecture which has sometimes astonished grave and condescending Panjandrums in those fields. He is staying with a Signora Casandi (who I think is a relative of Yvonne Hamilton) at Fiesole,

---

[10] Östen Undén (1886-1974), Professor of Law at Uppsala University 1917–37, Swedish Foreign Minister 1924–6 and 1945–62.
[11] T-R's two *Sunday Times* articles, published under the general title 'The Secret of Franco's Rule', were 'How Spain Kept Out of the War' (7 June 1953) and 'Is Franco a Fascist?' (14 June).
[12] Nicky Mariano's sister Alda (b. 1883), the I Tatti librarian 1929–62, was beloved by Kenneth Clark for her skittish chatter. She married Baron Egbert ('Bertie') von Anrep, who was the highly effective estate manager at I Tatti until his death in 1955.
[13] Nicolas Tate (b. 1934). After retiring from the Confederation of British Industry, he ran the Salisbury Cathedral Spire Trust.

for a fortnight or so from 6th July, and I told him that I would write to you in case you should be able to receive him at Vallombrosa, if you are there (he has a car & could find his way there), or would allow him to see I Tatti.

I suppose you have followed the great literary scandal about Simon Harcourt-Smith and the Borgias, revealed in the *Times Literary Supplement* in March in a brilliant review which was written, I understand, by Mario Praz?[14] As you will know, Harcourt-Smith – who, I understand, is a mere crook and was dismissed from the diplomatic service for embezzlement in Brussels – simply plagiarised Maria Bellonci's *Lucrezia Borgia*, publishing, under his own name, an unacknowledged English translation of it and pretending that this was the result of his own research in the archives of Ferrara.[15] (Enquiries of the archivist at Ferrara have revealed that Harcourt-Smith has never even visited that repository.) The result of this exposure has been four lawsuits, a good deal of discredit to Peter Quennell, who puffed the book in the *Daily Mail* as the book of the month, and the withdrawal of the book from publication. Harcourt-Smith, pursued by the officers of the law, is alleged to have fled abroad, but is in fact living in a cellar in Paultons Street, Chelsea, with a mistress who goes above ground to buy food once a day ... Such are the risks of that literary life which we have so hazardously adopted! Since you appreciate style and exquisite malice, and know the good Miss Haslip and (the perhaps less good) Harold Nicolson, and don't – I think – take the *Observer*, I am enclosing, for your amusement, a review which touches lightly on this now famous controversy and may also give you a little pleasure.[16] Might it also elicit some more news from you? Do please forgive, and forbear to imitate, my dilatory habits in correspondence. I long to hear from and about you all. [...]

PS. Do you know the Romanellis at Bello Sguardo? If so, and if they should bring to you a girl called Phoebe Hichens[17] who is staying with them, do be kind to her – I know you are always *very* kind to feminine visitors even

---

[14] Mario Praz (1896–1982) demonstrated the wholesale plagiarism in Simon Harcourt-Smith's *The Marriage at Ferrara* (1952) in 'The Borgia Tradition', *TLS*, 13 March 1953, p. 170. Harcourt-Smith's book was withdrawn shortly after being chosen as *Daily Mail* book of the month. Praz, who taught Italian literature at Manchester University and English literature at Rome University, translated BB's *Aesthetics and History in the Visual Arts* into Italian.

[15] Simon Harcourt-Smith (b. 1905) entered the Foreign Office in 1928, served in Peking in 1930–33 and was appointed Second Secretary at the Brussels Embassy in 1936; but left diplomacy in 1938.

[16] Sir Harold Nicolson (1886–1968) contributed a weekly book review to the *Observer* 1949–63. His review of Joan Haslip's *Lucrezia Borgia* (1953) explained that 'she describes her [Borgia] villains with neat straightforwardness, as if she were writing of the squabbles between a clergyman's family at Chelmsford and their uncle, a former Civil Servant, living in discontented retirement at Torquay. This makes the whole thing easier to understand.'

[17] Phoebe Hichens (b. 1929) of North Aston Hall, Oxford.

though I have seen you critically quiz the masculine variety! – she is a friend of mine. But I think she will have gone when you are back in Tuscany.

To the delight of Berenson and Mariano, they received an unexpected telegram from Trevor-Roper in early July, proposing a visit later in the month; Trevor-Roper was travelling with his new love, Xandra Howard-Johnston, and introduced her at I Tatti on 23 July, as Berenson recorded in his diary:

24 July 1953
'Arrival of Hugh Trevor-Roper and Lady Alexandra Howard-Johnston. Youngish woman with wooden angular profile, Celtic blond colouring, fairly good figure, no interest or talk to entitle her to frequent us or to be travelling with Hugh. She is Dawyck Haig's sister and daughter of the general of the First World War, and perhaps that is enough. Hugh, awkward gestures, shrill yet pleasant laugh as of musical glasses. No flow of continuous talk. Reports that Winston Churchill has had two slight strokes, one while in the House, but quickly recovered.'

25 July 1953
'Lady Alexandra improves on acquaintance. Would not know she had ever read a book, but of good judgment and sound sense about people, and she seems to know many of the governing class societishly as well as politically. Hugh explained that if Churchill resigns he can propose his successor, and it will be Eden, of whom he, Hugh, thinks little, boring and pretentious. Could not draw him about Butler. Hugh thinks Salisbury the ablest person in the Tory Cab., and would have him as prime minister. Says there is no reason why a peer should not be.'

1 August 1953   Christ Church, Oxford

My dear Nicky,
    How very kind of you it was, at such short, sudden and laconic notice, and when all your plans for the great summer migration had been made, to receive us so hospitably at I Tatti! I was delighted to see you and BB again, and find you both looking so well, and to be exhausted again by BB's physical energy in leading us over those rough and stony mountains; and Xandra (who is now in Scotland and will no doubt be writing to you from that strange, arctic, almost Eskimo country) never ceased to bubble with enthusiasm at the recollection of I Tatti. We didn't stay at the Palazzo Ravizza in Siena, as it is rather a long way from the centre of life and our time was so short; but at the Toscana, which is central & convenient and, we

thought, attractive. We arrived back in London in good order on Tuesday. Xandra's husband, having discovered that she had gone abroad by Newhaven & Dieppe, and knowing that she would have to be back on 28th July, with great craft had all the boat trains from Newhaven met; but we, with superior craft, had the tickets changed in Paris and returned *via* Calais and Dover, thus giving him the slip. Incidentally, since you asked me about that formidable character, and since I'm afraid that my answer was perhaps somewhat fragmentary, I took an opportunity to cross-examine her in detail on one or two points of his personality. To complete my sketch I should therefore add

(1) he is *very* good-looking, especially in naval uniform, bedizened with medals commemorating heroic exploits at sea.

(2) he is always in a hurry and, being accustomed to brisk nautical commands, will not tolerate any delay in business. Other people's recreations are also unwarrantable delays in business. His own recreations count as business and are therefore allowed.

(3) his own recreations are, in winter, wild-fowling and, in summer, fish-spearing (both pastimes being conducted in solitude). When he was stationed in England, he spent all his spare time in the centre of a bog near Portsmouth, sitting in a hip-bath which he had specially transported thither, and disguised as a clump of bulrushes, in order to spy unobserved on the wildfowl of those dismal marshes; and when he was stationed for two years in Greece, although he never visited the Parthenon, he speared a large number of fish. Indeed he carries about with him, and shows liberally to acquaintances, a photograph not (Xandra complains) of his wife and children but of himself and a large fish.

(4) He is extremely mean (I have seen some very comic evidence of this); but allows that his own tastes may properly be gratified. Thus, when he was in China, he wrote to Xandra telling her that it was quite unwarrantable for her to employ a nurse for the children when he was 'stinting and starving' himself to save money. Afterwards Xandra discovered that he had, at that time, in his personal service, five cooks! At present, in France, he has for himself alone three cars. Incidentally, the five cooks seem particularly unnecessary since I understand that his favourite food is the potato.

Having elicited these interesting details I asked Xandra why she married him when really almost any of her other candidates – even Sir Bernard

Docker (with whose recent antics you are doubtless familiar),[1] Alfred Potocki (whose peasants had to kiss his toes as he rode out hunting and whose pigs had each a warm bath daily),[2] or Lord Glentanar (from whom she hid in a cupboard for a week-end)[3] might have proved a little better. She answered by referring me to (1) above, and to the general disordination of the faculties caused by being bombed in London in 1940.

Of course it is conceivable that some of the above details may be slightly exaggerated. Unfortunately, since I am obliged to avoid him now, I cannot confirm or deny the evidence at first hand. As I think I mentioned, I have only met him once; and on that occasion, since I never stopped talking, he had no opportunity of expressing himself on any subject whatever!

Please don't retail any of this – or indeed anything else that can still be buried in discreet silence – to that *incorrigible rattle* D. Hill! You know he lubricates his passage up ducal stairways by spreading precisely such stories as these about those benevolent friends upon whom he relies to turn those golden keys!

I got your postcard about the 'catalogues' before visiting Bain,[4] and my quick intellect fathomed its occult meaning at the fourth reading. So I have so far done nothing. But how do I communicate with Luisa to pass on these useful documents? Or have you written to her? I await advice, or rather orders, and will promptly execute them.

Ever since I reached England I have been totally crippled by a sudden attack of lumbago. They tell me, in a genial way, before quickly passing on to more attractive subjects, that it will go as rapidly as it came. I wish it would do so. At present I creep about with a forest of sticks and a can-tankerous facial expression, looking like

> The foul witch Sycorax, who with age and envy
> Was grown in a hoop.[5]

Kind friends give me a good deal of advice, mostly contradictory and some of it (e.g. 'Drink more port') almost certainly disastrous. [...]

---

[1] Sir Bernard Docker (1896–1978), who had been forced to resign earlier in 1953 from the boards of Midland Bank and Guardian Assurance after being prosecuted for breaches of the currency regulations on foreign travel, was notorious with his wife for ostentatious luxury and drunken antics.
[2] Count Alfred Potocki (1886–1958), Polish landowner and international sportsman, owned the castle of Lancut and its treasures until dispossessed under the Soviet occupation in 1945.
[3] Thomas Coats, 2nd Baron Glentanar (1894-1971) inherited a fortune derived from Scottish thread manufacturing.
[4] James Bain was a London bookseller who supplied the I Tatti library.
[5] Lines spoken by Prospero in *The Tempest*: I, ii, 258–9.

9 August 1953   Christ Church, Oxford

My dear BB

You can hardly believe what pleasure you gave both to me and Xandra by allowing us to come – and at such short notice, and in answer to so brief and peremptory and elliptical a telegram, and (I fear) at such inconvenience to yourselves – for those three delightful days at I Tatti. We both enjoyed our visit immensely, and it was delightful to see you all well and active. I hope we didn't disorder the well-regulated mechanics of life too seriously, and that you are now installed at Vallombrosa just as if no such sudden barbarian invasion from the North had occurred, and that you are not too heavily beset by lawyers – or rather, I should say, by legalities – but can stroll peacefully in the cool summer air meditating and conversing, like epicurean gods upon that comfortable Olympus. Nevertheless, I am glad also that we caught you in the plains. How else would I ever have discovered (or rather, been shown, for I would never have discovered it myself) Bagazzano? I am amazed to think that I could have visited you so often and have been so long unaware of it. Have you yet more such experiences to produce as suddenly from your inexhaustible surroundings?[1]

Since I came back, I have been sitting entirely alone in my rooms in Oxford, writing a wicked little book on the *Roman Catholic Revival in 19th Century England* which will no doubt, on its publication, cause many a social door to shut against me.[2] But I hope it will also give some pleasure and some instruction to some people! Anyway, I'm not quite as interested in the openness of social doors as some of my acquaintance! Here in Oxford, I find, I rather like being alone, – for a time. The place is totally empty: that is, it is full of bland-faced tourists whose strange clothes, voices, gestures and apparent interests make one feel far more insulated from humanity than would mere neuter vacuity. From morning to night I see no known face except that of my servant who comes in once a day and deposits a cold meal on my dining-room table (rather like an old peasant housewife putting out a bowl of milk and a few cheesecakes for the hobgoblin); but I read and

---

[1] Xandra Howard-Johnston had written to BB on 4 August: 'I had heard so much about you and I Tatti that I have always longed to meet you [...] I feel it was a tremendous compliment to Hugh that you should have delayed your departure to Vallombrosa by two days in order to receive him & a lady friend! You said to me, "Italy is a paradise on earth," well, I think I Tatti is a Heaven on earth. I have never known such beauty, such peace, as I found there. All cares, all pre-occupations, fell away from me, though, I must admit, I would have been more at my ease if Hugh had told me before my arrival, instead of after my departure, that you did not like blue-stocking women!'
[2] See T-R's letter of 17 June 1953.

write away, and – you may have noticed – I *publish* nothing! I know you
think I publish a lot. I submit that statistics, as distinct from general
impressions, confirm that I publish very little! I can assure you that I have
observed with care the sad effect which hebdomadal publication has had
upon the quality of the work of Desmond MacCarthy,[3] Raymond Mortimer[4]
and others, and am fully determined *never* to fall into that fatal trap! Is this
a vain thing to say?

I expect to stay here till the end of August; then I go to Scotland for a
week; then I shall either come back here or (if I feel I can spare the time –
which depends on my rate of progress now) I shall go for a fortnight to
Spain, to visit the archives of Simancas and see, if I can, the few Spanish
historians whom I respect. What wonderful subjects of history there are in
Spain, if only there were historians to exploit them – or rather, if only
Spanish historians had, as English and French and Italian historians have,
the antiquarian researches of two centuries on which to base their work!
But alas, except for the work of the Duke of Alba and his *Real Academia*,
there is almost nothing: the history of Spain has been written almost
entirely – as to the 16th & 17th centuries – from Venetian ambassadors'
Relazioni, from *Don Quixote*, and from the 500 surviving comedies of Lope
de Vega. (Thank God the other 1,000 have been lost!) [...]

*Berenson replied on 23 August: 'Lady Alexandra wrote alarmingly & entertainingly,
hinting at gossip most unexpected in New Testament Scotland. Do encourage her to
send more & be more detailed as well as precise. Yesterday we had to lunch Patrick
Lindsay who brought a Miss Jebb as well as two yg. Pakenhams. The last two I
teased about their popery, & they passed the test splendidly. I begged them to urge
their father to come to see me.'*

2 September 1953   20 Bondgate Without, Alnwick

My dear BB
I am so sorry to hear that you have been unwell; I hope you are now as
fully recovered as the gaiety of your letter suggests. As soon as I get back to

---

[3] Sir Desmond MacCarthy (1877–1952), literary editor of *New Statesman* 1920–28, principal book
reviewer for the *Sunday Times* 1928–52.
[4] Raymond Mortimer (1895–1980), literary editor of the *New Statesman* 1935–47, joined the *Sunday
Times* as a book reviewer, and succeeded MacCarthy as principal reviewer in 1952.

the south – I write this in Northumberland – I shall no doubt have from the young Pakenhams[1] & Vanessa Jebb[2] (as I have already had from Nicolas Tate) a properly deferential account of their visit to your small but distinguished principality. (I regard I Tatti as a little independent political unit, of high civilisation, and with a very elegant Renaissance court, like the Duchy of Urbino.) But on one point I must remonstrate. You command me, and I have of course at once obeyed your commands, to tell Xandra to be more explicit about the scandalous gossip at which hitherto, with a proper feminine reticence, she has only hinted: gossip, you add, 'unsuspected in Old Testament Scotland'. My dear BB, have you not read the Old Testament? It leaves the most advanced circles in Ecclefechan and Clackmannan nowhere! Cast your eye through the book of Leviticus, or even Deuteronomy ...

Xandra can tell you more than I can about the Lindsay–Pakenham romance: at least she hears the gossip from the Lindsay, I from the Pakenham side.[3] Briefly, comparing our notes acquired in these different camps, we deduce that the Pakenhams have great hopes, the Lindsays great fears. My position with the Pakenhams is in danger of great complication owing to my booklet on Popery. In a moment of genial malice I suggested to Frank Pakenham (who tells everyone that he has great hopes of converting me) that I should dedicate the work to him. He said that, in general, he would be prepared to risk excommunication in the good cause of bringing me nearer to the truth; but in particular he reserved his answer. Shortly afterwards he approached me and said he hoped there was no danger of my retreating on my *promise* to dedicate the book to him; and about the same time Elizabeth, his wife, came to me and said they were all so touched at this *promise* of mine, etc. etc.; so I am now pretty well committed. Since then I have discovered that Frank had taken the

---

[1] Thomas Pakenham (b. 1933), Frank Pakenham's eldest son, became a travel writer and historian. During lunch at I Tatti he asked loudly and inconveniently how the money had been made to pay for such grandeur. His sister Antonia (b. 1932) worked at Weidenfeld & Nicolson from 1953 until her marriage in 1956 to the Conservative politician Hugh Fraser. Afterwards a successful biographer, she married the playwright Harold Pinter in 1980.

[2] After graduating from St Hugh's College, Oxford, in 1954, Vanessa Jebb (b. 1931) went to work for the publisher André Deutsch, but in 1956 replaced Antonia Pakenham in the offices of Weidenfeld & Nicolson, where she remained until 1960. BB described her as 'ivory dark with beautiful chiselled features, and face serious, almost melancholy, but with a quiet and persuasive distinction' (diary, 22 August 1953). In 1962 she married the historian Hugh Thomas (afterwards Lord Thomas of Swynnerton).

[3] Hon. Patrick Lindsay (1928-1986), daredevil sportsman, aviator and motorist, had been Derek Hill's paying guest in the I Tatti *villino* and an almost daily visitor to the library in 1951–2. At this time he was enjoying a romance with Antonia Pakenham. He became a director of Christie's in 1955 and ran their Old Masters and English pictures department.

precaution of consulting, in the interim, a sagacious Jesuit, who had evidently told him to accept the dedication in order to get an advance copy of the text into his hands and then pass it to them for scrutiny. This means that they would know the contents several weeks before publication and would have a useful period in which to decide their attitude and work up their counterblast. Consequently I am looking for a way out of that genial suggestion which has suddenly been converted into a 'promise'. Unfortunately, even if I avoid showing the work to Frank, my retreat is now blocked by another obstacle of my own heedless manufacture. For the work in question is to be published by George Weidenfeld, a smart, smooth, enterprising émigré from Vienna,[4] who, having got Nigel Nicolson as a sleeping-partner to make the firm socially presentable,[5] and the heiress of those great multiple-purveyors, Messrs Marks and Spencer, as a wife, to make it economically solvent, is now setting out openly with the intention of reducing all other and more conservative publishers to bankruptcy. (Jamie Hamilton, whose firm threads its precarious, funambulatory course by seducing ready-made authors rather than discovering new ones, and who now sees a rival and bolder and more successful seducer in the same market, now goes a sickly green at the mere name of Weidenfeld.) Well, this George Weidenfeld, who incidentally published my edition of Hitler's *Table-Talk*, owing to his very success in cutting the throats of more somnolent publishers, is now expanding his business and looking for bright young graduates; and being himself, owing to his Viennese youth, out of touch with the English market, applied to me. Always eager to oblige my friends by making them give jobs to my *protégés*, I at once supplied two: one a former pupil from Christ Church,[6] the other – Antonia Pakenham! So now, even if I keep the MS out of the hands of her father, I fear that an extra set of galley-proofs will reach the Reverend Fathers of Farm Street from young Antonia in the publisher's office; who will no doubt acquire the honour of beatification for so holy and meritorious a fraud. Or do I misjudge the moral teaching of her Church, the versatile casuistry of her accomplished confessors?

Such are some of the deep, insoluble dilemmas which now face me.

---

[4] George Weidenfeld (b. 1919), chairman of the publishing house of Weidenfeld & Nicolson, received a life peerage in 1976.
[5] Nigel Nicolson (1917–2004), who first met BB in Italy in 1945, was a Conservative MP 1952–9, and ultimately became a distinguished man-of-letters.
[6] Nicholas Thompson (b. 1928) was Gladstone memorial exhibitioner at Christ Church in 1949, joined Weidenfeld & Nicolson after graduating in 1953, and became its managing director in 1956.

> Ah me undone! which way shall I flee
> Infinite wrath and infinite despair?[7]

But no: on second thoughts, this is too extreme a statement of my plight. Have no fears on my account: I doubt if I am losing much sleep over the problem. In fact, my morale is almost indecently high. It is the journey north that does it. Though intellectually the North of England perhaps lags some paces behind the vertiginous steps of the stony-hearted metropolis, I must admit that when I cross the river Trent, going north, I always suddenly feel the elation of going home, and it takes me a good two days before I as suddenly discover the painful thinness of the conversation in these northern *salons*. However, I have only had one day so far, so the elation is at its height. How delightful to look into the air and see, not, as in the dank and stuffy valley of the Thames, torpid cabbage-butterflies generated in those dismal flats, but terns and oyster-catchers: and friendly red squirrels peeping coyly out of the leaves, instead of grey squirrels grinning unashamed on naked tree-stumps! This world begins in Yorkshire and lasts up to Northumberland; then comes the river Tweed and beyond it a geographical darkness envelops the *terra incognita* of Old Testament Scotland: which darkness, however, I shall, in a few days, timidly penetrate; but not, of course, far: one must always take care to be within shouting-distance of an English rescue-party.

You will notice (I hope) that I am keeping my promise and writing nothing for the Press. All literary activity has been concentrated solely upon the papists. This is not entirely, I must admit, the result of scholarly purism; for I was indeed persuaded, the other day, to write a diatribe for the *Sunday Times* against the *Daily Mirror*. The *Daily Mirror*, I suspect, is not much known at I Tatti. It is the lowest of all English papers. Its avowed philosophy is that what 'the people' want is 'sex and crime'; its chosen diet must be presented to it in the palatable form of pictures, not the indigestible form of prose. This philosophy is justified by its results, and therefore I presume, at least according to the doctrines of your great compatriot William James,[8] true: for the daily circulation of the *Daily Mirror* is now four-and-a-half million copies. The editor has now written a book boasting of the methods by which this enviable result was achieved.[9] I should add that Lord Kemsley,

---

[7] A misquotation of canto I of Shelley's poem 'The Wandering Jew'.
[8] The doctrines of the Harvard philosopher William James (1842–1910) had a profound influence on the young Berenson.
[9] Hugh Cudlipp (1913–1998), later Lord Cudlipp, author of *Publish and Be Damned! The Astonishing Story of the Daily Mirror* (1953), was the newspaper's editorial director but never its editor.

owner of the *Sunday Times*,[10] suffered a dismal defeat at the hands of the *Daily Mirror*, for he owned a rival picture-paper, the *Daily Sketch*. Seeing that it was impossible to be more indecent than the *Mirror*, he began a rival campaign in the name of purity, under the slogan 'All the news & pictures fit to print'; but unfortunately this virtuous crusade did not succeed and therefore presumably (still according to William James) its philosophy is untrue: so untrue that the *Sketch* gradually subsided into total bankruptcy and has just been sold to Lord Rothermere for a song.[11] Consequently Lord Kemsley feels rather sore about the *Mirror*, and when this disagreeable yellow-jacketed vulgar book boasting of its methods and its success under the uncivil title *Publish and Be Damned!* appeared, and was found to be particularly funny about Lord Kemsley's unfortunate 'tut-tut campaign', he naturally felt an itch to bite it with his only remaining tooth, *viz:* the *Sunday Times*. I was accordingly asked to write an article on the crimes of the *Mirror*, to be splashed in the centre page of the *Sunday Times*. To this congenial task I did not demur. I set to work. I had hardly written a paragraph when the telephone rang: it was a personal message from Lord Kemsley enjoining me 'not to be too mild'. (You see what my reputation is – one who coos like a sucking-dove.) I sharpened up a few epithets. Then the telephone rang again. His Lordship was having cold feet. Would not any publicity, even if damaging in substance, nevertheless be of benefit to his victim? Might not the hated *Daily Mirror*, already victorious over his disastrous 'tut-tut campaign', now rise, through his denunciation, to the 5-million mark? I was asked to stay my hand until the weekly meeting when the temperature of his Lordship's feet could be ascertained. Yesterday, when I arrived in Northumberland, I found a telegram advising me that all was over. And so, thanks to the sudden refrigeration of the baronial feet I have been enabled to preserve (in publication at least: for my friends insist, and my enemies complain, that I still rattle away in private) my Trappist silence. [...]

22 September 1953   Christ Church, Oxford

My dear BB

How mobile you are! I feel ashamed by comparison, sitting sedentarily here in Oxford, to which I have just returned after my tentative expeditions

---

[10] As editor-in-chief of the *Sunday Times* 1937–59, Gomer Berry, 1st Viscount Kemsley (1883–1968) trebled his newspaper's circulation.
[11] Esmond Harmsworth, 2nd Viscount Rothermere (1898–1978), Chairman of Associated Newspapers and proprietor of the *Daily Mail*.

across the northern border of civilisation. Fortunately, of course, there are islands of culture even among the rude Caledonian natives – houses of Anglicised magnates, like those Romanised landlords, in ancient Gaul or Burgundy, among whom the reluctant, fastidious bishop Sidonius Apollinaris found himself;[1] and it is only to such houses that I have dared to resort. What news can I bring you thence? Or has Xandra already forestalled me in conveying it? You will have heard, perhaps, of Derek Hill's recent movements. Letters addressed to him started arriving at Bemersyde, and it was therefore supposed, for a time, that he was about to propose himself for a visit; but afterwards Dawyck was asked to forward them to another address, and we learnt that Derek's programme had become very crowded. I understand that the pursuit of pure art has led him to a passionate admiration of the works of Sir Edwin Landseer; and in consequence of this he had found it necessary to go to Balmoral to inspect some of the originals[2] ... And then you will no doubt have heard how the great siege of Floors Castle has at last been raised and the Duchess has marched out with all the honours of war and a substantial slice of the ducal revenues as indemnity.[3] I forget if I kept you up to date in this famous and protracted campaign: how the Duchess, sitting silently at breakfast one day with her morose and boorish spouse, was handed, by a flunkey, a letter upon a silver salver; which, when slit open with an armigerous paper-knife, proved to be a communication from the Duke's lawyers ordering her to leave the castle forthwith – such being a husband's rights according to Scots law; and how, when the Duchess declined to comply except after the negotiation of an adequate economic settlement, the Duke proceeded to starve her out; whereupon the Duchess retreated to a distant wing of that vast and hideous mausoleum and, from this stronghold, with the assistance of one maid, launched her *défi* and prepared to stand a siege. Then you will have heard how the Duke cut off the water, heat and electricity; and how, when the Duchess contrived to fill a bath with water, as a reservoir from which to draw a carefully measured daily ration, the Duke's agent, a man of feudal obedience and heart of stone, came and pulled up the plug so that the

---

[1] Saint Sidonius Apollinaris, a patrician and senator of Rome, was appointed Bishop of Avenna in 472.
[2] Following Hill's visit to the royal family at Balmoral, BB wrote to Xandra Howard-Johnston (12 October 1953): 'Derek's real mission is to know all the Kings of the earth.'
[3] Lady Mary Crewe-Milnes (b. 1915), the tall, dark and intelligent daughter of the Marquess of Crewe, had married George ('Bobo'), 9th Duke of Roxburghe (1913–1974) in 1935. Subsequently the Duke acquired a girlfriend, Mrs Elizabeth Church (1918–1983), the petite, red-headed, horsy wife of a lieutenant-colonel of the Argyll and Sutherland Highlanders, and in 1952 demanded a divorce. The Roxburghes were divorced in December 1953, and in January 1954 the Duke remarried.

precious fluid gurgled irrevocably away; and how, when Lord Ellesmere[4] furtively conveyed to the captive Duchess a small paraffin-stove (for this, I think, was in February when the gigantic stone rooms and flagged corridors of Floors Castle disponge a dank and penetrating chill), he received from the Duke's lawyer a letter advising him that in the event of Floors Castle being accidentally burnt to the ground in consequence of this dangerous importation, he would be held financially liable; and how, when other relief forces had been turned away by ducal levies, armed with pitchforks, sporrans, skene-dhus, shillelaghs, cabers and other barbarous instruments, Dawyck and Xandra, who, being neighbours, knew of secret approaches to the castle, came by night and fed the Duchess through a crack, while their neighbours the McEwens of Marchmont,[5] through another crack, similarly sustained the heroic maid . . . Well, all is now over, and the Duchess, whom Xandra & I found regaining her strength in another castle, now seems refreshed in spirit, as in pocket, by the victory, while the otherwise unemployed aristocracy of the Borders are busily arranging a new and, it is hoped, less turbulent marriage for her. The Haddingtons are recommending Alan Pryce-Jones, the Duchess of Buccleuch her new *protégé* John Foster (a bounding lawyer and fellow of All Souls).[6] It is not known that either of these gentlemen have been consulted on the matter; but you must understand that the Scottish aristocracy, being accustomed to shift villages across the Atlantic in order to improve their grouse-moors (see the good Marx on the Duchess of Sutherland) sometimes forget about such formalities as consent. No Magna Carta was ever signed on any Caledonian Runnymede.

How calm and orderly, by contrast, is the social life of England! Admittedly, on my return to Oxford, I find myself as effectively expelled from Christ Church as even the Duchess of Roxburghe was from Floors, since the decorators, who ought to have completed their work a week ago, are still busy, or rather squatting, in my rooms. Consequently I am having to picnic a quarter of a mile away, and if ever I wish to replace a collar-stud, or verify a reference, I have to set out, with galoshes and umbrella, across the intervening wastes, equipped to plunge under a tropical jungle of dust-sheets, and there to burrow among inverted cupboards and precariously

---

[4] John Egerton, 5th Earl of Ellesmere (1915–2000), later 6th Duke of Sutherland, lived in the same county as the Roxburghes.

[5] Sir John McEwen (1894–1962), of Marchmont, had a numerous, mischievous and lively family.

[6] (Sir) John Foster (1903–1982) had been since 1924 a Fellow of All Souls, where he was reckoned Isaiah Berlin's only rival as a brilliant conversationalist. A barrister, and since 1945 a Conservative MP, Foster was renowned for his ebullience at parties and prodigious success with women, but he never married.

stacked *pots de chambre*. No wonder all intellectual work is temporarily at a standstill, and instead of ruminating on Roman Catholics I am writing these somewhat diffuse and prolix letters to my friends.

You ask why George Weidenfeld has not approached you, and what other works of merit he has published. Well, he would approach you instantly if he dared, and grasp you in a perhaps inextricable embrace; and he has published Lali Horstmann's *Nothing for Tears*, Rose Macaulay's *Pleasure of Ruins*, Isaiah Berlin's essay on Tolstoy, Peter Quennell's *Spring in Sicily* and many other fashionable works. Maria Bellonci's *Lucrezia Borgia* and Franco Venturi's *Populismo Russo* are shortly to appear in English from his cramped, bulging and feverishly active office in Cork Street. Are you really interested? I mentioned your name to him yesterday, lunching with him and a seedy Swiss[7] who is peddling the literary remains of Martin Bormann. But perhaps before committing yourself you had better obtain a grave and prosaic account of him from his other Oxford author, Isaiah Berlin. At any rate, his affairs are not quite so confused as those of your (and my) publishers Messrs Macmillan, whose once united firm is now atomised into four mutually warring offices which have long given up any interest in books except as convenient missiles for enraged directors to hurl to and fro across the Atlantic at each other's heads.

I must stop. The night of the term is about to close in upon me, and already I hear that ominous noise, the mumble of undergraduates creeping ever nearer, like a returning high tide, after the happy interlude of vacation. When shall I next see you? As you will have seen, the Ashley Clarkes are assuming ambassadorial rank in Rome.[8] Xandra & I are dining with them in London tomorrow and we will urge them to call on you. They should I think be an improvement on their predecessors,[9] – and useful for us. If the complexities of her life allow (it is *very* complex) may I perhaps suggest bringing her out at Xmas? But perhaps she will be child-bound. She is only really free in the school term, and then I am not. And of course there is the Admiral to be considered, who even at this moment is gathering his forces for a carefully planned Trafalgar campaign[10] [...]

---

[7] François Genoud: see T-R's letter of 24 July 1952.
[8] Sir (Henry) Ashley Clarke (1903–1994), British Ambassador in Rome 1953–62, was a connoisseur whose diplomatic efforts in Italy were all the more successful for being cultural rather than economic or political. He had married Virginia Bell of New York, but she left him for the Rome manager of British European Airways. BB wrote of the Clarks: 'He agreeable, good-looking [...] Wife much younger, bird-like, twirling, hopping, twittering' (diary, 29 November 1953).
[9] The previous Ambassadress, Lady Mallet, treated BB 'as if I were a bad smell' (diary, 21 November 1952).
[10] Admiral Howard-Johnston was preparing divorce proceedings against his wife.

Berenson wrote on 5 November, praising Trevor-Roper's essay 'The Gentry 1540–
1640' and soliciting his paper on the Elizabethan aristocracy. 'The Lewis Namiers
are here & he shares my enthusiasm over your Gentry article. Both are good
company & thus far I perceive nothing grumpy & withering about him. On the
contrary most generally enthusiastic.'

8 November 1953   Christ Church, Oxford

My dear BB

I was delighted to get your letter and hear your news, and learn about
the visit of the Namiers: you must have controlled him admirably, because –
except in the presence of the very great – he can be very overpowering! I
think she is charming. I am also delighted that you approve of my article
on *the Gentry*. So far there has been no squeak from the opposition – indeed,
I feel almost ridiculous, having advanced, thus armed and equipped, into
the heart of the enemy's territory only to find it not only undefended but
even unoccupied. There has not been so much as a blow-pipe or an assegai
visible among the bushes, or a fugitive black bottom flickering among the
jungle trees; and the Old Man of the Trees, Tawney himself (who refused
even to see the article before publication), being totally invisible, inaudible
and even unmentioned, is now being dismissed, by the advanced anthro-
pologists of my expedition, as a myth. However, perhaps they are all cooking
up some slogan of defiance in some oracular cave in the unexplored depths
of their country!

As for my article on the Elizabethan Aristocracy, for which you ask,
you shall of course have it.[1] Here it is. Perhaps I should also explain its
circumstances. (I didn't send it to you before because I felt that, though
necessary, it was too negative.)

Stone, the writer whose errors I touch lightly upon in the article, is an
Oxford historian who is, in my opinion (and now, I think, in everyone's
opinion), a charlatan.[2] Energetic, unscrupulous, and impatient, he decided
to get well known quickly; and the terrifying thing is that he succeeded. He
rushed round England & France, attending conferences; pushed himself
before the notice of professors; advertised himself, through his father-in-

---

[1] 'The Elizabethan Aristocracy: an Anatomy Anatomised', *Economic History Review*, 2nd series,
III (1951), pp. 279–98. Described by J.H Hexter as 'a magnificent if terrifying work of destruction'
(*Reappraisals in History* (1961), p. 138) and by John Kenyon as 'one of the most vitriolic attacks
ever made by one historian on another' (*The History Men* (1983), p. 247).
[2] Lawrence Stone (1919–1999), lecturer at University College, Oxford 1947–50, Fellow of Wadham
College, Oxford 1950–63 and Dodge Professor of History at Princeton 1963–90. His books included
Anatomy of the Elizabethan Aristocracy (1948) and *The Crisis of the Aristocracy 1558–1641* (1965).

law, a French medieval historian called Prof. Fawtier, in France;[3] and then wrote articles which, by the triple technique of a challenging thesis (generally a mere exaggeration of a borrowed thesis), a dogmatic *ex-cathedra* style, and a portentous array of documentation – appendices, footnotes, statistics – were taken everywhere, even by the elect, as being important contributions to scholarship. The peak of Stone's career of success was his massive article entitled *The Anatomy of the Elizabethan Aristocracy* – 41 pages of text and 12 pages of statistical appendices – which dominated and almost exclusively filled one number of the official publication of the Economic History Society. In consequence of this article, before which all the professors at once (except J.E. Neale, who remained aloof in contemptuous silence) bowed down in servile adoration, Stone was put on the Council of the Economic History Society and pressed for professorships; the then Professor of Economic History at Oxford (W.K. Hancock) wrote that 'in ten years' time no economic historian in England will be able to hold a candle to Stone';[4] his successor,[5] then at Cambridge, told me when I visited that provincial university that 'to economic historians now there can only be one question of interest, and that is, what is Stone working on now?'; and for another year the Professor of Economic History at Cambridge,[6] who edits the *Economic History Review,* gave pride of place in his journal to every new pronouncement by the oracular Stone. Then I wrote the article of which I am sending you a copy. There were immense difficulties in getting it published – just as there were in getting the article on *the Gentry* published (which was turned down by the Economic History Society and only afterwards accepted when the Council discovered that I had signed a contract to publish it elsewhere!) – but in the end it appeared and the whole Stone myth completely dissolved. Afterward I was sniped at a good deal for having used such heavy guns against poor Stone, whom no one had taken seriously. This argument was especially used by those who (like the Professors of Economic History in Oxford, Cambridge and London) had themselves hailed Stone as the genius of their subject,

[3] Robert Fawtier (1885–1966) held a pre-war chair in medieval history at the University of Bordeaux and a post-war chair at the Sorbonne. He published several editions of medieval charters, deeds and royal accounts, and wrote *Les Capétiens et la France* (1940).

[4] Sir Keith Hancock (1898–1988), Fellow of All Souls 1924–30, Chichele Professor of Economic History at Oxford 1944–9, Director of the Institute of Commonwealth Studies in the University of London 1949–56, Professor of History at the Australian National University 1957–65.

[5] (Sir) John Habakkuk (1915–2002), historian of land and labour markets, Chichele Professor of Economic History and Fellow of All Souls 1950–67, Principal of Jesus College 1967–84, Vice-Chancellor 1973–7.

[6] (Sir) Michael Postan (1899–1981), Fellow of Peterhouse, Cambridge 1935–65, Professor of Economic History at Cambridge 1938–65 and editor of the *Economic History Review* 1934-60.

and who now, in the words of Samuel Butler, when they had made stepping-stones of their dead selves, certainly jumped upon them to some tune. Since my article was published, a curious silence has overcome the previously vociferous Stone. Nothing by him is now published in the learned journals, and professors of history, when his name is mentioned, pretend either not to hear, or not to have heard of his existence. The greatest of modern French historians (in my opinion), – Fernand Braudel, – tells me that he was just about to have a full translation of Stone's article published in his periodical *Annales; Civilisations, Sociétés, Economies* (the best historical periodical in the world) – the article, he explains, had been so unanimously extolled in England and by his own colleague, Stone's father-in-law, Prof. Fawtier; and his thesis was certainly *'une thèse seduisante'* – when the appearance of my article saved him from such an unfortunate act.

Such is the history of my now famous article the *Anatomy Anatomised.* As you will realise, from my previous silence, I don't boast much about it. It was a necessary operation to destroy a charlatan. But I am glad I did it: first, because it was necessary; secondly, because the whole story gave me a vivid experience of the ease with which a charlatan can impose himself even upon those who think themselves the elect; and finally because it was in consequence of the research which I was impelled to undertake in that cause that I first discovered how vulnerable was the other hitherto accepted orthodoxy: the orthodoxy of Tawney; and I feel that through my examination of Tawney's thesis I have been able to advance a constructive (and not merely, as in my *critique* of Stone, a destructive) thesis.

Now let me turn from the guerrilla-warfare of the cloister to the heartier rough-and-tumble of the World. Your papers – even the polite pages of *The Times* cannot entirely conceal the fact – will have shown you that there is now in England a highly farcical witch-hunt against homosexuality: a phenomenon which, it appears, has just been discovered thanks to the arrest, on a charge of importuning (a charge only known, I think, in this puritan country), of Sir John Gielgud, Kt.[7] (Noël Coward's chances of a knighthood have now slumped, of course, to *nil.*)[8] For a fortnight newspapers, clergymen, politicians have been wringing their hands and calling for a *jehâd* or holy war; the *Sunday Pictorial* (which claims to echo the elusive voice of the People) and the *Daily Express* (which only amplifies the

---

[7] The actor John Gielgud (1904–2000), who had been knighted in the Coronation Honours of June 1953, was arrested on 21 October on a charge of soliciting men in a Chelsea lavatory, and fined £10.
[8] Noël Coward's knighthood, which was not gazetted until 1970, is said to have been deferred because of the Gielgud case.

voice of that stern New Brunswick Presbyterian Lord Beaverbrook) have both demanded that all suspected homosexuals be imprisoned for life;[9] Lord Samuel, in the House of Lords, with the Book of Leviticus in one hand and his order-paper in the other, has declared with Sinaitical vehemence that 'the sins of Sodom and Gomorrah are stalking through our land' and has called for a salutary descent of fire and brimstone from Heaven;[10] and the Bishop of Exeter, preaching to the illiterate yokels of the West Country, has invoked the learned disapproval of the Latin Fathers upon their supposed activities.[11] Now, I am told, in the panic fear which has swept through the brotherhood, the plainest of women are finding themselves in great demand, feminine company being, in society, the only protection against grave imputations. Meanwhile, while Frank Pakenham's commission on crime has been converted into a commission on vice,[12] and the police forces of England are concentrating all their activities on boudoir-espionage, all real forms of crime are naturally enjoying a safe boom: girls are being done-in and buried under floor-boards in ever-increasing numbers, cat-burglaries are perpetrated with impunity in every great house, and the Duchess of Buccleuch, afraid to part company even for an instant with such an heirloom, sleeps with her tiara tangled round her toes in bed.[13] The civilised Latin peoples must regard us as *very* odd!

My dear BB, when shall I next see you all? I have a *chance* of coming in December. A friend of mine, who is valuing, for Sotheby's, the treasures of ex-King Farouk in the Abdin Palace, Cairo,[14] has invited me there for Xmas and I am sorely tempted to go. So far, it seems as if nobody from the outer

---

[9] In the *Sunday Express* (25 October), its editor, John Gordon, railed against this 'widespread disease' which 'infects politics, literature, the stage, the Church and youth movements' as well as 'the exotic world of international politics'. A similar refrain was audible in *Sunday Pictorial*, 25 October 1953, p. 5 ('A Page That Faces up to the Shock We Feel When Manliness Deserts a Male').

[10] In the House of Lords, on 4 November, the veteran Liberal politician Viscount Samuel warned 'that the vices of Sodom and Gomorrah, of the cities of the plain, appear to be rife among us. If they spread, if they become common, then retribution will be found, not in earthquake or conflagration but in something much more deadly, an insidious poisoning of the moral sense.'

[11] Robert Mortimer (1902–1976), author of treatises on gambling and private penance, was a former colleague of T-R, having been Canon of Christ Church and Regius Professor of Moral and Pastoral Theology at Oxford until his preferment to the bishopric of Exeter in 1949.

[12] Pakenham had received funding from the Nuffield Foundation in 1953 to conduct a two-year investigation into crime. Although he detached himself from the inquiry during 1954, he wrote a personal account of its work, which Weidenfeld & Nicolson published in 1958 under the title *Causes of Crime*.

[13] Mary ('Molly') Lascelles (1900–1993), who had married the 8th Duke of Buccleuch in 1921, often entertained T-R at her husband's houses.

[14] King Farouk I of Egypt (1921–1965) had been deposed in 1952 by an uprising of the Free Officers Movement subsidised by the CIA. The nineteenth-century Abdin Palace in the centre of Cairo was the official residence of the Egyptian royal family from 1874 until 1952.

world is allowed to see them – the Stevensons (Sir Ralph Stevenson is our ambassador in Cairo) paid me a visit today and they say that they have never got in – and my informant has given me most tempting accounts of them.[15] They are to be sold, apparently, in April; but some of them, and in particular the large collection of 18th century pornographic watches, are apparently going to be destroyed by the puritan military dictator, that Egyptian Cromwell, General Neguib.[16] My plan would be to come to Italy and then go on to Egypt. Xandra is also very anxious to see you all again, and *thinks* that she could come at that time. She is child-bound from 19th December, and I am college-bound till 8th December; but we hope that between these dates we might be able to visit you [...] in what Isaiah calls 'that small but distinguished principality' of I Tatti. [...]

Trevor-Roper visited I Tatti for a second time with Xandra Howard-Johnston for the week beginning 9 December 1953. On 16 December he left for Israel, 'this squalid, bouncing, pioneering, combustible, fascinating country' (letter of 23 December to Nicky Mariano), before returning to I Tatti on 28–9 December. 'He found [Israel] fascinating, but not at all to his liking,' Berenson reported to Hamish Hamilton on 31 December. 'Nor do I understand why he went there – perhaps a secret mission.' Afterwards BB mused in his diary (13 January 1954) about 'how unexpectedly and suddenly the look of people changes. A couple of weeks ago, Hugh Trevor-Roper returned from Israel. Had not been away a fortnight, but came back looking hand-somer, more distinguished, as well as more mature than when he left.'

---

[15] Sir Ralph Stevenson (1895–1977) was Ambassador to Yugoslavia 1943–6, to China 1946–50 and to Egypt 1950–5; and afterwards a local politician and casino director on the Isle of Man.
[16] Mohammed Nagib (1901–1984) led the military coup of July 1952, was installed as Prime Minister and became the first President of Egypt in June 1953; but in November 1954 he was supplanted by another young officer, Colonel Nasser, as Egyptian head of state and president of the Revolutionary Council.

1954

7 February 1954   Christ Church, Oxford

My dear BB

How long, I feel, I have owed you a letter; how rapidly the time has flown since I left I Tatti after that welcome respite from the physical discomfort and boring, earnest, welfare-state conversation of the Judges of Israel! (Incidentally, a glance at the map shows that whereas historic Israel is ruled by the Arabs, modern Israel is the land of the Philistines; but this, like so many other thoughts that occurred to me then, is a thing that I must be careful not to say in the hearing, direct or indirect, of the kind Israeli ambassador who sent me there!) Almost as soon as I got back, I was struck down by a strange disease and was rather ill for about 10 days. Doctors came and drank sherry at my bedside, and learnedly speculated, and inserted into me almost as much penicillin as they absorbed sherry themselves; but they never came to any conclusion except that it was doubtless some strange Palestinian virus, perhaps the Botch of Egypt with which the genial God of the Old Testament so often scared his naughty people.[1] Then, as I began to recover, we agreed that the difficult problem of diagnosis could be ignored, and it was left for Isaiah to identify it afterwards, by some Arabic name which I have since forgotten. He says that it is non-recurrent, so I am satisfied. I was worried at the time lest it should be infectious and lest I should have been dangerously incubating it at I Tatti; but as Nicky's letter of 22nd January announced no such domestic disaster, I was encouraged to suppose that the danger-period was safely past. I do hope so: it would indeed be unforgivable to repay such hospitality by scattering Oriental blights!

Now I will bring you up to date in the dramas that are raging on the Scottish Border and in the shady alcoves of solicitors' offices in Whitehall and Woburn Square. Briefly, the Admiral, discovering by the systematic interception of private letters (really Xandra is *most* incompetent at protecting her correspondence!) first, that a case for cruelty is being prepared against him, and, secondly, that his general and congenital jealousy can now be directed on to me, has decided to get in first. Consequently, without waiting to prepare his case or check his evidence very carefully, he has

---

[1] 'The Lord will smite you with the Botch of Egypt, and with the emerods, and with the scab and the itch': Deuteronomy, 28: 27.

launched a petition for divorce, citing me, and asking for custody of the children. Concurrently with this firm gesture, he has tried to undermine resistance from within, in the hope that we will surrender at the mere blast of the trumpet and thus give him an undefended victory. He has done this in two ways: first, by secret threats and hints to me, conveying, by four different channels, dark insinuations that he has 'something on me', can 'blacken my character', ruin my career, etc. etc., in the hope, presumably, that I will press Xandra not to fight; secondly, by intense public propaganda, in the twittering groves of Borderland, about his impregnable legal position. In particular, he has announced that he has secretly possessed, for the last three years, a large *cache* of Dawyck's private letters to Xandra which he will use to discredit Dawyck if he is produced as a witness – and of course, in the cruelty case, Dawyck is an invaluable witness: indeed the Admiral probably thinks (but if so, he is wrong) that he is the only witness. By these secret insinuations and this open propaganda, the Admiral, though his real position is very weak, hopes to undermine the defences, break into the demoralised citadel, and carry off the children as captives to the cave of his ogress-mother in the Savoy Hotel, Lausanne.[2]

However, as you will perhaps have deduced from the general tone of this *communiqué*, the citadel is far from demoralised. For first, we regard his insinuations and his propaganda as signs of weakness, not strength. If his hand were really strong, the best way of frightening us into surrender would be not to boast about its strength to third parties but to show it to us and thus persuade us of the inutility of resistance. Nor do we think that he can discredit Dawyck, even if he has stolen a lot of his letters. It is true, he may frighten Dawyck – but Dawyck, by a fortunate chance, happens, at this crucial time, to be out of earshot, in Rome; and anyway, since all Xandra's other relatives (with the sole exception of her sister Doria,[3] who is a quisling) have come strongly out in her support, have urged her to fight, and have slammed the door in the Admiral's face when he has tried to visit them and utter his propaganda to them, I think that Dawyck, even if the Admiral's threats reach him, will nevertheless be drawn by family solidarity, if by no other motive, into the witness-box. And secondly, I must admit that we are not much impressed by the Admiral's manifesto; for in his petition of divorce, which is a sworn statement, he has not only contrived to state every fact about Xandra and me incorrectly, but has even given the dates

---

[2] Comtesse Pierre du Breuil St Germain.
[3] Lady Victoria Haig (1908–1993) had been divorced in 1951 from Brigadier Claud Montagu-Douglas-Scott.

of birth of *all three* of his own children incorrectly![4] We feel that even if the worst should come to the worst, he would find it difficult to persuade the Court, in the face of such evidence, that he is a very devoted or attentive father.

So the net result is that we are calling his bluff. We are demanding better and fuller particulars of his charge; have stated that his petition will be resisted; and are going ahead with the cross-petition of cruelty. Meanwhile, there is room for manoeuvre behind the battlefronts. Xandra's morale was high when she was in the south and in touch with our lawyer; but now she is back in Melrose, surrounded by RC peeresses and defeatist neighbours still rocking from the effects of the Admiral's lightning propaganda-campaign in those parts; and of course she misses Dawyck very much. So if you should happen to write to her, do please encourage her.

You will understand that, what with this major campaign, not to speak of a few colonial skirmishes with papists, infuriated by my innocent little article on the English Catholics, and socialists, infuriated by my innocent little broadcast on their philosophical errors,[5] and with being ill, and with having to lecture, I have found my time pretty full and my pupils have had to put up with some very casual attention (but I firmly and conveniently believe that undergraduates really only learn by teaching themselves). So, I'm afraid, have my correspondents. And I have had almost no social life. But I can report that d'Entrèves and Katkov and Isaiah, all of whom I have seen, are flourishing. Owing to his father's death, Isaiah has terminated his stay in America and is now back here: he spends the week here and the week-end with his mother in London. He has also, as a result of his father's death, suddenly found himself the proprietor, managing director and sole shareholder in a business specialising in the export and import of pig's bristles. As you can imagine, Isaiah, gifted though he is, finds himself somewhat at sea among these abstruse, hair-splitting mysteries; so he, like me, although for different reasons, finds himself rather preoccupied.

And now that I have, belatedly I fear, broken my reprehensible silence, I hope I shall hear from you. How are you? I hope you are well. Is spring already appearing at I Tatti? Or are you, like us, in the icy grip of winter? Here for a fortnight we have been icebound, and squeals of dismay have been arising (instantly to be frozen into glacial hieroglyphs on the lips of their utterers) from the habitual dwellers of this soft, dank valley of the

[4]James Howard-Johnston (12 March 1942); Xenia (11 March 1944); Peter (25 September 1950).
[5]T-R's BBC Third Programme radio lecture was printed as 'Human Nature in Politics', *The Listener*, 50 (10 December 1953), pp. 993–5. His replies to his critics were printed in *The Listener* of 14 and 28 January 1954.

Thames. But I, I must admit, delight in it – whether because it dries the air into the semblance of the air of Northumberland, where alone I always flourish, or because, as in rotten meat, the process of physical decay in me is arrested by refrigeration, is a question which I cannot answer. But at any rate, in I Tatti, I am sure, there are none of these violent oscillations to which we are subject. There, as in Elysium, thanks to that ingenious adjustable hot-air-blower whose mechanism I never cease to admire, there comes not rain nor hail nor any snow; and I hope you are all living there a proper Elysian life of even temperature, exquisite regularity and rarefied high-class conversation. Who are the fortunate visitors who come every now and then to commune with those high spirits and seek wisdom from the oracular cave? Do tell me; and tell me of course news of all the other tutelary divinities of the place, especially Nicky, to whom I send my thanks for her kind letter – a welcome document in my illness – and, as to you, and all others at I Tatti, my love. [...]

17 February 1954   Christ Church, Oxford

My dear BB

I was delighted to hear from you,[1] and Xandra tells me that you have written a charming letter to her too, which greatly raises her morale. At present all the peeresses in Scotland are giving her conflicting advice as to how *they* managed *their* divorces, which is very confusing, especially as their recollection is thickly clouded by romantic ignorance of the law. Did I say 'all the peeresses'? Of course I should have said 'all the *Protestant* peeresses'; for half the peeresses of Scotland are sunk in deep, not to say abject, popery, and they of course, are singing another song:

> Comfort's in Heaven, but we are on the Earth
> Where nothing lives but crosses, cares and grief.[2] etc. etc.

However, Lady Haddington, who is either outside the range of logic, or has a Jesuit confessor, or is a better friend than papist, has quietly told her Protestant lawyer to offer to Xandra's lawyer any help that may be necessary and has even instructed him to say that she will, if necessary, give evidence; so I am feeling more warmly to her now!

---

[1] BB had recently written that he felt 'the deepest and most affectionate interest' in the divorce proceedings, and asking to be kept informed.
[2] Spoken by the Duke of York in Act II, scene ii of Shakespeare's *Richard II*.

The other day I sent you a book; Gerald Brenan's *Face of Spain*.[3] You may remember that I sang its praises and crammed it down your throat (as Logan would say), at I Tatti; I will tell you about the author, who is a hero of mine, and the book.

I know nothing about his origin. I suppose, from his name, he is Irish – though his mind isn't and he is a Protestant. I think he fought in the First World War, and then, for reasons of health, went to Spain, where he farmed in the uplands near Granada. I know nothing about his education. I suspect that he was not formally well educated – he gives the impression of being a man of intense self-education, who has been driven to study deeply everything that he has studied through a passionate, almost puritan love of the truth, or rather (perhaps I should say) hatred of inadequate or evasive or second-hand answers. Possibly he was at an English public school (socially he is of the educated class) and went early to the war and took to intellectual things with the intensity born of known belatedness. At all events, I am sure that even so he never intended to write anything. He just farmed above Granada and studied Spanish history and life and literature and got to know it as no foreigner seems to me ever to have known it. Furthermore, he knows it as Doughty knew Arabia: both loving and hating it. I don't believe people can really *know* a country unless they *both* love it *and* hate it: the words at any rate of Englishmen Italianate and the Englishmen Hispaniolized (I have just discovered this expression used by Sir Walter Raleigh) and Englishmen Arabicised seem to me very superficial because, in their appreciation, they swallow everything and dehumanise the countries of their choice. But Brenan, though he is by choice or residence a Spaniard, has never ceased to look at Spain with critical English eyes; and, compared with him, the professional RC Hispanophiles seem to me of an incomparable triviality.

Then, in 1936, came the Spanish Civil War, and at once there arrived in Spain a host of Left-wing English intellectuals who brought out to that African society, with its incomprehensible complexity, their ready-made Marxist formulae which they hastily applied to Spanish society and then sent back, interspersed with a few Spanish words, to their London papers. This went tediously on for three years; then suddenly, in 1939, there was published Brenan's book, *The Spanish Labyrinth*.[4] It is really an astonishing

---

[3] T-R had initiated his correspondence with Gerald Brenan (1894–1987) in 1951. He wrote to him (11 March 1968): 'Ever since I read *The Spanish Labyrinth*, I have looked upon you as my ideal historian – you *see* the past in the present, and the present in the past, imaginatively, and yet with corrective scholarship, and you express it in perfect prose – and I would rather write for you than anyone else.'

[4] *The Spanish Labyrinth* was first published in 1943, but covers the period to 1939.

work. The richness of the historical knowledge, the heroic intellectual integrity, the rejection of all ready-made formulae, the monumental learning behind it, the burning lucidity of the style – it made everything else written on Spain seem pitifully shoddy. I was immensely impressed on reading it: there is still nothing like it; and although it ostensibly deals with the Civil War of 1936–9 only, I make my best pupils studying 16th & 17th century Spain read it, for I think there is more profound analysis of 16th century Spain between the lines of Brenan's book than in the explicit statements of any work written directly on the subject.

Brenan has since told me how he wrote it. He says that he was driven to write it by indignation: indignation not with the Right – they of course were wrong, but, as he says, one *expects* the Right to be wrong and is not irritated by their errors or concerned to go round correcting them – but with the Left, who ought not to have been such fools. The amount of work which he did for it was phenomenal. For instance, I know that to explain Spanish anarchism he worked through the majestic collection of anarchist literature – the completest collection in the world – in Amsterdam. When he had finished, I suppose he had worked off his indignation: anyway, he said he was never going to consider Spanish politics again: he was only interested in literature. He wrote two wonderfully good essays on St John of the Cross in *Horizon* during the war (nos. 88 & 89), and an extraordinarily good *History of Spanish Literature* after the war. The little travel book which I have sent to you was written in 1949. From about 1937 until a year ago he was living in England, in Wiltshire. At that time he told me that he had finished with Spain and was never going back there. But in the winter of 1952, when I visited him in England, he had changed his mind, and since the beginning of last year he has been living in his house in Churriana, near Málaga, working on a book on St Teresa. I had been thinking of going out there to stay with him this spring: to me he is almost the BB of Spain, the ever-fresh fountain of understanding in that difficult land; and as you will have gathered from my language, I have an enormous intellectual respect for him. But I now think I shall be arguing in the divorce-courts, not in his pleasant Andalusian garden, at that time.

Well, this is the mind, or rather my version of the mind, whose casual by-product I have sent you. I hope you won't disagree too much with my interpretation!

Now I must stop. Midnight is long past. Best wishes to all of you. I will write to Nicky shortly with, I hope, the latest news of the Admiral, who is still, in the words of our lawyer, 'seeking for the evidence he professed to have'. Do keep me supplied with the always interesting news of I Tatti.

On 17 March Hamish Hamilton reported to Berenson that Trevor-Roper and Xandra Howard-Johnston had been recent guests at their house, 'and after dinner took Yvonne aside and Told All. I gather that you are not only conversant but have been aiding and abetting. A very good cause, as we both feel that marriage will make Hugh more human and perhaps a soupçon *less malicious. Yvonne is prepared to wager large sums (which she hasn't got, so I wouldn't advise anyone to venture) that Hugh has never slept with anyone, and wonders what your views are.' BB replied on 20 March: 'Naughty Yvonne's guess about Hugh may hit the mark. More women than men, and all Italian women, smell a virgin male afar.' A month later (24 April) Hamilton gave Berenson another glimpse: 'Hugh T-R came to dinner, and was in sparkling form, challenging, mischievous, confiding about his matrimonial projects and complications, and evidently revelling in the whole situation.'*

30 March 1954   **Christ Church, Oxford**

My dear Nicky,

How are you all? I long to hear news of I Tatti, which must be enjoying now the beginning of spring. How I wish I could visit you at this time of year! But I must be content to listen at second hand to travellers' tales. As you can imagine, life is rather complicated at present. I forget what the state of affairs was when I last wrote. At present all is total uncertainty and suspense. The Admiral, fortified by a huge and most damaging haul of my private letters, has now launched a petition in which he quotes huge extracts, including as many names as he can work in, just to spread the damage as widely as possible; we have built up a case of cruelty (always difficult owing to the absence or natural reluctance of witnesses); the Admiral has declared an economic blockade, cutting off Xandra's money in the hope that she will give up the children through incapacity to pay the nurse's wages; Xandra, however, by some brisk operations on the London stock-market (she has shown a speculative agility you could hardly credit her with) has kept the beleaguered garrison alive so far; the Admiral, through devious channels, has suggested a compromise – either no divorce at all or a divorce in ten years' time (!); the situation has been enlivened by the desertion to us by a few small craft from the Admiral's flotilla and by a broadside, which has seriously disconcerted him, from Admiral-of-the-Fleet Lord Mountbatten,[1] from which a sulphurous cloud still hangs over the entire battlefield; the lawyers on opposite sides silently and

---

[1] Louis Mountbatten, 1st Earl Mountbatten of Burma (1900–1979), ex-Viceroy of India, was at this time Commander-in-Chief of the Mediterranean Fleet. Howard-Johnston was chief of staff to the flag officer in central Europe.

anonymously rake in their casual spoils as each wrecked reputation drifts blazing by; and, as at Jutland, both sides implausibly claim some kind of a victory. Meanwhile of course all scholarship, research, reading, writing, etc., is indefinitely suspended.

In the midst of these tense operations I was suddenly disconcerted by an imperious *ukase* from my slave-owner, the *Sunday Times*. I was ordered to Germany. I had no desire to go: I didn't wish to avow my reasons; I didn't wish (in view of ever-growing lawyers' bills) to quarrel with that useful source of income. What was I to do? I decided to face the Editor, an economist, formerly a Fellow of All Souls, grey-haired, grey-faced, grey-souled and grey-minded.[2] I went to London and lunched with him in the grey air of the Athenæum. I explained that to go to Germany at this moment was very difficult: my health, my work, my plans, etc. . . . I saw that I was getting nowhere. So then I began to explain how inconvenient it would prove for *them*. Over my potted shrimps I deployed an almost evangelical eloquence. I felt I was making an impression: the project was evaporating from the grey mind of the editor, and a total vacuity was replacing it. However, I knew well that editorial minds, like Nature (which they do not otherwise much resemble), abhor a vacuum: if I left it at that, the German project, temporarily dispersed, would soon re-enter that uncomfortable void and there condense again, ten times more dreadful and deform. So I decided boldly to block re-entry by filling the void with another project. Feeling desperately in my mind for the nearest idea, I hit on the grim thought of Israel, and I suddenly became, over a mutton cutlet, enormously eloquent on that boring subject. The result was a triumph. I am *not* going to Germany; but I have had to pay for my escape by writing on Israel instead; so now all other work is suspended while I try to recapture those happily lost impressions of virtuous discomfort in an East-European social-democracy planted incongruously in the valleys of Philistia and the hills of Judaea.

But I am determined not to be nearly so entertaining at the expense of Israel as I feel (through a romantic haze, no doubt) that I was in January. In this critical posture of my affairs I have decided, for a time at least, to make *no more enemies*, only friends. I seem recently to have made an enemy of my old friend, or at least contemporary, Philip Toynbee (see *Sunday Times* of recent date).[3] Do you know him? Has he ever been to I Tatti? I

[2] Henry Hodson (1906–1999), Fellow of All Souls 1928–35 and editor of the *Sunday Times* 1950–61.

[3] Philip Toynbee (1916–1981) had been a history scholar at Christ Church and first Communist president of the Oxford Union. Subsequently a book reviewer, novelist and poet.

suspect not; but if he has, you would not have forgotten, for he would indubitably have smuggled a whisky-bottle into his bathroom, fallen down the stairs before dinner, and perhaps seduced Augusta afterwards.[4] He is the son of our famous English prophet, the Apostle of the Half-Baked, Arnold Toynbee, whose ten volumes on the Philosophy of History are often referred to (though less often read) in the Middle West of America. But it is on the female side that the eccentricities have descended. In order to produce Philip, Arnold Toynbee married the daughter of that distinguished Hellenist, Gilbert Murray;[5] in order to produce Mrs Toynbee, Gilbert Murray married the daughter of the 9th Earl of Carlisle; and in order to produce Lady Mary Murray, the 9th Earl of Carlisle married that famous priestess of temperance, the teetotal Countess of Carlisle, who, on her husband's death, signalised her emphatic detestation of the Demon Drink by emptying thousands of hogsheads of choicest hock and claret (the contents of the nobleman's cellars) over the battlements of Naworth Castle into the medieval moat.[6] You see the rest: it follows automatically. The 10th Earl of Carlisle, understandably piqued at his mother's free and easy way with the family wine-cellars, solaced himself with bought and borrowed bottles; and his mother, in indignation, contrived to divert the inheritance of Castle Howard to her obediently teetotal daughter, the Lady Mary (who fobbed it off on a younger brother). Lady Mary introduced her passionate hatred of alcohol into the Murray household in which, when I was an undergraduate, I had many a glass of lemonade; and two of her sons died of drink.[7] Her daughter, Mrs Toynbee, drowned her mind in an even more potent and permanent narcotic: she was converted to Popery. And her son, Philip, that sad, bohemian intellectual of the *Observer*, has consequently oscillated all his life between Drink and Dogma, between Bolshevism and the Bottle. How rash of me to have provoked (so soon after my encounter with the similarly enflamed doctrinaire Evelyn Waugh) that formidable combination of intoxicants.

Thus you see the zigzag progress of my life, buffeted from day to day by

---

[4] Augusta Pratesi was Nicky Mariano's personal maid.
[5] Gilbert Murray (1866–1957), Regius Professor of Greek at Oxford 1908–36, had married Lady Mary Howard (1865–1956). BB had first met him in 1888, and they maintained occasional contact for seventy years. A militant teetotaller, Murray challenged the legality of selling wines and spirits at Christ Church, and tried to prohibit undergraduates from using motor-cars because they facilitated fornication. This proposal was defeated in the Hebdomadal Concil by the counter-argument that if undergraduates wished to fornicate, they could as easily use trains.
[6] Rosalind Stanley (1845–1921) married George, 9th Earl of Carlisle. She was ostracised in London society for her tactless preaching of Irish Home Rule, and became president of the British Women's Temperance Association.
[7] Denis Murray (1892–1930) and Basil Murray (1902–1937).

enraged husbands, enraged papists, exacting editors, inebriated Bolsheviks. Oh for the calm of I Tatti, that earthly Jerusalem (but no, in the circumstances that would be the wrong image), that other Eden, demi-Paradise. [...]

PS. I met Sylvia the other day at a party given by my brother. Later, seeing her standing alone & Rose Macaulay also standing alone, I buzzed up, full of eagerness to show my social utility, and introduced them to each other. At once there was a noise as of nuclear fission, and they sprang apart with a loud hissing noise and furious gestures. Alas, I don't move in the literary world, don't really know what is going on in those pastoral alcoves. It seems (too late I learnt it) that Rose Macaulay had written a book, and Sylvia had reviewed it![8]

Berenson replied from I Tatti on 21 February that in 1933 he had read Brenan's picaresque novel Jack Robinson. *'The book touches bottom as far as I ever had read. My only objection was that the bottom so very often was of a slop-pail. But I have never forgotten it, & got many readers to it. I fear few admired it as I did.'*

22 May 1954   Christ Church, Oxford

My dear BB

How long it is since I had one of those ever-welcome letters from I Tatti! But whose fault is that? I ask myself; and uneasily I answer that it must certainly be mine. So now I am taking my pen to wipe away, as I hope, that reproach and elicit from you, I also hope, some news of you and Nicky. A little, of course, dribbles through. I understand you have been in Venice; but tell me more. Now I suppose you are at I Tatti. Would that I were there, as the hymnologist says. I imagine the water running in your stream as sinners enviously imagine the comforts of paradise – which (St Augustine tells us) only increases the malicious self-satisfaction of the saints. Meanwhile I can tell you little of movement here, for I have not moved. I think I told you how I avoided being sent to Germany in March by writing up my views on Israel from January. I did indeed go to Northumberland for a few days in April, and saw Xandra – owing to the fact that I can't be seen with her in my home county of Northumberland, or she with me in her home county of Roxburgheshire, we had to meet in a lonely spot in the

---

[8] T-R had first met the novelist (Dame) Rose Macaulay (1881-1958) as a fellow guest of Pearsall Smith's. Her most recent book, *The Pleasure of Ruins*, had been published by Weidenfeld & Nicolson in 1953.

Lammermuirs. Otherwise I have been in Oxford, as it seems, ever since I left your hospitable doors in January.

As for *things*, they haven't moved much more than persons; but they have moved a bit. The Admiral continued to show confidence – indeed a kind of tyrannical confidence – until March. Then, quite suddenly, since our morale seemed to hold out, his seemed to give in. He was summoned to Malta to see Mountbatten (of whom he stands greatly in awe); he discovered some facts which showed that the cruelty case was not bluff; he appears to have been in some way reprimanded or threatened by Mount-batten; and then, quite suddenly he offered to surrender on all fronts provided that no cruelty case were brought and provided that the public record appeared in his favour. That is, whereas he will not *grant* custody of the children, which would make the public record wear an unsatisfactory look, he will not *apply* for it, and so there will be no court order, and behind the scenes he will arrange a practical surrender. He is even prepared to pay his own costs provided that it doesn't publicly look as if he had done so. Thus (if all goes well) there will be no battle, he will have the form, and we the substance of victory. Of course it hasn't been all as smooth as my narrative suggests: *Nervenkrieg* and *Blitzkrieg* have been his weapons throughout: he has even tried to have Xandra summoned from Scotland, at a few hours' notice, before a court in London – a summons was delivered to her out of a clear sky although he had actually telephoned her the previous night and given no inkling of this manoeuvre either to her or to her lawyer: and there is still time for things to go wrong; but in general the tendency is in the right direction, and now that the children have in fact, under all kinds of legal safeguards, been abroad & spent part of the holidays with him, I think that the parties are adjusting themselves. Meanwhile, although I am keeping some control over publicity in Oxford and North-umberland, we are no longer concerned to suppress the facts, and indeed in London they are well known, so I expect all our common friends know everything and there is no longer any ban on any conversation.

I said that I had escaped from Germany; but not, I think, for long. I think I shall certainly have to go back in August. The awful thing about Germany is that although I really dislike it, I am irresistibly drawn back to it. I don't like the people; their conversation bores me; their tastes, their pleasures, their language, their scholarship all seem to me coarse and dreary; their food is dreadful; and although I like their wine, it is simpler and cheaper for it to come to me than for me to go to fetch it. But one can't get away from their politics which alternately threaten and fascinate, and I suppose I must go. And if one must go, what can one do to mitigate the tedium of the place? What pleasures are there in those gross provincial towns in Saxony and Bavaria, those Cyclopean factory-cities of the Ruhr, and the now irremediably Americanised Heidelberg? I once went to a wonderful performance of *Fidelio* in Berlin, in 1950; but otherwise I can remember, in Germany, no pleasure, no, none at all. How much I would prefer Italy, Greece, Spain ... but I suppose I must go. But perhaps I shall be able to slip down into Austria, perhaps even to Italy, for a rest from that thick caliginous northern air. Would I then find you perched up upon your eyrie at Vallombrosa?

And now what can I tell you of English affairs? What indeed that has not already reached you from your more regular correspondents here: for doubtless the Hamiltons have kept you in touch with every gesture and vacillation of the *beau monde* in which they so feverishly gyrate. I sometimes think they are like teetotums whom only social momentum keeps upright, ceaselessly spinning in their not always appropriately assembled collections of inkwells and coronets. And as for Jamie's great rival, George Weidenfeld, who captured I Tatti by his charm, he, I fear, is about to decline in the publishing world. So if George Weidenfeld is pressing you for your next work, don't leap *too* eagerly into his arms just yet!

Now I must stop. This has not, I think, been a very interesting letter. But when I stop to think, I am really astonished that I ever put pen to paper to write any letters at all after the dreadful Incident. Have I described to you that nadir of my recent fortunes? If not, I will do so. It was quite an episode, I need hardly say, in the long war of manoeuvre against the Admiral. I knew, of course, that the Admiral had contrived to steal one or two of my letters; and one day I contrived to ensure that copies of these intercepted letters should be sent to my lawyer. When this had been done, I went to my lawyer's office to glance through them and see the extent of the damage. With gay and nimble tread, spurning the sedentary lift, I gambolled up the office stairs and asked for the documents. Then, what a shock I received! Did I say 'one or two'? What seemed a whole book, the bulk of an American doctoral thesis, was placed in my hands. I took and read: at least two dozen letters, sometimes 16 or 20 pages long, had been captured and had now been copied by typists, and distributed from secretary to secretary in two solicitors' offices, and passed to Counsel, and ruminated over by clerks. My heart sank as I read. It took the whole morning to read them. I must admit that sometimes I was forced to laugh – there were some particularly happy passages about the Admiral which must have given less pleasure to him than to me – but more often the solemn silence of that legal office was broken by deep and dismal groans. The intimacies, the personalities, the gossip and scandal of those now copied and circulated letters appalled me, as it appals me still in retrospect. How does one know who may have read them? After all, Xandra's niece works in a solicitor's office. How can I be sure, I asked, that the Bishop of Exeter may not have a niece in the office of Messrs Vertue, Churcher and Gush (for this, believe it or not, is the name of the Admiral's solicitors)? And then how shall I face the Bishop again after that happy turn which I had done, describing him extenuating over the port the sins he had been denouncing from the pulpit? And then there were those intimate observations about the private life of the Duchess of B ...¹ and those irreverent speculations about X, Y, Z ... I assure you that from that day I went into a deep decline, and resolved never to write a personal letter again. However, as you see, I have now recovered a certain capacity although Xandra assures me that my letters to her have never been the same since that day. [...]

'I never begin a letter to you', Nicky Mariano wrote from Venice on 25 May, 'without having to say that I am deeply ashamed of myself for having left one of your wonderful epistles unanswered for months [...] In your case my belated answer procures me the enjoyment of rereading your letter and of laughing again over your priceless description of Philip Toynbee and his background. I have never met him but heard of him, as he is a great friend of Ben Nicolson's. Various astonishing accounts of his original behaviour have reached us from other quarters. Which makes me think of the Sunday Times and its editor, one answering to the name of Stodson; highly recommended by Raymond Mortimer and John Russell, and I wonder if he corresponds to the person described in your letter as 'grey-haired, grey-faced, grey-souled and grey-minded'? If so, I feel rather relieved that we are missing him in Florence, and that Alda and Luisa have the privilege of receiving him at I Tatti. [...] we saw in Florence just before leaving, Hamish Hamilton, and both he and his wife spoke with great appreciation of you but also with a certain concern of the Admiral's attitude and Xandra's difficult position. The same I heard from Lady Ashley Clarke whom we met a few days ago in Casa Cini at lunch. I gather from all this that the whole affair has become common property and that too alarms me. Lady Clarke seemed to think that Xandra would never manage to get a divorce from the horrible admiral and might lose her children as well.'

28 May 1954   Christ Church, Oxford

Dearest Nicky,

But I never *expect* you to answer letters! I know how busy you must be with all your more official letters and all those guests, so I write to you

---

¹The Duchess of Buccleuch was enjoying *une amitié amoureuse* with Alan Pryce-Jones whose earliest known sexual experiences, according to Robert Blake, had been with John Betjeman.

(when I do, which I'm afraid isn't very often) without expecting any reply, and any reply which comes, like your letter which I have just received today, brings all the added delight of an unexpected pleasure! I greatly enjoyed reading it and getting news of you and BB. I wrote to BB a few days ago, at I Tatti, but I will write and tell you all I can too, in case I left anything out, although nothing significant has happened since then.

I don't think the position is nearly as black as Jamie Hamilton and Virginia Clarke have suggested. *On the face of it* all looks promising, the Admiral, as I told BB, having apparently undertaken to surrender on all points of substance in exchange for a victory on points of form. It all depends really on his *bona fides*, and to judge that we must know what is going on in his mind. This, unfortunately, we don't know; but I have my suspicions. I have some reason to suspect that Mountbatten has led the Admiral to think that he *may* get another command (I think that he hinted at a hypothetical possibility in Indo-China), but that he certainly *won't* do so if he causes trouble in this matter; and that it is this hint which has caused the Admiral, whose sole interest is in the promotion of which he had, until then, despaired, to change his tune so suddenly – especially when it became clear to him that he really would have to face a cruelty case unless he agreed on terms. If this reasoning is correct, then it would seem that all may now go well.

The only danger that I can see is that the Admiral may be playing for time, showing a conciliatory spirit to protract negotiation and postpone a battle until he knows whether he will be promoted or (as seems more likely) not. But his own lawyer has told our lawyer that if the Admiral tries to cheat, he, the lawyer, will refuse to represent him any longer. The fact that the lawyer can say this suggests that he doesn't altogether exclude the possibility by his client; but on the other hand I think that it is also some guarantee that the Admiral's tendency to cheat, if it is there, will be controlled. So on the whole we are optimistic.

I wonder if I was unfair to Hodson (not Stodson!), the editor of the *Sunday Times*? Perhaps he is not as grey as I suggested. Perhaps I look for too much superficial vitality in people and neglect the sterling qualities that lurk behind many a dispiriting mien and manner. Perhaps I ... but, oh dear! How dangerous it is to began the never-ending process of intro-spection which is so often cut short by lunacy, suicide, or – what is a blend of them both – religious conversion! Suffice it then to say that Hodson has always *seemed to me* a typical editor of a respectable Sunday paper: harassed, unadventurous, methodical, perpetually tired, completely unoriginal, without personality, thoroughly familiar with the stretch of railway along which he travels in regular, hygienic, *Times*-reading comfort between his

The teacher – Trevor-Roper at the end of Michaelmas Term of 1950.

The traveller – Trevor-Roper flies into New York in 1949.

Above: The broadcaster – Lord Samuel, Trevor-Roper, Bertrand Russell and Norman Fisher discuss 'The Limits of Tolerance' on the BBC radio programme *London Forum*, February 1950.

Below: The controversialist – A. J. Ayer and Trevor-Roper listen to Arthur Koestler at the Congress of Cultural Freedom in Berlin, June 1950. Franz Borkenau stands behind them.

Trevor-Roper at work in his rooms in Christ Church in the mid-1950s.

Robert Blake conferring with Trevor-Roper in the same room.

Berenson working at I Tatti in 1948: he was in bed when he wrote many of his scrawling letters to Trevor-Roper.

Opposite page: Nicky Mariano reading aloud to Berenson at I Tatti in 1948: on high days she read and reread a fresh new letter from Trevor-Roper.

Xandra and Hugh Trevor-Roper on a Christ Church roof in August 1957 during his final month as a Student of the college.

Opposite page: Berenson and Nicky Mariano strolling in the grounds of I Tatti in 1948.

Above: The Trevor-Ropers outside Marylebone Presbyterian Church, 4 October 1954. 'We determined to stop the mouth of criticism by having a proper church wedding.'
Below: Chiefswood, 'the only Regency house in the Borders, built in 1820 by Sir Walter Scott for his daughter', where the Trevor-Ropers lived 1959–87.

The Library at I
Tatti, where Trevor-
Roper worked with
grateful happiness.

Berenson at his
desk in 1957.

Berenson, aged 92, contemplates a sculpture at I Tatti in 1957.

Opposite page: Berenson in 1953. 'We must look and look and look till we live the painting and for a fleeting moment become identified with it,' he had recently written.

Trevor-Roper gossiping with Randolph Churchill and Young Winston outside the Oxford Divinity School on the Chancellorship election day, 5 March 1960.

Harold Macmillan being toasted by Brasenose hearties after his installation as Chancellor of Oxford University in April 1960.

country house and his London flat, a member of the Athenæum, unhappy at gay parties in the *beau monde*; happy only when he is going through the familiar motions of solemnly stroking his nose before uttering a cautious but obediently accepted statement in his deferentially approached, conventionally furnished office. But of course it is always there, or in the Athenæum, that I have met him, and perhaps, when he is in the country, or on holiday, he breaks out. I try to envisage him in moments of rapture: struggling with a 30 lb salmon, reciting Swinburne on a mountain-top, swept off his feet by Padre Pio or a Punch-and-Judy Show ... but no: somehow I can't. Do tell me (if you meet him) whether I am really quite wrong.

I also had doubts after I had written to you about Philip Toynbee. Someone told me that he was now reformed, and I reflected that although the last time I saw him he was, as on all previous occasions, totally drunk, that was some years ago; and perhaps I ought not to have assumed that he is unchanged. However, he came to Oxford the other day, and all is well: I mean, my generalisation still applies. The details do not need recording.

I wish I was in Venice – at least while you and BB are there. The first time I visited it, how wonderful I found it! But I must admit that on my last visit I was rather put off by the crowd of stout, loud-voiced, summer-suited Americans who filled the Piazza San Marco and fought for access to that wayside shrine of the transatlantic tourist, the American Express Office [...]

8 September 1954   Christ Church, Oxford

My dear BB

I feel very remiss. Yes, I owe you a letter and have done so, I fear, for a long time. Well, here it is and I will tell you the latest developments.

Xandra is divorced. The admiral has surrendered. In return for a victory of form, he has surrendered all points of substance. He was a not a minute too soon, as Xandra discovered that he has been living for the last two years (i.e. since he got the post in Fontainebleau) with an Egyptian woman resident in Lausanne! Nor is that the only thing that she has discovered. However, the essential thing was to win on substance, not on form, so we didn't boggle at that, and now all is over. We contrived to control publicity fairly successfully, and I expect I shall have to control certain clerical rumblings from the Chapter here; but I am confident all will be well. We hope (unless there are legal objections, which we don't anticipate) to be married on 4th October.[1] We would invite you and Nicky, but as we know you couldn't come, we merely ask that you attend in spirit the select party which Dawyck is giving for us on that occasion. Xandra has promised not to prevent me from working, so you must entertain no fears on that account: I hope still to study a little and write a little, in spite of matrimony!

Now you are up to date in our affairs: bring us up to date in yours. How are you both? I hope you are well, enjoying the clear air of Vallombrosa. What visitors ascend that pilgrim-trodden mountain and commune with the Oracle in that comfortable cave? Whom have you seen from the dwindling *beau monde* of the Western World?

But no: you are not yet an Oracle; or rather, there is still an Oracle more oracular than you can hope, or indeed (I think) would wish to be. I have today received the last four volumes of Arnold Toynbee's great 10-volume work on *History*. My dear BB, do not let it reach you! Keep it at bay! Deny it any foothold in the incorruptible Biblioteca Berensoniana! I'm afraid that portentous mind has now become totally unhinged. My eyes popped as I read. The egotism is quite unbelievable. There are 30 pages of acknowledgements – 'to Marcus Aurelius, who taught me to bear greatness with humility' etc. etc. Endless trivial details about the infant experiences of 'the writer of this study' (like those *minutiae* of the childhood of Jesus elaborated by pious Franciscans in the 14th century) in order to show how the great mind was formed. And all pretence at scientific method now thrown overboard. Toynbee has now become a Seer. He assures us that he knows what he is talking about (which is incidentally the most arrant rubbish) because he has six times been carried off into the past, 'rapt into a momentary communion' with ancient events, and once even 'directly aware of the passage of History gently flowing through him in a mighty current, and of his own life welling like a wave in the flow of this vast tide'. After that, of course, there is no need of argument: what he says, goes. He compares himself with Ezekiel; and I must say that his language is often as unintelligible.

I have got to review this rubbish. What *can* I say?[2]

Xandra and I have been to Austria for a holiday after the battle. We took the car and looked at baroque churches and rococo palaces in Austria and Bavaria; and just to ensure that she varied the diet with a dash of reality, I took her also to a couple of German concentration camps: grim prisons

---

[1] They were married on 4 October 1954 at St Marylebone Presbyterian Church, George Street, London.
[2] T-R indicted Toynbee for 'intellectual hanky-panky' and 'a terrible perversion of history' ('Testing the Toynbee System', *Sunday Times*, 17 October 1954).

where gas-chambers and crematoria, morgues and gibbets are still preserved by the Occupying Powers as a reminder to the scowling natives – who, of course, would pull them down and bury them if they could. We were very unsocial, avoided both Vienna and Salzburg, and visited no one except the Hofmannsthals,[3] whom perhaps you know. We have been back about a fortnight (Xandra is now in Scotland with her children); and I found your letter on my return. I am now alone, leading a hermit's life at Oxford, writing my book on the English Roman Catholics, and also an essay to be published in a *Festschrift* for Namier, to celebrate his 68th birthday, or his retirement, or his 17th rejection for a chair at Oxford, or some such recurrent anniversary. It is on *Oliver Cromwell and his Parliaments* (a suitable offering, I thought, for the historian of parliament and dictator of English historical study!).

Now you are up to date in the bare skeleton of our lives. What more can I tell you? Alas, nothing: my eremitical life has kept me away from the great world in which gossip is interchanged. Why, I don't even know what happened to Freya Stark and Derek Hill in darkest Armenia; I haven't seen a publisher, or even a *déracinée* Mayfair countess, for months; I haven't even been to Edinburgh, that new summer metropolis of our island. So I look to the sociable Florentines for news, and all I can send you in return is, at present, this bare chronicle, to save the remnants of my reputation (if I ever had one) as a faithful correspondent. [...]

24 October 1954   Christ Church, Oxford

My dear BB

Oh how scandalously out of date is all my correspondence![1] I suppose you were beginning to think that it had ceased altogether. But no, it was only in suspense during a period of vertiginous reorganisation, and now, though slightly shamefacedly in view of my omissions, I resume it and will seek to bring it up to date again. I think I last wrote to you towards the end of September, telling you that Xandra and I were being married on 4th

---

[3] The T-Rs lunched on 4 August at Zell-am-see with Raimund von Hofmannsthal (1906–1974), the dashing son of BB's friend Hugo von Hofmannsthal, the Austrian poet, playwright and librettist. In London he sold advertising for *Time Life* magazine, at whose expense he gave brilliant dinner-parties. His wife, Lady Elizabeth Paget (1916–1980), the intelligent, beautiful daughter of the Marquess of Anglesey, was admired, or adored, by many famous men. 'Raimund von Hofmannsthal was a man of incandescent aesthetic feeling,' Isaiah Berlin wrote. 'His view of Society was of a piece with this: he saw human beings in aesthetic and emotional terms – Society, the great world, was, to him, a stage, a pageant, a dream or a nightmare' (*The Times*, 26 April 1974).
[1] Two letters from BB dated 15 September and 15 October had been left unanswered.

October and soliciting your good wishes on that day. Well, I will now give you a brief summary of the events since then.

First of all, on the diplomatic front all is well. Xandra has the children; the Admiral has surrendered; the lawyers have fixed the details; and there have been no hitches. The Admiral had the children over in France for three weeks or a month in the summer, but so far from kidnapping them, he put them in a hotel in Normandy and only bothered to visit them twice; so no great possessiveness on his part is to be feared in future. I think he only pretended an interest in them while the battle was on, and now that the battle for the divorce is over, he has dropped the interest which he had assumed as a matter of tactics only. The children themselves seem to have accepted everything with perfect equanimity. The Admiral, we are told, has now given up his Egyptian mistress and has proposed marriage to the young daughter of a Parisian dress-designer, who, at the moment, is considering her reply. As a tactical move, he has first taken the precaution of deleting from *Who's Who* all references to either his first or his second marriage. He will thus be able to pose to his third victim as an eligible bachelor.

Our wedding was successfully organised. Here too certain tactical preparations were judged necessary. As a matter of general philosophy, I have long ago come to the conclusion that in all doubtful situations it pays to attack, or at least to keep the flags flying. In accordance with this general rule, we decided to launch a general defiance against such elements in English society as showed a tendency to disapprove of our affairs. The clergy, for instance, and the Roman Catholics, and certain academic doubters, and certain defenders of strict morality on either side of the Cheviot Hills ... And then there was a certain head of an Oxford College, whom I had thought a personal friend, and to whom I had written telling him the facts in advance, but who declared, in reply (not to me but to a friend), that he did not intend to commit himself until he saw which way the other grave academic cats had jumped ... Well, we decided to make the first cat jump our way by a little preliminary conditioning and a sharp word of command, confident that a general landslide of unanimous unthinking secondary cats would follow its lead. In this I think we were pretty successful.[2]

The first step was to prevent publicity of Xandra's divorce, which was usefully timed to occur in the depths of the summer vacation. This succeeded beyond our expectations, thanks to a certain number of friends

---

[2] This anecdote describes (Sir) John Masterman (1891–1977), Provost of Worcester College, Oxford 1946–61 and Vice-Chancellor 1957–8. As a Christ Church history tutor he had taught T-R. During 1941–5 he chaired MI5's XX committee.

and, I think, genuine goodwill in the Press. I was not even identified by the Press. Then we determined to stop the mouth of criticism by having a proper church wedding. The Presbyterian Church of Scotland, of which Xandra's father was an Elder, is much more liberal in these matters than the Anglican Church, and decides such cases on their merits, not by an absolute rule. I found a sensible minister, submitted the evidence, and discovered that he was willing. We then invited all the most respectable people (or at least the holders of the most respectable offices) to the ceremony and the reception, which Dawyck held for us in London; and, ever since, the air has been dark with the precipitate one-way leaping of hitherto hesitant cats. Xandra finds herself courted by bishops, heads of colleges, RC priests, professors of moral theology and many others who had previously been poised to leap emphatically in the opposite direction. All this has been very enjoyable to watch, and I find my sceptical view of human society agreeably reinforced by it.

Of course this doesn't mean that our problems are over. Far from it. The moral and diplomatic battles have merely given way to certain less exciting practical problems. Where are we to live? Oh dear, how difficult it is! Are there no elegant Georgian houses on salubrious hilltops surrounded by deferential villages within eight miles of Oxford? Alas, it seems, none. What houses we have visited! What verminous thatched cottages, oak-beamed and ingle-nooked, sinking slowly into festering swamps! What red-brick ecclesiastically arched medievally turreted villas in demure suburbs of Oxford! Of course we have turned them all down. Fastidiously we still insist on what we want, not on what we can get; and meanwhile we lodge as we can, and Xandra oscillates like a somewhat irregular pendulum between Oxford and Melrose. Ultimately, we hope, we will find something before we have ruined ourselves in the search; but sometimes it seems very desperate.

This means that we cannot, alas, very intelligently answer your very kind question about a wedding present. We have as yet no carefully measurable niches to fill, no cellars to stock, no dressers to adorn. All we can say is that anything which brings your good wishes will delight us, although in fact our memory of I Tatti hardly needs such artificial stimulation! Only not a decanter, of which about a dozen now sit empty and menacing upon my sideboard!

Now I will revert to mere gossip. Whom of your friends have we seen? The Hamiltons of course. Not indeed at our wedding; for although we allotted special seats for them in the church (next to their great rivals the Weidenfelds, so that the light badinage of temporarily reconciled publishers might provide an appropriate undertone to the nuptial ceremony), they didn't even reach the reception party until Xandra and I had changed and were departing for Scotland. Doubtless – such is the press of social life – they had found it necessary to fit in a preliminary party before it.[3] And of course the Weidenfelds. What a success George Weidenfeld had at our wedding! He had to have a special party himself a few days afterwards to cement all the alliances he had then briskly made in the literary world, and to remind the guests of the books that they then promised to write. George is now on a dozen new social lists and has a dozen new books advertised as forthcoming; all of which, we insist, he owes to us. As for Derek Hill – he, alas, could not attend. He was, as he explained to us at Bemersyde just before, buried in Ireland, devoting himself to art, and burning in the bogs of Donegal with a hard gem-like flame. (It is true that we met him a few days later, in London, having luncheon with a duchess.) How engagingly good-tempered he is! I am quite converted to him, especially after his stories of travel in the Moslem East with Freya Stark. He described that famous journey to us at Bemersyde, to the delight of all.

And now what of your goings-on? Or rather, of the goings-on of others around you? Who is coming, who going, in the shady avenues and deliciously echoing *coulisses* of I Tatti? I do hope you are fully restored to health, and that Nicky is well and that all the household flourishes. And I do hope – we both hope (I must remember always to write in the plural number now) – that we shall hear from you soon, with news of all your activities. I hear that Sylvia has been to see you and that something about you is soon to be expected from that nimble (though not always discreet) pen – published, no doubt, by either H. Hamilton or G. Weidenfeld. But though I hear from Sylvia I haven't seen her for a year. What is afoot? I long to know everything, and know it at first hand too. [...]

On 29 October, Berenson sent Xandra Trevor-Roper a cheque for $100 as a wedding present. Meanwhile Trevor-Roper addressed Nicky with the following letter, heedless of her habit of promptly reading aloud to BB any Trevor-Roper letters she received.

---

[3] Hamilton had reported to BB on 12 October: 'we arrived so late that we caught a glimpse only of the bride and groom and missed all the people like Isaiah, Roy Harrod, Molly Buccleuch whom we would like to have seen. Hugh had changed and wore the usual undergraduate costume of sports coat and grey trousers and looked the part. The bride looked like his mother. But I've no doubt it will do them both good.'

5 November 1954   Christ Church, Oxford

My dear Nicky

How are you all? I do hope you flourish. We are living in a somewhat chaotic hand-to-mouth way, while looking for a house, which we have not yet found. At the moment Xandra is in Scotland but the Admiral has now discovered an antique Scottish law whereby he can claim, or thinks he can claim, all her property in Scotland, which includes half the house and all the contents; so we can't consider the battle altogether over. Fortunately, by patient research and the cultivation of sociable Belgian financiers, we have discovered some dark facts in the history of the Belgian private banker who handles the Admiral's secret hoards of money (investing them, to avoid taxation, in the Belgian Congo – doubtless in the slave-trade!), so we may be able to use counter-threats.

No doubt you may be thinking that in all these circumstances I can hardly be applying myself to much in the way of scholarship. Well, I am at any rate still aware of its existence; and the thought which chiefly exercises me at the moment is the one on which I wish, if I may, to seek your advice. It concerns BB's 90th birthday, which, if my calculations are correct, falls on the 26th June next year. What offering is the intellectual world (as distinct from the social world, which will also no doubt pay its tribute) preparing for him on that occasion? More important, what offering would he appreciate most? A hecatomb of corpses after a brilliant gladiatorial contest in his honour by the virtuosi of the Warburg Institute? Somehow I think not. A chorus of self-styled admirers each secretly blowing his own trumpet? Somehow I think not either. In my perplexity I have written to K. Clark (now wholly immersed in the problems of commercial television) to ask whether he knows of any plan. He replies that he knows of none, and that in any case he is not an enthusiast for *Festschrift* publications. 'They do not always please the recipient, and they successfully conceal useful articles from all future researchers.' Which is no doubt true. But what do *you*, who know BB's secret mind so much better than anyone else, really think he would most appreciate from those of his friends who would be prepared to take some time and trouble to produce something to please him? Do tell me, if you have any idea, and the time and trouble will be taken [...]

This enquiry prompted a response on 8 November from Berenson:
'Excepting billets doux Nicky & I read each other's letters aloud to each other. She was reading yrs this morning about received threats of the admiral. As a good fighter you may enjoy the fun & I fervently hope the issue will be in yr. favour. She

*read on & bumped on what was to be done by "you folks" in Engel-land about my
90th birthday.*

'*I never was more delighted in my life than by what happened on my 70th
birthday. I opened* The Times *for that day & on the leader page there was a brief
reference to the day & to me, signed by a number of people.*

'*The only tribute for the 90th birthday would be something of the same, signed
by as many "hommes de lettres" as felt inclined, e.g. Harold Nicolson, Priestley,
Compton Mackenzie, Raymond Mortimer, Rosamond Lehmann, some "art-
niggers", & perhaps a few scholars in other fields.'*

*Trevor-Roper did not try to appease Berenson's startling vanity by organising a
90th birthday letter in* The Times; *but he did try unavailingly to arrange through
Raymond Mortimer for the publication of a tribute in the* Sunday Times *on 26
June.*

11 December 1954   Churriana, Málaga

My dear BB

I must write to thank you for the very generous present which you so
kindly sent, and which, though addressed to Xandra, will be spent to the
advantage of both of us. We shall certainly seek, in spending it, to get
something worthy of the gift and appropriate to the giver. Alas, at present
we are still homeless: we so nearly had a house – it was the house at Cumnor
down whose stairs Amy Robsart[1] so mysteriously fell; but at the last moment
we lost it, betrayed by our own agent; and now, in frustrated retrospect, it
seems to possess even more virtues than it had. So the great problem
remains and at this moment Xandra is in Melrose, celebrating Christmas
with the children, and I (rather unwillingly in the circumstances) have
yielded to the pressure of that literary pasha, the editor of the *Sunday Times*,
applied myself to the galley-oar, and am making my way to the Barbary
Coast. The way is long and slow; climatic convulsions have interrupted my
journey; a tornado in London postponed my departure; floods on the
aerodrome of Málaga made it impossible to land there and I had to return
to Madrid; and I am now pausing to repair my oar-blistered hands in the
friendly port of Churriana. That it to say, I am stopping for three days with
Gerald Brenan, that Englishman hispaniolised whose works I think I have
crammed down your throat and whom, as a scholar, a hispanist, a historian
and a writer, I so venerate. After tomorrow I fly to Tetuán and thence to

---

[1] The tragic Elizabethan heroine of Scott's novel *Kenilworth* (1822) is lured into falling through a
trapdoor at Cumnor Place.

Rabat, Fez and Marrakesh, well prepared by, or laden with, the words of
Augustin Bernard,[2] E.-F. Gautier,[3] and (for lighter hours) Edith Wharton.[4]
When I have absorbed some information and some experience of Morocco,
of which at present I dare not speak (for I have no doubt you know it well),
I will write to you again. At present this is an intermediate letter to send
you most grateful thanks for your very kind present and to wish you all my
best wishes for Christmas.

Oh, and of course to tell you just a little news from the world, if I can
think of any which has not yet been conveyed to you by your numerous
visitors, of whom I hear that Raymond Mortimer has been one. What can
I tell you that you do not already know? Of whom shall I speak? Of the K.
Clarks, now settled in a Kentish castle, and the great party which one of
the local magnates gave to the entire neighbourhood to meet them – a
party to which, however, the Clarks themselves failed to come, so that
the county of Kent now murmurs, as counties so often do? Of George
Weidenfeld, whose social ascent still continues: having graduated from the
world of journalism to the world of literature, he has now risen (according
to some standards of hypsometry) still higher, and from literary duchesses
has ascended to the world of pure duchesses, duchesses who, so far from
even dabbling in literary fashions, are totally illiterate? Or of Dominic de
Grunne, that fashionable aristocratic intellectual handsome social bon-
vivant *abbé* who, in the inevitable Toynbean parabola of social *Yin* and *Yan*
(or is it *Yang?*), is now, alas, in decline? He has become, by his too indefatigable acceptance of fashionable (and even unfashionable) invitations, a
social figure of fun; and now even the English Roman Catholics have turned
against him. By some curious chance, a Protestant friend of mine went
recently on a sponsored RC trip to Rheims. All the *élite* of English Roman-
ism were there. Ostensibly they went to pray at the consecration (if that is
the correct process) of a new window; but in fact they devoted more
practical attention to the local champagne (for, as you know, English RCs
regard good living as an eighth sacrament). My friend found Evelyn Waugh
on his right, pouring into his right ear denunciations of me; on his left was
Douglas Woodruff,[5] pouring into his left ear denunciations of Dominic de

---

[2] Augustin Bernard was author of *Maroc* (1913) among other works on North Africa.
[3] Emile-Félix Gautier (1864–1940), historian, geographer and Saharan explorer, wrote *L'Is-
lamisation de l'Afrique du Nord: les siècles obscures de Maghreb* (1927) and *Genséric, roi des Vandals*
(1932).
[4] Edith Wharton (1862–1937) had been an intimate friend and correspondent of BB. Her travel
writings included *In Morocco* (1920).
[5] Douglas Woodruff (1897–1978) converted to Catholicism at the age of thirteen and was editor of
The Tablet 1936–67.

Grunne. The interesting fact was that the denunciations were in almost identical terms: we were both said to be disastrous influences, ruinous to the great cause of Catholicism in England, and neither Waugh nor Woodruff is going to rest until Trevor-Roper and de Grunne have been eliminated from the holy fishing-pool of Oxford which these heretics are so disastrously polluting.

I wish I had some other news for you; but alas, I can think of none. But I will send you a report on my travels in Morocco. How I wish I could come back via Florence and visit you on the way; but time is so short that I don't think it is possible. The term, that odious institution, bears down upon me; and how can I visit the Blue Men of Rio de Oro[6] and the Glaoui of Marrakesh[7] in so brief a visit and yet deviate, as I would like, via Italy? But perhaps I may come later and bring Xandra, who, I think, would never forgive me if I visited you alone. [...]

<hr/>

[6] The Blue Men of Rio de Oro, Arab nomads from the western Sahara, were so named because they wore indigo robes.
[7] El Hadji Thami El Glaoui (1872?–1956) had succeeded his brother in 1911 as hereditary Sultan of the Atlas mountains and paramount Pasha of Marrakesh. He kept an unusually large harem, was obsessed with golf and was wounded on seventeen occasions while suppressing revolts against his authority. The French colonial government ensured his support by a large annual subsidy.

1955

5 February 1955   Christ Church, Oxford

My dear BB

I am ashamed at not having written to you for so long, but glad to hear, first from Nicky, then from you, that you are getting over your most unpleasant fall.[1] I was very alarmed to hear of it, when I was in Paris on my way back from Morocco, and most relieved to hear that you had not been seriously hurt and are now about again.

At present we are living in a very hand-to-mouth way. We have not yet got the kind of house we want. We very nearly succeeded in December, but were betrayed by our agents, and the result is that we are still homeless. Perhaps we are too exacting in our requirements. Meanwhile the Admiral is on the war-path again. With the prospect of retirement ahead of him, with infinite leisure for his machinations and the large, secret resources of his equally enraged and equally vindictive mother behind him, he has now changed his lawyers and is preparing to claim Xandra's house in Scotland, to sabotage the education of his children, and, by pleading 'poverty' (his wealth being safely concealed from the law), to escape from his financial obligations. However, we have not yet given up hope of defeating him, and although it is a nuisance having to write so many letters to lawyers instead of to friends, I am not being entirely distracted from more serious writing. I have written a long essay for a forthcoming *Festschrift* for Namier, of which you shall have an offprint when it is printed,[2] and am at work on another essay which I hope will be as effective as my essay on *the Gentry* in removing some of the obstructions to historical study in England! As soon as we have a house, I have plans for a book on the 17th century. Oh, how I wish we could find one! At present we are living in the Cotswolds, 24 miles from Oxford and 6 miles from the nearest shop, in a perfectly charming little house which has very kindly been lent to us by Michael Astor.[3] It is

---

[1] BB suffered many weeks of discomfort after falling down a steep, rocky slope on 14 December. He wrote to TR on 15 February: 'My pirouette in empty space has made a coward of me. I scarcely dare to plan leaving I Tatti again.'
[2] 'Oliver Cromwell and his Parliaments' became the opening essay in Richard Pares and A.J.P. Taylor (eds.), *Essays Presented to Sir Lewis Namier* (1956).
[3] Hon. Michael Astor (1916–1980), a Conservative MP 1945–51. Red Brick Cottage, which he lent to the T-Rs, is a Queen Anne dower house on the Oxfordshire edge of the Cotswolds. His friendship with T-R soured at a dinner party at which a guest asked what Guy Burgess would find to do if he returned to live in England and T-R quipped, 'He would go to work at the

most beautiful, and since it is on the Astor estate (Bruern Abbey) we can get both domestic help and enjoyable society. But Xandra finds it a little remote in the middle of the week! And we only have it till March, when we must make some other arrangement. As the Admiral is threatening to come and live in 'his' house in the Borders in the spring, we expect a general crisis about that time!

I enjoyed my visit to Morocco. At least, I found it most interesting, although politically I can see no answer and physically I found it rather exhausting, and was taken ill in the most inconvenient spot, on the Sahara side of the Atlas Mountains. I expect you know Morocco well. I found Marrakesh disappointing, but I was delighted by the Chellah outside Rabat, and Volubilis, and Meknes; and the Atlas Mountains fascinated me. What a difference it makes to one's idea of Moorish Spain, to have seen Berber Morocco! When one sees the Berber irrigation in the Sahara oases and compares it with the lazily scratched soil of Andalucia, one gets a picture of the meaning of 'Castilianisation' and the expulsion of the Moriscos more vivid than any book has conveyed to me. I felt that I learnt a great deal about history in Morocco. I have also discovered some new historians: Ibn Khaldoun[4] and a modern Frenchman of genius (and some wild ideas), E.-F. Gautier. Do you know his works? They include a most interesting book on the Vandals (*Genséric*) and a fascinating work on the early history of North Africa, *Les Siècles Obscurs de l'Afrique du Nord*. As to politics, – I have published two articles in the *Sunday Times* (23rd & 30th Jan), – which have suffered a good deal of editorial mutilation.[5] Now that Mendès-France has fallen, I feel that trouble throughout North Africa will begin again.[6]

We are rather disconcerted by some news which we receive from Italy. A friend of ours, Lord Hambleden, who is young and rich (thanks to the family ownership of W.H. Smith's bookstalls),[7] has become engaged to

---

Observer.' Astor, the host, laying down his cutlery, said furiously: 'My father owned the *Observer*, my brother edits the *Observer*, and I will have no one speak of the *Observer* in that offensive way in my house.' The T-Rs left the party early.

[4] Ibn Khaldūn (1332–1406), Islamic official, statesman and philosopher: see T-R's article 'Ibn Khaldoun and the Decline of Barbary' (*Historical Essays*, pp. 24–9).

[5] 'Morocco, a Land of Crises and Contrasts: France Has Exploited Her Resources But the Moors Exploit Each Other', *Sunday Times*, 23 January 1955, p. 7; 'Protectorate Must Go, Say New Moors: Impatience with Old Men and Old Régime', *Sunday Times*, 30 January 1955, p. 7.

[6] Pierre Mendès-France (1907–1982) resigned on the day of this letter (5 February) as Prime Minister of France, and Minister of Foreign Affairs, after being defeated on a vote of confidence on his North African policy.

[7] William ('Harry') Smith, 4th Viscount Hambleden (b. 1930) joined the board of W.H. Smith & Son Holdings in 1956.

the daughter of Attolico, the former Italian ambassador to Berlin.[8] Virginia Clarke now writes the most terrible account of Signora (or is it Contessa?) Attolico, the ambassador's wife, who – according to this account – is not only a fascist, a howling snob, and an odious woman, but also acquired a large fortune by means far less innocent than the honest foundation of multiple railway-bookstalls. Do write and give us the truth as known in that great centre of intelligence at Settignano.

Meanwhile what news can I give you? The saddest is the fate of your visitor of last year, George Weidenfeld, whose social ascent in the smart and intellectual world has been so fast and high, that now, like the Comet, he has suffered a most ignominious crash. I think I told you how, at his last party, he had graduated, through intellectuals, to intellectual duchesses, and finally to pure (or at least purely unintellectual) duchesses. Well, that party was a climax and a turning point not only socially but also domestically. You will remember that George Weidenfeld was accompanied, when he visited you, by a doting young wife of many charms, not the least of which was her status as the heiress of that great firm, Marks and Spencer, with whom George Weidenfeld has now not only this family alliance but also a very lucrative business contract. Unfortunately, it now seems, Mrs Weidenfeld does not share her husband's social ambitions. In fact, as has been increasingly obvious at his increasingly grand parties, she is bored stiff by society – both by intellectuals and by duchesses. As she surveyed the *débris* of her husband's last party, at which she had carried round drinks, with ever-increasing *ennui*, to ever giddier groups of loquacious peeresses, gossip-writers, fashionable novelists, and professional party-goers, and saw the carnage of empty champagne bottles, crushed lobster-shells and trodden caviar, she decided she could bear it no longer. Seizing her child, she slipped away to her parental home, where she has ever since remained, obstinately refusing ever to return to the social life of 11 Chester Square. George tears his hair in his deserted house, which he had just had newly decorated in the style of a high-class and rather *risqué* Jewish café in Vienna; and the spring list of Messrs Weidenfeld and Nicolson is likely to be, this year, rather late.

Another social crash which I see looming ahead (for with practice I am becoming quite a skilled social astronomer) is that of the once all-conquering fashionable Roman Catholic priest, Fr Dominic de Grunne. The English RCs, that bristling defensive phalanx of sensitive conformists, who first launched him as a handsome, intellectual, aristocratic *abbé* likely

---

[8] Count Bernardo Attolico (1880–1942) was Italian Ambassador to Brazil (1930–35) and to Germany (1935–40). His formidable widow was Contessa Eleonora Attolico di Adelfia (d. 1980).

to make converts among the *jeunesse dorée*, have now discovered that he, like Bishop Colenso among the Zulus, instead of converting the natives, has been converted by them;[9] and they now regard him as a pernicious corrupter of pilgrims, but in fact, instead of scallop-shells and magical amulets, they had equipped themselves with vintage-cards and swizzle-sticks. Needless to say, it was from one of these sceptical eavesdroppers, Sir Charles Petrie (who is not RC at all),[10] that I learnt of the plot there hatched to ruin Fr de Grunne. So far nothing has been done, but I cannot think that Fr de Grunne improved his chances of survival by attending our wedding (which all the Anglican clergy politely declined). I couldn't resist inviting him because I knew that, if invited, he wouldn't be able to resist the invitation.

I must now stop. Xandra has just penetrated into my study under the roof of our cottage to say (1) that I must descend to dinner, and (2) – for she was swathed in a *chic* kitchen apron, created by Jacques Fath of Paris[11] – that alas, she cannot write to you since her life is spent among pots and pans. [...]

PS. Xandra has just seen this letter and protests shrilly that her apron came from Marks & Spencer and cost 3/11d. I have been obliged to insert this erratum slip for the sake of domestic peace.

'You ask about Countess Attolico,' Berenson replied from I Tatti on 15 February. 'I am told that she is handsome, masterful, bigoted, with five daughters to provide for. A doubtful mother-in-law for yr Englishman.' A month later he was trying to assess his prospects after the death of Bela Horowitz of the Phaidon Press, who had undertaken to publish his four-volume catalogue of Italian paintings; and who was, he judged, 'the Duveen of publishers [...] as unlike most publishers as Duveen from other dealers' (diary, 16 July 1953). 'If you, as you alone can, hear anything about the firm, please let me know,' Berenson asked Trevor-Roper on 15 March.

---

[9] John Colenso (1814–1883), who was appointed Bishop of Natal in 1853, felt obliged to tell Zulu converts that much of the Bible was factually untrue, and was unable to present Old Testament massacres as the will of God when he was preaching that warfare was ungodly. This led to the quip that Colenso, having gone out to convert the heathen, had been converted by them. He was convicted of heresy and excommunicated.
[10] Sir Charles Petrie (1895–1977), a historian specialising in the Spanish ruling classes, the Stuart royal family and Jacobites.
[11] Jacques Fath (1912–1954) had been one of the great post-war Paris couturiers with a lavish shop on Avenue Pierre 1er de Serbie. His clothes were elegant, playful and risqué, with hour-glass waists and plunging necklines.

23 March 1955   Christ Church, Oxford

My dear BB

I am so sorry that we had to postpone – though I hope only for a time – our visit to I Tatti. The fact is that we have not been able to keep our present house over the summer. The owner of it, Michael Astor, had promised it to someone else, and although he thought that the promise was sufficiently vague to enable him to let us have it, he discovered that in fact the other people had come to rely on it, so he felt that he had to let them have it.[1] So we are really rather preoccupied here. Quite apart from that, the Admiral is now at war on all fronts. It seems that he is now being retired and has nothing to do but to plan revenge, and that his mother has promised to pay all legal costs if he fights for everything: he has therefore gone back on every one of his previous promises, is trying to send the boy, instead of to Eton, to a merchant-navy school, and the girl to a convent in Switzerland; has refused to return any of Xandra's property; is claiming her house in Scotland; and has put the burden of appeal to the court on to us. So we shall have to go to court. It is all extremely tiresome. Xandra has made concession after concession in the hope of reasonableness from him, but it is useless: it is like dealing with my old friend Hitler. Anyway, the result is that our lawyer did not want us – quite apart from our house problem – to go abroad at such a crucial time. I had already undertaken to give a lecture in French at the Sorbonne last week, so we went over for that purpose and stayed with the Jebbs[2] and with Diana Cooper[3] at Chantilly and saw a lot of friends, including the Gileses; but alas, our plans to go further, to Italy, had to be reversed. We were so disappointed; but once the Admiral has been defeated, we hope to come and see you in less difficult circumstances.

Just before going to Paris, I had a visit, in Oxford, from Sylvia, who tells me, *inter alia*, that you are going to Tripoli in June – which surely will be very hot; but I understand that you will be in a palace, fanned by relays of deferential black eunuchs. I hope you will enjoy it. Even while Sylvia was

---

[1] Red Brick Cottage was taken over first by Victor Cunard (*The Times* correspondent in Rome, 1922–7), and next in 1956 by Stephen and Natasha Spender.

[2] Sir Gladwyn Jebb (1900-1996), later 1st Baron Gladwyn, British Ambassador in Paris, had married Cynthia Noble (1898–1990), one of the great diplomatic wives of her generation.

[3] Lady Diana Manners (1892–1986) was the widow of a previous British Ambassador to Paris, Duff Cooper, and the putative daughter of Harry Cust, who (wrote BB) 'I loved so much.' In the mid-1950s she paid several visits to I Tatti: 'it's so disarming a man of 92 being so demonstratively affectionate,' she said; 'he makes you feel that he needs to hold your hand and that he must have one more embrace.'

telling me this, a young Cicogna[4] was sitting for an examination to get into Christ Church. I don't know if he succeeded, as since then I have been away, first in Paris, then in our country cottage.

I enjoyed my lecture in Paris. As I have probably told you, I have an enormous respect for the French historians there – Lucien Febvre, Fernand Braudel & co.; and I was flattered to be invited by them and glad to work for a few days at the Ecole des Hautes Etudes there and get to know the group of historians who, in my opinion, are asking entirely new questions and creating a new type of history. They are very cosmopolitan: the best are French, Italians, Portuguese and a Hungarian (Balazs)[5] who is working on Chinese history. There are no Germans – the Germans have not progressed since 1870 – and (although their work is known in England) no Englishmen; but I hope to do what I can to convert England. So please envisage me as a new missionary to the English, an *Augustinus Redivivus,*[6] proselytising in the unpromising milieu of pagan Oxford!

The death of Horowitz[7] is a great blow, but I hope it will not upset your plans. The firm will presumably go on under Goldschneider.[8] I will set my agents to work at once and report to you. I hope I shall be able to report fairly soon.

My brother has been operating on Percy Lubbock.[9] Once again, owing to my visit to Paris and my inaccessibility in the country, I am out of touch with the news and don't know whether the operation has been successful; but I hope so. This country cottage in which we live has many charms: it is rural, beautiful, quiet, and we have servants; also I find I can work well here; but it is rather out of touch with the world. I only wish we could have kept it over the summer. Once we reach the autumn, all is well – we have a house from then on. It is only for the summer that we are homeless. It is

---

[4] BB was going to stay in Tripoli with Countess Anna-Maria Cicogna (b. 1913), daughter of the powerful Italian industrialist Count Giuseppe Volpi di Misurata and wife of Count Cesare Cicogna Mozzoni. Her son was never an undergraduate at Christ Church.

[5] Etienne [István] Balazs (1905–1963), a refugee who had been rescued by Braudel from a mortifying job as a French provincial schoolmaster in 1949, became one of the greatest European scholars of Chinese history.

[6] Augustine reborn.

[7] Bela Horowitz (1903–1955) had founded Phaidon Press in pre-war Vienna, but came to London after the Anschluss in 1938. His ambitious post-war publishing programme established Phaidon as pre-eminent art-book publishers. 'Horowitz, wreathed in smiles, insinuating, subtle, abstains from arguing, but takes [...] other paths to reach his goal, which is to make you do what he wants' (BB diary, 17 July 1954).

[8] Ludwig Goldschneider (1896–1973) was a Viennese art historian and co-founder of the Phaidon Press: in the event, Horowitz's son-in-law Harvey Miller took over responsibility for the business.

[9] As an ophthalmologist Patrick Trevor-Roper had been consulted by Lubbock about his failing sight.

maddening that this temporary homelessness should coincide with the Admiral's most violent and unremitting campaign! [...]

'It is too long since I heard from you,' Berenson complained from Sainet Volpi, Contessa Anna-Maria Cicogna's villa near Tripoli, on 13 May. 'You are busy, no doubt, house-hunting, fighting the Admiral, & writing articles to find time for one of your magnificent epistles. Yet I suspect you did find the time to persuade your Hebdomenal Council to offer me a doctorate in letters honori causa. Unfortunately I cannot accept it as it would necessitate my coming to Oxford to receive it. I cannot imagine who but YOU would have inspired the working members of the Council (who probably never heard of me before) to do me such honour [...] My going to England is out of the question. Not only the journey but all I would encounter there would kill me in no time.'

28 May 1955   Christ Church, Oxford

My dear BB

As so often, I am ashamed at my epistolary indebtedness. I owe you, I think, for three letters. And I have to explain, further, that I was *not* responsible for the offer to you of an honorary doctorate. Of course I think that you ought to have one – indeed ought to have had one long ago; but I think that offers should not be made if they are conditional on an impossibility, and I have long supposed that a journey to England would be, for you, an impossibility. I understand that the proposer this time was Kenneth Clark, who is evidently convinced that you would come to England: indeed he is said by the Vice-Chancellor to have said that you were visiting sites in Tunisia (*sic*) on a donkey? Is that true? I hope so, although it rather deflated my arguments about your temporary fragility. I insisted that on the contrary you were reclining in an air-conditioned palace in Tripoli, receiving sherbet and salaams from deferential black eunuchs; and on the strength of this assurance I suggested that, on the old principle of the mutual approximation of Mahomet and the mountain, the degree be conveyed, by a high-powered delegation (including, of course, myself), to you. But it seems that this is a constitutional impossibility. And now Jamie Hamilton assures me that K. Clark is almost right, and even if the detail about the donkey is inexact, you went to Tripoli not, as I had supposed, smoothly by air, but in a storm-tossed caïque or felucca across the raging Syrtes; and if this is not mobility, what is? So altogether I am beginning to think that really you *could* have come here, and I am delighted to think that you are again so agile; but I am sure you are wiser to stay in the Mediterranean area and insist that your friends visit you there –

especially this year, which has not yet seen, in these islands, even the first faint beginning of summer.

Now what news can I give you to atone for my long silence? First, the cause of it all; which, I need hardly say, is the Admiral. The Admiral is now more than ever on the war-path, seeking revenge by every means at his disposal, trying to strike Xandra through the children, trying to claim her property in Scotland, and in every way seeking to make life burdensome to her. He has already defaulted on every agreement made at the time of the divorce, and we are having to appeal to the court for enforcement. Backed by the large but secret financial resources of his mother, he is capable of infinite litigation, but at the same time, because they are secret, he can pretend, when it comes to getting any order against him, to be poor. He is also an expert in the war of nerves, moving entirely in the dark behind a fog of war; and he has the psychological advantage of knowing that he can terrorise Xandra's Haig relatives: he only has to say Boo and they all dive for cover. His latest move is to declare that he is going to take up residence in 'his' house in Scotland next week, and that Xandra must clear out and leave all her furniture there for him. I am in favour of resistance. Xandra could simply refuse to go, like the Duchess of Roxburghe, with the added advantage that (unlike the Duchess) the house is in fact partly hers and is in her, not his, country. However, Xandra is terrified of the Admiral and doesn't feel capable of such defiance, so she is going to let him in. I fear that once in it may be difficult to get him out, and we may find that in the autumn, when we move into our house in Oxford, we cannot get at her furniture. In addition to this he is causing infinite trouble by trying to default on the children's education, switching the boy from Eton to a tough unsuitable merchant-navy school and the girl to a Swiss convent.[1] However, we think we have scotched that. All this is very tiresome, and very wearing to Xandra; but if we can keep him at bay over the summer I think all will be well. Xandra is at this moment in Scotland: she went there to vote in the General Election. She comes back to Oxford next week. If the necessities of coping with the Admiral allow, we may be able to go abroad in July. Will you be at I Tatti then, just in case it should so happen that we are able to go to Italy? It is a very long chance, but it *might* be possible for us.

In spite of all this, I have been doing a good deal of work. I have written a long essay for Namier's *Festschrift*, which I shall send you in due course; also a longish article on Erasmus in *Encounter* which I will send if you don't

---

[1] The Admiral tried to insist that James Howard-Johnston be sent to Pangbourne Nautical College, even though the boy's uncle Gavin Astor had undertaken to pay most of the Eton fees.

already have it;[2] and I have produced (with a joint-editor) an edition of a second-rate Jacobean poet.[3] I am also trying to found a new historical school here, to bring English historical studies out of their backwater by applying the methods of the French school. I have collected a group of young zealots and am mobilising arguments and programmes in order to persuade the Rockefeller Foundation to support it. There is an immense amount of work to be done in this direction, but I don't see why it shouldn't be done. I have also been reading Jacob Burckhardt again. What a wonderful historical mind! I had to write about the new English selection of his letters (an article in the *New Statesman*, not yet published),[4] and this led me to read the German edition of Kaphahn, and then to re-read the other works on the Renaissance and Constantine the Great and his *Weltgeschichtliche Betrachtungen.*[5] They really are a wonderful re-discovery to make. What 19th century historian saw historical forces so clearly? I am still excited by the experience.

Incidentally I think I mentioned that I went to Paris to give a lecture about six weeks ago. This was part of my campaign of Anglo-French historical *rapprochement.* I promised to send you the text of the lecture when it was printed in the *Annales*; but since it is not yet in print in French and now has been printed in English (in *History Today*) I shall send you, in a day or two, the English text instead.[6]

So much for intellectual life. Now what of social life? I watch it furtively from the periphery, and every now and then catch a glimpse into the merry-go-round. It gets giddier and giddier, like a Hieronymus Bosch fantasy. Some are climbing up, some precariously poised on some perilous and unsubstantial social summit, some suddenly and painfully being cast down. Among the latter, I fear, is your *quondam* visitor George Weidenfeld[7] who, it was noticed, was only at the crowded, promiscuous, unfashionable election-party last Thursday night and was *not* at the more select luncheon-party on the following day. His day, it is thought, is now past, and the peerage are quickly selling out such shares in him as they had bought. Alas, how recently they bought them, and at the top of the market too! When I

[2] 'Desiderius Erasmus', *Encounter*, IV (May 1955), pp. 57–68; *Historical Essays*, pp. 35–60.
[3] *The Poems of Richard Corbett*, edited by T-R and J.A.W. Bennett, published by Oxford University Press in 1955.
[4] T-R's review of Alexander Dru's *The Letters of Jacob Burckhardt* was published as 'The Faustian Historian', *New Statesman*, 6 August 1955, pp. 164–5, and reprinted in *Historical Essays*, pp. 273–8.
[5] Felix Kaphahn edited Burckhardt's letters; *Weltgeschichtliche Betrachtungen* = Reflections on World History.
[6] 'The Social Origins of the Great Rebellion', *History Today*, V (June 1955), pp. 376–82, is an abridged version of 'La Révolution Anglaise de Cromwell', *Annales*, X (July 1955), pp. 331–40.
[7] Weidenfeld had first visited I Tatti in February 1951.

meet him now, he cuts me dead: I fear he thinks that I have hastened his decline; and indeed it is true that I gave an imprudent but (I thought) highly entertaining account of his social activities to Randolph Churchill, who then treacherously passed it on to Weidenfeld. Now I, of course, cut Randolph Churchill.[8] Another social casualty, on a much narrower front, is Derek Hill, who is now *brûlé* with a Duchess; which causes him social agony. But that, I am sure, is a temporary mishap only: on other fronts he remains triumphant. The one social performer whose performance is still faultless is that exquisite Belgian *abbé*, Dominic de Grunne, whom all the pious rage of the English Catholic bigots has not yet succeeded in driving out of Oxford. Dominic de Grunne has recently added to his social accomplishments (which are many) by becoming a first-rate cook. His dishes are really delicious. He has great flair and manipulates the kitchen utensils with the choreographical virtuosity of a papal chaplain serving the altar. He is in great demand among the *beau monde* and whenever there is an exquisite, informal, aristocratic dinner-party in London, the *abbé* de Grunne can be seen scuttling off from Oxford with his saucepans and his *soutane*. Xandra and I had dinner with him the other night. He killed the lobsters with his own hands (being bloodless, such murder is allowed to the clergy), and cooked them in whisky according to some special Benedictine recipe recommended for *jours maigres*.[9] And as he served them, he diverted us (and two emancipated Catholic guests) with some exquisite imitations of less sophisticated Roman Catholic priests. You can imagine how the purse-faced and puritanical English RCs hate him!

Thank you for the cutting from the *New York Times*. It amuses me that after ten years the little dishonesties (or at least a part of them) of General Truscott should be revealed.[10] I have always kept completely silent, at least in print, about that incident; but *magna est veritas et praevalet*,[11] and I get a little private satisfaction to see that it is in America that the truth has at last leaked out.

I am glad you liked my article on Namier (who incidentally is receiving a degree here in June: fitting if belated recognition from the university

---

[8] Randolph Spencer-Churchill (1911–1968), political journalist and clubman. T-R's memoir of him begins: 'The late Bernard Berenson used to divide humanity, for some purposes, into two classes: the life-enhancing and the life-diminishing. It is a categorization which I have found very convenient – indeed, for social purposes, academic appointments, etc., absolutely fundamental. Randolph Churchill was one of the most life-enhancing of all my friends.' (Kay Halle, *Randolph Churchill* (1971), p. 267.)

[9] Religious days on which the eating of meat is forbidden to Catholics.

[10] Lucian Truscott (1895–1965), US major general, formed and trained the Rangers, an American force modelled on the Commandos, and led assault troops in the liberation of Italy.

[11] 'Great is truth, and it prevails' (2 Esdras; Apocrypha).

which so often refused him a professorship). You say you wish someone would say something similar of your work. So do I. But who? Alas, the art-critics, even more than the historians, have turned themselves into sectaries and microscopists. When I read the *Burlington Magazine* I feel very sad. The humanity seems to have gone out of the subject. Or is it merely my ignorance? Whom would you like to be your interpreter to the world?

I must now stop. I am sending this letter to Settignano. I hope you have by now returned safely and in good health across that uncertain sea. I hope that your change of air has done you good and enabled you to face without alarm the celebration of your ninetieth birthday. [...]

On 8 June, Berenson wrote from Calabria, which he had last visited in 1908. 'I then suffered too much physically to do it justice. Now that I travel en prince, *rooms comfy & roads perfect, I have the leisure of body & of mind to enjoy the landscape.' He lamented that 'all the honours that are to be showered on my 90th birthday are for my longevity, scarcely for what I have done.'*

20 July 1955   [Lurs, near Forcalquier, Alpes-de-Haute-Provence]

My dear BB

Now that the climacteric date is past, and you are used to being 90, and back (I suppose) at I Tatti, I write to tell you our news and solicit yours. When I last heard from you, you were in Calabria, on your way back from Tripoli. I hope you are still in as good health and as high spirits as you seemed, from your letter, to be there. And I hope that the birthday cele-brations, which you seem largely to have escaped, were not too exhausting to you.

We have also been having a somewhat exhausting time, which however, is now past. The source (I need hardly say) was the Admiral, who turned Xandra out of her house in Scotland, has refused to do anything for his children (except turn them out too) and tried to prevent his children from getting an English education, even to the extent of refusing the Eton scholarship which James won and forcing him into the Navy which he does not want to join. However, in the end, all has come well. Xandra went to court over the children's education and won on all points; the Admiral's behaviour in Scotland has so damaged him that his new wife (he has married, *en troisièmes noces*, the daughter of the painter Helleu)[1] has pre-vailed upon him to sell out his share of the house, and with it his nuisance

---

[1] Paul-César Helleu (1859–1927), painter and etcher, whose work was described by Degas as *le Watteau à vapeur.*

value there (I need hardly say that he is demanding a large profit for himself!); and we *think* that everything will become easier thereafter. But of course it has been a great strain for Xandra; who however is now having a holiday here in Provence, where we are staying in a charming little hotel at Forcalquier, and she can spend the days painting. We have to go back next week, before the children return from school.

One thing I regret, as an omission, in connexion with your birthday. I remember your remarks about my little note, in the *Sunday Times*, on Namier, and I had hoped to persuade someone, qualified to do so, to publish something for your birthday showing the difference, in art-criticism and art-history, between the pre-Berenson and the post-Berenson eras. For this, it seems to me, is the real measure of achievement, and enables one to distinguish, for instance, in my field, between Namier and Pirenne, on the one hand, and historians like Trevelyan,[2] on the other hand, who have enjoyed great celebrity but who, when this question is asked, are found to have left their subject in exactly the same state as they discovered it. I am sorry that I failed to get anyone to do this for you in time for your 90th birthday; but it will have to be done, and I shall try to ensure that you have it to read on your 100th.

I think I mentioned to you that I had been re-reading Jakob Burckhardt. What a good writer he was! What a revolution in the study of history – being the study not of politics but of society and culture – the development of art history *as a branch of history* has caused. I am thinking also of Emile Mâle,[3] whose works were a revelation to me. Now this visit to the Vaucluse has reminded me of another work which I first read at Logan's instigation, Voigt's *Wiederbelebung des Classischen Alterhums*.[4] Winckelmann,[5] Wolff, Justi,[6] Burckhardt – it is astonishing to think that it was in Germany that this revolution took place (for I suppose that Burckhardt, though Swiss, must be accounted German by his formation). But I think that that spirit has left Germany altogether now, and has migrated elsewhere. I have just written a short article on Burckhardt, *à propos* of his newly translated *Letters*, for the *New Statesman*. I don't know when they will publish it.

I am full of projects. Despairing of the present historical school at Oxford,

---

[2] George Macaulay Trevelyan (1876–1962), Regius Professor of Modern History at Cambridge 1927–40 and Master of Trinity College 1940–51.
[3] Emile Mâle (1862–1954), who was elected to the chair of medieval archaeology at the Sorbonne in 1908, wrote three important volumes on the iconography and symbolism in French medieval religious art.
[4] Georg Voigt (1827–1891) wrote a major study of the revival of classical antiquity.
[5] Johann Winckelmann (1717–1768), German archaeologist and historian of ancient art.
[6] Carl Justi (1832–1912), a German art historian who studied the cultural context of art.

I am trying to set up a new historical institute in England to direct study in the direction which interests me, and to publish work for which, so far, it has been difficult to find publishers. Fernand Braudel, the French historian, is my great ally, and has promised to help; I have already got a publisher who, if guaranteed against loss, will produce the results; and I am beginning with a *seminar* next term. The Oxford Professors will no doubt be furious: this however does not seriously disconcert me! My ultimate aim is to have something in England corresponding with the Ecole Pratique des Hautes Etudes in Paris, something which will take note (as our present professors and the timid publishers they advise do not) of the new attitude towards historical studies created by the introduction of such new branches: what the French call *interhistoire*. It will also give me some pleasure to steal back from the Marxists some of the clothes they have stolen!

Did you read an article I wrote on Erasmus in *Encounter*? If not, and if you would like to read it, I have a copy in Oxford which I will send you on my return. I shall be back there on 29 July, and then expect to spend August in Scotland. In September I may have to go – I say 'may have to go' but really I should say 'am all agog to go' – to Poland for the *Sunday Times*. How distant are your recollections of that strange country, whose history fascinates me but whose language, alas, I shall never be able to understand? I fear they will be – considering the revolutions to which it is subject – very distant. Even Xandra's memories and contacts (she used to stay with the Potockis before the war) apply to a vanished age. But can you recommend me any good books on Polish life before 1939? I remember you once quoted to me an account by a Polish Jew of life in the household of Prince Sapieha;[7] but I have forgotten the author. Can you remind me of him? Do tell me anything you can.

I must now go out and see if Xandra is all right at her easel. She is full of alarms at being alone in this hospitable country because we are in the very parish in which Sir Jack Drummond, his wife and child were all murdered a few years ago by the still uncondemned peasant Dominici.[8] Indeed the Drummonds are buried in the cemetery here, and Dominici's sister washes the dishes in our hotel. But Dominici awaits the result of his appeal in prison in Marseilles, and I don't really feel that his example is

[7] Solomon Maimon (1754–1800), a Talmudic scholar from Polish Lithuania, translated scientific works into Hebrew and impressed contemporaries with his commentaries on Kant and Hume.
[8] Sir Jack Drummond, the biochemist who devised a balanced diet for British civilians during the war, had been shot dead in 1952 while camping near the banks of the Durance river at Lurs. His wife was also fatally shot, and their daughter bludgeoned to death. The capital sentence on Gaston Dominici (1876?-1965) was commuted in 1957, and he was pardoned in 1960.

catching in this delightful locality. However, I am under orders and must go [...]

27 August 1955   Bemersyde, Melrose, Scotland

My dear BB

You must excuse my unconventional writing paper. I am staying with Dawyck and cannot cramp my epistolary style within the narrow limits of his parsimonious Scottish writing paper. For I feel that I owe you a long letter, and now I have abstracted myself from the house-party to write one.

First of all, thank you very much for the exquisitely produced *Bibliografia*. I was delighted to receive it, am delighted to own it, and am particularly delighted that something so appropriate has been written for your birthday. I am so glad that some record of your work has been compiled after all, and that Willy Mostyn-Owen has been so well employed and has deserved so well of the republic of letters.[1]

You may be asking, why am I not in Poland. Of course I ought to be; but there has been a hitch, indeed a fatal hitch. Of course I wanted to go. The *Sunday Times* also wanted me to go. And the Poles wanted me to go too and invited me to go as a guest of the Polish Academy (an invitation which the *Sunday Times*, jealous of their authority over me, intercepted and refused on my behalf, without telling me about it). But at the last moment a fatal question of *prestige* intervened. The Poles promised me a visa on a particular date. I agreed to the date. So did the *Sunday Times*, to whom the date was anyway quite immaterial. Then suddenly Lord Kemsley heard what happened. 'What?' he cried, 'shall the *Sunday Times*, that respectable engine of enlightened opinion, accept dictation as to dates from the Poles? Shall a coroneted English peer bow down before a communist bureaucracy?' And he insisted that, to avoid even the appearance of such an imputation, the date should be altered by one week. Thereupon the Polish Embassy in London was equally filled with dark clouds of rage and slighted self-importance. 'What?' cried the Polish Counsellor, whose polysyllabical name I despair of spelling, 'shall a People's Republic accept dictation from a plutodemocratic newspaper-peer?' And thereupon, in Kemsley House and Portland Place blood-pressures and temperatures rose, and the treaty that was so nearly signed was torn up, and Trevor-Roper remained in the calm rural solitudes of the Scottish Border, having read laborious pages about Polish history and Polish politics and Polish economy in vain.

---

[1] *Bibliografia di Bernard Berenson*, compiled by Mostyn-Owen, had been beautifully printed in Milan earlier in 1955.

Not indeed that I am not perfectly happy on the Scottish Border, which is my home and to which I become (as I think that all natives of that enchanted land do become) every year more attached. *Ille terrarum mihi praeter omnes angulus ridet*[2] etc.; and now we have (for the time being at least) driven the Admiral out of Xandra's house in Melrose – to which, however, he will doubtless return, when he has got his second wind, with a pitchfork. And yet, I must admit, there are some disadvantages in living among these romantic rural solitudes, with no Bodleian Library or Parker's Bookshop round the corner, with my own books so far away and the wrong ones (as always happens) in the wrong place; and of course the conversation of Cheviot farmers is always, when intelligible, rather thin: I miss the fountain of more sophisticated conversation which, in Oxford, can always be found playing in Isaiah's rooms in All Souls. So on Wednesday I go back to Oxford, only spending three days with Dawyck first, for the Edinburgh Festival. Xandra has gone to the even wilder north, with her children, to stay with her rich Astor relatives.[3] I had declined this invitation, thinking I would be in Poland. Anyway I dislike shooting parties: I can't hit the birds or compete in the conversation; and Dawyck assures me that the rest of the party will be *very* dull.

Isaiah, incidentally, – as you have no doubt already heard from numerous well-placed sources – is engaged in a complicated romance with Aline Halban, *née* de Gunzbourg, whom perhaps you know.[4] Her husband, a nuclear physicist, has been given his *congé* and told to accept a grand position as atomic adviser to the French government. A divorce will be arranged in the civilised French fashion; the re-marriage will take place next year. Aline Halban is very beautiful, very rich, and has great taste; but I don't find her very interesting. She is a hereditary director of the Ritz, Paris; her great-grandfather, who began (I understand) as a pedlar of paraffin, ended as a partner of Sir Henry Deterding;[5] she belongs to the social *enclave* of the Paris Rothschilds; and in all her marriages (Isaiah will be her third husband) she has kept strictly within the Jewish world.

Now what can I tell you from Oxford? There (as you may have deduced

---

[2] 'This corner of the earth pleases me more than any other.' Horace, *Odes* 2, no. 6, ll.13–14.
[3] Her youngest sister Irene (1919–2001) had married Gavin Astor, later 2nd Baron Astor of Hever, who owned an estate, Tillypronie, in Aberdeenshire.
[4] The marriage of Aline Halban (b. 1915), the wife of a physicist working in Oxford, collapsed in 1954 after she and Berlin collaborated on a French translation of *The Hedgehog and the Fox*. She married Berlin in 1956.
[5] Henry Deterding (1866–1939), Director General of the Royal Dutch Petroleum Company, had received an honorary British knighthood in 1920 as recognition of his support of the British war effort.

from *The Times*) all intellectual speculation has given way to the great question of the Road through the Christ Church Meadow, which has totally convulsed City and University alike, rendering all old politics useless and all pretence of scholarship irrelevant. In case the numerous letters and round-robins, ministerial utterances and inter-academic bombardments, have seemed to you, in the pure rarefied air of Vallombrosa, rather obscure, perhaps you will allow me to simplify it by extracting from the complicated mass of polemical details the simple explanation of it all, the character of our Vice Chancellor, A.H. Smith, Warden of New College.[6]

Have you ever read that great work, Creighton's *History of the Popes*? If so, you may remember one Pope (I forget his name) of whom Creighton writes that, arriving later at power, he sought to cram into his brief reign the gratification of the ambitions, resentments and jealousies of a lifetime. Even such is also that seemingly mild, mildly eccentric, longwinded Victorian aesthete, Warden Smith. But I will proceed at leisure and give you the facts, beginning with a brief biography of this new human volcano which has suddenly erupted in our midst.

Warden Smith, it is essential to understand, is not only a philosopher and an aesthete, but one whose views both on philosophy and aesthetics have always, in the past, been treated with some hilarity by his colleagues. Some years ago he sought to bolster up his *ego* in the world of philosophy by applying for a doctorate of letters; but unfortunately the committee of scholars who examined his works in order to judge his worthiness of such a title, decided that they did not really reach the required standard. Frustrated, Warden Smith then decided to exert himself in the aesthetic field. Prying about in the corners and the archives of New College, he discovered that the elegant Georgian windows in one of the quadrangles had once been gothic. He therefore determined to restore the whole quadrangle to its primitive gothic character; and after weeks of assiduous intrigue, skilful purchase of votes, dangling of patronage, and delivery of long speeches which wore out the opposition and drove the neutrals into timorous hiding, he ultimately prevailed upon the Governing Body of the College, by a narrow majority, to approve the re-gothicisation of *one* window only, as a tentative experiment, at a cost of £300. Accordingly, this was done; but when the Fellows of New College saw the result, a slight shift in the voting caused the Warden's narrow majority altogether to dissolve,

---

[6] Alic Smith (1883–1958) was a civil servant in the Scottish Office before his appointment in 1919 as a Fellow of New College and tutor in philosophy there. Subsequently Warden of the college, he was a busy committee-man, a master of tactical ruses and Vice-Chancellor of the university 1954–7.

and he has never since been able to continue his architectural follies, of which the only concrete result thus consists of one gothic window absurdly spoiling an otherwise perfect Georgian quadrangle. Thus, it seemed, the career of Warden Smith was about to end on a note of comic failure, when suddenly an extension of the retiring age and the frail health of a rival unexpectedly advanced him to the Vice-Chancellorship, and Power at last lodged itself in his astonished hands.

At once Warden Smith, now Vice-Chancellor Smith, saw golden opportunities of glorifying his reign. The philosophic views which had failed to obtain a doctorate in 1948 were now expressed, in long speeches, to distinguished audiences imprisoned at academic dinners and public feasts; Kings and Emperor were summoned from the Gothic North and blackest Ethiopia to receive doctorates at his hands; and he now resolved, instead of merely gothicising one window in an obstinately Georgian quadrangle, to medievalise the whole university. Instead of laboratories and reading-rooms he would build a pillory and a pest-house; Berkeley[7] and Hume should be driven out by Duns Scotus[8] and Erigena;[9] and instead of serving as a thoroughfare for buses and motor-cars, the High Street, newly cobbled and grassed, should accommodate only maypoles and morris-dancers and bare-footed monks singing Vespers through the nose.

But, you will object, how could such anachronistic views ever become practical politics? The answer is simple. First, Warden Smith, like all who arrive at executive eminence in our universities, is a past-master of *intrigue*. Secondly, he has discovered allies in an unexpected quarter: the great race of Motorists.

For the British Motorist, having invested large sums of money in his motor car, naturally expects some return on his investment. He expects, in fact, to be able to move faster in his expensive car than on his gratuitous feet. He is therefore mortified to discover that, when thrusting his way through Oxford, he is continually held up by traffic-blocks and has to witness armies of low-class pedestrians sweeping past at 3 miles per hour. Away, he impetuously cries, with these obstructions, these university buildings which impede the march of petrol and progress! Let us have a huge turnpike road that ignores such obstacles! And Warden Smith, hearing their voice, sweetly sings, shouts a little louder, until the noise reaches the Ears of the Mighty, into which I shall then whisper the solution: a Road through the Meadow and a Grass-Grown High Street.

[7] George Berkeley (1685–1753), Bishop of Cloyne, philosopher and immaculate prose stylist.
[8] Joannes Duns Scotus (1265?–1308?), a Franciscan monk and philosopher.
[9] John Erigena (or Scotus), a ninth-century Irishman whose writings foreshadowed medieval mysticism.

This in fact is what has happened. Of course the solution is no solution at all: the first breath of common-sense dissolves it; but the breath of common-sense has long since been drowned by the cry of the Motorists, 'Do Something, Do *Anything!*' and the whisper of the Vice-Chancellor, 'Do This, Do This!' The only possible result, if his voice were to prevail, would be a road through the Meadow without of course any closing of the High Street. All the motorists would then hope that *other* motorists would take the new road, leaving them to go faster along the old road. But as the new road would not lead to the shops to which they are all in fact going, no one will in fact take it, and the situation will be the same as before except for the ruin of the Meadow. This will be an appropriate sequel to the Affair of the New College Window.

Of course, as you can imagine, the Opposition is organising furiously. Ministers are being lobbied in country houses, and the fact that half the House of Lords were at Christ Church is not being left unexploited by my more active colleagues. Warden Smith's sinister intrigues are being uncovered; petitions to the Chancellor for his removal are being discussed; and the interests of the shopkeepers of the High Street, who have no desire to be cut off from American motorists and reduced to the custom of impecunious pedestrians, are being ventilated with a sympathy and tenderness which they have never received before. So busy is everyone on this great matter that I have decided that no effort is required of me and I can concentrate calmly on my books, which I prefer; merely observing from a safe distance this new outbreak of *furor academicus*, this new by-plot in *la comédie humaine*.

Now to return to my own studies. I will certainly send you a copy of my essay on Erasmus. I have no copy here or I would have sent one earlier, but I will send one from Oxford next week. Before long there will also appear in the *New Statesman* a particularly malicious article which I have written comparing the English Catholics and the French Protestants, whose haunts I visited while in the Midi in July.[10] I have enjoyed writing it; but Xandra is full of base apprehensions about its publication: so many of the Scottish

---

[10] T-R's review of E.G. Léonard's *Le Protestant Français* and of Stuart Schram's *Protestantism and Politics in France* was published as 'Huguenots and Papists', *New Statesman*, 5 November 1955, pp. 579-80. Describing nineteenth-century English converts to Catholicism he wrote, 'they were the casualties of change: intellectuals tired of thinking, aristocrats unable to compete in society, worldlings weary of the world. How well one knows the face of certain converts to Catholicism – that smooth, exhausted look, burnt-out and yet at rest, as of a motorist who, after many mishaps and mounting insurance-premiums, has at last decided to drive himself no more, and having found a chauffeur with excellent references, resigns himself to safer travel in a cushioned back-seat.'

aristocracy in these parts are now sunk in abject popery. 'Will the children ever be asked to stay at Tyninghame again?' she sadly sighs." But I assure her that none of her Roman Catholic friends read the *New Statesman*. Most of them do not read at all. The only danger is Lady Hesketh, who gives herself intellectual airs, writes reviews in *The Tablet*, and is being carefully built up by social priests as an intellectual giantess.[12] She will no doubt discover the heretical article and communicate a rapid electric shock which will pass from Marchmont to Mellerstain and from Mellerstain to Abbotsford and from Abbotsford to Paxton (these being the great convert houses of the Border).[13] So now, in order to save the situation, I am trying to evolve some scheme to prevent Lady Hesketh from seeing the article. Perhaps she could be invited to Rome during the crucial week. I think an invitation from the Pope would *certainly* be effective. If I gave you notice of the date, could you procure one?

So much for England. Now will you tell me something from Italy? Do you know anything about a young man (at least I think he is a young man) called John Fleming, who lives in Italy (I don't know where) and who has discovered Robert Adam's Journal of his Italian tour? He has published an article on it in the current number of the *Cornhill Magazine*.[14] He has also written a good book on Scottish houses; and I understand that he is writing a history of the Adam family.

Derek Hill, as you know, has 'settled' in Donegal.[15] At least he has gone there; but the general view is that it is not for long, and that a house in Donegal will soon be for sale at bargain price. I am told that he has been writing to all his friends urging them to go and stay there to avoid the deadly monotony of painting. Dawyck refuses firmly to go: he says that art should be undisturbed by society. I doubt if this is Derek's philosophy.

Dawyck has some Italian guests here, Prince & Princess Boncompagni-

---

[11] Tyninghame Castle, overlooking Hedderwick Bay, near Prestonkirk in East Lothian was the home of Lord and Lady Haddington. T-R published an essay, 'Tyninghame Library', in 1976.

[12] Christian ('Kistie') Hesketh (1929–2006) had been widowed by the death of her young husband Lord Hesketh in June. She served four terms between 1981 and 2003 as a trustee of the London Library, where she was shrewd, modest and humorous.

[13] Marchmont was the house of Lady Hesketh's father Sir John McEwen; Mellerstain was another home of the Haddingtons; Sir Walter Maxwell-Constable-Scott lived at Abbotsford; and Paxton was held by the Home-Robertson family.

[14] John Fleming (1919–2001), historian of architecture and the decorative arts, wrote (among other distinguished works) 'Robert Adam the Grand-Tourist', *Cornhill Magazine*, 168 (1955), pp. 118–37, and *Robert Adam and his Circle in Edinburgh and Rome* (1962). Later he settled in a villa near Lucca with Hugh Honour.

[15] In 1954, encouraged by Henry McIlhenny and (as he thought) by Dawyck Haig, Hill had bought an old rectory on the shores of the Lake of Gartan in County Donegal. He kept the house until the end of his life.

Ludovisi: christian names Alberico and Letizia.[16] Do you know them? Can you tell me anything about them? She seems intelligent and I like her, but I find him rather a bore. However, having a Pope in the family, I understand that he has a hereditary right to grant dispensations which can be useful, as he has just been staying with an RC shooting party and allowed them all to eat grouse on Friday.

We have had an astonishing summer here. I never thought that I would ever feel, as you Mediterraneans feel, *bored* with the sun. It has shone incessantly for two months, and I find myself wearing tropical clothes to motor in an open car into Edinburgh to the opera at night. Perhaps we are undergoing a climatic change such as occurred after 1600: in which case we may look for harder winters, and the Thames frozen over, and plague in summer, and all those other phenomena which my fellow-historians, in their perplexity, now bring forward to account for the *crise de contraction du 16e siècle.*

Incidentally all my fellow-historians seem to be in Rome now. But I hate moving in crowds, and out of the 3,000 historians I suppose that 50 at the most deserve the name: the others have gone for the jaunt, or in the hope of ventilating their claims to notice and promotion, or pushed by their wives, anxious to buy silk underwear. So I shall not be among them, but will come more privately and pay, if we may, a discreeter visit to that less crowded intellectual capital on the hill at Settignano. [...]

PS. 30/8/55 Derek has telephoned and is arriving from Ireland. He took the precaution of asking who was here, but, finding that the company is socially all right, is on his way, and art and the bogs of Donegal are abandoned.

Berenson replied on 7 September that 'the Ludovisi girl is the daughter of Count Pecci-Blunt. Said Pecci-Blunt (né Blumenthal), a New York Jew banker, whose cable address was "Blunt", married a great niece of Pope Leo XIII. They hold high festival in an Aladdin style at Marlia, a fairy palace near Lucca, & entertain the great world in Rome. The daughter seems nicer than either of the parents.'

There was no immediate response from Trevor-Roper, and on 30 November Sylvia Sprigge wrote to him from I Tatti that Nicky Mariano's left leg was encased in plaster of Paris after breaking a bone in a fall. 'There's no pain now, but 35 days more of not being able to walk downstairs. This means a sad little Christmas. Do write to

---

[16] Prince Alberico Boncompagni-Ludovisi, Prince of Venosa (b. 1918), younger son of the 9th Prince of Piombino, had married in 1941 and was divorced in 1982. Laetitia Boncompagni-Ludovisi (b. 1920) was the daughter of Count Cecil Pecci-Blunt (d. 1965), and of Anna Laetitia Pecci-Blunt (1885-1971), great-niece of Pope Leo XIII. Contessa Pecci-Blunt was a patron of the arts and a prominent hostess.

her. [. . .] As for BB – he longs to see you & Xandra – oh do pop out for Christmas/or New Year, do. I notice such a big change since last we met. He is wonderful at times, very deaf at others, suddenly very tired & breathless, & often his memory is confused. He clings enormously to life.' She added a postscript: 'If you see Isaiah Berlin, do try to persuade him to come here to stay – why don't you come together? You'd be so welcome, I know.'

3 December 1955   Christ Church, Oxford

My dear Nicky

I was just going to write to you to say how delighted we are to be able to come and see you both, when I got a letter from Sylvia saying that you are immobilised, in plaster-of-Paris, with a broken ankle. How maddening for you: I do hope you are comfortable and are mending well inside the plaster, and that we shall find you otherwise well and cheerful in this adversity. I hope you find, as I found when I was in plaster with a broken back, that the pain soon goes and the plaster becomes almost a welcome (as it is certainly an inseparable) companion. But then with a broken back one is completely mobile – indeed can go for long walks – but you must find locomotion very difficult. However, I hope we may still see you both. Xandra is at present in Scotland (being child-bound there during the nurse's holiday), but we meet again on Thursday, in Newcastle-on-Tyne, the grim metropolis of the North, and will, unless you command otherwise, travel down to London that night and not draw breath until we arrive in Florence on Saturday 10th December, by the Rome express to Pisa. I am not sure of the time of arrival; but no doubt it is known at Villa Berenson.

We are greatly looking forward to seeing you both. It seems ages since we were at I Tatti – nearly two years, if not quite two years. We shall have a great deal to tell you and to hear from you. We have now got a house in Oxford and it has been very exhausting getting into it, especially for Xandra; but I think progress is being made.[1] And then what distractions! I think I have never had so exhausting a term. And in the middle of it all that wretched valet of Hitler[2] came back from Russia and I had to fly to Munich

---

[1] The house, belonging to Christ Church, was 8 St Aldate's. The T-Rs remained entrenched there after he left Christ Church to become a Fellow of Oriel in 1957 despite the urgings of the college Treasurer that they should move out. Indeed they remained unmoveable until T-R became Master of Peterhouse, Cambridge, in 1980. Harold Macmillan, as Chancellor of the university, rather unfairly sympathised with T-R on the 'Rachmanite behaviour of your old college.'
[2] Heinz Linge (b. 1913), Hitler's valet, had (like other crucial witnesses to Hitler's last days) been imprisoned by the Russians for ten years, but was released in October 1955 and published his recollections in a Berlin newspaper.

and perform some hasty research to prevent the dangerous possibility of heresy or error on that subject upon which I am now the infallible Pope ...[3]

Incidentally, what antics the other Pope – I mean *your* Pope, the Italian Pope – is up to! I suppose it is all Sister Pasqualina's doing.[4] I look forward to all kinds of information from you on this subject. Have you read *Les Clés de St Pierre* by Roger Peyrefitte, the man with whom I travelled across Sicily some years ago, when I made a *sortie* from I Tatti to the south?[5] But I must go back and resume the thread of my narrative: back to Munich, to which I made a flying visit a month ago.

I must admit the visit made me more anti-German, or at least more anti-Bavarian, than ever. In Munich I hired a car to take me out to Pilsensee where I hoped to catch a man who had been Hitler's pilot and had recently returned from Russia. He was a well-spoken man who had been a chauffeur in private service, and we talked all the way and got on very well with each other. In the course of conversation he told me that he had been a prisoner in Russia and had been closely interrogated by the Russians. Why? I asked. Because, he said, – and he said it in the calmest, most natural way in the world – 'I happened to watch the shooting, in Simferopol, of 20,000 Jews.' He explained that he had not taken part in the shooting himself – he was a corporal in the Wehrmacht and the shooting was done by the SS – and that fact seemed to him sufficient to discharge his conscience of any awkward emotions in the matter; but he had had the good fortune (*das Glück*) to have a friend in the SS who took him there as a *Zuschauer*,[6] so he had been able to see the spectacle. He added that he disapproved of it in principle; but he said all this in so calm and dispassionate a manner that I was quite revolted and thought it would have been better if he had been activated by fanaticism than by this cold-blooded neutral curiosity. He also told me that he had been captured in Courland where the German Army was

[3] T-R interviewed Johann Rattenhuber, who commanded Hitler's bodyguard, in Munich on 30 October, and Hans Baur, Hitler's pilot, at Pilsensee next day. Both men had just been released from Soviet captivity.
[4] After a grave illness, Pope Pius XII was felt to have fallen deeper under the influence of Pasqualina Lehnert, the German nun who had been his housekeeper for nearly forty years and had come to be nicknamed *La Pappessa*. He made several reactionary pronouncements during 1955, but T-R is probably referring to the Vatican's denunciation of Roger Peyrefitte's new novel (see below).
[5] Roger Peyrefitte (1907–2000) was a retired French diplomat whose first and best novel, *Les Amitiés particulières* (1944), concerned the love between boys at a French boarding-school. His novel *Les Clés de Saint-Pierre* (1955), which accused Vatican officials of duplicity, greed and superstition, sold massively in France and Italy after being denounced by the Vatican as 'lewdly libellous'.
[6] Spectator.

surrounded. 'We hung on,' he explained, 'expecting the Americans to come and rescue us and drive the Russians back *aber Sie waren zu Dumm; und jetzt ist es zu spät.*[7] I am afraid this view is still common in Germany. I find it very depressing. I am in favour of keeping the country permanently divided!

I do hope BB is keeping well and has quite got over his fall. It is depressing that you should both go in for such antics. But I hope we shall find you both full of loquacity. Immobility of the limbs gives greater energy to the other faculties, and we have a lot to hear. How is Percy? I hope the operation has proved successful. What news of Luisa? And of whom would you like news? Isaiah is in Chicago till January, when he gets married. Mrs Cyril Connolly has gone back to Cyril, and George Weidenfeld, now totally discredited, pants, like fallen Icarus, at the bottom of a deep, neglected social pit. But Sylvia, now a very metropolitan figure, centrally placed in the heart of Mayfair,[8] will have been a far more useful guide to these events than we poor provincial mice can hope to be. We shall have to confine our conversation, *faute de mieux*, to the Good, the True and the Beautiful. Anyway we are all agog to see you on Saturday. [...]

The Trevor-Ropers arrived at I Tatti on Saturday, 10 December and left on the 13th. 'Xandra adores him, and listens open-mouthed, still in love,' Berenson reported to Hamish Hamilton afterwards. While there they were presented to the ex-Queen of Romania. The Trevor-Ropers then spent a week as guests of the British Ambassador and his wife, the Ashley Clarkes, at the Embassy in Rome, and had two meetings with Sir D'Arcy Osborne, formerly British Minister to the Holy See and afterwards Duke of Leeds, who took Trevor-Roper to call at the Vatican.

28 December 1955   Birchfield, Melrose

My dear BB

We are now back in Scotland, not without certain adventures (see below), and I write to tell you how much we enjoyed our visit and how glad we were to find you so well and, on the anniversary of your fall, so agile. I do hope Nicky is now a little more agile, and can migrate at least from floor to floor. Thank you both very much for receiving us so hospitably: we only wish we could have stayed longer; but our free time is severely rationed by children's holidays. As it was, we arrived in England too late for our

---

[7] 'But you were too stupid; and now it's too late.'
[8] The Sprigges had moved into chambers in Albany, Piccadilly.

connexions: the aeroplane was ten hours late in leaving Rome, as we only discovered when we arrived at the aerodrome, having said goodbye to everyone, dismissed the driver, and generally cut off our retreat. The result was that we arrived in London at 2.0 in the morning, with nowhere to stay, and Xandra had to travel up to Scotland a day late. Nor was this all. When her train was sitting in a station in rural Yorkshire, deep in snow, at 4.30 in the morning, another train ran into the back of it and smashed it. Xandra was in the tail sleeper, which was completely shattered: the engine of the offending train actually penetrated, having wrecked the guards' van, into the lavatory immediately adjoining her compartment. She was unhurt, but got a considerable shock. Fortunately the train was going very slowly because of the snow – 15 miles an hour instead of the usual 60 – otherwise there would have been terrible casualties. However, all is now well, and we have survived the horrors of Christmas and we shall be going to Oxford soon after the New Year.

We greatly enjoyed our stay in Rome too. One of the people we met there was a friend our yours, I think, *viz*: Harold Parsons,[1] whom we found both charming and interesting. He took us to the Etruscan Museum at the Villa Giulia, and to other places including the church of Santa Francesca Romana to see the 5th century encaustic painting which Cellini discovered there and which I think you have seen.

Can you tell me anything about the inner history of Roger Peyrefitte's *Les Clés de St Pierre*? I mean, about the circumstances of its composition? The subject came up when we were having luncheon with the Boncompagnis. Letizia Boncompagni questioned me about my journey across Italy with Peyrefitte and showed a good deal of disapproval of the book (although she admitted that the Pope had gone too far in his latest antics). But she never let out, what I afterwards discovered, that Peyrefitte had spent three months staying in the Pecci-Blunt palace, gathering information for the book. What do you make of all this?[2]

As yet I can't give you any report about the election of Professor Wind.[3] That must await my return to Oxford, the essential centre of all such

---

[1] Harold Parsons (1882–1967), an American connoisseur, had known BB for over forty years.
[2] Princess Boncompagni-Ludovisi's parents owned Palazzo Pecci-Blunt in Rome. Her discretion about Peyrefitte's visit may have had other roots: his homosexuality was no more discreet than Cecil Pecci-Blunt's relationship with an English footman named Cecil Everly.
[3] Edgar Wind (1900–1971), Fellow of Trinity College, Oxford and Professor of the History of Art 1955–67, was a Berliner by birth and training who left Germany after Hitler's accession to power and held chairs in art, and philosophy and art, in the USA 1942–55. As guest Chichele lecturer in Oxford in 1954 he gave such dazzling performances that he was chosen as the first incumbent of the university's new chair in the history of art. His belligerent temper was disguised under a suave manner.

information. But I shall not forget. As soon as I am back in these gently susurrating *coulisses,* I shall unfurl my antennae and record whatever I can of the buzzing. Unless, of course, it should transpire that (as sometimes happens in these academic matters) some *grande dame* has been behind it. In that case I may more profitably begin my researches here in the wilds of Scotland, while our own local duchesses are gathered together for the barbarian feast of Hogmanay.[4] [...]

---

[4]The T-Rs reached Melrose on Christmas Eve, had tea on Christmas Day and lunch on 5 January with the Duke and Duchess of Buccleuch, and also visited the Ellesmeres (the future Duke and Duchess of Sutherland).

1956

On 11 January 1956, Berenson sent a woeful letter explaining that he had been unwell since Christmas. 'The whole of that "holy night" I passed in violent spasms of retching with intervening moments of extraordinary mental clarity. In one of them I realized that the doctor was whispering to Nicky and Emma that my end had come, and it amused me so much that I laughed out aloud, to their horror. Of course they thought that I had gone out of my mind. I hadn't, only it seemed so funny to be given up for dying when I felt so much alive.' He had since developed cystitis, and was still confined to bed. He asked for inside information about Edgar Wind's recent election to the chair of art history at Oxford.

12 February 1956   Christ Church, Oxford

My dear BB

You wrote an alarming letter about your attack of cystitis. I do hope you are now completely recovered. It sounds horrible. Xandra, who has had it, says it is, and that it is due to draughts, *courants d'air* such as I had imagined were never admitted to I Tatti. But I hope all is well now and that your next letter will tell me that you are free of cystitis and Nicky of plaster and that you are both looking forward to that wonderful phenomenon, the spring at Settignano. Meanwhile I send you what I'm afraid can only be called the first instalment of my news on the election of Professor Edgar Wind.

The truth is, it is difficult to get an impartial verdict because my friends in the University seem – I regret to say – to have been all on one side. My main source, since I haven't yet seen Isaiah (he has been in America, and then getting married) is Maurice Bowra. He tells me that Wind is a spellbinder, a wonderful lecturer, and that being a man of great resourcefulness, when he runs out of matter, he invents. This does not greatly differ from your picture of him, so I went on to ask how, in that case, he got nominated and elected. The answer was that the opposition hadn't got a candidate. The opposition consisted, it seems, of Tom Boase,[1]

---

[1] Thomas Boase (1898–1974), general editor of the *Oxford History of English Art* in eleven volumes, Director of the Courtauld Institute and Professor of the History of Art at London University 1937–47, President of Magdalen College, Oxford 1947–68.

Michael Maclagan,[2] and Norrington:[3] the pro-Wind party were the Vice-Chancellor,[4] Bowra, K.T. Parker and Seznec. The opposition, who do, I fear, represent the party of Dry Old Sticks in the University, looked desperately around for Someone, Anyone, to put up against this terrible charlatan of Smith College; but in fact they could think of no-one except a very boring old hack called Pächt who delves laboriously in some recess of the Warburg Institute.[5] How, I was asked, could anyone really vote for Pächt? I had to admit it was difficult. And so, it seems, all the various talents of the Vice-Chancellor and his party were deployed in favour of Wind. Cultural respect-ability was supplied by K.T. Parker, the Panjandrum of the Ashmolean; cosmopolitan *aperçus* by Seznec; noises off by Bowra; and at their head, the Vice-Chancellor ... but how can I do justice to that splendid character, that Protean figure, compounded as he is of the Ancient Mariner, the Welsh Wizard, King Arthur, St Athanasius *contra mundum*, and the Foul Fiend Flibbertigibbet, and drawing his various arts alternately from Winchester College, Tammany Hall, and those ancient rocks on which the sirens sang? Would poor old Tom Boase and a pair of dry sticks do against such a combination? Of course they were helpless. Wind, they feebly protested, doesn't know anything. But does that matter? asked Sir Maurice (whose own scholarship is not always judged exact by the critics); after all, there is no *school* of Art-History in the University which he can lead into error by his ignorance: he will be but a professor lecturing in the void to susceptible *femmes du monde*; at least his errors may stimulate interest. A fig for learning! Who would you prefer? It was unfortunate that the opposition could only think of one name. 'Pächt' chanted Tom Boase and the two Dry Sticks in timorous unison, and Echo feebly answered 'Pächt'; whereupon the Vice-Chancellor flapped his wings and hooted derisively at them and they were scattered; and so Professor Wind, fleeing from Smith College, arrived at Oxford, to the delight of some – the gay and frivolous, I fear – and the chagrin of others, the grave scholars who know that he is a plausible humbug. I fear he is a humbug. The other day we consulted him about a good portrait-painter to paint the Prime Minister for our college hall.[6]

---

[2] Michael Maclagan (1914–2003), Fellow and tutor in medieval history at Trinity College, Oxford 1939–81, sometime Lord Mayor of Oxford and Visitor of the Ashmolean Museum, Portcullis Pursuivant 1970–80, and Richmond Herald 1980–9.

[3] (Sir) Arthur ('Thomas') Norrington (1899–1982), President of Trinity College, Oxford 1954–70.

[4] A.H. Smith: see letter of 27 August 1955.

[5] Otto Pächt (1902–1988), a refugee from Vienna, wrote on medieval book illuminations, early Dutch painters and cognate subjects.

[6] Sir Anthony Eden (1897–1977), later 1st Earl of Avon, Prime Minister 1955–7, had read Persian and Arabic as a Christ Church undergraduate, and was elected a Student there in 1941.

Wind did not pause to think. Tcheritchev, he exclaimed with instantaneous enthusiasm.[7] As far as I know Tcheritchev only paints fashionable women with long seductive hands. But these, I suppose, are the only circles in which the Professor now moves. I believe his lectures are crowded by culture-loving duchesses who go there to be seen listening in rapture as he slides over the gaps in his knowledge by brilliant improvisation. All this, I must admit, I have built up largely on the basis of one conversation with Maurice Bowra. However, determined as always to hear both sides, I have invited the Maclagans to dinner next week (it will be a stiff evening: what trials one undergoes in the pursuit of knowledge!). I shall then get the Opposition view, which no doubt will give me the material for another letter.

Meanwhile what other news can I give you? I have found the man who buried Hitler's bones.[8] So, dropping my more serious studies and abandoning my pupils, I nipped over to Bremen a fortnight ago and knocked on his door. I now have a fascinating story to tell, full of macabre detail: I am busy writing it up and you shall see it in due course.[9] But otherwise my visit to Germany was not a success. I missed my aeroplane and smashed my car on the way out; and on my way back, after making four attempts to land at London airport, and failing because of the fog, I was taken back and deposited in Brussels while Xandra, who had been waiting at the airport, had to drive home again in the fog. Life at Oxford is, of course, still entirely dominated by the great question of Roads. The other day a science professor was walking along South Parks Road and met the Vice-Chancellor and his dog on a lead. They fell into conversation. Suddenly the Vice-Chancellor uttered the phrase 'Inner Relief Roads'. Promptly his dog, who now knew his master's conversational habits by heart and had been obliged to listen to many an interminable monologue on that subject, gave a great yawn, curled up, and fell asleep on the pavement. Do you remember the splendid passage in Mark Pattison's memoirs, describing how the Oxford Movement, as a topic of conversation, was killed in Oxford Common Rooms, after Newman's secession, by the Railway

---

[7] The efforts of Pavel Tchelitchew (1898–1957) to create a sequence of paintings showing a soul's journey to immortality, and his images of Hell, Purgatory and Paradise, led Edith Sitwell to call him 'the greatest living painter – indeed as great a painter as El Greco'. He was best known as a stage designer.

[8] Harry Mengershausen, an officer in Hitler's detective bodyguard, buried the corpses of Hitler and Eva Braun on wooden boards, three feet underground, in a bomb crater outside the bunker in Berlin. Held in captivity by the Russians for eleven years, he was interviewed by T-R in Bremen on 27 January 1956 after being returned to Germany.

[9] See T-R's articles 'Hitler's Fate' in *Sunday Times*, 18 and 25 March 1956, and 'The "Mystery" of Hitler's Death', *Commentary*, XXII (July 1956), pp. 1-12.

Mania, King Hudson, and finally the crash of 1847?[10] Even so today in Oxford all intellectual conversation, all speculation, all learning have been driven out by the Road Mania. Such feeble energies as we have left are concentrated on the great problem of whether Mr Asquith did or did not spend the morning of 12 June 1916 playing bridge (see *The Times, passim*, for the last month). And of course the Trevor-Ropers have a further pre-occupation in our perpetual litigation. The Admiral, indefatigable in his worrying tactics, is now pursuing us in the Scottish courts, and I am having to learn an entirely new language in order to discover the meaning of portentous documents, written in the archaic idiom of Lady Macbeth's attorney, which issue from some Caledonian peatbog in his name. Xandra, who makes such a show of being Scottish, is even more at sea in the face of her national literature than I am, and tries to save her face by insisting that they are not written in Scottish at all but in medieval Latin.

I must now stop and go to bed [...]

13 April 1956   **Rabat, Morocco**

My dear BB

You must think that I have become a very bad correspondent. Doubtless you ascribe it to matrimony; but that is not the fact. The fact is that I realise you expect from me *long* letters, and so I have become ashamed to send you the customary brief intercalary letters which, in ordinary life, fill the gaps between the occasional long letters. And now, after so long a delay, I am almost ashamed to write to you at all. But I hope you will forgive me for this long silence. I hope also that you are now thoroughly recovered and enjoying the spring which, I hope, has come to Settignano.

By its non-arrival in the rest of Europe (except, I understand, Scotland, whence Xandra writes that it is wonderful) I have been reduced to a low physical ebb and now lie in Rabat gasping like a fish cast upon these Atlantic shores. We went for a few days, after the end of last term, to Paris, so that Xandra could replenish her stock of exotic hats. Then she went back to Scotland for the children's holidays and I went on to Spain partly for my own purposes (I wanted to study some documents in the Biblioteca del Palacio), partly for the *Sunday Times*, for which I aim to write two articles.[1]

---

[10] Mark Pattison (1813–1884), Rector of Lincoln College, Oxford, abandoned his high-churchmanship after John Henry Newman became a Catholic in 1845. The railway speculator George Hudson (1800-1871) was ruined by the discovery of railway financing frauds in 1849.

[1] 'Ferment Under Spain's Surface: Youth and Labour Critical of Franco's Regime', *Sunday Times*, 15 April 1956, and 'Franco and the Moors', *Sunday Times*, 22 April 1956. General Franco (1892–1975) had been confirmed as Spanish head-of-state for life in 1947. T-R had sided with the Popular Front government in Spain against the militarist insurgents during the civil war in the 1930s.

This also enabled me to stay for a few days with Gerald Brenan, of whom, or of whose works, I think you know. He lives in Churriana, a village near Málaga; and I find his house there the most stimulating intellectual centre of any after I Tatti. I told the *Sunday Times*, at the beginning of March, that there was bound to be some sort of a 'Morocco crisis' in Spanish politics; so I arranged also to go to Tetuán and Rabat. I didn't realise how right I was. In fact I was in Madrid when the Sultan arrived and I pretty well followed him back via Tetuán to Rabat.

Spanish politics do seem to me exceptionally interesting at the moment. Every base upon which Franco's monarchy is based seems to me to be split. The old opposition is dead – a few *émigrés*, a few liberal intellectuals, uttering outworn slogans. But *within* the previous supporters of the *régime* there seems to be a real crisis, social, intellectual, colonial. The only basis of the *régime* which is not shaken seems to me to be the general apathy of the people. If Franco's power were to crumble – and at present a revolt in Rio de Oro might cause it to crumble – nobody seems to have any ideas of how to replace it: it would probably have to be set up again.

And then Morocco – what a difference since I was last here, just over a year ago, in the reign of that poor puppet Ben Arafa,[2] who has now secretly fled from Tangier to a well-appointed villa on the Côte d'Azur! The restored Sultan is thoroughly enjoying his triumph, but seems to have reflected a good deal on the mutability of human affairs, and other such important commonplaces, during his exile in Madagascar. I think he is now determined, in spite of their treatment of him, to co-operate with the French in order not to be swallowed up by the Moorish Nationalists, and the French, relying on this, are equally determined, in spite of their humiliation, to cooperate with him. They assure me that the Sultan, whom, a year ago, they had described as 'quite impossible', is really a man of superior intelligence, Western, progressive, civilised. My only doubts on this score (apart from the suddenness of this new discovery by the French) arise from meeting his intimate and trusted personal adviser, Comte Clauzel,[3] to whom Roland de

---

[2] In August 1953 the French government, which had exercised a protectorate over Morocco since 1912, deposed Sultan Mohammed V Ben Yussuf and installed his kinsman Moulay Mohammed Ben Arafa as their puppet sultan. Ben Arafa abdicated in October 1955 and Mohammed V was restored as Sultan in November. In March 1956 the French government recognised Moroccan independence, and pledged to help Morocco recover control of the Spanish zone and Tangier. During the Sultan's state visit to Spain (4–9 April 1956), a joint declaration acknowledging the sovereignty and territorial integrity of Morocco was signed in Madrid.

[3] Ghislain, Comte Clauzel (1907–1992), was a diplomat renowned for his handsome bearing, immaculate appearance and punctilious manners. He was posted to Rabat in 1949 as Conseiller des Affaires Chérifiennes, and served as the liaison between the French Resident and the Sultan.

Margerie, the head of the Quai d'Orsay,[4] gave me a letter. I thought Clauzel – who anyway injured my vanity by assuming that I was much less intelligent than I think I am, and tried to fob me off with absurd answers – a soapy, shifty snob. Yesterday he asked me to come and see the Sultan's procession to prayers from his window at 12.15 and then to have luncheon. By 1 o'clock I had found his manners to be so inconceivably egotistic and insolent that I decided to leave rather than accept hospitality from him. I find that my view of him is shared by most Frenchmen, but not, I fear, by the Sultan.

All this has been interesting, but unfortunately, owing to the truly dreadful weather in Spain and Africa, I have been consistently ill and travel has been a nightmare to me. I feel I shall never make the long journey back from Rabat to Scotland, and yet I shall never recover here: which fills me with gloom. However, if the doctor allows me, I shall fly to Paris tomorrow: at least then I shall *feel* nearer home.

I have now made further enquiries about Professor Wind. The general view is that he is admittedly a charlatan, but a charlatan of something akin to genius, and that as there is no School of Art History at Oxford as there is at American Universities – i.e. no one can read the subject for a degree – he cannot do any positive harm, whereas his undoubted gift of exposition – even if erroneous – may interest people in the subject. Isaiah Berlin says he took no part in the election, but he says that if he had taken part he would in fact have supported Wind. The prime mover seems to have been d'Entrèves, supported by Maurice Bowra and K.T. Parker. I have not myself been to any of Wind's lectures, but I understand that they are a great draw. I fear that Art, as a subject, is becoming very fashionable: there is no function (as it seems to me) at which the feminine *beau-monde* is so eager to show off its headgear as a Lecture on Art (with slides, of course) by a Fashionable Connoisseur. K. Clark started it, at least at Oxford, with Jane Clark's hats. For his lectures Sybil Colefax used to be brought down from London in a crate, and elegant dinner-parties of the *élite* were *de rigueur* afterwards.

I'm afraid there is a great cult of Art among the young now. You are largely responsible. Your *Italian Painters* (the illustrated edition, of course) is the one book, I am assured, which every undergraduate possesses. (Next

---

He left Morocco in 1952, returned there in 1956–7, and later served as French Ambassador to Pakistan and to the Philippines. After retiring in 1972, he became a director of the Möet et Chandon champagne company.

[4] Roland de Margerie (1899–1990) had been an affectionate, protective friend to Xandra Howard-Johnston while her first husband was *en poste* in Paris. Appointed Director-General of Political Affairs at the French Foreign Ministry in 1955; subsequently Ambassador to the Vatican, Spain and Germany.

on the list is G.M. Trevelyan's *English Social History.*) But I fear they don't
read it. Indeed, they don't read anything. The classics – in any language –
are mere names to them. They look at pictures, listen to music; but books,
nowadays, are no part of their intellectual furniture.

I sometimes think what a fine turn could be done on the antithesis in
human history between the Image and the Book. It seems to me one of the
permanent conflicts in humanity. The Middle Ages believed in the Image,
the Reformers in the Book. In the 16th century they were locked in strife.
The Reformers printed ever more books – books mainly denouncing
images – and the Catholics invented the *Index Librorum Prohibitorum*[5] and
burnt those books and built ever more images, which the Reformers then
decapitated, pulverised, destroyed. The Enlightenment was a great age of
the Book. Today we live in a world of the Image. Hence the popularity
of Catholicism, which relies on the senses, not the intellect. Today the
Protestants are the Marxists, who are still the People of the Book. As a
natural Protestant I regret this: I regret that the cult of the book should
have dwindled to a sect – and the sectarians of such a Book too!

But good heavens, to whom do I say this? Am I not uttering heresy to
the High Priest himself? I please myself with the thought that I am not. No
doubt, I say to myself, the High Priest is horrified by the success of his own
teaching, or rather by the consequences that others have drawn from that
teaching. And anyway, what of the *Biblioteca Berensoniana*, that great
depository of Books! So I am determined to regard you as an ally in this
great battle which anyway I have perhaps altogether imagined. [...]

10 June 1956   8 St Aldate's, Oxford

My dear BB

Please send a short letter and tell us how you are. We long to hear from
you. I do hope that after your unpleasant winter you are now well and
comfortable, and that summer has come to Settignano. We keep hearing
of you, or getting questions about you, from our common friends – the
Notesteins, who are in Oxford now, Baron Franchetti,[1] whom I met again
last night – but we should like to hear from you direct too!

Meanwhile what news can I give you? Isaiah we have hardly seen. He

---

[5] The Index of Prohibited Books that Catholics were prohibited to read was imposed by Pope Paul
IV in 1557, periodically revised and finally abrogated in 1966.
[1] Probably Baron Carlo Franchetti (b. 1895), a descendant of the first Italian Jew to be ennobled
(in 1858 for financing railway-building in Piedmont). Educated at Eton and New College, Oxford;
interested in alpinism, speleology, etching and architecture. Possibly the same Baron Franchetti
who was Yvonne Hamilton's first husband, befriended Ernest Hemingway and collected fast cars.

lives withdrawn in Headington House and, except to meet Bulganin and Khrushchev, hardly emerges.[2] Namier perhaps you have seen, for I think he is just back from Italy. Notestein, incidentally, agrees with you about Wind. He says he will be a great success for two years, and then someone will start checking his references ... The Hamiltons we have not seen for a very long time: I suppose they still exist. Dawyck is getting married next month to a girl whom we think very nice and suitable. She is called Adrienne Morley and makes tiles in a kiln in Hampstead. Derek I saw staying at Bemersyde last month. He was on a social round; but I think he is now buried in Donegal. I had promised to go and stay a couple of days with him a fortnight ago, when I was in Belfast listening to some lectures by my friend, your compatriot, John Nef,[3] but it proved impossible. So I'm afraid I can't report on his life as 'a Protestant hog in a bog'. We, as you see from this writing-paper, are now settled into our house in Oxford: in fact, we are having a great house-warming party next week. I wish you were near enough to come!

Do you know some people called Corsini? I have a pupil called Nicolas Gage who is going to Florence in July to learn Italian and is to stay with them. He is intelligent and engagingly dotty – a dottiness which comes (I think) from his mother, *née* Imogen Grenfell, daughter of Lord Desborough.[4] I have promised to find out anything I can about the Corsini, so do tell me anything you can.

Do you know the work of Moses Finley, *né* Finckelstein?[5] May I recommend you his little book on *The World of Odysseus*? It was published in America about two years ago and is now appearing in England. I think it is wonderfully good; fresh and clear and illuminating: I have never read anything so fresh and exciting on the Homeric age, and so completely free from pedantry. Also he asks new questions and gives, in my opinion, satisfying and stimulating answers. I discovered his work a year ago when there seemed a chance of getting him to Oxford. He was at New Brunswick but was driven out by Senator McCarthy. I don't *think* he is (or was) a communist, but he was clearly at least *marxisant*. I was so excited by his

---

[2] The visit to Oxford on 21 April by the Soviet leaders Nikolai Bulganin and Nikita Khrushchev was enlivened by undergraduate pranks as well as a meeting with Berlin.

[3] T-R admired the work of John Nef (1899–1988), an economic historian at the University of Chicago, who gave the Wiles lectures at Queen's University, Belfast, in May 1956.

[4] Nicolas Gage (b. 1934), later 8th Viscount Gage, was grandson of Lord and Lady Desborough, hospitable Edwardians.

[5] (Sir) Moses Finley (1912–1986) left Rutgers University, New Jersey, and moved to England in 1954. He was appointed university lecturer in classics at Cambridge in 1955, elected to a Fellowship at Jesus College in 1957, was Professor of Ancient History 1970–79 and Master of Darwin College 1976–82.

work that I determined to get him to Christ Church. Of course there was a panic on the Right Wing, but after a tremendous struggle I persuaded the Governing Body of Christ Church to make him an offer. Unfortunately, by that time my old classical tutor, Denys Page,[6] being now Regius Professor of Greek at Cambridge, persuaded Cambridge to make him a better offer, so we lost him to our rival university. I really recommend his book to you. It is not too long for you! I am going to write something on it in the *New Statesman.*[7]

Incidentally I have sent you an essay I wrote on 'Oliver Cromwell and his Parliaments'; which you mustn't bother to read: it is just to complete the small collection of my works in the Biblioteca Berensoniana. It was written for a *Festschrift* for Namier, which is now published. I shall also send you, when it appears, an essay I have written for an American official publication *Problems of Communism.* The essay, which I think might amuse you, is on 'Marx and the Study of History'. Meanwhile, I am working on the subject of the Reformation and Social Change – two processes which, I now think, are quite distinct. What confusion has been caused by those German sociologists – Marx, Weber,[8] Troeltsch,[9] Sombart,[10] etc. – who confounded them! But I suppose they have set a lot of new ideas in motion by that confusion. If only they didn't write so portentously!

At the end of the month I go to Paris for two days to a conference on the Renaissance. I don't know if it will be interesting or not: some of the participants promise to be interesting. But I shall reserve judgment till I have been, and will then send you an account of it [...]

PS. We went to the famous Plesch Ball (see *New Statesman* on the subject).[11]

---

[6] T-R had many early contacts with (Sir) Denys Page (1908–1978), classics tutor at Christ Church 1932–50 and a senior figure in wartime deciphering of enemy signals at Bletchley. Elected Regius Professor of Greek at Cambridge in 1950 and Master of Jesus College, Cambridge in 1959.
[7] 'The World of Homer', *New Statesman*, 14 July 1956, pp. 45–6; *Historical Essays*, pp. 6–11.
[8] Max Weber (1864–1920), author of *Die protestantische Ethik und der Geist der Kapitalismus.*
[9] Ernst Troeltsch (1865–1923) was a liberal theologian, philosopher and historian who like Weber investigated the connections between Calvinism and capitalism.
[10] Werner Sombart (1863–1941) sought to refute Weber's theories. 'Sombart's book *The Jews and Modern Capitalism,*' so T-R had written in 1951, 'is [...] rich, suggestive, intellectually irresponsible and its political consequences ultimately disastrous. Himself a Gentile, an admirer of Jews, he became involuntarily a Founding Father of anti-Semitism.' (*Historical Essay*, pp. 156–7.)
[11] The Hungarian financier Arpad Plesch (1889–1974) had in 1954 become the sixth husband of Maria Anna ('Etti') von Wurmbrand-Stuppach (1914–2003). They gave a lavish coming-out ball at Claridge's hotel in London on 16 May for her only child Countess Marie-Anna ('Bunny') Esterhazy and another debutante, Florence ('Flockie') Harcourt-Smith. An anonymous article entitled 'Bunny, Flockie and Co.' in *New Statesman* of 26 May denounced 'the upper-class spending spree' at Claridge's as 'tedious bad taste', 'cocking a tentative snoot at the masses' and 'a fake revival of the leisured class'. The prig who wrote the piece consoled its readers with the improbable suggestion that the Pleschs' guests had been served 'bad champagne and dubious caviare'.

Incidentally do tell us your information on the Pleschs – no two sources seem to agree! There, larger than life, circulating nimbly among the bogus foliage in Claridges, was George Weidenfeld, larger than ever, with a succession of slim and elegant *débutantes*. So his social decline has been very temporary, or at least, if he hit the bottom, he bounces.

Berenson replied on 15 June that Nicky Gage's hosts, the Corsini, were 'the most respectable family of Florence. Prince Tommaso overwhelmed by care of innumerable estates all over Italy that bring in little.' He wrote again, on 13 August, to praise Trevor-Roper's 'clinching paper' entitled 'The "Mystery" of Hitler's Death' published in Commentary *in July. 'The mystery that remains is why Stalin and his troops refused to admit Hitler's death. [...] I still suspect that they kept in reserve the possibility Hitler was still alive on the chance of launching somebody as a false Hitler for their own purposes as the Poles did after Boris Gurdunov.'*

18 August 1956   8 St Aldate's, Oxford

My dear BB

   I was taking up my pen to write to you when your letter came. I'm afraid I have been very long silent, and really our *rôles* have been reversed; for whereas you always say that you can't pick up a paper without seeing any evidence of me, this has been definitely untrue for a long time, and now whatever paper I pick up I find in it (with pleasure) evidence of you. *The Times* the other day carried your photograph; Annigoni quotes you in a published letter;[1] the *Literary Supplement* is full of you;[2] and now even from distant Mexico, that glittering shop-window of the otherwise empty Spanish world, I receive a picture of you in *La Gaceta*,[3] whereby I keep in touch with the intellectual life of central America; to which I have a passion to go, but to which I seem never to be able actually to find the way. Perhaps it is really very disappointing. I have an irrepressible feeling that its intellectual life is bogus where it is not borrowed. Still, I am glad to see that it is being borrowed from the right sources.

   As for me, I can account for my withdrawal from the world. I am trying to write something on that controversial subject, the Reformation and the economic growth of Europe. What a morass I now find myself in! What

---

[1] *The Times* of 4 August printed a photograph of BB as well as Pietro Annigoni's letter, 'Cleaning Old Pictures', which quoted a message from BB.
[2] 'The Making of a Connoisseur', a review of Mostyn-Owen's bibliography, was the lead article in *TLS*, 29 June 1956, pp. 385–6; and 'Restored Portrait of an Italian Painter', *TLS*, 20 July 1956, p. 438, reviewed the revised edition of BB's *Lorenzo Lotto*.
[3] A newspaper published by Universidad Nacional Autónoma de México.

infinite books I have had to read, and in German too! What numerous changes of mind I have gone through! How many pages have I written, only to tear up again! However, it keeps me quiet. For a time progress was very slow; but then I took a firm line. No more social life, no more London balls, no more weekends in the country, no movement from Oxford till I had completed 100 pages; which I have now done, and tomorrow I go to Scotland, whither Xandra – unable to endure this rigorous anti-social regime, and burdened by children – went off last week. There I shall *try* to vegetate (how does one do it?), as I have been suffering for some time from some eye-trouble and may have to stop using my eyes much for a time. But is this possible? What else can one do?

Do you read the *Spectator*? It is really an excellent paper now. Ian Gilmour has transformed it.[4] It is full of controversy. At present there is a highly diverting spectacle provided by those never-failing comedians the English convert RCs.[5] I have written a brief letter to help the controversy on, as from the Vatican City, signed Pius †; but I fear that the editor may suspect its genuineness, – though not, I am sure, on the grounds of any deviation in it from Catholic orthodoxy.

Isaiah has gone to Russia – not, I hasten to add, as a refugee, like Burgess and Maclean, but as a tourist, disguised as an *honorary attaché* at the British Embassy. Aline has gone with him: I think she will hate it; but I greatly look forward to their return and his accounts of life there. He went in the war, and dined out for months afterwards on the narratives he brought back.

I hope you enjoyed the Destalinisation episode. It has given me endless pleasure. The antics of British communists are as enjoyable as those of British Catholics; and this time they have been as disconcerted as the English papists would be if the Pope were found to have been a Protestant all the time. They are all bickering about it like mad. As for the facts behind it, I am completely persuaded by the article by Geoffrey Hudson (for whom I have a great respect) in the *Twentieth Century*: an article which proves to me that Khrushchev murdered Stalin.[6] I have been offered enormous sums of dollars by the American press to write about the Last Days of Stalin; but – with some difficulty – I have preserved what remains of my literary and historic virtue.

---

[4] Ian Gilmour (b. 1926), afterwards Lord Gilmour of Craigmillar, had become proprietor-editor of *The Spectator* in December 1954 and was elected as a Conservative MP in 1962.
[5] Evelyn Waugh, in weekly issues of *The Spectator* from 3 to 24 August, pursued a truculent correspondence about the dogmas of the Immaculate Conception and of the bodily assumption of the Blessed Virgin Mary into heaven.
[6] G.F. Hudson, 'The Heirs of Stalin', *Twentieth Century*, 160 (August 1956), pp. 99–113.

What else can I tell you? Oxford is very dull. I made a careful computation the other day which satisfies me that there are in this university only 19 intelligent people, of whom six are hermits or otherwise unsuitable for social life and eight are so social that they can never be found, always being in Paris, London, or some such place. So I am becoming a hermit too, and only reading books. Also my circle of friends is, I fear, shrinking. I had to go to Ireland recently, to Belfast, that centre of Protestantism in the otherwise dotty isle. Derek, whom I had met staying with Dawyck in the spring, invited me to stay; but Xandra was so indignant at my going there when she was not with me (for she drew the line at Belfast) that I weakly complied, wrote to Derek, said I had to go to Dublin on business, and went instead to stay with a splendid, monstrous, outrageous master of foxhounds in County Kildare.[7] But alas for human prevision! My excellent host decided that it was his duty to enliven the conversation in his house by bringing in the garrulous neighbours from adjoining counties to dinner; and so I found myself next to a formidable elderly lady who engaged me in needless rattle. Too late I discovered that she was Derek's aunt, even then on the way to stay with him ... Soon afterwards I had from Derek a dry postcard beginning, 'My aunt, Madam O'Malley, tells me ...'[8] Soft answers have failed to turn away his wrath, and I now fear that I am eternally in the shadows, as seen from the glowering hills and bogs of Co. Donegal.

But not, I hope, as seen from the serene beech-shaded hills of Vallombrosa where you, I hope, have escaped from all but the choicest company and are doubtless preparing some new and, I hope, heretical publication. I wish we could be among those few visitors. But instead we send you, across the intervening distance, all our best wishes; and when you descend again into the valley, with its brisk social life, I hope we may both come and visit you again and find you in good health [...]

26 September 1956   **Christ Church, Oxford**

My dear BB

I was so glad to get your telegram and to know that we may visit you from 21st to 28th October. We have decided to make a brief expedition to

---

[7] After a meeting with Conor Cruise O'Brien in Dublin on 25 May, T-R went to stay with Michael Beaumont, formerly MP for Aylesbury, at Harristown House near Brannockstown. After the dinner party on 26 May, the Beaumonts took T-R for a Sunday visit to Sir Alfred Beit's art collection at Russborough.

[8] Hill's aunt Grace, Madam O'Mahony [*sic*], was married to Dermot Gun O'Mahony, whose father had assumed the title of The O'Mahony by deed poll in 1912. In a letter of 10 June 1956, Hill described his aunt as 'very fierce like a general with a noble weather-battered leathery face'.

Italy – no further south than you – and shall spend one week in motion, one at rest. The week of motion will be in the Valle Padana. I resolved, some years ago, never to go to Venice again: the crowds of the less cultured of your compatriots, who stood shouting in the Piazza S. Marco, or sat boasting in Florian's, or queued noisily up to the *American Express* office, were too much for me. But Xandra wants to go and I suppose that in October the foreigners may have gone home again. I also want to go to Vicenza, where I have never been; and we will go to Ravenna, which I would gladly see again, before coming on to you. I believe that the Palladian villa of Marina Volpi-Trotalong (but I know I must not use that word: is the correct form Luling?) is near Vicenza, or near Venice, and visible.[1] Is that so? We should very much like to see it if possible. We have heard about it from Dawyck, who saw it. Anyway, after whatever movements, we greatly look forward to seeing you both, and hope we shall find you well.

So far we have not moved this summer except within the narrow orbit of Oxford and Scotland. I have been scratching away with pen on paper, and then re-scratching it all out again. Here we continue our circular dance around that gothic Pied Piper, Vice-Chancellor Smith, now quite uncontrollable, having succeeded (so far) in both his ambitions. Has he not added to his triumphal academic car, after the King of Sweden and the Emperor of Ethiopia, that greatest monarch of all, Nikita Khrushchev, with gory heads still hanging round his belt? Has he not persuaded the Minister of Transport to double-cross all to whom he has ever promised anything, and to declare – while the Cabinet with its five Christ Church members is preoccupied in the Middle East – not only a Road through the Meadow but a Medieval High Street? Of course we rural peasantry of the Meadow are going to fight back, with our Stone Age implements. The essential aim will now be to ruin the minister.

> Rege incolumi mens omnibus una est;
> Amisso rupere fidem.[2]

If you read the *Spectator* (if not, you should: the new regime has gayened it up beyond belief), you will see the first attack on Friday.[3]

---

[1] BB adored Marina Volpi (1907–1977), daughter of the Italian industrialist Volpi, sister of Anna-Maria Cicogna and wife of Count Enrico Luling. Her father in 1935 gave her the villa of Maser, which had been built by Palladio and was decorated with frescoes by Veronese.

[2] 'While their king is safe, they are all of one mind; but when they have lost him, they have lost their confidence.' Virgil, *Georgics IV*, 212–13.

[3] Robert Blake, 'Ploughing the Sandys', *Spectator*, 28 September 1956, p. 412, is a trenchant criticism of the proposal to build a road through Christ Church Meadow.

Unfortunately I can play no part in this congenial battle, at least *in propria persona*: I must egg my fellow-peasants on from behind, perhaps even furtively sharpening their pitchforks for them, but I must myself remain securely concealed in the long meadow grass. Once I did rashly venture out into the open: I read, in the Cathedral on Sunday, a carefully chosen First Lesson – what long vigils with the Concordance it cost me to find that text! – a commination of divine wrath against those who drove roads through other people's Meadows. But that was some time ago. Now I must be very discreet.

The reason? Of course it is the usual academic reason. I have a protégé whom I particularly want to insert, as a Research Fellow, into All Souls College. But the Warden of All Souls, John Sparrow, with whom I must, for this reason, on no account quarrel, is a fanatical supporter of his fellow-Wykehamist, the Vice Chancellor[4] ... so you see we are up against the Wykehamist international (you know that in England we are governed by Old Etonians led by the nose to disaster by a Wykehamist Underground). However, as at Suez, ancient tribal nationalism still shows that it can survive in our technological age, so we do not despair.

Meanwhile I scratch away about the 16th century and find that as I solve, or think that I solve, each minor problem, the unsolved problems get larger and more numerous as they are approached. But I suppose all writing is like this. Then, in despair, I suspend work. I look forward to suspending it at I Tatti. We shall let you know exactly about our arrival when plans are made: probably by bus from Ravenna. Do tell us if there is anything we should not miss at Vicenza, or near it (Ravenna I know: but how glad I shall be to see it again! What about Verona? Or Mantua? I know neither). [...]

On 11 October, the Trevor-Ropers left England for Italy, where they visited Verona, Vicenza, Venice and Marina Luling-Volpi's Villa Maser before reaching I Tatti on 21 October. They found the rakish English author James Pope-Hennessy staying there: other callers at the house included the French philosopher and dramatist Abbé Gabriel Marcel, the Italian diplomat Giuliano Cora, and Victor Cunard, who had succeeded them in Red Brick Cottage on the Astor estate. They lunched with Prince

---

[4]John Sparrow (1906–1992) had been an undergraduate pupil of A.H. Smith's at New College, and retained a lifelong affectionate respect for him. Sparrow was a barrister, book collector and bibliographer as well as Warden of All Souls 1952–77. 'We like him personally – at least in small doses – but as an intellectual figure I'm afraid I regard him as ridiculous and as a university figure a disaster. He is very learned, but all his learning is concentrated on absurd trifles [...] Similarly in university affairs, he spends all his time (which is immense, since he has no academic duties) in elaborating ingenious reasons for preventing anything from happening anywhere. This can be maddening.' (T-R to Nicky Mariano, 23 March 1962.)

Paul of Yugoslavia at Pratellino, and visited Harold Acton at La Pietra, before returning to Paris.

'The Trevor-Ropers left after a week's stay,' Berenson noted in his diary on 29 October. 'She looked haggard and years older than Hugh, but very well dressed, and is not by any means as stupid and dazed as she looks. He is in the first flower of his years and career. Handsome in a Nordic way, though not particularly distinguished-looking. Angular Pinocchio-like gestures, sawing up and down, and finishing arguments with clenched fist. Cock-sure, arrogant, but without insolence, and no effort to assert himself, seems to think it is not worthwhile. Seldom starts, but when cranked up goes on endlessly with infinite detail, and detective awareness and marvellous capacity for taking trouble to convince himself, and to convince his hearers. Seems to have known everybody, or at least everybody who has counted, in the last 30 years. Can recite entire sagas about them. A fascinating letter-writer, indeed an epistolary artist, brilliant reviewer of all sort of books, very serious historian and formidable polemicist.'

13 November 1956   **8 St Aldate's, Oxford**

My dear BB

Little did I think, when you sighed for a psalm *In introitu Israel in Aegyptum,*[1] that God, who clearly pays heed to your lightest wish, should have granted it even before I could write to tell you, as I now do, how much we enjoyed our stay at I Tatti! We were in Ireland when the news broke,[2] and constrained to silence by ignorance of the circumstances in the midst of the suspicious natives; and since we have been back in England, I have felt constrained to silence too, in order not to partake of the braying and counter-braying of my asinine colleagues. But I find the whole affair very mortifying. All my worst suspicions of Eden are confirmed. The facts were perfectly clear – have been clear since September 1955, when the Czech arms-deal was arranged. All the British government had to do was to prepare opinion for the inevitable Israeli attack, so that Egypt would in any case appear as the true aggressors, and build up diplomacy and force in the full sight of the Arab powers. And yet in fact all that this vain, ineffectual Man of Blood has done is to travel in the pro-Arab 'bus until the seizure of the Suez canal and then jump desperately on to the anti-Arab 'bus and throw his weight about with the uncontrolled, panic-stricken, bewildered irresponsibility of a last-minute convert. So we are condemned by all,

[1] 'Israel came into Egypt' (Psalm 105: 23).
[2] On 29 October, following the Egyptians' nationalisation of the Suez canal and a secret pact between Britain, France and Israel, Israeli troops had invaded Egypt. British paratroopers followed.

haven't secured the canal, have put it out of action, haven't got rid of Nasser, and look like making a present of the Middle East to Russia. Was ever a good case so wantonly bungled? The pro-Eden press is now loudly claiming (1) that we have stopped a general war; (2) that we have 'revealed' the extent of Russian penetration in the Middle East. It seems to me that (1) is doubtful, and anyway there were less disastrous ways of achieving it, and (2) was well known already. As *The Times* has pointed out, the 'disclosures' about Russian arms in Egypt only differ by ten fighter-planes from the estimates of such arms published before the 'invasion'.

However, this letter is not sent to bore you with politics. It is a letter of thanks. We were both delighted to be at I Tatti again and to see you both looking so well. What a pleasure it is to come to rest in that ever-hospitable house and enjoy such excellent company! We couldn't have enjoyed it more. Thank you both very much for letting us come.

By now, I suppose, you will have had the King of Sweden; and you will have savoured your triumph over the Florentine pictures. Perhaps, after this triumph, you will come to the aid of certain other pictures too. For when we were in Ireland, staying with the Moynes,[3] a sinister figure turned up in their hospitable house. Bryan Moyne's eldest son is a flibbertigibbet called Desmond Guinness whose mother, a Mitford, has since run off with Sir Oswald Mosley to whom she is now married.[4] As if this double connexion with Nazism were not enough, he has now married the daughter of a Prince of Urach-Württemberg who, before the war, cultivated Hitler and obsequiously painted his portrait (he is now more innocently employed selling Mercedes-Benz cars).[5] Well, this young man came over to luncheon one day and brought with him – *horresco referens*[6] – David Carritt.[7] It

---

[3] The T-Rs stayed at Knockmaroon (30 October to 3 November) as the guest of Bryan Guinness, 2nd Baron Moyne (1905–1992), poet and vice-chairman of Arthur Guinness & Company.

[4] Desmond Guinness was Bryan Moyne's second son: see letter of 23 March 1952. His mother Diana (1910–2003) and his aunt Unity Mitford (1914–1948) had both admired Nazism.

[5] Prince Albrecht von Urach (1903–1969), Count of Württemberg, was cousin or nephew of several reigning monarchs. A painter and Nazi photo-journalist, he endured many hardships before joining Mercedes-Benz's public relations department in 1953.

[6] 'I shudder as I recall it' (Virgil).

[7] As an ingratiating and very self-confident youth David Carritt (1927–1982) had visited BB at I Tatti on 9 September 1947: asked afterwards by a friend, who met him in a Florence bar, where he had been, he replied, 'Up at I Tatti correcting a few attributions.' A month later, as a Christ Church undergraduate, he called on T-R and listened with him to a radio broadcast by Alys Russell. Carritt, who for some years provided BB with photographs of pictures and art-world news, worked at Christie's, opened his own Mayfair gallery and was art critic of the *Evening Standard*. Among many lucrative finds, he discovered a Tiepolo ceiling in the club-house of Hendon golf course, a set of vast Guardi canvases rolled up in an Irish stables and an unknown Caravaggio in Cumbria. He also bought for £8,000 a Fragonard that no one else had noticed at the Mentmore sale.

appears that Desmond Guinness is helping to organise an exhibition of works of art from Irish country houses. Carritt is going round with him, theoretically to advise him about the pictures which they find in Irish country houses; but in fact he is using this opportunity to spy out the land as a dealer; and no one doubts what the consequence will be. Before long, the country houses of Ireland will be stripped bare, at low prices, of their treasures; and Carritt (who is already looking very prosperous and is twice his former bulk) will be flourishing hugely on their resale.

We greatly enjoyed our visit to Ireland, – where, incidentally, we saw Derek, but in Dublin, not Donegal. The Moynes live about five miles out of Dublin, beyond Phoenix Park. But I think Xandra found the conducted tours of the Brewery rather too extensive. Bryan seems convinced that all visitors have an insatiable passion for the complex and recondite details of his brewery, and we were taken over different parts of it no less than three times. What vast acreage of skimming vats, fermenting tuns, aluminium containers we uncomprehendingly surveyed! What infinite series of great cauldrons, in which thick brown liquid infernally seethed! 'And now', said Bryan, 'you *must* come up to the top of the Brewery: it is the highest point in Dublin.' We stumbled on. Wherever we went, we walked on perforated metal flooring and Xandra's high-heels perpetually got stuck in the per-forations, her Jacques Fath hat got caught by its plumage in the steaming overhead pipes. But Bryan, who is a poet when not brewing, didn't notice these practical hitches. 'It's a pity the lift isn't working,' he observed casually, 'but it's only seven storeys up'; so we struggled up, seven storeys of enor-mous height, while great torrents of Guinness swirled past us like a moun-tain-stream and occasionally a Caliban-like figure deferentially, through the steam, touched his hat to the agile patron who darted between the cauldrons. When we finally reached the top, 'There', said Bryan proudly, 'lies the whole of Dublin'; and we looked down into a thick, uniform, obscuring fog in which nothing was visible. On three separate days we thus followed our host round different stretches of the brewery, all equally unintelligible to us; and Bryan seemed quite upset, for our sakes, that on the fourth day some inconvenient social alibi prevented us from a visit to the cooperage-department.

I gave four lectures, on four successive days, in Dublin, and then we came back here, and I have been trying, after so much travel, so much pleasure, and so much distraction by political events, to reacclimatise myself to work on the 16th century; which I am doing, I fear, very slowly. Life at I Tatti makes one in love with *douceur de vivre*, and it is a great effort to put pen to paper again. However, little by little, I push the reluctant instru-ment – never reluctant when writing to you, only when trying to write a chapter of grave historical matter. Meanwhile your *Sunday Times* will show, for the next two weeks, that I am still active,[8] and I have just posted to you an article which I wrote for an American paper called *Problems of Communism*.[9] I *was* quite pleased with it at one time, when I had just written it; but alas, the sub-editors have been at work and I can hardly recognise it now: they have edited it out of the English in which I wrote it into another language which I don't always understand. Meanwhile I have come to terms with my publishers, so my new edition of *The Last Days of Hitler* should soon be out. A copy will be sent to you [...]

'At last,' Berenson replied on 18 November, 'thanks to yours of the 13th, I begin to understand Eden's mistakes & the consequent hue & cry against his policy in the near East. [...] Now it is Eisenhower who is forbidding you to touch a hair of Nasser's head. I am too disgusted, too sick. What a welter!'

25 November 1956   **8 St Aldate's, Oxford**

My dear BB

I write to give you some account of the atmosphere in England after the heroic follies (culminating in the Flight to Jamaica) of our worthless Prime Minister.

My own view of the merits of the case is quite clear. The case against Egypt was overwhelming; the need for action was clear; but since the timidity of America and the squeals of the virtuous Asiatics were predictable, it was necessary that the action be not only sharp and effective but that it be carefully planned and against a background of favourable opinion, which it was perfectly possible to prepare. In fact the action was ineffective (instead of ruining Nasser and securing the canal, we secured Nasser in power and ruined the canal); it was ill-planned – reactions were not foreseen and Russian threats were enough to stop it half-way; and nothing whatever was done to prepare opinion. Now we have done what may be very serious damage to our economy and have given the Russians an open door into the Middle East. I find it very difficult to regard this as anything but disastrous.

---

[8] 'Nazi Secret Service', *Sunday Times*, 18 November 1956, was T-R's review of K.H. Abshagen's biography, *Canaris*, and of Walter Schellenberg's *Memoirs*; 'German Alibi?', 25 November, was his review of Gerald Reitlinger's *The S.S.*

[9] A historical survey printed as the Introduction to *Why I Oppose Communism: A Symposium* (London, 1956).

However, these clear and simple views which I have advanced are very heretical. The mass of my countrymen shout, from opposite massed choirs, either (a) that we have been wicked to think of using force against this tinpot Egyptian dictator or of ignoring the craven (or interested) squeaks of India, Bolivia, Saudi Arabia, Rumania etc.; or (b) that the Prime Minister is the greatest leader we have ever had and that our action has been characterised by heroism, genius and disinterested magnanimity. View (a) I regard with contempt. (Particularly contemptible, in my opinion, is the attitude of the virtuous Indians, who extenuated the Russian action in Hungary and have conveniently forgotten what notice *they* paid to a UNO resolution that they should leave Kashmir.) It is view (b) which fascinates me. It fascinates me because it has created an atmosphere which I have known only once before, but which was then identical with the atmosphere today: the atmosphere of 1938, of Munich.

How shall I ever forget Munich? My friends were divided, families were divided, social life was forced into new patterns. The cleavage cut society into novel forms: it did not correspond with any of the old cleavages of political party, economic activity, social class. And while the virtuous Left uttered pacifist nonsense, the Chamberlainites declared, in ever more strident tones, that Chamberlain was the greatest leader we had ever had, a genius, an immortal, a Messiah ...

It is incredible how similar the atmosphere is today. With the true-blue tories who, with absolute unanimity, declare forth the genius of Eden, it is quite impossible to argue. However great the losses, those – they say – were a small sacrifice in view of the great gains won by our brilliant Prime Minister (gains which they seldom very clearly specify). And now again, as in 1938, society is divided and it is hardly possible to speak across the divisions. In London, people are excluded from dinner parties &, in the country, from shooting parties, if they do not proclaim the genius of Eden. Moreover, it seems really true that support for the Prime Minister has positively *grown* since this fiasco.

Often, in the past fortnight, I have reflected on the social basis of this irrational support for a policy which seems to me rationally indefensible; and I conclude that there is in England, as in other countries, a fascist world: the world of lower-middle-class conservatives who have no intelligence but a deep belief in violence as a sign of self-importance; who hate foreigners, especially if they come from 'inferior' races; and who, gratified with the spectacle of such violence against such people, even if it fails in its object, are prepared to shout, in unison, 'il Duce ha sempre ragione'.[1] In ordinary

---

[1] 'The Leader is always right': an ironic saying by dissidents of the Mussolini era.

times, and given good politics by their leaders, these people remain below the level of public notice, quietly reading the *Daily Telegraph* and cultivating their gardens. But these are not ordinary times and the politics of our leaders are not good; and so out of frustration this extraordinary and disquieting spirit breaks forth.

I was advancing this view the other day to Ian Gilmour, the Editor of the *Spectator*, in his club; but when I came to the words 'lower middle-class' he took me up, and was about to give instances to confound my interpretation when we were interrupted by Lord Linlithgow, who came and joined us.[2] Five minutes of conversation with him were enough to show that it is by no means only the lower-middle-classes who utter these incredible sentiments. But I still keep to my original view. All that Lord Linlithgow did was to show how it was that even the *haute aristocratie* of Italy and Germany found it easy to join the fascist movement.

However, I think that I begin now to detect a change. The flight of Eden has helped. I now find that those of my more intelligent friends who had surprised me by supporting the follies of the government are now beginning to make admissions. Moreover, with that flight, I think that there is a genuine improvement in the situation which, if only Eden's successors show reasonable skill, may be exploited. Nasser has shown that Eden is not the only ass. His expulsion of the British and French civilians at this stage, and his attempts to call the tune as if he had ever had a good case, and as if he had not been militarily defeated, seems to me *Yβρις*[3] which may yet turn, if properly handled, to our advantage. And slowly – through no virtue of ours – the other Arab States (who have already shown the real solidity of the Arab League) are beginning to realise what Russian patronage may mean. I still hope that in spite of our huge mistakes, and the unnecessary cost, Nasser's days may be numbered. But our method has been that of burning down the house in order to have roast pig.

The question one has to ask is, what has happened to Eden, to make him behave in this extraordinary way. The flight to Jamaica, at the height of the crisis, is in keeping with his previous follies. Never before has a Prime Minister fled a whole hemisphere away in the middle of a crisis which he has himself provoked. If he were in need of a rest, why (it is asked) could he not go and stay with friends in England? Or go to Jamaica and put it

---

[2] Charles Hope, 3rd Marquess of Linlithgow (1912–1987). Gilmour had written to T-R on 19 November: 'Eden is indeed unspeakable. In the present semi-fascist atmosphere up here it is considered treacherous to whisper a word of criticism. When I go into my Club [White's], I feel as if I had been cheating at cards or something vile like that! Still we go plugging on even though our readers leave us in shoals.'
[3] 'Overweening presumption'.

out that he had gone to stay with friends in England? Is it possible that he can survive in politics after such a comedy? But perhaps this is what Toynbee describes as the essential phase in the life of a Great Man, the phase of Withdrawal and Return. Can it be that Eden is a disciple of Toynbee?

Everything is possible; but my own view is that this is all the result of Lady Eden,[4] who now completely manages her vain and foolish husband: a determined, ambitious woman whose understanding of the public is sufficiently shown by the public speech into which she broke out just before the Withdrawal, in which she declared that in the last few days she had felt as if the Suez Canal ran through her drawing-room. And who manages Lady Eden? I understand that just as the Prime Minister only listens to her, so she only listens to one voice, one Rasputin: Cecil Beaton.[5] Do you know Cecil Beaton? He is a fashionable – no, *the* fashionable, the only – English photographer: the Hoffman[6] of the new fascist court; and he is, of course, *uno di quelli*, as I believe the polite Italians say, and of course, being one, a friend of the Queen-Mother who also has a particular taste for *quelli* . . .

But I am now getting ribald. I must stop. Already I am losing all my friends owing to my nonconformity in the present political furore. I dare not call at the *Sunday Times* office lest I be dismissed for deviation. I think I am the only person in Oxford who refused to sign either of the two petitions, one denouncing the government for its lack of virtue, the other praising it for its genius. So I must walk warily, uttering (for a time) only sedate platitudes, such as would not bring a blush to the cheek even of the best-behaved Wykehamist. Which however reminds me (before I fulfil this undertaking) of one small fact. You know that the American Press reported a mass-protest by members of the British Foreign Office against the Suez adventure. Well, you also know that members of the British Foreign Office simply don't do that sort of thing; so writing to Patrick Reilly,[7] our ambassador-designate to Moscow, – a *very* discreet Wykehamist – I touched on this obvious *canard*, drawing a felicitous but avowedly incredible picture

---

[4] Clarissa Spencer-Churchill (b. 1920) had worked for George Weidenfeld before her marriage to Anthony Eden in 1952.

[5] (Sir) Cecil Beaton (1904–1980), photographer and stage designer, took splendid photographs of BB at I Tatti in 1955, and described his visit in *The Face of the World* (1957), pp. 49–51. T-R had met him at a small luncheon given by Lady Jebb at the British Embassy in Paris on 12 October 1956.

[6] Heinrich Hoffman (1885–1957) was appointed as Hitler's official photographer in 1924, and made a fortune from photographic royalties and fawning Hitler picture-books.

[7] (Sir) Patrick Reilly (1909–1999) had become T-R's friend when holding a pre-war Fellowship at All Souls. Minister in Paris at the onset of the Suez crisis, he was recalled to London in October 1956 to be Deputy Under Secretary of State at the Foreign Office, and took over the Moscow Embassy in February 1957. Ambassador in Paris 1965–8.

of an army of Wykehamist councillors in black suits gesticulating in wild passion in the office of Sir Ivone Kirkpatrick.[8] To my astonishment he replied saying that the report was 'greatly exaggerated'. He did not say it was untrue. So I think it can safely be said that there was some kind of protest even by the Foreign Office. Patrick Reilly's comment was *Quem Deus vult perdere* (Wykehamists are always classical scholars).[9] I understand from Ian Gilmour that Kirkpatrick was seen walking down the corridor of the Foreign Office wringing his hands and saying 'He's mad! He's mad!' which seems to be the same sentiment in English (Kirkpatrick is a Roman Catholic so his education doesn't run to Latin quotations except from the liturgy).

Now I must really stop and the era of discretion will begin. We saw Morra[10] the other day: now I know how you get such inside information about the Weidenfeld *ménage*. So you will know that Weidenfeld is now in America and Mrs W. has gone to stay with Cyril Connolly.[11] Xandra has tried to get in touch with Clotilde Marghieri,[12] though much inhibited, first by the inefficient service at her hotel, and secondly by her own perplexity, not knowing whether she has a title and if so what. But she (Xandra) has now written and I hope we shall see her (CM). I hope the Serocalcin pills will keep you free from colds: we both find them miraculous. If you have any difficulty in getting them in Italy, tell me and I shall send more. [...]

Berenson replied from I Tatti on 2 December: 'Hard for me to understand the unanimity of the literary world, of the intelligentzia *in general, in disapproving the move against Nasser. They express disapproval in terms taken from Soviet propaganda which they suck avidly like mother's milk. What makes them do that?*

'I wonder why people in the "Western World" seem so unwilling (or is it unable) to see that Nasser means the stagnation punctuated by violence & chaos of the Muslim world. If that world is encouraged or even passively allowed to dominate, the Mediterranean may return to the Moriscos. Franco would cheer their invasions & join them.'

---

[8] Sir Ivone Kirkpatrick (1897–1964), formerly UK High Commissioner in Germany, was Permanent Secretary at the Foreign Officer 1953–7.

[9] *Quem Juppiter vult perdere dementat prius*: 'Whom God would destroy He first sends mad'.

[10] Count Umberto Morro di Lavriano, historian, critic and translator, was a regular visitor to I Tatti, and published *Colloqui con Berenson* in 1963.

[11] Weidenfeld had married Cyril Connolly's ex-wife Barbara Skelton in August 1956. A few months later, when Weidenfeld was in the USA, she began an affair with Connolly.

[12] BB was besotted with Clotilde Marghieri (c.1892–1981) during the early 1930s, and remained her devoted admirer. She lived in amicable independence from her lawyer husband at La Quiete, in the village of Santa Maria La Bruna, on the slopes of Vesuvius.

10 December 1956   8 St Aldate's, Oxford

My dear BB

British politics remain suspended while our dear Prime Minister basks in Jamaica. Educated opinion is divided between those who hate him for going into Egypt and those who hate him for going out, and those who despise him for going to Jamaica, and those who think he ought to be impeached, and those who think he ought to be certified. However, astonishing to relate, his position seems to be stronger than ever, firmly based on the half-baked semi-fascist lower middle class (represented by the Queen and half the aristocracy) – and, I suspect, on the opposition between Butler[1] & Macmillan[2] in the cabinet. The situation is really like the spring of 1940, without a Churchill: as if we had been defeated in Norway and had all wanted to get rid of Chamberlain, but had then to choose between (say) Lord Halifax, Sir John Simon or Sir Samuel Hoare.[3] So in the end nothing is done and we are governed by the personal dictatorship of a bruised film-star in a transatlantic Berchtesgarden. The maddening thing is that whereas the crises of 1938 and 1940 were at least caused by the dictator of the most highly industrialised and formidably armed people in Europe, that of 1956 is caused by a twopenny Levantine demagogue who at any moment may be pushed aside by the Egyptian pro-communist party.

Two facts now seem to be emerging from the fog of conflicting verbiage, charges and countercharges, leakages, conjectures, recriminations. First, I suspect that the Israelis spoilt everything by attacking Egypt two days ahead of schedule. This put our time-table out, and it was by the margin of those two days that we failed to seize the whole canal and destroy Nasser. But the government can't avow this good reason because it means avowing that we knew in advance of the Israeli plans and had indeed concerted plans with them. Secondly, it seems clear that at the moment of crisis Eden lost his nerve. The Russians threatened to drop atomic bombs on London (which I am certain was bluff), and at the same time the Americans refused any support against Russia unless we stopped fighting and thus lost the canal which we could have taken in two days. Bohlen, the US Ambassador in Moscow,[4] appears to have pressed Washington to spare no means to ruin

---

[1] Richard Austen ('Rab') Butler (1902–1982), later Lord Butler of Saffron Walden, was then regarded as Eden's likeliest successor as Prime Minister.
[2] Harold Macmillan (1894–1986), later 1st Earl of Stockton, beat Butler in the contest to succeed Eden as Prime Minister in January 1957. He was T-R's publisher, and became Chancellor of Oxford University in 1960 after a campaign masterminded by T-R.
[3] Members of the Cabinet in 1939 known for their conciliatory temper and uninspiring leadership.
[4] Charles Bohlen (1904–1974), US Ambassador to the Soviet Union 1953–7 and to France 1962–8.

our plans. Under the combined pressure of both Russia and America, the British Cabinet met for four hours, during which Eden was outvoted by the Butlerites (Butler, of course, is an old Appeaser). He could have dismissed a few ministers and gone on; but he threw up the sponge and fled to Jamaica, leaving Butler and Macmillan to mop up the mess. Now, though they both despise him, it seems probable that B would rather go on with Eden than serve under M, and M would rather go on with Eden than serve under B. I cannot be sure of all this, but I think it is the most likely reading of the facts that do come my way.

One result is a very widespread hatred and contempt for America. The irrational hate America less for stopping us than for being in a position to stop us; the rational for consistently refusing to see that there was a crisis in the Middle East, for cynically exploiting the evidence of crisis in the interest of the American oil companies, and for sabotaging an attempt (however ill-timed and ill-prepared) to solve it by an overdue show of force. I'm afraid I rather sympathise with the latter view. My contempt for Eden is boundless; but I cannot see that the West gains either materially or morally if we all forbid each other to tread even on the imaginary corns of a jumped-up petty dictator in the East.

I shall leave this dispiriting subject, which has shed discredit, as it seems to me, on everyone involved, and turn to the lighter world of mere gossip.

I got to this point two days ago, and then slammed my right hand in the car door and now have difficulty in writing, so will postpone my account of Xandra's attendance at Wind's lecture and her report thereon till my next letter. [...]

Berenson replied from I Tatti on 28 December: 'I cannot exaggerate my distress, my misery over the conduct of Washington in this affair. [...] If only your government hadn't lost nerve in July and gone straight forward! "Cosa fatta capo ha" [what's done is done] would have prevailed.'

1957

My dear BB

I am always sorry to see a typed letter from you. I do hope you will be well, and completely well, soon, and that your next letter will be in your own hand, as a sign that you are recovered. Do recover quickly and completely.

Of course you may show my letter to Walter Lippmann if you think it worth showing. Since I mentioned the alleged pressure by Bohlen from Moscow, I think I should give you my source. It was told to me by Isaiah (himself a close friend of Bohlen, and one, therefore, who would not have passed it on unless he himself believed it), who had it from Hägglöf, the Swedish Ambassador here.[1] Hägglöf had just returned from Sweden, so it is natural to assume – though it is only an assumption – that he had it from the Swedish Foreign Office. My suspicion is that what caused the British Cabinet to lose its nerve was not so much the Russian threat as the absolute American refusal to co-operate if the Russians intervened unless we first cleared right out of Egypt. But in any case there was clearly enough division in the cabinet already. The maddening behaviour of the Americans – now made more maddening by their belated admissions – doesn't seem to me to excuse the fatally unprepared, hole-and-corner way in which Eden acted. It seems to me that it was quite unnecessary so to act that *everyone* was unprepared for the action and so disastrously bewildered by it.

My hand, as you see, is now completely repaired (except for the loss of a finger-nail), so I can write with fluency and will now go on to tell you the tale of Xandra's attendance at Wind's lecture – a fatal attendance, I may add, for while she was there, inaccessible to the world, all her various agents, who for nearly two years had been utterly silent, suddenly broke into cry at auctions and sale-rooms throughout the land, and bid for and bought grand pianos; with the result that when she emerged from the lecture-room we found ourselves irrevocably possessed of *four* such objects. Nor, I feel, from her account of it, did the lecture compensate for such a snowstorm of unwanted pianos or the administrative problem, which we now face, of getting rid of two or three of them. For according to Xandra the lecture,

---

[1] Gunnar Hägglöf (1904–1995), Swedish Ambassador in London 1947–67. Berlin considered Chuck Bohlen 'one of the most delightful, talented, upright and attractive human beings I have ever known' (*The Times*, 11 January 1974).

though undeniably interesting and novel (we will not risk saying whether it was – to use those archaic adjectives – *right* or *wrong*) was of an incredible and sexual vulgarity. You know, no doubt, what Wind looks like – a leering, lecherous, gloating face, with hideous, but perhaps – who knows? – hideously fascinating features and large, lecherous eyes. Well, you can imagine him standing there in the artificial twilight (for of course there were lantern-slides), slowly moving his fat, Germanic hands round imaginary aërial replicas of some naked breasts by Rubens, at that moment represented on the screen above him; and as he fondled and re-fondled these globular but insubstantial objects, he uttered, in thick, German accents, sexual words which, says Xandra, she had previously thought, and in fact still thinks, are normally excluded from educated conversation. Altogether, she says, it was disgusting. And yet, she insists, the substance of it was also – whether right or wrong – interesting. But her predominant emotion was disgust. All the same, I think I now see why those elderly ladies from perhaps prim or repressed homes in America so love to listen to him. I now find him more horrible than ever to meet – I have not had much conversation with him, but physically he repels me. I have not seen Seznec for some time: I don't know what he now says about his former *protégé*, – in fact, his creation.

I write this in Melrose, where we have been spending Christmas and New Year, more or less immobile for lack of petrol.[2] But immobility has its advantages. I have now read *The Paston Letters*.[3] How fascinating they are! Is there anything like them in any other country? What a wonderfully complete picture they give of life in a really pre-capitalist, or at least non-capitalist, society! No wonder the civilised Italian envoys from 'bourgeois-capitalist' cities like Venice found the English barbarians! Always as I read (I am rather ashamed of not having read them before), I was reminded of Morocco – the great *caïds* of the Atlas who built up, by ways very like those of our 15th century dukes, similar ephemeral empires of patronage, violence and corruption, and (one must add) similarly built great temples and fortresses and tombs for the admiration and amazement of posterity. Really it is to Morocco or Persia that our medievalists should go to study feudal life, to see what it *really* meant. But alas, they insist on reading only monkish *words* and build up a ridiculous never-never-land of Christian Unity: kings with folded hands and nuns demurely knitting, in shady cloister pent ... I have just written something on this for the *New Statesman* (that ever more

---

[2] From 17 December 1956 until 15 May following, petrol rationing was imposed in Britain: private motorists had an allowance enough for them to drive about 200 miles a month.
[3] *The Paston Letters*, correspondence between members of a prosperous Norfolk family c.1420–1503, had recently been republished in John Harrington's edition.

contemptible rag, the weekly Bible of the Half-Baked); but of course there was far too little space to say all I wanted on such a splendid theme.[4]

As for my article on *Stalin*, which I read to you, that has fallen the victim of a sad fate. The American magazine in which it was to appear ceased circulation the week before it was to be published, after the article had been set up and advertised and illustrated. So now you are the only member of the public whom it has reached. Still, I am glad it was you rather than any of the four million readers of the now defunct *Collins Magazine*. And after all, since it's an ill wind that blows no one any good, I have discovered some positive advantage in this misfortune. I often sadly reflected that that article, if published, might prevent me from going to Russia. This particularly saddened me because our new ambassador to Moscow, Patrick Reilly, is one of my closest friends and had invited Xandra and me to go out and stay with them when they are established there (they go in February). How tiresome, I reflected, if that wretched article should now prevent me from getting a *visa* ... But now the problem has solved itself. All the same, I regret all that wasted labour.

But no! How can I regret it? It was on the profits – or at least on the expectation of the profits – of that article that we made our journey to Italy in October and were able to visit you. How we enjoyed that visit! One of the pleasures was to see you so well. Do get well again so that we may give ourselves that pleasure again soon. [...]

22 March 1957   8 St Aldate's, Oxford

My dear BB

I fear it is I who owe: it always is; so here, after some delay comes a letter, to bring love to you both from Xandra and me. We long to hear from you. We do hope you are already feeling the coming of spring – we have had no winter here, only a long, slow, wonderful spring – and that we shall have some chance of visiting you before long. Meanwhile let me bring you up to date, as far as I can, in the affairs of Oxford, which have never been more vertiginous than in this mild and stimulative winter in which governments, ministers and vice-chancellors have all been dethroned in the midst of their deepest plots and darkest manoeuvres.

---

[4] T-R's reviews of *The Paston Letters* – 'Up and Down in the County', *New Statesman* (19 January 1957), pp. 73–4 – likened the fifteenth-century Dukes of Suffolk to a twentieth-century 'pasha, who has cornered water-rights, distributed uneven justice, prospered in war, subjected other tribes, built up a private empire of patronage, which suddenly dissolves with his death: a man like the late El Glaoui, Pasha of Marrakesh'.

The great speculation is over the Regius Chair of Modern History. But when I think of this topic, my heart quails within me. How can I do justice to the dramas, the intrigues, the by-plots, the plays within plays, of this great struggle? A letter is too brief and feeble a medium. The subject requires a book, and a book by Balzac. But within the brief compass of a few pages, I will do what I can.

First, you must know that the Regius Chair of Modern History in this university has for thirty years been held by Medieval Manchester Mice. These men, succeeding imperceptibly to each other, like Amurath to Amurath, have gradually throttled and strangled the subject, reducing it to petty clerical antiquarianism, destitute of spirit, devoid of ideas, without range, without depth, without philosophy. Moreover, in these thirty years, they have sought to ensure that the unfortunate subject shall never revive, by the simple expedient of planting junior mice from their own mouse-nest in all other chairs both in this and in other universities. We now have, in this university, seven professors of history only one of whom has ever written so much as one book on a historical subject, and two of whom have never even committed so much as a single antiquarian review. This school, moreover, takes itself very seriously. The mice are not in the least ashamed of their slender output, their narrow views, their utter obscurity. This, they say, is what Professors should be like. And when they sense opposition from what may be called the party of Gaiety (they *detest* gaiety) and Life (they *abhor* life), they naturally prepare, by their accustomed means, to defend themselves.[1]

The leader of this party at present is the present Regius Professor, one Galbraith: a plebeian character who seeks to divert attention from his historical failings by low buffoonery.[2] I write, of course, entirely objectively; though it is incidentally a fact that he seems animated by a particularly violent detestation of me. He does not in fact know me, neither recognises me in the street nor has ever spoken to me. But somehow he seems to sense in me a desperate enemy, and certainly he has gone to very great lengths in his opposition to me. Three years ago, when a committee of

---

[1] During the autumn of 1956 T-R had promoted the candidature of Steven Runciman for the Regius chair. 'He would be a Professor of the right kind: a distinguished historian who has written original, scholarly and highly readable books, and who would lend distinction to the chair instead of merely owing any distinction he had to it [...] There is a liberalism, an elevation, a vitality about his work which makes that of our local antiquaries, nibbling away in their narrow sectors, look mean and stale' (letter to J.C. Masterman, 13 December 1956). But Runciman declined to be a candidate.

[2] Vivian Galbraith (1889–1976), Fellow and tutor in modern history at Balliol 1928–37, Regius Professor of Modern History at Oxford 1947–57.

electors proposed to make me a professor, Galbraith held them up to ransom for three months, threatening to resign if I were appointed, etc., until finally the exhausted electors gave way and elected a mouse, who had never been heard of before and has never been heard of since.[3] Last November, when I was a candidate to give certain important lectures for this year, Galbraith adopted similar tactics and tried to slip through a special decree to suspend the lectures for a year in order to avoid seeing me appointed. In this he failed – or rather, his manoeuvre being discovered, he was defeated by a counter move; but the battle is still in suspense and purple smoke arises from the University Buildings whenever the electors are gathered together to consider whom they ought to have elected last November to the still unfilled position . . .

But now Galbraith is due to retire and the Regius Chair must be filled. Consequently a tremor of apprehension runs through every mouse-nest. For whereas, by their mere numbers, they reckon that they can now put their fellow-mice into all chairs which are filled by election – election, that is, by themselves – this one chair is an exception to that rule, for it, the grandest of historical chairs, is filled by nomination: nomination by the Crown, that is, in practice, by the Prime Minister. Imagine therefore how the sensitive whiskers of the Mice are trembling to catch and transmit the rumours and suggestions which float, or may be made to float, along the labyrinthine corridors of Downing Street!

At first, it must be admitted, the Mice were quite confident. The Prime Minister, they thought, would naturally consult them, and as naturally accept their suggestions. All that was necessary was for them to select a good reliable Mouse, groom him, put him through certain paces which are regarded as upward steps in Mouseland, and then, when asked, to draw the attention of the patronage-secretary to the Mouse whom they had thus placed at the head of the queue. This therefore they did. For the past two years confidence reigned. The succession of one Southern was considered to be already fixed: as fixed as the succession of a nominated Caesar to a reigning Augustus.[4]

But alas, what are the hopes of Mice in days such as these, with dotty politics and tumbling thrones? Just when all seemed firm and fixed, the thunder and lightning shot from the clear sky; and amid the convulsions

---

[3] R.B. Wernham: see T-R's letter of 6 July 1951.

[4] Galbraith's pupil (Sir) Richard Southern (1912–2001) succeeded him in 1937 as a Fellow and history tutor at Balliol. His deservedly high reputation as a scholar was established by *The Making of the Middle Ages* (1953). Elected Chichele Professor of Modern History at Oxford in 1961 and President of St John's College in 1969.

the panic-stricken mice, when they had gained the safety of their incon-
spicuous holes and had timidly poked their quivering noses out again into
the open air, discovered that after all it was not they who governed the
affairs of the world.

Who in fact did govern them? The first claimant was our old friend,
whom I think I have described to you, Warden Smith of New College, the
Vice-Chancellor, who by now – I am referring to the end of last year – had
been raised to the dizziest pinnacle of triumph and euphoria. Had he not
triumphed over all opposition? Had he not, thanks to a côterie of devoted
Wykehamists and political methods which would have been regarded as
miraculous in Tammany Hall, succeeded in suppressing all evidence of
opposition to his cherished project of Gothicising the University and
driving an *Autostrada* through the Christ Church Meadow? Had he not,
on the personal invitation of his friend and fellow-administrator Nikita
Khrushchev, been to Russia, to study, and perhaps to teach, the refinements
of absolute government through bogus committee? Now, he thought, he
would crown his work by a signal appointment. He would make the new
Regius Professor. So, tossing off a glass of peppered vodka, he sent for his
faithful creatures and showed them a letter he had written to the chancellor
of the University, Lord Halifax, in which he urged him to see that the Prime
Minister appointed the right man to the post.[5]

Whom did Warden Smith wish to appoint? He wished, of course, to
make a personal appointment: one that would be remembered as *his*
appointment, distinguishable from all others by that same quality of heroic,
machiavellian eccentricity which marked all his own gestures. He wished to
appoint someone whom no other Vice-Chancellor would ever recommend,
someone who would go down in history (if the study of that science should
survive the shock of such an appointment) as Warden Smith's Regius
Professor, just as the Red Dean of Canterbury lives in history as Ramsay
Macdonald's Dean.[6] In fact he urged an aristocratic chancellor and a conservative Prime Minister to appoint the irresponsible left-wing demagogue,
the Tom Paine of British television who had publicly declared that the
Queen should live in a bed-sitting-room, the giddy Bevanite columnist of
the *Daily Mirror*: A.J.P. Taylor.

Such was the position in January 1957. But now storm followed storm,

---

[5] Edward Wood, 3rd Viscount and 1st Earl of Halifax (1881–1959), formerly Viceroy of India,
Foreign Secretary and British Ambassador to the USA, had been Chancellor of Oxford University
since 1933.
[6] The Labour Prime Minister Ramsay MacDonald had in 1931 nominated as Dean of Canterbury
an eager Soviet apologist named Hewlett Johnson (1874–1966).

and the astonished Mice, still cowering in their cosy holes, saw yet new wild beasts of the forest trampling and snorting through their sacred preserves. For in that very month Warden Smith found his power slipping from him. Politics, he discovered, were not so easy after all: the enraged opposition, who at first had been outwitted because they simply could not believe that the Vice-Chancellor could possibly have been as unscrupulous as all that, now at last were hammering back at him; and the Vice-Chancellor, overwhelmed, frustrated, and broken in health, suddenly abdicated his throne. Whereupon the new Vice-Chancellor promptly wrote another letter to his old friend the Chancellor telling him not to think of suggesting that nasty radical A.J.P. Taylor but to recommend that sound, reputable conservative character H.R. Trevor-Roper.

Of course Warden Smith was furious. Steam rose through the one gothic window which he had contrived to insert into New College. He is said to have written an outraged letter to the Chancellor roundly denouncing his successor as a man of no principles and base conservative prejudices – which was perhaps unwise, as the new Vice-Chancellor, J.C. Masterman, is a lifelong friend of Lord Halifax. As for Galbraith, his fury (and his expression of it) knows no bounds, and steam rose also from the professorial rooms in Oriel College, thick, strong and coarse-smelling, as from a boiling sewer. However, this conjuncture of events did not last long, for within a few days yet another storm broke upon our heads. Our dear Prime Minister, like our dear Vice-Chancellor, found politics too much for his health, and suddenly he too had a successor: a successor, moreover, who from the start made it clear that he had his own views in the matter. Was he not himself a scholar, an amateur of history, a man who neither despised nor feared the academic world and who firmly believed that history is of current political importance? Harold Macmillan lost not time in letting it be known that neither Mice nor Vice-Chancellors nor Chancellors nor patronage-Secretaries would make this appointment, but the Prime Minister himself, and he alone.

Whom would he appoint? At once a new claimant appeared. A.L. Rowse, the Cornish egomaniac, suddenly moved about Oxford with a new assurance. Was he not a convert to Churchillian toryism of precisely the kind favoured by Macmillan? Was he not a devout cultivator of duchesses, and particularly of the Dowager Duchess of Devonshire, the Prime Minister's mother-in-law? Were not his books published by Macmillan? Had he not for years been assiduously licking the boots of both the Macmillans and the Cavendish family? Surely now his hour had come. He could afford to walk serenely in Oxford. For a time he did.

Yes, for a time. But after a time, a sudden change came over that serene figure. Suddenly, it was noted, he was filled with rancour and hatred, and in conversation with those few people to whom he will still speak in Oxford, he would declaim against the rottenness of England, the uselessness of its government, the necessity of dollars, and his own future plans of a happy life, lucratively lecturing to the more appreciative audiences of Mid-Western Women's Clubs ... One is forced to conclude that, for whatever reason, Rowse has decided that he will *not* be offered the chair. Why? We do not know. Possibly the Prime Minister has too much sense. Or possibly he has heard the great scandal now going round the London clubs, the scandal of 'the Cornish Waif' – the poor Cornish old-age pensioner whom Rowse (who is himself a Cornish peasant and has the character of a medieval village usurer) has contrived to defraud of some £3,000.

At all events, speculation is now once again free for all. The Prime Minister, by all accounts, is enjoying it too: he discusses it at parties with empty-headed countesses and fashionable undergraduates. There is a general feeling that whoever is appointed will *not* be A.J.P. Taylor *or* one of the mice. The mice go about looking very grave, as if all sound scholarship, all high standards were now in jeopardy together with their empire. A.J.P. Taylor, on the other hand, does not look grave: he is not capable of gravity. The gravity of the mice is further increased by the recent election of Isaiah to the Chair of Political Economy. That was a great victory for the Party of Gaiety. Can it be that the rule of virtuous, left-wing, nonconformist Wykehamist (or adoptive Wykehamist) nonentities is at last coming to an end?

All this, as you can imagine, has imposed a heavy strain on me. My friends have insisted that for the time being I must be discreet.[7] But 'the time being' has gone on so long! I have hardly dared utter a squeak since last January. And this, incidentally, is the explanation of an article, which I have sent to you in proof, and which you may already have received, on the *Millennium of Arnold Toynbee*. It is, as you will see if you read it, entirely innocent and anodyne; and it was accepted for publication by *Encounter*.[8] But now my friends, who seem to spend their whole time restraining, imprisoning and silencing me, say No: it must not be published, or at least not yet. In vain I have pointed out that it cannot possibly make any difference: that my friends are firm friends, that my enemies are firm

[7] The friends were his Christ Church colleagues Charles Stuart and Robert Blake. 'It is', Blake wrote to T-R on 10 January after Eden's resignation, 'of paramount importance [...] that you should under no circumstances commit yourself in public on the politics of Suez. I know that you feel very strongly about it, and the temptation to make an adverse crack must be almost irresistible. Resist it!'
[8] 'Arnold Toynbee's Millennium' was finally published in *Encounter*, VIII (June 1957), pp. 14–28.

enemies, that there is no floating vote, and that if there were the Prime Minister would not listen to it. Professor Berlin, speaking seriously from the responsibility of his new position, gave me my orders. 'Even though the risk may be only one-thousandth of one-per-cent,' he said gravely, sipping his brandy with hieratic ceremony in the Ritz hotel (of which his wife is a *directrice*), 'there is no point in taking that risk at this moment.' Consequently I have been forbidden to publish and have sent the proof to you instead; and tomorrow, so that I may be out of mischief for the next month, I am going off to Persia to utter my indiscretions to the waste Iranian mountains.

But why do I trouble you with these details about hypothetical professors? You, as a practical man, a realist, are no doubt concerned only with real professors, like Professor Edgar Wind. So let me tell you that the University, at its last meeting, resolved to build, at huge cost, an auditorium four times as large as the largest lecture-hall at present available, for the sole purpose of accommodating the audience of Professor Wind, and preventing the recurrence of such sad incidents as have recently happened, when the Warden of All Souls, after queuing for half an hour at the door, was turned away through lack of space. There are some who deplore this new extravagance, thinking that a marquee would be less expensive to erect and easier to dismantle next year, when the fashion has passed; but such sceptics are naturally and rightly disregarded by the numerous and triumphant devotees of the Professor.

I must now stop and pack for Persia. Tomorrow I go first to Eton to see my stepson confirmed in the religion of the Church of England & then to Baghdad to see large numbers of people who have somehow avoided these self-evident truths. Please write to me, c/o the British Ambassador, Tehran, and tell me how you are and what is happening to you and around you both. [...]

2 June 1957   8 St Aldate's, Oxford

My dear BB

I have owed you a long letter for a long time, – ever since I received yours in Persia.[1] How infinitely remote in time my visit to Persia now seems; and yet it is only just a month since I returned. And how complacent I feel at

---

[1] BB had written on 30 March recalling Toynbee's visit to I Tatti in 1922. 'Greeks in Asia Minor were being massacred by Turks with Italians & French grinning & conniving. Toynbee spoke dogmatically [and] enthusiastically about the Turks & heartily approved of their uprooting a Greek civilization that had been there for 3,000 years. I never wanted to see him again.'

having been to some place unknown to you! Of course you must go. But if
you go, may I give you one piece of useful practical advice? Don't go by bus
from Baghdad. I did. In retrospect I wouldn't have missed it for worlds.
But in prospect ... never, never, never again. It was a pilgrims' bus: the
pilgrims go from Persia to Iraq, from the land of ancient bigotry to the land
of secularism and reason, in order to bury their dead in the holy cities of
the Shi'ites there; and having done so, they return by bus, with the empty
coffins and such additional passengers as may choose to travel with them.
The journey takes two days, and very long days too, from 6.0 a.m. to
midnight. And it was full of incident. There were violent quarrels between
passengers and driver, which I would like to think were about some abstruse
point of Muslim theology, but which more probably concerned the fare.
There was a splendid scene when attempts were made to vaccinate all the
passengers by force in a rural dispensary where the chaos of flashing needles,
screaming children, and protesting heretics was still further confounded
by squealing pigs and squawking chickens. And finally there was the
caravanserai where we spent the abbreviated night at Kermanshah: a caravanserai over whose squalor I hastily draw a decent veil. But even so, in the
end, I ask myself, would I have missed that journey? And I always answer,
and must answer, No. For I hate aeroplanes and aerodromes: their uniform
western style, their impersonal, international, disinfected, devitalised iden-
tity; and by travelling into Persia in that bus I saw more of the country and
the people, and breathed more of the atmosphere of the country, than I
would ever otherwise have done. Besides, by the purest chance, and unaware
of the fact, I entered Persia on the 13th day of the Persian New Year, the day
on which the Persian women put on their brightest clothes and the Persian
families go out of doors to eat their meals in ritual picnic. So, once we
had crossed the frontier from garish, modern, stable, sanitary, secular,
prosperous Iraq, into thwarted, violent, ancient, bigoted, poverty-stricken
Persia, we suddenly came upon a series of wonderful human spectacles.
Never have I seen such colours. The Persians have a truly wonderful, natural
instinct for colour. Even these peasant women in those remote villages were
dressed, that day, like Byzantine duchesses, and wandered over the fields in
imperial purple, blue and green, under their open black *chadors*,[2] and with
tiaras on their heads. Not even in Italy, not even in Greece, have I seen such
natural love of beauty, and especially of beauty in colour, as in Persia. And
the daylight too is like the Greek daylight: bright but not too clear, thin and
sparkling at that great height (the whole country being – except for the

---

[2] A *chador* is a black outer-garment worn by Muslim women in Iran and enveloping the wearer
from head to toe.

Gulf coast – 4,000 feet above sea level), infinitely subtle and various. The weather while I was in Persia was generally foul – cold and wet – and I was never able to go to the Caspian, the Elburz mountains being impassable; but even so I was able to travel about a certain amount and some of the country, especially in the south, is wonderfully romantic: the country round Persepolis, for instance, and the oasis in which Isfahan lies – an incredibly beautiful city, as rich in architecture as Toledo and yet not dead, as Toledo is, not a mere museum, or corpse in which tourists, like highly coloured active maggots, wriggle and feed, but a living city, with a life and industry of its own, – and Shiraz also, a pleasant fragment of Persia, that huge, naturally decentralised country; but it was a wonderful fragment, and I long to go back and see more.

And yet if Persia is a fascinating country, it is also a very dispiriting country. The contrast with Iraq is immense. Iraq is efficient, energetic, prosperous, complacent: a Levantine Switzerland. There is no danger of revolution there.[3] Persia, under a film of artificial stability, seemed to me full of revolutionary strains. It is a country of butterflies and dung. This of course makes it all the more interesting. The butterflies are fascinating: but at times the dung is very depressing.[4]

In many ways the country reminds me of Spain. Both, after all, are ancient countries upon which the Arabs and Islam imposed only a super-ficial, transient conquest. Both are high, bare, and disunited. Both are naturally poor. Both, in social habits and social structure, are incurably 'Oriental'. And the government is very much the same too: a usurping despotism that is kept in place by the selfish fears of a frightened upper class which has tasted revolution. The Shah seems to me very like General Franco.[5] He is anomalous and unloved, but socially indispensable; and he keeps his position by ceaseless meddling, by cutting off (metaphorically) every head that rises too high, by destroying his own servants whenever

[3] Despite T-R's confidence, the proclamation of a union between Iraq and Jordan in 1958 provoked a revolution during which King Faisal II was killed. In 'Land of Two Rivers', *Sunday Times*, 19 May 1957, he presented Iraq as 'the one stable Arab power, the firm pivot of the anti-Communist, anti-Nasser axis in the Middle East'. The country's oil wealth 'does not provide merely concrete palaces and shiny Cadillacs for the royal family, as in Arabia, nor merely a pourboire for Gov-ernment officials, as formerly in Persia: it spreads outwards and downwards, enriching the whole country through great public work'.
[4] In 'Heirs of Darius', *Sunday Times*, 2 June 1957, T-R wrote: 'Landlord wealth insults peasant poverty. The profit of great enterprises sticks to few hands. The mullahs of the holy city of Qum scowl at the new oilfield which threatens to convulse their jealous backwater. And Persian pride, Persian individualism, Persian suspicion and sophistry both hasten and cloak that gradual disintegration of all effort which is the despair of Western officials in this ancient, fascinating, dispiriting country.'
[5] Mohammed Reza Pahlavi (1919–1980), Shahanshah of Iran 1941–79.

they acquire any support or reputation which might dim his own. The government rackets are very like those in Spain too. The Shah and his family and his ministers go very profitably into business: and woe to the foreign contractor who fails to ensure that lucrative subcontracts are awarded to those firms of which his Imperial Majesty the Shah-an-Shah is director! Only in one respect do I see a real contrast between Persia and Spain. Of that proud, sullen, reserved, equalitarian obstinacy which is so obvious in Spain there is in Persia no trace: instead there is an Irish blarney, an Italian subtlety, a Jesuitical sophistry.

Whence did this art, this charm, this love of beauty and colour come? When I looked at the ancient art of Persia, I found no trace of such qualities. At Persepolis the great monumental reliefs have about them an utter deadness: the deadness of endless, repetitive carbon-copies, which, I suppose, is what they are. For I presume that Cyrus brought from Babylon both the style and the artists for his triumphal buildings, and that later native workmen simply copied them for ever and ever. Certainly there seems no development of style: the reliefs on the tombs of the last Achaemenids are identical with those of the first. And what a difference between them and the Assyrian reliefs which I saw in Baghdad, Mosul and Nimrud, bursting with violent, cruel vitality! The Sassanian reliefs too seemed to me lifeless, though in a different way, loose and blowsy, not clear and hard and dull like their predecessors. And yet Persian art of the late Middle Ages is so full of life and charm and the whole Persian character is now, and has so long been, colourful, sensuous, almost volatile in its lightness. It cannot have been the Arabs who brought in this new character to a once dull, majestic people. I suppose it must have been the Northern invaders, the Mongols, the Afghans, the Cossacks of the Steppes.

Now I have obeyed your instructions and written 'a long letter about Persia'. Now I feel in that happy position of being, for however brief a time – for I always marvel at the punctuality of your correspondence, which I cannot equal – on the credit side of our account. So now you can write and bring me up to date in your affairs. How are you all? How is I Tatti? I do hope you are well and that we shall have an opportunity of seeing you before long. Meanwhile write and tell us how you are and what you are doing and whom you are seeing. And thank you also for your kind remarks and comments on my wicked article on Toynbee which, altered a little since I received your letter, will shortly reach you in print, in *Encounter*. I do not know whether it will provoke the great man to launch a thunderbolt or a writ against me – *Encounter*'s lawyers, who do not seem to know the law very well, and are, like all lawyers, inconceivably timid, declared that the article was 'libellous and actionable *per se* and *in toto*' – nor do I know from what quarter of his Heaven such a thunderbolt or writ would come. When I last heard of Toynbee he was on the third lap of his non-stop pilgrimage round and round the world, and was on his way from Baghdad to the ancient Arbela, in order (I presume) to feel 'still unspent reverberations of psychic events' on that squalid and malodorous mound. For I am sorry to say that Toynbee has a great reputation in the East. Like other Messiahs – Buddha and Christ, Calvin and Marx – he has been unsuccessful in his native land but has convinced the Gentiles. He is the Prophet which an unappreciative Europe has bestowed upon Asia as a belated return for Christ.

And now before ending this letter perhaps I should bring you up to date in the great matter of the Regius Chair of History here. I forget what the position was when I last wrote, but I think that that was the time when our new Prime Minister, who, above all things, wants to be original, to cut a dash, to be as different as possible from his tediously conventional predecessor, was contemplating a woman-professor, and, having consulted his old friend Sir Lewis Namier, was promptly told to stuff in Namier's prize pupil, Lucy Sutherland.[6] Lucy Sutherland is a dull, competent woman who knows a lot about the politics of the East India Company in London in the 18th century, but has – as far as is known – no interest at all in any other historical subject. On the other hand she has a profound interest in power. Head of a Women's College, Member of Hebdomadal Council, Member of the Visitatorial Board, Member of one Royal Commission after another, she is essentially a practical woman who, as the daughter of a South African gold-mining magnate, has an inherited love of bossing people about. Therefore, about a fortnight ago, when the Prime Minister wrote to her, in pursuit of Sir Lewis's instructions, offering her the chair, she briskly replied that she would gladly accept it, provided that she could keep all her other offices as well. After all, is she not an energetic, managing woman, capable of holding any number of offices in plurality? Why should she turn out of her numerous other seats of office in order to sit exclusively in one chair, however grand? No: her nimble bottom, she declared (though not perhaps *totidem verbis*),[7] was capable of a rapid rotatory act of musical Chairs: she could sit in the Regius chair on Mondays, on Hebdomadal Council on Tuesdays, on Royal Commissions on Wednesdays, on the Visitatorial Board on Thursdays, and on the Principal's throne at Lady Margaret Hall for the

[6] (Dame) Lucy Sutherland (1903–1980), the first woman undergraduate to speak at the Oxford Union (1926), was a Fellow of Somerville 1928–45, Principal of Lady Margaret Hall 1945–71 and pro-Vice-Chancellor 1960–69.
[7] In so many words.

rest of the week. Unfortunately this view was not shared by the Prime Minister, who understandably thought that if a historian were to accept a chair, and particularly the grandest chair in Oxford, he or she should sit firmly in it. Consequently Lucy Sutherland was forced to choose, as all other professors, in such a position, had previously been forced to choose; and when it came to this hard choice, she naturally chose the seat not of learning but of power. So that was the end of that attempt to make history by effeminating the Regius Chair.

And what is the position now? The University, of course, as usual, furiously speculates. Last week the *Observer* confidently declared that Sir Lewis's next nominee would be A.J.P. Taylor, and that A.J.P. Taylor would therefore infallibly be appointed. But the *Observer* can always safely be distrusted, and less absurd prophets feel quite certain that there was never any prospect that Macmillan would appoint that irresponsible radical to such a position. The majority view is that the Prime Minister is still determined to have a woman, and that, this being so, the only question is, which woman? There are some who, supposing that it can only be a woman sponsored by Namier, profess to fear the sudden elevation of Miss Ninetta S. Jucker, one of those obedient hacks who 'namierise', under his general and peremptory orders, some particularly unimportant segment of 18th century parliamentary history.[8] Miss Jucker, it is noted, in her preface to her edition of *The Jenkinson Papers*, has laid her flattery of Sir Lewis on in the manner which he prefers, *viz*. with a trowel. Surely then, they argue, she must have her reward. But the majority view, almost the dogma, is that the new Regius, or rather Regia, Professor will be that amiable, scholarly but (in my view) superficial historian, Veronica Wedgwood, who writes prettily about the 17th century.[9] As a matter of fact I very much doubt whether this assumption – it is very widely taken for granted here – ever had any basis of fact. The PM may have considered Veronica Wedgwood, but I doubt it. I suspect that the whole idea is a mere *canard*, taken up and given currency by Raymond Mortimer. Another feminine runner who has been tipped by know-alls is Cecil Woodham-Smith, an amateur historian, the wife of a rich city lawyer, who writes excellent, readable, scholarly,

[8] Ninetta Jucker (b. 1913) was neither considered for the Regius chair nor a hack constitutional historian. She went to live in Paris with her Italian lover in 1939, gave birth to his child there in 1940, and decided to remain with him throughout the German occupation: a challenging experience described in her memoir *Curfew in Paris* (1960). Her study of the first Earl of Liverpool, *The Jenkinson Papers 1760–1766* (1949), contains matter-of-fact, rather than obsequious, references to Namier. She settled in Rome after the war, and later wrote a history of modern Italy.
[9] (Dame) Veronica Wedgwood (1910–1997), a successful narrative historian, had no desire for academic responsibilities.

gossipy, profitable books on Florence Nightingale and the Crimean War.[10] But I do not think that she was ever a serious runner.

In fact – if I may return from these interesting speculations to anything so dull as mere facts – the Prime Minister wrote offering me the chair some ten days ago, i.e. (I think) immediately after Lucy Sutherland had reluctantly chosen power, and I replied last Monday accepting it, or rather, agreeing that he should recommend my name. Of course there may still be a hitch. The PM may change his mind, or the Queen may dissuade him ('Oh Mr Macmillan, have you forgotten dear Sir Arthur Bryant?');[11] but barring such hazards, I presume that I shall be appointed and the appointment published any day. And yet, one must remember, Derby Day is not till 6 June, and until that important event is over the Queen may well have no time for any papers except the sporting papers. So it may still be that this letter will bring you the first news. In that case I confidently ask you to be discreet until the appointment, if it is confirmed, is published. I don't want to make a fool of myself, like Lucy Sutherland, by premature publicity! So far only a few very close friends, whose advice I have needed, know about it: and now you [...]

Berenson wrote from Rome on 22 June with renewed congratulations on Trevor-Roper's appointment to the Regius chair: 'I all but wired to Macmillan to congratulate him.'

10 July 1957   Astoria Hotel, Leningrad

My dear BB

I have now written, with my own hand, 270 letters of thanks for letters of congratulation, and I have left over, to be answered more at leisure and more at length, the letters which I valued most, such as yours. So you will excuse the delay which is the sign of election. Now, sitting in our richly furnished Edwardian suite in Leningrad, I have found the leisure, and I hope I will be able to supply the length, which you deserve.

First, I will say something of the reactions to my appointment.[1] At Oxford I appear to be quite uncontroversial. In fact, after the episode of Lucy Sutherland, I think there was a general swing of the floating vote towards me: people were afraid of a purely erratic choice, or they were afraid of

---

[10] Cecil Woodham-Smith (1896–1977) became an honorary Fellow of St Hilda's College, Oxford in 1967.
[11] Sir Arthur Bryant (1899–1985) was the prolific author of patriotic historical best-sellers.
[1] Announced in *The Times* of 6 June 1957; Galbraith did not retire until September.

A.J.P. Taylor (who really, in my opinion, never had a chance: not that he did not deserve it, but because his politics and those of Harold Macmillan are such poles asunder). So in the end, as far as Oxford was concerned, I was wafted in with the breath of favour, even relief, and the existing Regius Professor, who had publicly declared that he would resign his chair if I were elected even to the meanest chair of history in Oxford, was among the first to write his hypocritical congratulations. Even the clergy joined the applauding throng, and, ignoring the shrill cries of 'à bas l'anti-cléricalisme' which issued from those who really opposed me on quite other grounds (e.g. the *Observer*, which is hopping mad on account of my shots at its great Panjandrum Arnold Toynbee), three bishops and an archbishop wrote paeans of pleasure at my appointment. Most comic of all, I fear, was the behaviour of our old friend Sir Lewis Namier, the only begetter of the famous but now farcical candidature of Miss Sutherland. All these months that famous oracle had kept silent in his cave in the Grampians, W8:[2] only to the Prime Minister had he uttered, like Egeria to King Numa Pompilius, his secret wisdom. Then, quite suddenly, when his plan had openly and completely failed (and when the Prime Minister's letter was already in my pocket), he rushed out to back another horse. He telephoned Alan Taylor and asked him to assure me that he, Sir Lewis, had never given his favour exclusively to Lucy Sutherland but had always coupled her name with Taylor's and my own. 'I must admit', Alan Taylor wrote, in dutifully passing on this news to me, 'that I do not altogether believe this; but I do not hold it against him'.

Taylor has throughout behaved with great magnanimity, – especially, I think, in respect of the Great Man. For I think it is clear that Sir Lewis abandoned Taylor, his oldest and truest disciple, the editor of his *Festschrift*, the constant singer of his praises. Of course it may be that Namier decided, as he rationally might decide, that Taylor was simply not *papabile*, and that therefore there was no point in pressing his claims. But I fear there is also some truth in the sad story of Alan Taylor's review in the *Manchester Guardian*. For you must know that Sir Lewis, like most Masters (you must have experienced this sad fate yourself), has now acquired an army of unimaginative imitators: scribes and hacks who tediously apply his technique in unrewarding fields, 'namierising' the obscure politics of obscure back-benchers in unimportant parliamentary debates. There was Miss Jucker on *The Jenkinson Papers*; there was Mr Brooke on *The Chatham*

---

[2]Namier lived in The Grampians, a nondescript block of flats on Shepherds Bush Road, the London postcode of which was W12. Arnold Toynbee's postcode, however, was W8.

Administration;[3] and these writers did not omit to preface their works with lavish hecatombs of words to their great patron, Sir Lewis. Moreover, it must be admitted, Sir Lewis – whose critics have recently accused him of *megalomania* – did not spurn these rich sacrifices. His nostrils dilated with the savour thereof and his ears drank in the hymns of praise, and he declared himself well pleased with the fruitful labours and pious demeanour of his servants Jucker and Brooke. It was therefore unfortunate, in some respects, that just as He was expressing peculiar benedictions upon Mr Brooke, Alan Taylor, that *enfant terrible* of English historical studies, wrote an excellent and timely review of Mr Brooke's work in the *Manchester Guardian*, the gist of which may be expressed thus: '*Vicisti Galilaee!*[4] You have conquered, Sir Lewis! We are all Namierists now, we surrendered at our discretion long ago. Therefore, why must you go on? Spare us, spare us these unremitting attentions of your clergy!' The cry was a heartfelt cry, with which we all sympathise. But alas, Sir Lewis, who loves his priests, was not at all sympathetic: he turned away his countenance in wrath, and the shadow of his great wrath fell even upon Magdalen College, and the name of A.J.P. Taylor was blotted out of the Book of Life for ever. And that, I fear, is why Sir Lewis favoured instead the more docile follower of his Holy Word, Lucy Sutherland; and why, when that sound old mare (if I may suddenly change the metaphor) unexpectedly crossed her legs at the last fence, he made his sudden, belated, undignified dash from the Royal Enclosure to the bookies to place a saving bet not on Taylor (that erratic quadruped) but on the safe conservative creature that was running a constant third, Trevor-Roper.

Of course it is rather an anti-climax to find everyone in Oxford suddenly satisfied after all, and to find myself regarded as a compromise candidate, welcomed for the good old academic reason that my appointment has at least kept someone worse out. However, there is some compensation to be found in the fury which my appointment has aroused in more distant quarters. I have mentioned the *Observer*, that declining organ of virtuous Germanic Wykehamist apocalyptic socialism. The Further Left are even more furious: a high level of farce was reached in the joint post-mortem conducted by the *Tribune* (the Bevanite organ) and the *Daily Mirror*. According to the *Tribune*, the only question was, why had Macmillan

---

[3] John Brooke (1920–1985), author of *The Chatham Administration, 1766–1768* (1956), took over the editorship of the three-volume *History of Parliament 1754–1790* on Namier's death and completed Namier's study of *Charles Townshend*. He toiled on the staff of the Historical Manuscripts Commission rather than in academia.

[4] 'You have won, Galilean.' Dying words attributed to the Roman emperor Julian the Apostate.

appointed someone who, for once, was not one of his own relations? After sagacious exploration it decided that I must be regarded as a quasi-relation since I publish with Macmillans, and the firm is an extension of the family. To this the *Daily Mirror* was able to retort that no such refinements of argument were necessary: I *am* related to the Prime Minister: is not my sister-in-law's first cousin (Lord Astor) married to Lady Dorothy Macmillan's niece? As this Astor marriage only lasted for a few months, the connexion seems to me somewhat tenuous; but then so are most of the arguments of the English Left.

I am glad to say, however, that it is not only the English Left that has expressed fury at my appointment: the European Right has not been far behind. A neo-nazi paper in Germany, *Der Reichsruf*, has sounded the clarion-call, and *Die Zeit*, of Hamburg, ends a long article on 'Der Mephisto von Oxford' with the sad conclusions that 'unhappily we cannot congratulate either Oxford or England or Europe on this appointment'. I'm afraid *Die Zeit* over-estimates the influence of an Oxford Regius Professor.

For what, in fact, is my new position? In return for a loss of income and extrusion from my college (I have to migrate to Oriel College, the dingiest, dullest college in Oxford), I have acquired indeed a throne: but I am like a German Prince who has been elected to the glorious but impotent throne of Poland. All around me I see the other German Princes, the Provincial Professors, firmly established as tyrants in their narrow domains, while I, on my more ancient, more splendid throne, am rendered powerless by a highly organised *szláchta*[5] of college tutors, whose turbulent Diet, with its *liberum veto*,[6] prevents me from ever doing anything. What then am I to do? What indeed but go to St Petersburg and take lessons in despotism from my neighbour the Czar. To St Petersburg therefore we have come.

In coming, we have left behind us not only the noise of dissent at my appointment but also another noise which mingles discordantly with it: the response to my article on Toynbee. On the whole I have been surprised by the general agreement: of all the letters I have received, not one has been hostile; and the editor of *Encounter*, the paper in which it was published, has had much the same experience. On the other hand the Holy Family of Toynbee is of course furious. Apart from their organ, the *Observer*, which has censoriously announced that anyone who so dissents from the Master is not fit to be placed in a position from which he might corrupt the young, Philip Toynbee has written to *Encounter* declaring that his father, so far from entertaining messianic views, is, in his private life (but was not also

---

[5] Polish nobility.
[6] In the eighteenth-century Polish parliament, the Sejm, a single 'No' vote could veto a measure.

Nietzsche?) of 'a famous, almost excessive modesty'.[7] At almost the same time Arnold Toynbee, in Beirut, received the Press and, as if to illustrate this famous, almost excessive modesty, defended himself against the charge of defeatism by saying that 'I, above all others' preached resistance to Hitler in the 1930s. I must admit that I have so far failed to find any evidence of this activity of Toynbee as the genius of resistance. All I can discover is an interesting fact reported by Thomas Jones in his *Diary with Letters*.[8] According to Jones, Toynbee came to stay in a house-party at Blickling in 1936. While the others were playing golf, Toynbee and Jones went for a walk and Toynbee, who had been lecturing in Germany and had had a long private audience with Hitler, reported that he was convinced that Hitler seriously desired peace and should be cultivated. Jones was so impressed that he asked Toynbee to put his views down in writing, so that he could pass them on to Baldwin[9] and Eden. Further, since my article was published, I have heard indirectly from Margaret Lambert,[10] the editor of the German Diplomatic Documents, who worked with Toynbee during the war, that in 1940 Toynbee drove his subordinates (and his wife) mad by publicly pre-paring himself for the rôle of the new St Augustine: the founder of a new church based on the repentance of the West, justly destroyed by the invincible Vandals. And this is the man who now claims, in retrospect, that 'I, above all others preached resistance to Hitler'!

However, in one small detail I must modify my article. In it I suggested, as a remote, hypothetical fantasy, that after the cult of the Mish-Mash had been established, Toynbee's study in 45 Pembroke Square would no longer be in London but, by a miraculous levitation and aerial transportation, like that of the Virgin's house to Loreto, would have reached America. Now Peter Calvocoressi,[11] who worked under Toynbee until he could bear it no longer, tells me that this has in fact already happened: the contents of Toynbee's study were in fact transported by air to America in 1954, to feature

[7] 'My father's modesty is famous – perhaps excessive': Philip Toynbee, 'The Toynbee Millennium', *Encounter*, IX (July 1957), p. 71.

[8] Thomas Jones (1870–1955), a retired civil servant and well-intentioned meddler, had published *A Diary with Letters 1931–1950* in 1954.

[9] Stanley Baldwin (1867–1947), later 1st Earl Baldwin of Bewdley, was Prime Minister at the time of the Blickling conversation.

[10] Hon. Margaret Lambert (1906–1995) joined the Royal Institute of International Affairs (Chatham House) in 1936, remained after the Institute became the wartime Foreign Office Research Department, with Toynbee as director, and then worked as an intelligence officer, monitoring Eastern European reactions to BBC wartime broadcasting. British editor-in-chief of German Foreign Office Documents 1951–83.

[11] Peter Calvocoressi (b. 1912) was employed under Toynbee at the RIIA editing the Institute's annual *Survey of International Affairs* 1949–54.

in 'a televised theophany'. So I'm afraid that my fantasy was not fantastic enough: it merely expressed the facts.

But now I have left behind all these rumbling noises, and as no letters are being forwarded to me here, I live entirely in the present in this strange new world behind the Iron Curtain. What a strange world it is! We have only been here two days and yet already I could fill a book with my impressions (in fact Xandra has already done so). We decided to come because the new British Ambassador in Moscow, Sir Patrick Reilly, is an old friend of mine and invited us to stay with him and obtained visas for us. So we sailed to Sweden and came via Helsinki to Leningrad, *en route* for Moscow. Here we are staying at the Intourist Hotel, the Astoria, where we find ourselves in a large suite, consisting of a bedroom, a bathroom, a dining-room, a drawing-room and a study, all richly and heavily furnished with bronze statues, ferns and huge ormolu clocks. (In the city of Leningrad itself, as in all Russian cities, the housing shortage is acute, and few families have apartments to themselves.) Everywhere around us the thing which most impresses the visitor is the immense respect paid to 'culture'. All the old palaces and churches have been restored, repainted, re-gilded, quite regardless of cost: never, since they were first built, can they have looked so splendid. The palace at Tsarskoye Selo, shattered by German occupation in the war, is being completely restored. The Peterhof is completely re-gilded, and the great gilt statues, carried off and melted down by the Germans, have been exactly replaced. Moreover all this has been done with great taste; and the new public buildings – the underground stations, the railway stations, etc. – show great taste too: they are severe, classical, and again incredibly costly. And yet, once one has observed all this, and expressed one's admiration of it, another reflection inevitably follows. All this culture is completely divorced from ideas. The classical past is venerated; classical art and architecture are worshipped – from outside. But the ideas which lay behind such 'culture' are utterly banned. Nothing can be read except safe propaganda. No foreign books, no foreign newspapers can be bought except those published or approved by the communist party. The contrast between the ownership of 'culture' on one hand and the absolute ban on thought on the other is almost terrifying, and in the new atmosphere of comparative liberalism – which is genuine, except in intellectual matters – I feel that it is bound to lead to some kind of explosion. The rule of the Party seems to me like the rule of the medieval Church: building great cathedrals and abbeys and filling them with images and paintings, and yet forbidding thought, indeed using this imagery to replace and smother thought. This was the contrast which led, at that time, to iconoclastic riots; one day, I feel, it will do the same here.

Another thing which has impressed us is the utter lack of any innovating spirit. Everything is slavish imitation. Just as the splendid new stations are built in heavy classical style – excellent indeed, but without a trace of originality – and just as our suite of rooms is fossilised in an Edwardian guise, so the general characteristic of all life seems to be the imitation of the bourgeois fashions of the last generation. The band in our hotel dining-room plays American songs of 1930 (so as least Xandra tells me, for I cannot identify such things). The ballet is no better. We went to a new ballet with the proletarian title of *Spartak*. It was like an infinitely long performance at the *Folies Bergères*, the worst kind of bourgeois music-hall spectacle, without unity, without form, without content; and the music was dreary conventional stuff fit to accompany it. Again and again we are driven to this conclusion: in matters of taste, communism (at least in Russia) is a desperate conservatism clinging to the bourgeois taste of a generation ago.

As for material life, our experience so far suggests that it is very jejune. Clothes, food, and goods in general (at least consumers' goods) are of very poor quality. It seems impossible to buy a postcard or an exercise-book – and these are the only things which, so far, we have sought to buy. However, I must not generalise too much on two days' experience: I will express myself with more confidence when we have been to Moscow and Kiev (which we hope to visit) and been able to notice more and make comparisons.

One regret which I have at coming at this moment to Russia, this intellectual wilderness, is that I had to leave behind, half-read, a wonderful work which is just going to be published. It is Jakob Burckhardt, *Historische Fragmente*, which has been discovered in Burckhardt's *Nachlass* by the indefatigable Werner Kaegi.[12] It is being published, I think in Vienna, this autumn, and I am writing an introduction to an English translation which will be published by the Beacon Press at Boston. What a great man Burckhardt was! I read everything he wrote with ever-increasing admiration. But I couldn't risk bringing abroad with me the only copy of the typescript now in England; so, reluctantly, I had to leave it unfinished behind. But do read it when it comes out: it is the kind of history that would appeal to you – though not, I fear, to Arnold Toynbee.

Now I must stop, not so much through shortage of matter (I could go on for pages) as through shortage of paper. But I will write again when I have been to Moscow. Meanwhile I will not entrust this letter to the open post at Leningrad, but will take it with me to Moscow tomorrow and

---

[12] Burckhardt's unpublished literary remains were traced and edited by Werner Kaegi (1901–1979).

send it to you, circuitously perhaps, but safely, through the diplomatic bag. [...]

'I received', BB wrote on 27 August from Vallombrosa, 'your fascinating letters from Moscow. Therein you spoke of going south & writing from there. Please try to make time to write about Kiev & other S. Russian places. It would interest me hugely.'

17 October 1957   Savile Club, 69 Brook St., W1

My dear BB

I am conscious of owing you a letter for a long time, but oh, how overwhelmed with work I have been since we got back from Russia, and all my correspondence is scandalously in arrears. In fact we never went to Kiev. Time was short and there was so much to do in Leningrad and Moscow; and then Kiev was a long way and although we should have liked to see it, we decided that we did not want to go so far for a couple of days only – for we had to be back in England on a certain day – and in a Russian aeroplane, of which we found one experience (we flew from Leningrad to Moscow) quite enough. We took care to return by the Swedish plane which flies once or twice a week from Moscow to Copenhagen.

Russia was an extraordinary experience. When we were in Helsinki on our way there we met our ambassador in Moscow who was there to meet his daughter. I said to him, flippantly, 'are you glad to be in a free country now?' He replied, to my astonishment, with a heartfelt yes. How absurd, I thought to think of Helsinki, this miserable parochial peasant-come-to-town northern backwater, as a haven from that fascinating, vast, mysterious, animated, monstrous country Russia! Then we went into Russia, and were kept busy for three weeks being fascinated by it. But when we came to leave – and not before (for we were too preoccupied before) we both suddenly and independently felt the same emotion. We longed to escape from that dreadful prison. When we looked down from the Swedish plane and at last saw the island of Bornholm, with its trim, identical, dull, Danish farms, we felt like shipwrecked sailors who at last have sighted a friendly vessel; and when we landed at Copenhagen, that dull, bourgeois city, I could have kissed the tarmac of the aerodrome, such was my relief: we felt that a nightmare was over; a nightmare whose full horror was not appreciated till we were emerging from it. Then I remembered the incident in Helsinki. I also remembered a remark made to me by Mrs Menon, the wife of the Indian ambassador. The Indian ambassador is accredited also to Poland and Hungary. How interesting! I exclaimed, thinking of the

fascinating political situation of both countries. 'Oh how I wish', interpos-
ed Mrs Menon, 'that it was Helsinki!' In spite of its boring, provincial,
sub-arctic, philistine, small-town character, Helsinki, to the civilised
diplomatists besieged in Moscow, really is Europe: the nearest accessible
part of European civilisation.

Of course, when we became aware of our emotions, we asked ourselves
the cause. Why did we find Russia such a prison? Why were we so relieved
to escape to the dull, bourgeois world? Russia – in all respects visible or
perceptible by Europeans – is very uncomfortable. The food is uneatable,
the rooms and atmosphere squalid, there is nothing to buy, no trace of
material civilisation, or ordinary everyday efficiency. There are neither
goods nor services. But although this was very apparent to us, we did not
suffer from its direct, physical impact: for we lived in the Embassy, with
efficient service (even though the servants, supplied by the Russian government, are all spies) and good food (all flown out from England). What
wore us down was the atmosphere. Although I am certain that it is *far*
better now than under Stalin – the *mystique* of the secret police is now
broken, irremediably broken, although all the apparatus of coercion may
remain: people are no longer afraid of it as they were – it is nevertheless an
atmosphere of restraint, coercion, suspicion, made visible everywhere by
the dingy squalor and inefficiency of everyday life. We never saw anyone
smile all the time we were in Russia. At the Embassy the atmosphere of
surveillance and suspicion was everywhere. The ambassador's voice has
dropped several pitches since he went there, since there are microphones
everywhere (the building is owned, serviced and repaired by the Russian
government). At first I was sceptical about this; but since my return here
George Kennan, the former US ambassador, has told me how he actually
found one of the microphones in the US Embassy, concealed in the wall
behind the ambassador's desk.[1] Whenever anyone – ambassador, guests,
embassy staff, anyone – leaves or enters the building, the Russian guards,
posted night and day at the gate, telephone to their headquarters to report
the fact; and of course on expeditions – the scope of which is minutely
circumscribed for diplomats – one is always followed.

And then, apart from these personal considerations, there is the low level
of human life everywhere, – intellectual, aesthetic, physical. All activity, all
ingenuity, all resources of the human mind and human labour, are diverted
to secret activities which of course one cannot see, but which one naturally

---

[1] George Kennan (1904–2005) had been declared *persona non grata* as US Ambassador to the
Soviet Union in 1953. A visiting professor at Oxford during 1957–8; his Reith lectures of 1957 were
published as *Russia, the Atom and the West* (1958).

assumes to be the pursuit of industrial and military power; and the whole range of human life which consists of civilisation in our sense of the word is left as a neglected slum. At every level one soon became aware of this. Intellectually – I had two interviews with Russian historians. They were represented – and obviously resented that representation – by a jumped-up historical commissar with soapy manners and unctuous doctrinal orthodoxy; but it was clear that their standard was very low. They do not believe in their own orthodoxy (nobody in Russia seems to believe in anything), but mechanically apply it. Aesthetically – we found some wonderful works of art, and two magnificent collections of French Impressionists (made, of course, by civilised merchants before 1917); but they were quite neglected by the Russians, who trooped through vast gallery after vast gallery of hideous, anecdotal, politically virtuous 'socialist realism' – which is the taste of our Nanny, only on the heroic scale made possible by unlimited funds. Physically – I went to visit the grandest collective farm near Moscow, and found a squalid affair that would be condemned out of hand and the manager evicted for bad husbandry in any western country. And yet, we had continually to remind ourselves, what we see is merely the slum side of Russian life. Elsewhere, behind guarded walls, in remote provinces, secretly, a huge material power is being efficiently built up, to be used by these baboons. It was this thought, as much as the inefficiency which we actually saw, that depressed us.

On the other hand everyone, as it seemed to us, was eager to meet foreigners from the West. Anyone who could speak Russian (as we cannot) would have no difficulty in making direct contact. People came up to us in crowded picture-galleries and other convenient places and tried to talk to us. One man who approached me in the Hermitage at Leningrad, and who spoke German, seemed very promising, but our Russian guide descended on me and he had to flee. Russian officials make tremendous, but laboriously discreet efforts to prevent foreigners from meeting unreliable Russians, or from seeing native conditions; and of course equally laborious, but perhaps not equally discreet, efforts to prevent Russians from meeting unreliable foreigners or from seeing foreign conditions. Nevertheless, my impression was that ordinary Russians now know perfectly well that their standards of life are far, far behind ours, though they have very little idea of what ours are really like. I think that if the Iron Curtain were to dissolve, it would be their society, not ours, which would prove explosive under the strain of contact. I put this, on my return, to Kennan, and he agrees. He told me that just after the war 50,000 Russian soldiers deserted in Rumania alone – and that not even for the fleshpots of Bucharest but for the comparative paradise of peasant life in Rumania. If the Russians came to the

West, he said, 'they would simply explode, like those fishes which live five miles below the surface of the sea and blow up if they are brought to the surface.' Having been to Russia, I now completely understand the case of Nina the female discus-thrower who went mad at the sight of the London shops and stole five cheap and horrible hats.[2] Xandra, as advised by our hostess, took only very old and plain clothes to Russia, but wherever we went the women stared at her as if she was a creature from the moon and sometimes fingered her clothes as we passed.

Intellectually the Russians seem quite cynical. Nobody, as far as I could discover, believes in Marxism, or indeed in anything. They are very interested in non-Marxist ways of thought, which however are almost taboo; but Kennan says that they have more intellectual curiosity than capacity: their method of education does not enable them to think persistently. Of that I cannot judge.

Since we came back I have been working hard on my *magnum opus* on the English Revolution, and am now working on my inaugural lecture, which I shall give on 12 November and of which I shall send you a copy when it is in print, as it will be by then or soon after.[3] I have also sent you a copy of my little collection of essays, many of which you have already read in the *New Statesman*. All this has kept me busy and I have not been very social, but we have had news of you from John Pope-Hennessy[4] and the Hamish Hamiltons. [...]

7 November 1957   8 St Aldate's, Oxford

My dear Nicky,

Of course BB may show my letter, or copies of it, to Prince Paul and Jamie Hamilton. He does not need my permission. Other people do, but not those whose discretion I trust as I do his (I have also some *very* indiscreet friends!). I am so glad the letter interested you. I forget how much or how little I told you. I remember that I told you about the universal depression of Russian life. Did I tell you about my meetings with the Russian historians,

---

[2] Nina Ponomareva (b. 1929), an Olympic gold medallist of 1952 who was visiting London for an Anglo-Russian athletics match, caused a diplomatic incident in August 1956 when she stole five hats worth £1 12s. 11d. from C and A Modes in Oxford Street.

[3] Reprinted as 'History: Professional and Lay' in *History and Imagination: Essays in Honour of H.R. Trevor-Roper* (1981), pp. 1–14.

[4] (Sir) John Pope-Hennessy (1913–1994) 'has many gifts as a scholar, is good, helpful, and yet his dull aspect, his voice, his old maidish, rather surly, camel-like look, puts me off' (BB to Hamish Hamilton, 12 August 1954). An art historian and museum curator, he wrote of BB with sympathetic insight in *Learning to Look* (1991) and *On Artists and Art Historians* (1994). T-R had first met him through Pearsall Smith.

about the river journey to Ryazan (where I terrorised the spy, who was sent to spy on us all the way, by perpetually spying on him), and about that dreadful hotel – the newest grandest Intourist hotel at Vladimir – with its universal decay (before even it was finished) and its armies of carnivorous bedbugs? I expect I did, so I will not risk repeating myself, though I happen to be at leisure to write at length, being in bed with what seems a second attack of Asian 'flu. We both had it three weeks ago; Xandra went to Ireland and recovered; I, thinking of my duties here, stayed and tried to recover here. I have failed and am now back in bed feeling very low.

I hope BB has had a copy of my essays.[1] I have enjoyed the reviews of them so far. Having given one or two knocks now & then, I expect to receive one or two in return, and I know that, as one reviewer writes, 'many daggers are at the draw.' However, none was inserted with such feline malevolence as Harold Nicolson's.[2] But of course he wrote in the *Observer*, which pursues me with particular ferocity on all occasions, partly out of general antipathy (the *Observer* hates clarity, gaiety, pleasure and believes in self-mortification, Germanic *Weltanschauungen, Angst* and mumpery, and socialism as a means of reducing pleasure and relieving a guilty conscience), partly out of a new and particular hatred owing to my *Millennium of Arnold Toynbee*: the Holy Family of Toynbee are heavily entrenched in the *Observer*. However, Harold Nicolson is said to have little or no influence now; the vindictiveness of the review is generally regarded as self-cancelling; and anyway it has provoked Cyril Connolly to rise in my defence! The review which I have most enjoyed was in the Bevanite paper *Tribune*. *Tribune* specially asked for a review copy, and I feel pretty sure it was in order to slang it: it had already denounced my appointment as Regius Professor (instead of the Bevanite hero A.J.P. Taylor) as a nepotistic job. However, in fact it has come out with a great puff.[3]

It is rather embarrassing to find myself far more popular on the Left than on the Right, but I'm afraid there is a reason. On the whole there is

---

[1] *Historical Essays* (published in October 1957) contained forty-two essays collected from various periodicals: 'This book', wrote A.J.P. Taylor in a phrase that amused BB, 'has a unity, so much so that it seems like an original work and will enable Mr Trevor-Roper to conceal for some time the fact that he has not yet produced a sustained book of mature historical scholarship' ('A Corner in Rationality', *New Statesman* 19 October 1957, p. 503).
[2] 'The Professor, for all the fine finality of his judgements, lacks the daring scope of Toynbee, the majesty of Namier, the incisive wit of A.J.P. Taylor, the taste of Miss Wedgwood, the humanity of Trevelyan, or the charm and modesty of Dr A.L. Rowse [...] with Professor Trevor-Roper we feel that there is an absence of even average human compassion.' Harold Nicolson, 'The Regius Professor', *Observer*, 20 October 1957, p. 18.
[3] Raymond Fletcher, 'Hitler's Outsiders', *Tribune*, 1 November 1957, p. 13, praised T-R as 'one of the ablest of that peculiarly English breed – the fighting historians.'

far more humbug in England on the Right than on the Left. For instance, on the Right one must not tilt at *any* sacred cows, even if they are unorthodox sacred cows, for the sanctity of such cows is more important than the truth of any doctrine or idea. The English Right may not have much use for English Catholicism, but one must not say so: for the English Catholics, however erroneous, vote straight, they are on the side of 'the Establishment' (are they really?), and by an unwritten concordat their sacred cows must be ostensibly revered. The same is true of Toynbee. His apocalypse may be antichristian, obscurantist and intellectually dishonest, but it is expressed in the language of reverential religiosity (or, more briefly, cant), and therefore must be publicly praised. In consequence of this sad fact, I find myself disapproved of by the Right (to which I belong) for not respecting the taboos which, through timidity and lack of logic, they cravenly worship, and supported by the Left (which I repudiate) for opposing not the Right but the humbug of the Right. Of course this doesn't apply to the miserable *Observer*, which contrives to combine all the cant of the Establishment with all the error of the Left!

I shall send you a printed copy of my inaugural lecture which – if I am up and about by then, as I sincerely hope – is to be delivered on Tuesday. One of my predecessors, Sir Charles Firth, was boycotted in Oxford for 24 years after his inaugural lecture (in which he had been so rash as to suggest that a university, among other things, was also a place of learning).[4] If I last out my time until the retiring age, I shall have 24 years; so I must be careful what I say on Tuesday.

Owing to my illness I have seen no-one, or almost no-one, since I last wrote: nor have I read or written anything. I had one lucid weekend which we spent at Stratfield Saye with the Duke of Wellington whom you probably know: a learned, interesting and cultivated man, but so fussy that by the end of the week-end we were reduced almost to paralysis by fear of touching a treasure or dropping a spot on the carpet.[5] We went and visited the Colvilles, who are great friends of ours, and who live in the old rectory at the ducal gate: they told us that they had a continual stream of visitors seeking relief from the same strain.[6] Fellow-guests were General and Mrs

---

[4] Sir Charles Firth's inaugural lecture as Regius Professor of Modern History in 1904 provoked most Oxford college history tutors to sign and print a retort.

[5] Gerald Wellesley, 7th Duke of Wellington (1885–1972), architect, connoisseur and intimate friend of Mary Berenson's lover Geoffrey Scott.

[6] (Sir) John Colville (1915–1987), principal private secretary to Churchill 1951–5, and subsequently a bank director, had married a courtier, Lady Margaret Egerton (1918–2004), sister of T-R's Roxburghshire neighbour Lord Ellesmere.

Aspinall-Oglander.[7] They are of value to me because the general owns some very interesting family papers – indeed the whole Trevor-Roper interpretation of the whole history of England in the 17th century hangs upon one crucial sentence in the notebook of Sir John Oglander.[8] Mrs Oglander is a howling intellectual snob and claims familiarity with everyone who is anyone in the intellectual world, calling them all by their Christian names (generally the wrong Christian names). She is, of course, a great friend of BB. Does BB agree? (I need hardly add *this* letter is *not* to be circulated!).
[...]

[undated; mid-December 1957]   8 St Aldate's, Oxford

My dear BB

Alas, I see no prospect of getting away, but I live in hope of visiting you before long, and meanwhile I write to send you both our best wishes and tell you such news as I can. In order to disperse my critics, I am now writing a huge book, in three volumes. I know you hold the Alexandrian view that a big book is a big evil, but I have decided that the subject requires it. It is on the Puritan revolution. It was going to have been published by Jamie Hamilton, but I'm afraid I suddenly decided that I *couldn't* publish a serious book with that pathetic wobbler – he came and visited us, and seemed feebler than ever, and I just felt that he really can't be taken seriously at all – so it will be a Macmillan book after all.[1]

You see I am taking myself very seriously. But I must admit that my efforts to pose as a grave member of the Establishment have not so far proved very successful. I have had a sad *débâcle* with the Church, which I will now sadly explain.

It all began when I was asked to appear on television as one of a panel of

---

[7] Brigadier General Cecil Aspinall-Oglander (1878-1959), historian of the Gallipoli campaign and biographer of Lord Lynedoch, assumed his surname in 1927 after marrying Mrs Florence Kennard (1884–1961), heiress to the Oglander estates on the Isle of Wight.

[8] The crucial passage from the diary of Sir John Oglander (1585–1655), together with T-R's interpretation, can be found in *Historical Essays*, p. 181.

[1] T-R's rupture with Hamilton is described in a sequence of letters between St John's Wood and I Tatti. 'Some time I must tell you about our visit to Oxford, where we were received v. frigidly by Hugh, for no reason we could discover, and were thankful thereafter to warm our hands and hearts on Isaiah. *What* a strange mortal Hugh is' (Hamilton to Berenson, 8 December 1957). 'It has been rather a wretched week [...] Hugh Trevor-Roper has torn up his contract for the "Cromwell" book on the pretext that we announced it before he intended us to do so. In fact we consulted his agent first and did so only in order to stake a claim on the tercentenary and warn others off the grass. Hugh is certainly unpredictable, and I mind his decision (though it's a blow to the firm) less than his rudeness to Yvonne three weeks ago' (Hamilton to Berenson, 22 December 1957).

grave and respectable pundits giving advice to a young man who was, or believed himself to be, assailed by religious Doubts. I said to myself, Now you are a Regius Professor and a member of the Establishment, you must be very careful what you say. You must resist all temptation to enlarge this young man's Doubts. You must show him the way into the Church, not the way out of it. So I thought gravely and respectably about it, and in due course, when the young man had expressed his doubts, and a canon of Salisbury cathedral had told him that high-church Anglicanism would soon put him to rights, I opened my mouth and stroked my nose and uttered some statesmanlike opinions, calculated, as I thought, to make the crooked straight and the rough places plain so that there would be a broad and tempting highway into the Church.

Young man, I said (or words to this effect), these doubts are nothing. You think certain doctrines of the Church unplausible. Of course you are quite right: they are. But why should you expect them to be plausible? How can you seriously suppose that doctrines devised to befuddle the senses of illiterate peasants in the pre-scientific Middle East should stand up to our exacting tests? The doctrine of the Church, that extraordinary patchwork garment, which nevertheless has a certain archaic beauty, is not tailor-made to fit you. It is a reach-me-down garment, somewhat moth-eaten in places, as needs must be; but it has fitted many a good man in the past, and will fit you, if you wear it lightly and don't go about drawing attention to the admittedly numerous holes which now make up the major part of it ...

So I spoke, and I must say, I thought I had done rather well, and opened a new breach in those prohibitive doctrinal walls which keep so many men out of the Church. Having said so, and put the canon right on one or two points of theology, and forced him, for the sake of his own consistency, to admit that he didn't believe in the Athanasian creed, I set off back to Oxford full of self-congratulation, all agog to receive the compliments of the Anglican hierarchy and news of my election to the House of Laymen in the Convocation of Canterbury.

Alas, what are the hopes of men! I was gravely deceived. Next day the Archbishop of Canterbury,[2] after a substantial luncheon of roast-beef and claret, sent for pen and ink (he would have sent for fire and faggot if the old statutes had not unfortunately been repealed at the Reformation), and wrote to Sir Ian Jacob, director of the BBC,[3] saying that he trusted soon to have an assurance that a young man called Trevor-Roper, whom he

---

[2] Geoffrey Fisher (1887–1972), Archbishop of Canterbury 1945–61 and afterwards Lord Fisher of Lambeth.
[3] Lt-Gen Sir Ian Jacob (1899–1993), Director-General of the BBC 1952–9.

understood to be a student just down from Oxford, would never be allowed to speak on the radio again. A week later I met the bishop of Exeter – a convivial prelate from whom I once won a bottle of port in consequence of a bet on a point of theology. He told me that last Sunday he had been woken from slumber in his episcopal stall by the voice of his own Dean preaching a sermon against me in his cathedral, and he threatened to send me a large bill for the postage which he had incurred, writing letters to calm down the indignant lower clergy in his diocese. So now I am fleeing to Scotland, outside the reach of the Established Church.

Nor have I been entirely successful in establishing my new respectability in the lay world either. I'm afraid my inaugural lecture has caused a good deal of mumping among the Manchester medievalists, and the former Professor of Latin, Eduard Fraenkel, a German of the most boring kind, the author of the $3\frac{1}{2}$ kilo commentary on Aeschylus' *Agamemnon* to which I made a discreetly veiled reference, is furious.[4] He wrote to the Regius Professor of Greek asking him, as a member of the Governing Body of Christ Church, to see that I was properly disciplined.

However, I shall survive these blows of fortune, I expect. A timely withdrawal beyond the Cheviot Hills – how I wish it were beyond the Alps – will give these light English breezes time to drop and the temperature even in Lambeth Palace time to cool. And next time I can get away it will be to Italy. Xandra and I both long to revisit you: it is maddening that she is always so child-bound when I am free; but perhaps by skimping my duties I can get away for a week even in term now. I have already cancelled a visit to America this spring because I want to work on my book: might not this free me for a short visit? [...]

---

[4] Eduard Fraenkel (1888-1970), a German Jewish classical scholar, was forbidden to teach when the Nazis came to power in 1933. Elected to a Fellowship at Trinity College, Oxford in 1934, he held the Corpus chair in Latin from 1935 until 1953, and pioneered the use of the German seminar method in Oxford.

1958

My dear BB

I write to send you our best wishes for the New Year and to thank you both for your Christmas card. I hope you are keeping well and not having too many visitors, and occasionally getting out in the mild Tuscan winter.

We have had a very disordered Christmas. I had to give two lectures in Glasgow, so I set off to Scotland two days early; Xandra, children & servants were to follow. When I got to Melrose, children & servants had arrived, but Xandra had been removed to hospital in Oxford; so I had to set off south again. On arrival I found that she had pneumonia – virus-pneumonia, which doesn't respond to the new antibiotics. She has been there ever since, and only today, after 12 days of high temperature, is beginning to revive. I think all will be well now, but she will emerge very enfeebled for the worst part of the winter. Meanwhile I have been picknicking in a deserted house, without servants and surrounded by obstinately closed colleges. I want to try to get Xandra away for a rest, if I can arrange it, instead of letting her fuss about getting the children back to school; but I don't know if I can stop her from doing that. Anyway she is now well enough to take some notice of the world and to send you both, as she does, her best wishes.

Of course all this is a tiresome dislocation of my work. I am engaged on a vast operation, so ambitious that I sometimes despair of it, especially when subject to all these interruptions. I never tell people what it is, lest their knowledge of it, and questions about it, then begin to plague me and disconcert it. But I will tell you. It is on the English Puritan Revolution, and I call it 'vast' and 'ambitious' because I am trying to treat it in a new way.[1]

Briefly the problem is this. The old historians wrote narrative history. This was readable, but unfortunately it often did not solve problems or even necessarily state them. It was perfectly satisfactory for describing the making of policy, or the conduct of politics, or war; but in revolutionary periods it somehow fails, because it cannot penetrate to the depths of society which are then stirred up, or the heart of those intractable problems round which human muddles are woven like some great untidy cocoon.

---

[1] This was one of several books that T-R neither completed nor published.

More modern historians, interested in these problems, adopt an analytic method. The Marxists do this; but, in my view, wrongly. So does Namier, but only in a limited, unrevolutionary period. Outside that period, I don't think that his technique can be applied, though some of his generalisations can. I think that Namier is better than the Marxists because (among other virtues) he doesn't try to deal with revolutionary periods: in other words because he avoids precisely that problem which I, perhaps over-ambitiously, want to face. And the reason for this is, I believe, that whereas only the analytic method can reveal the social depths, such an essentially static method cannot explain the movement which, by agitating the surface, stirs up those depths and brings out the horrible monsters that lurk there. These movements, I believe, are caused not by the inherent contradictions of social systems (as the Marxists would say) – in fact I believe that there are no social contradictions which cannot be kept quiet by good politics, no social system which is not 'impossible', 'revolutionary' etc., if subjected to the Marxist microscope; through which, however, they only look at the societies which actually have exploded – but by events and the intellectual impact of events, their cumulative pressure on the human mind. What happened before seems to me just as important, in the history of social revolutions, as what lies beneath. Social analysis must, to be effective, be fitted into a narrative form.

But what a problem of form this necessity imposes! The good Miss Wedgwood writes excellent, readable narrative history: but only the surface of society moves: nothing is explained. The sociological historians dive into the depths: but there is no movement at all. How can one *both* move *and* carry along with one the fermenting depths which are also, at every point, influenced by the pressure of events about them? And how can one possibly do this so that the result is readable? This is the problem. Nicky once referred to one of my reviews as 'three-dimensional'. I wasn't quite sure that this wasn't a euphemism for unreadable. But what I would like to do is to write a book on this intractable subject which could be described as three-dimensional and yet readable. In fact, I had written 400 pages by last autumn and decided that it was getting formless and would be unreadable; so I have begun again and have written about 200 pages in a new form. But then the interruptions of life, the necessities of lecturing on quite different subjects, the pressures of this and that occasion, the dislocation of illness, etc. .... That is why I sometimes despair of it and feel that, in the end, this letter may be the only evidence of this ambitious but abortive project.

Meanwhile, realising that I cannot write, I read. Particularly I have been reading Hume. I regard him as one of the great forebears. Hume, Millar,

Adam Smith ... what a revolution in historical study they started![2] How ridiculous that its results should have been seized and stirred up in the witches' cauldron of Hegelian rubbish in order to end in the horrible *olla podrida*[3] of Marxism! For I believe that this is what happened: that Marx owed all the *rational* part of his historical philosophy (which he admitted was unoriginal) to Hume and Adam Smith; and then the wretch went and bedevilled it all with his mystical dialectical mumbo-jumbo, which I suppose was more taking in 19th century Germany. Oddly enough, I have discovered an almost exactly parallel case in the 17th century. The more I read of Francis Bacon, the more I am impressed with his social and historical understanding.[4] He seems to me the greatest, profoundest, acutest intellect that ever studied the contemporary social problems of England. And yet, in the years after his death, he had no *direct* influence at all. Such influence as he had was at second hand. His ideas were transported from England to Eastern Europe and came back to England from Poland and Transylvania, where they had become mingled with messianic rubbish about Armageddon, the Millennium, the Ancient of Days and the Number of the Beast. In this form, and in this form only, were they acceptable to the generation younger than himself.

I have just finished reading Hume's Letters, in Greig's edition, supplemented by Klibansky & Mossner.[5] What a splendid letter-writer he was: so genial and gay as well as full of ideas! And his best letters, I notice, are all to Scotsmen – John Clephane, William Strachan, Gilbert Elliot, Adam Smith. How can one account for this extraordinary phenomenon of the Scottish intellectual ferment of the 18th century, the sudden appearance of eccentrics and geniuses in a country which, hitherto, had only produced hell-fire preaching dominies and cattle-thieving squireens? I wish I knew a good book on the subject. Can you tell me of one?

And then, too, I have been reading *Dr Zhivago*. Have you read it? I thought it a wonderful book, Tolstoyan in its vast, panoramic complexity. But I don't wonder that it didn't please Mr Khrushchev and the panjandrums of literary orthodoxy in Russia. It would be a thaw indeed that

---

[2] David Hume (1711-1776) in his six-volume *History of England*, from Caesar's invasion to the Glorious Revolution of 1688, treated literature and science as well as statecraft, and established a new standard in narrative history; the jurist John Millar (1735–1801) wrote a work of proto-sociology, *Observations Concerning the Distinctions of Rank in Society*; Adam Smith (1723–1790), author of *The Wealth of Nations*, edited Hume's autobiography.

[3] Spanish spiced stew containing a wide variety of meats and vegetables.

[4] Francis Bacon, Viscount St Albans (1561–1626), Lord Chancellor of England, philosopher and essayist.

[5] Raymond Klibansky and Ernest Mossner had edited *New Letters of David Hume* (1954).

allowed such a growth to spring up in that dreary winter landscape. And how good the English translation is! The translator, Max Hayward, is a lecturer in Russian at Leeds.[6] (He helped me when I was working on the Russian evidence for *The Last Days of Hitler.*) He has been described to me as the only Englishman who speaks Russian so perfectly that he could genuinely be taken for a Russian. But how good his English is too! I wonder if he can be lured from Leeds, that city of barbarous provincialism. But perhaps I am being purblind. No doubt this is what metropolitan Englishmen said – in fact it is what Dr Johnson said – about 18th century Scotland. Perhaps (since Scotland is now intellectually moribund) Leeds is the new Athens of the North.

And now I see that I have got to page 6 of my letter without giving you any gossip of any kind. But how can I? I am a hermit. All life has drained away from Oxford. Even the Regius Professor of Ecclesiastical History – a fossil survivor from the days of Queen Anne, the Non-Jurors[7] and Dr Sacheverell[8] – is less eremitical than I: he has stumped off, looking like a bundle of black rags (he last untied his clothes in 1935), with a flat hat on his head, an alarm clock tied round his neck, and his pockets bulging with three weeks' supply of college stationery and college toast, to spend the Christmas season above a book-shop in Tunbridge Wells.[9] And if even he has flown, how can you expect the gay *mondain* society of the Berlins and company to be here? Of course they are not. Our Vice-Chancellor, Tom Boase, you may even have met: for he is, I think in Florence, trying to humour an eccentric millionaire who wants to leave his rational cash to the University provided that (like Bacon and Hume) it is mixed up with the teaching of some mystical rubbish. We naturally suppose that Tom Boase is plausibly persuading him to leave it unconditionally to Magdalen College instead. The benefactor's name is Whitaker: do you know of him?[10] [...]

In a letter to Hamish Hamilton on 12 March, Berenson lamented: 'Now that Hugh

---

[6] Max Hayward (1924–1979) studied in Prague and worked in the British Embassy in Moscow before joining the Russian department at Leeds University. Afterwards a Fellow of St Anthony's College, Oxford and a member of the Russian and East European Centre there, he translated Pasternak's *Doctor Zhivago* jointly with Manya Harari.
[7] Beneficed clergy of the Church of England who refused to swear oaths of allegiance after the Glorious Revolution of 1688.
[8] Henry Sacheverell (1674–1724), a clergyman of violent Tory opinions, whose trial for seditious libel led to the downfall of the Whig ministry in 1710.
[9] Claude Jenkins (1877–1959), Regius Professor of Ecclesiastical History and Canon of Christ Church since 1934, had nominally been T-R's graduate supervisor, but neglected his responsibilities.
[10] Unidentified.

is Regius Professor I seldom hear from him and I miss his letters.' The correspondence faltered as Berenson's strength failed and Trevor-Roper was preoccupied by his new responsibilities. All but one of the final letters sent to I Tatti were addressed to Nicky Mariano, and read aloud by her.

13 August 1958   8 St Aldate's, Oxford

My dear BB

I believe you owe me a letter – that is if you got my letter about Mexico, as I hope you did. But all the same, I feel guilty at not having written for so long. Let me now make excuses and amends. My excuse is that I find myself writing my book all day and cannot hold a pen by the evening; also I have had rather a distracted term, Xandra being ill – as at I Tatti – with this tiresome internal complaint (now diagnosed as pancreas trouble, but not cured). She is now staying with her aunt Violet in Anglesey, where I hope she is getting a rest. I am going up there for the week-end, but meanwhile am alone. How are you? I do hope your back-trouble is better and that you have been able to go to Vallombrosa. Do write, or perhaps Nicky will write, and tell us about yourself if either of you has time.

What can I tell you about life here? Since getting back from Mexico, that horrible country, I have been very static: but even in our static condition we have had one or two dramas. For instance, the visit of those two very different musicians, Poulenc and Shostakovitch who both came to receive honorary degrees.[1] Poulenc stayed with us, Shostakovitch with the Berlins, and we gave a joint musical party at our house at which they both per-formed. It was a nightmare in some respects: too many *prima donnas* in the house.

First of all Isaiah. Isaiah, as I have learned in the past, can be quite impossibly sensitive on trivial matters. And he was on this occasion. First of all he went round inviting verbally far more people than the house would hold, including some crashing bores whom he wanted to pay off, and who had no interest in music at all, and leaving very little room for our friends. When I meekly protested, he said it was impossible not to send them invitations now, as he had already asked them. 'Them' included the Winds. Then when I asked the Hodsons (he is editor of the *Sunday Times*), Isaiah suddenly announced that if Hodson came he would boycott the party. As Isaiah and Hodson are both fellows of All Souls & both came to dinner

---

[1] Francis Poulenc (1899–1963), French composer, and Dmitri Shostakovich (1906–1975), the great-est composer of Soviet Russia.

with us after my inaugural lecture, and showed no signs of anything but amity then, we were completely taken aback. Isaiah said Hodson had published something in the *Sunday Times* which he, Isaiah, could never forgive, and he absolutely refused to be in any room with him. We went down on our knees, told Isaiah he couldn't boycott his own party, etc.: but he was adamant: if Hodson, then no Isaiah. 'Perhaps Hodson will refuse,' we said, desperately deceiving ourselves with distant hopes. 'No,' said Isaiah, 'he never does.' 'But if he is aware of a *froideur*...' 'No,' said Isaiah, 'he is quite unaware of it. You ought never to have invited people to *our* party without first telling me!' 'But you asked 47 people without a word to us! The Winds!' And when I thought of the Winds, I clutched at them as at a lifeline in the argumentative storm. Really, though the Winds are great bores, and he is, I am sure, a total fraud, I can't say that I can't bear them; but now, as my only defence, I desperately pretended that I couldn't, so as to have some counter-grievance to set against Isaiah's grievance about Hodson. But it was no good. In despair, I thought of writing to Hodson and asking him not to come; but that, I thought, was too much: besides, he might refuse anyway, so why court trouble? So we waited. Then, at the last minute, the Hodsons answered: delighted to come. More dramas with the Berlins. In the end – having excoriated our knees in prayer on the rich Aubusson carpets of Headington House – we prevailed – Isaiah would come to his own party provided that he never saw Hodson, or had to speak to him, or was spoken to by him. With great skill we arranged the chairs, the supper, everything, to ensure this result. The Hodsons, immediately on arrival, were obsequiously hurried to comfortable but distant chairs at one end of the room: the Berlins firmly placed at the other. Supper was served to them in different rooms. All was peacefully past. Next day I discovered the reason for Isaiah's fury. Hodson, in a paragraph on Isaiah in the *Sunday Times*, had compared his eloquence to a Russian river melting in the spring. This seemed to me rather a happy image: but not, apparently, to Isaiah.

But was that the only drama? Certainly not. Shostakovitch was originally to have spent a night with the local representative of the British Council, Mr Frost. In his honour, the Frosts arranged a party and invited us. Therefore we invited the Frosts to our musical party. Then Mr Khrushchev suddenly launched out and made a furious attack on the British Council as an engine of imperialism, and Shostakovitch was told on no account to have anything to do with it. He was not to stay with the Frosts. He was to boycott the Frosts. He was never to meet them, see them, speak to them, be spoken to by them. If he met the Frosts at our party, there would be trouble.

Fresh drama. Should we put the Frosts off? I saw no reason why we should. We didn't. But then, on the very afternoon of our party, I was telephoned by the university registry and told that two members of the Russian embassy would be escorting Shostakovitch and must be asked to our party. I said that we had no room for them. In that case, I was told, Shostakovitch couldn't come. No escort, no Shostakovitch: how else could the Russians guarantee that Shostakovitch didn't see Frost? I stood firm. Universal blackmail all round. In the end all was well: Isaiah found someone to invite the escort to dinner and imprison them afterwards, in a series of remorseless parties, till 2.0 a.m. Shostakovitch came unescorted, played the piano splendidly (it has had to be repaired since), talked away to Frost, had as interpreters only reactionary bloodsuckers and oppressors of the people like Dimitri Obolensky[3] and bourgeois-capitalist plutocrats like Isaiah, and thoroughly enjoyed his evening. He was altogether charming, and that evening was the only time when he did not look a hunted man. At all other times it was quite pathetic. At the ceremony, on formal occasions, he looked paralysed with fear. If any stranger came up to him and spoke Russian, he started like a hunted rabbit. His spirit, Isaiah says, has been totally broken. But with us he was quite different and seemed really at ease. I was very glad we kept the escort away.

Since then, all has been peace again. Vacation has descended. Everyone has left Oxford except myself. I have scribbled myself silly. Today, I could write no more so I decided to read. I have just been reading John Chadwick's book on Michael Ventris' decipherment of Linear B script which has so convulsed all orthodoxies about Mycenaean Greece. What a wonderful man Ventris was! It is maddening that he should be killed at 34.[4] Champollion, Rawlinson, – they had cribs – bilingual or trilingual inscriptions which made their work possible.[5] Ventris did it entirely by deduction. I picked the book up full of doubts – it looks so formidable – and then couldn't put it

---

[3] (Sir) Dimitri Obolensky (1918–2001) had visited I Tatti at T-R's recommendation in 1951. Rescued in infancy from the Crimea on a British warship, he did not use the title of Prince after becoming a British subject in 1948. Student of Christ Church, Oxford 1950–85, Professor of Russian and Balkan History 1961–85. Admired for his literary sensibility and profound scholarship by T-R, who contributed the Introduction to Obolensky's memoirs *Bread of Exile* (1999), which were dedicated to T-R's stepson James Howard-Johnston.

[4] At the age of fourteen Michael Ventris (1922–1956) began trying to decipher the spidery squiggles written on Minoan clay tables which the archaeologist Sir Arthur Evans had found in Crete and had named Linear A and Linear B. He finally succeeded in deciphering Linear B script in 1952, and amazed scholars by proving that the language of Bronze Age Greece was Greek. T-R reviewed John Chadwick's *The Decipherment of Linear B* in *Sunday Times*, 7 September 1958.

[5] Jean-François Champollion (1790–1832) deciphered the hieroglyphics of the Rosetta Stone and compiled an ancient Egyptian dictionary; Sir Henry Rawlinson (1810–1895) deciphered the trilingual inscriptions (in Babylonian, old Persian and Elamite) carved on Darius the Great's orders at Bisitun in Persia.

down. I have now persuaded the *Sunday Times* to let me puff it in its astonished pages. Ventris taught himself Polish at the age of six and at the age of seven bought and studied a German book on Egyptian hieroglyphs. What a pleasure it is even to think of such a thing!

My brother Pat, to whom Nicky wrote a charming letter, is going to Italy soon and will write and ask if he can call on you. I have told him you will probably be at Vallombrosa, but he will find his way somehow. I hope you can see him and will like him. Everyone says that he is charming and very unlike me. I agree with both propositions separately, but don't like them put in such emphatic juxtaposition. He is a very good eye-surgeon, musical, easy-going, informal, and of a political *naïveté* which leaves me speechless.

Did you read any of Burckhardt's *Historische Fragmente*? What do you think of them? I think he is a marvellous historian – until suddenly I come up against that paralytic timidity which occasionally freezes up his thought – e.g. about Mohammed and Erasmus. I feel that there is something ungenerous about his fear of ideas, his clinging to 'culture', his neurosis about the destructive masses. But what a wonderful range! And if he is a pessimist, – well, I'm afraid all the best historians are. Macaulay isn't, Froude isn't, the Bismarckians Sybel and Treitschke aren't, Michelet isn't; but I feel that they are all a bit the worse for their vulgar optimism.[6] [...]

'Dearest Hugh,' Nicky Mariano wrote from Vallombrosa on 19 August, 'We were both delighted to get your letter and I have promised BB to give him a second reading of it. It was the first in a very long time for, alas, the one you mention, written from Mexico, never reached us and we had to content ourselves with the ST articles.' They were expecting Patrick Trevor-Roper to stay overnight at I Tatti on his way 'to the Buddha in Lerici', Percy Lubbock.

Berenson sent a message of his own from Vallombrosa on 3 September: it proved the final letter that Trevor-Roper received from him. 'I know that Nicky has thanked you for your wonderful letter,' he wrote. 'This is just to say your brother came, looked into our eyes and charmed us. I was amused to find so many traces of resemblance in look and gestures between you and him.' He suggested that Burckhardt had multiple personalities – 'they all unite in his hatred of the modern heresy that the artist lives the work of art he is producing' – but 'to write all I could say on this matter would take a book and so must wait until we meet again.'

---

[6] James Froude (1818–1894), one of T-R's predecessors in the Regius chair, wrote a multi-volume *History of England from the Fall of Wolsey to the Defeat of the Spanish Armada*; Heinrich von Sybel (1817–1895) edited Frederick the Great's correspondence and wrote a major study of the French revolution; Heinrich von Treitschke (1834–1896), the eulogist of Hohenzollern power, wrote a massive history of nineteenth-century Germany; Jules Michelet (1798–1874) was a Romantically overblown French historian.

9 September 1958   8 St Aldate's, Oxford

Dearest Nicky

Thank you so much for your letter. I was so sorry to hear that BB is still in trouble with his back: I do hope it is better now. I am slightly encouraged to think that it may be by a postcard from Pat – he only sends postcards, very brief and almost illegible: I don't think I have ever had a letter from him in my life – who clearly greatly enjoyed his visit to you and reports a sense of improvement at Casa al Dono: I am so glad you have been able to get up there, away from the heat of Florence. And I am so sorry to hear that you never got my long letter from Mexico. Not that it was of great interest in itself, but it was also my bread-and-butter letter, thanking you for so hospitably entertaining us on our last visit. You must think me very casual not to have written – but I hope you assumed that the letter was written and lost on the way!

Really, I hated Mexico. I tried to conceal this in my articles (unsuccessfully, to judge from some of the reactions), but I made no such attempt in my letter to you.[1] Somehow, in spite of the colours, the spectacular landscape, the strangeness and fascination of the country, it is repellent. There is no feeling of humanity there, just as there is none in Mexican art, which is impressive enough in detail, but which, when one sees it *en masse*, as in the Anthropological Museum there (a marvellous collection), is utterly barbaric, inhuman, uncivilisable. Everywhere there is an atmosphere, almost a smell, of blood, dust, hatred. Only in the old colonial areas, and in particular in the 18th century colonial areas, when the passions of conquest had been worn out, did I feel any spirit of civilisation. There is a perfectly charming town called Guanajuato, which was a boom-town of the late 18th century, based on the richest mine of Mexico: there alone did I feel at ease, among the elegant 18th century buildings, and the pollarded evergreen trees shading the *patio* and the streets, and the theatre and the municipal buildings in colonial rococo; and yet even there, when I actually visited the mine, the smell of blood and hatred came rushing up that infinite, disused shaft. As for Querétaro, where Maximilian was murdered,[2] I arrived there late one night, and fled from it at 7.0 the next morning: but that was partly because of the giant cockroaches in the

---

[1] T-R's three *Sunday Times* articles discussed Mexico's past exploitation and present Marxism (22 June), President Cárdenas' revolutionary achievements before 1940 (29 June) and the rapid industrialisation and ultra-modern trends since 1946 (6 July).
[2] Maximilian (1832–1867), brother of Emperor Franz Joseph of Austria, became Emperor of Mexico in 1864 as the result of intervention by Napoleon III's troops, but was captured, court-martialled and shot by republicans three years later.

vast, grand, squalid, decaying hotel. Altogether, though I enjoyed wonderful moments, I have no desire to see Mexico again: give me Europe; never have I felt so European as among those savage, bizarre mountains and their shoddy new skyscrapers, and those half-breeds staring with sinister, treacherous eyes at the glare of the sun. Even Spain seemed part of Europe there! [...]

Today I got a letter from BB. Please tell him I was delighted to see his signature again and to hear from him, and will write to him again soon. Xandra writes that she has seen Willy Mostyn-Owen at Edinburgh: I hope we may see him at Oxford before he goes back to Italy, and that we will be able to send more news to you with him. At present there is very little to tell you as I have been absolutely alone in this deserted city since I last wrote. What a horrible city Oxford is in August! It is like Baghdad, or Basra: enervating exhalations steam up from the river and only the Babel of foreign tongues is heard in the streets, which swarm like an oriental bazaar. One tries to seek refuge in the cloisters, or *medersahs*,[3] but is quickly overwhelmed by a bus-load of strangely clad, crop-haired, gum-chewing Americans, gaping after their raucous, inaccurate guide and distributing casual *baksheesh* to the natives who obligingly offer them snake-stones, basket-work and other local souvenirs ... But perhaps I am getting bad-tempered with isolation, toothache and bad weather. I will stop and write again later, when the fresher air of Scotland has revived my drooping spirits [...]

Nicky Mariano's message of 22 November enclosed a letter from Prince Alphonse Clary Aldringen, a Hapsburg nobleman living in Venice, about A.J.P. Taylor's 'rash statements' on German history.

3 December 1958   8 St Aldate's, Oxford

My dear Nicky

We were delighted to hear from you. Thank you so much for writing. And we were glad to hear that BB is feeling better, and not having too many exhausting guests! I hope he will go on getting better in the even, warm temperature of I Tatti, where even the mild Italian winter becomes milder still. How we would like to visit you, fleeing from this rude climate, and to see and talk to you both again! At present we must go to Scotland, for the children's holiday; but we promise to take you at your word and revisit you

---

[3] Traditional Muslim colleges.

soon. Meanwhile I write to send you our best wishes, and also to return Prince Clary's letter. Of course he is quite right about A.J.P. Taylor. Taylor has always been, in my opinion, unbalanced about Germany and Russia, believing in the unnatural wickedness of the Germans and (to balance it) the unnatural virtue of the Russians. When Russian virtue became too difficult to defend à l'outrance, he discovered that the really virtuous countries were Yugoslavia and Poland. I remember his visit to Czechoslovakia in 1946. He came back full of admiration. I went there the year after and he gave me letters to some of his communist and fellow-travelling friends. By the time I arrived, these communist & fellow-travelling friends were themselves in a state of panic (they included Clementis,[1] who was afterwards hanged for 'deviation,' and Ripka,[2] who fled to the west). But Taylor remains incorrigible. Recently, when President Heuss came to England, Taylor wrote an absolutely monstrous article in the *Daily Express* (he has now sold his soul to that detestable character, Lord Beaverbrook)[3] saying that the visit should be boycotted – not because Heuss's own anti-Nazi record was not perfectly reputable, but because *all* Germans must *always* be held responsible for Hitler, and Heuss's visit might involve a state visit, in return, by the Queen to Germany, – when she ought (he said) to go instead to virtuous Poland![4] I'm afraid that since my appointment Taylor has gone berserk: he no longer troubles about the truth. I think that originally his anti-German, pro-Russian attitude was not consciously dishonest. I think it sprang from a kind of *naïveté*. But now I think he will say anything, even if he knows it to be untrue.

I have been very busy, made busier by a visit to Paris in mid-term. I went as a member of the British delegation to the General Conference of Unesco.

---

[1] Vladimír Clementis (1902–1952), a Slovakian lawyer and Communist deputy from 1936, had been in charge of the BBC's wartime Slovak broadcasting. After Masaryk's violent death in 1948 he was appointed Foreign Minister of Czechoslovakia, but in 1950 was summarily dismissed and vilified for ideological deviation. In 1951 he was accused of treason, and subsequently condemned in a show-trial.

[2] Hubert Ripka (1895–1958), formerly a Prague newspaper editor, afterwards the anglophile Minister for Foreign Trade in the four-party coalition government, led the twelve non-Marxist ministers whose resignations in February 1948 prompted the Communist *coup d'état*.

[3] After Taylor replaced Robert Blake as Lord Beaverbrook's favourite historian, he was paid to write articles for his patron's *Sunday Express*. Taylor's first article, headlined 'Why must we soft-soap the Germans?' (27 October 1957), was fully as xenophobic and rabble-rousing as Beaverbrook could wish.

[4] Theodor Heuss (1884-1963), a liberal editor and progressive member of the Reichstag, was director of studies at the Deutsche Hochschule für Politik, the Berlin equivalent of Chatham House, until deprived of his posts by the Nazis. His books were burnt and he was prohibited from publishing further work. As first President of the German Federal Republic 1949–59, he paid a state visit to England in October 1958.

The whole thing is, I am now sure, a complete racket. I ought never to have gone, but I yielded, not to reason but to persuasion: persuasion by my former pupil, the boy-prodigy of the Tory Party, Sir Edward Boyle,[5] who pressed and flattered me into going, and, of course, equally insistent pressure (though not flattery) by Xandra, who simply wanted a visit to Paris. When I arrived, I soon found that there was absolutely nothing to do except to marvel at such grotesque extravagance. The new Unesco building seems to me, in its economic significance, like the Egyptian pyramids, or medieval gothic cathedrals: it has cost fabulous sums to build, and costs even more fabulous sums to maintain, and it keeps thousands of useless officials – priests and acolytes of the new nonsense-religion, monks and nuns,

> Embryos and idiots, Eremites and Friars,
> Black, white and grey, with all their Trumpery –[6]

in perpetual, expensive, meaningless, ceremonious circulation. But what else? I really think, nothing. Of course the Europeans and Americans, who do all the work, get nothing from it. On the whole, the Americans pay and the Asiatics and South Americans sponge. I was supposed to make a speech, and indeed took a lot of trouble to prepare it; but when I arrived, the timetable had been changed, the opportunity had already passed, and I never made it. Otherwise, we elected a new secretary-general of whom I thoroughly disapproved.[7] But Xandra was able to visit her *couturier* and order a new dress and a new hat; I was able to lay hands on some new *Hitleriana* (Hitler's last table-talk, when he realised that the war was lost) and arrange for its publication in *Figaro*; and we had dinner at the Jockey Club with Xandra's ex-mother-in-law who now, having a new daughter-in-law to hate, eats out of our hands!

Have you read *Dr Zhivago*? If so, in English, French, Italian or Russian? While the great drama of Pasternak's excommunication was in progress,

---

[5] Sir Edward Boyle (1923–1981), later Lord Boyle of Handsworth, was an enlightened Conservative MP who had pleased T-R by resigning as Economic Secretary to the Treasury in protest at Eden's Suez policy in 1956. Macmillan appointed him Minister of Education in 1962.

[6] Misquoted from Milton, *Paradise Lost*, iii, 474–5.

[7] The new Paris headquarters of the United Nations Educational, Scientific and Cultural Organisation were officially opened on 3 November. Luther Evans, Secretary-General of UNESCO, had been mistrusted by his staff since dismissing several fellow Americans for refusing to submit to questioning by US Loyalty Boards. He was forced to resign on 22 November, and was replaced by Vittorio Veronese (1910–1986), former President of the militant group Catholic Action.

Oxford was a very tense place.[8] Apart from Isaiah's part in it, many other people here were involved. Dimitri Obolensky had proposed Pasternak for the Nobel Prize; Katkov had obtained the Russian text, presumably from Pasternak, and – presumably with his connivance – had persuaded the BBC to broadcast it in Russian to Russia; and Pasternak's two sisters, who live in Oxford, alarmed by this provocation, for which they thought that Pasternak would have to pay, got Isaiah to go up to London and try (too late) to stop it. I don't know whether it was this 'provocation' which let loose the storm. Everyone who knows Pasternak agrees that he positively *wanted* trouble. Apparently he had a feeling of guilt and a desire for martyrdom. He was personally liked and protected by Stalin, and so survived when many of his friends perished, and is now ashamed of this. So at least Isaiah and Dimitri say: and he seems to have encouraged Katkov by giving him the Russian text; at least no one can think of another source from which Katkov can have got it. Apparently Pasternak has been quite open in speaking to visitors from the West. But why he suddenly surrendered in the end I don't know and haven't been told. Do you know Feltrinelli, or have you news from that source?[9]

Isaiah's inaugural lecture was delivered, to a vast audience, a month ago. It has not yet been published. Successive and ruthless prunings brought it down to an hour and a quarter. I hardly dare say so here (and do not say so here), but, secretly, I thought it disappointing. It was crammed with matter – so crammed that it was less easy to follow by ear than it will be by reading – but less general and also less original and less gay than I had hoped. In fact, it was almost a conventional piece of liberal school-philosophy, within rather narrow limits. I'm afraid Isaiah's genius is not really adapted to a formal lecture: like a natural, swollen, unharnessed torrent, its greatness depends upon its spontaneous overflow. He should talk, not write. But incidentally it was far more audible and intelligible than anyone expected. I think he took enormous trouble over his elocution: but that also reduced its spontaneity.

Did you enjoy the papal election?[10] Oxford, of course, lives from election to election, so we know all the gambits, imagine all the details, and relish

---

[8] Boris Pasternak (1890–1960) smuggled his novel *Doctor Zhivago* to the West when its publication was prohibited by the Soviet authorities in 1957. After being awarded the Nobel Prize for Literature in 1958, he was reviled by the Soviet Writers' Union, withdrew his acceptance and was obliged to grovel to Khrushchev.

[9] The Milan publisher and Marxist-Leninist enthusiast Giangiacomo Feltrinelli (1926–1972) had been the first to publish *Doctor Zhivago* in 1957.

[10] Cardinal Angelo Roncalli (1881–1963), Patriarch of Venice, had taken the name of Pope John XXIII after being elected Pope in October 1958.

all our imaginations. Did you read an article on it in the *New Statesman* by
Paul Johnson?[11] I firmly believe every word of it, though I must admit that
I don't like Paul Johnson.[12] He is the young prince of the *New Statesman*,
the present *protégé* of Kingsley Martin.[13] Kingsley Martin is subject to
successive *engouements*: recently it was for that brassy nihilist Malcolm
Muggeridge;[14] now it is for Paul Johnson, who is a Roman Catholic radical
casuist. He was educated by Jesuits at Stonyhurst, rebelled against his
education at Oxford, but now somehow has discovered that in reversing
one's direction one need not discard the envelope of the faith. At least I
think that he still regards himself as a Roman Catholic. His wife, whom he
recently married, converted herself to popery for the purpose, and went to
a desolate Hebridean island to produce her first child in the old Catholic
sanctity (and luxury) of some benighted Scottish recusant castle. At least
so I am told, although I may have telescoped some of the details. But I'm
afraid all English periodicals of any literary character are being rotted with
popery. The *New Statesman* is now thoroughly penetrated. It really is a
remarkable paper. When Kingsley Martin goes, I suppose it will dissolve
quite suddenly in mere ash and *débris*, leaving only radical rubbish and a
faint, sickly smell of popish incense. The *Times Literary Supplement* is by
now, of course, completely rotten. Alan Pryce Jones has killed it. It is only
held together by its anonymity. If that protection were to go, so that the
public suddenly saw the truth (*viz*: that it is written almost entirely by
Roman Catholic undergraduates), it would disintegrate at once. It is like a
bankrupt who keeps going on credit thanks to the secrecy of his bank
account. I must admit I find all this very depressing. Apart from anything
else, I now have no paper in which to write! For the *Sunday Times* is
impossibly stuffy. But perhaps this is really a good thing! I read instead,
and write lectures, and when I am free from writing or delivering lectures,
or sitting on committees (oh how I hate committees), or being dragged
this way and that on social occasions, I go quietly on with that great,

---

[11] Johnson, in 'Rome Goes Left', *New Statesman*, 1 November 1958, pp. 583–4, reported on the
sinuous intrigues surrounding the papal election.
[12] Paul Johnson (b. 1928) had joined the editorial staff of the *New Statesman* in 1955, and became
its strenuously left-wing editor in 1965, but later somersaulted into vehemently right-wing opinions. His article marking T-R's death, 'Hugh Trevor-Roper and the Monks of Magdalen', *The
Spectator*, 8 February 2003, p. 21, suggests that the dislike was reciprocated.
[13] Kingsley Martin (1897–1969), editor of the *New Statesman* 1931–60, had only recently relin-
quished his infatuation (*engouement*) with Stalinism.
[14] Malcolm Muggeridge (1903–1990) had been an unsuccessful editor of *Punch* 1952–7. 'I like poor
old Malcolm Muggeridge,' T-R had written in 1945. 'Alas, it must be admitted, Malcolm has
two fatal qualities: an appalling indifference to truth, and the dreary sneering cynicism of the
disillusioned radical.'

unending, formless, and at times dispiriting book which I am trying to write – of which I have already written and torn up and re-written 600 pages – on the English Great Rebellion.

But oh the distractions! The lectures, the opera, the pressure of this and that! *Es ist dafür besorgt, dass die Baüme nicht in Himmel hinaufreichen.*[15] However, I am trying to resist them all. I have refused an invitation to Formosa, from the Formosan government (if so we may call it), and intend to refuse every distraction to which mere economic necessity does not force me – unless, of course, it is to visit you at I Tatti again. I hope we may do that, and soon. Meanwhile, all our best wishes to you both, and love from us both, and don't exhaust yourself by taking too seriously (as Xandra insists on doing) the absurd pagan festival, so dear to the shopkeepers of all countries, Christmas! All the same, best Christmas greetings! [...]

---

[15] 'There is no need to worry that the trees will reach the heavens.'

1959

'BB is very grateful that you should not have stopped writing to him in spite of his not being up to writing himself any longer,' Nicky replied on 13 February 1959. 'We live very quietly and try to have one guest at a time or two at the utmost. John Pope-Hennessy was here over Christmas, then Baroness Ritter, our old friend, and then Morra came for a couple of days. [...] Just now we are alone and expecting the Kenneth Clarks next weekend. If only BB has one of his good days for them. Otherwise it will be very difficult.'

In December 1958, Xandra Trevor-Roper was again hospitalised with viral pneumonia, this time in Scotland. A letter to Nicky, in which Trevor-Roper proposed a last visit to Berenson as part of Xandra's convalescence, has not survived; but on 1 March Nicky wrote again: 'Dearest Hugh, got your letter yesterday and am very much at a loss of what to suggest in answer to your proposition. It is not a question of our having or not having room for you for we have really nobody coming to stay this spring. BB is no longer up to the effort of seeing guests except on some exceptional days when he is suddenly more communicative [...] I feel very sad at having to write such an inhospitable sounding letter but as I told you already, the change is very great [...] Perhaps it would be almost better for you to keep him in your memory as he was the last time you came when if I remember right, he was frail and spent a few days in bed [...] but still his own self intellectually.'

5 March 1959   Hotel Métropole, Beaulieu-sur-Mer

Dearest Nicky

Of course we entirely understand. We would certainly come even for two days if BB felt that he would like to see us, and we wouldn't like to be as near to you as we are without proposing it; but we see how difficult it must be for you and I'm afraid we must recognise the fact and live on our memories. But all the same, it is very sad not to see you, and we very much wish that we could. You must be having a very difficult time: we can only hope that we shall see you again before long.

We have now been here a week, and already Xandra is looking very much better and already I am beginning to feel bored, which (I suppose) is a sign of health. I feel like a battery-hen, stuck on this narrow perch, between the mountains and the sea, & forced to eat enormous meals without any opportunity of reducing their effect by exercise in a hen-run! Really, I must admit that I don't like the Riviera. The whole world here is so artificial. I like being in places where I can either go for long walks in pleasant, rural solitudes, or have a large room to myself full of books! Since we came here by air, Xandra not being well enough to face a long sea and train journey, I couldn't bring many books, and by now I have already read nearly all of them: all except the letters of Mme de Sévigné, whom I am now beginning to find rather a bore. In fact, I find myself in sympathy with Monsieur de Grignan.[1] Certainly I should feel pretty disgruntled if Xandra had a mother who wrote every other day the sort of letters which Mme de Sévigné wrote to her daughter. Admittedly some of them are wonderful; but there are so many in between!

We have lived a very vegetable life here so far. We went to Monte Carlo a few days ago to have luncheon with Lord Rothermere (the nephew of Lord Northcliffe, who founded the mass-circulation newspaper in England and died mad, believing himself to be Napoleon, in the 1920s). I found it very depressing. Lord Rothermere is, I suppose, one of the richest men in the world: at least his father left him £24,000,000, which seems to me quite a lot, but he is also one of the dullest, and is obviously entirely imprisoned by the frightening spectre of his own wealth. All his wives having fled from him, he lives in dreary solitude in a succession of large houses, and had driven out alone to his villa in Monte Carlo, which is horrible, & has no garden, and was living there, utterly bored. He told us he didn't even go to the casino – couldn't see the point of it (neither can I, but – I suspect – for different reasons: it can't be much of a thrill even to win 10,000 francs if one is already weighted down with £24,000,000). His other guests were Lord & Lady Arran, who are friends of ours (Lord Arran's brother, Lord Sudley, may have been known to you: he was a friend of Logan's): but they had to leave early, to catch an aeroplane, and by 2.30 Xandra & I were exchanging desperate looks & finally leaving.[2]

However, yesterday we had a more enjoyable social visit. We went to Grasse and had luncheon with someone whom I believe you know but whom we then met for the first time: Elliott Felkin.[3] We liked him very

[1] The possessive adoration felt by the Marquise de Sévigné (1626–1696) for her daughter, who had married Comte de Grignan, is expressed in the letters that she sent whenever they were separated.
[2] Paul Gore, Viscount Sudley (1903–1958), had died in December, following a cerebral haemorrhage, only ten days after succeeding his father as 7th Earl of Arran. T-R had been introduced to him by Pearsall Smith, and admired his translations from German. His brother David Gore, 8th Earl of Arran (1910–1983), worked for Rothermere as assistant manager of Associated Newspapers and deputy manager of the Daily Sketch; afterwards a Daily Mail columnist.
[3] Elliott Felkin (1892–1968), a scholar of King's College, Cambridge, joined the secretariat of the Reparations Commission in 1919, transferred to the League of Nations secretariat in 1923 and served as Secretary to the Permanent Central Opium Board, in Geneva and Washington,

much. He reminded us in many ways of Percy Lubbock – and yet not in all: for he himself cooked us the most wonderful luncheon. Somehow I doubt whether Percy has ever brandished a saucepan! His other guest was an Englishwoman who is now called Mrs Stadtländer (or is it Landstädter?) and who apparently held court in an intellectual *salon* in Paris. She kept tinkling intellectual names in the conversation, but as soon as it became clear that anyone else present knew the owners of those names, or their works, that bell would suddenly fall silent, and another name would start tinkling in the distance. We derived great pleasure from hearing these sudden campanological changes: so, I think, did our host!

We are now going to be here for another week and then will start on our way home. Xandra still has some more medical investigations to undergo, and I may have to go abroad somewhere for the *Sunday Times*. I don't want to go: I would really prefer to go to Scotland and see something of the children (whom I never saw at Christmas owing to Xandra's illness); but alas, one can't always control events. However, that will be decided later. Meanwhile, do write to us when you have time, and please give to BB (and take to yourself) all our love, and tell him how sorry we are not to see him on this visit, but we shall always think of I Tatti as the place we have enjoyed visiting, for the sake of you and BB, most of anywhere in the world. [...]

6 July 1959   8 St Aldate's, Oxford

My dearest Nicky

I have been a very bad correspondent. Please forgive me. And I have only the ordinary excuses, which wear thin with repetition. But I assure you we are often thinking of you, and hearing all we can. I'm afraid you must be having a very exhausting time; but I hope it is not too exhausting and that BB is comfortable. It was very kind of you to see my brother Pat when he was in Florence, and I was so glad to hear from him that he found you well.

I think I last wrote to you from Beaulieu, in March. Frankly, I didn't like Beaulieu; but then I hardly expected to. I don't like the Riviera, or any riviera. When I travel I like to be away from tourists, especially English tourists; and I like places where I can either go for long walks in remote and beautiful country or have friends and books around me. However, after Xandra's long illness it seemed that it must be either the Riviera or Switzerland; and when I thought of Switzerland, and of all those tourists with loud voices and skis and bobbles on their caps, moving about in troops

---

1938–52. He established the United Nations' post-war system for the surveillance of drug trafficking, retired to St Jacques de Grasse and had a loving expertise in the works of Thomas Hardy.

and clustering round bars, my heart sank further still and I decided on the Riviera. I was so exhausted, what with winter and work and Xandra's illness, that on arrival I sank into a chair and for four days quite enjoyed it; but then my morale and vigour returned, and I felt like a battery-hen on that narrow perch between the mountains and the sea, crammed daily with large, identical meals and denied any exercise; so I'm afraid I got very restive and in the end we shortened our stay and, after a short visit to friends in Provence, went home again.[1] Xandra had to go back into hospital over Easter, for examination, and then she went to Scotland and is now very much better. I had to go to Germany for the *Sunday Times*,[2] and although I found that very depressing, at least it wasn't as boring as Beaulieu. Since then we have had a term at Oxford, which now, thank God, is over; and I am back at work on my book.

But I will tell you about Germany. I went first to West Germany, which I always find very unsympathetic. The softness, the uninhibited, formless materialism of that bourgeois paradise is intellectually, morally, emotionally repellent to me. I stayed there as short a time as possible, and then went to Berlin, which is very different. The siege mentality of West Berlin creates a realism, an alertness, a mental vigour which is altogether absent from the cosy, heedless, smug *Schlaraffenland*[3] of the Rhine. The Berlin socialists are not like West German socialists, nor the Berlin christian democrats like West German christian democrats: and the difference is that they live in a real world. Then I went into East Germany. I had never been there before. I was told that I would never get there as a journalist, so I went as a historian, and called, in the Humboldt university, on a boring communist professor who had called on me in Oxford and who writes portentous marxist rubbish on English 17th century history.[4] He was very helpful and undertook to get me a visa to go to Dresden, Weimar and Rostock. He also said he would depute two of his *Assistenten* to act in turn as my guides.

'But my dear sir,' I expostulated, 'I would not think of immobilising your valuable *Assistenten*, and diverting them from their far more important duties of writing marxist rubbish' (or words to that effect): 'could I not go

---

[1] During the weekend of 13–15 March the T-Rs stayed at Château de Castille in Gard with the art collector Douglas Cooper (1911–1984) and John Richardson (b. 1924), later Slade Professor of Art History at Oxford and biographer of Picasso.
[2] T-R's two articles, 'Can Germany Stay Divided?' and 'Socialist Dupes of the Kremlin', appeared in *Sunday Times* of 19 and 26 April.
[3] Cockaigne, or land of milk and honey.
[4] Gerhard Schilfert (1917–2001), Professor at Humboldt University, Berlin 1956–82, wrote a Marxist study of the German revolutionaries of 1848 and *Die Englische Revolution 1640–1649* (1989).

alone?' 'Oh no,' he replied, 'that would be quite impossible. Apart from anything else, you would get into grave difficulty since you don't know German.' I must admit that this remark rather mortified me, since all our conversation was taking place in German; however, in the circumstances, I could hardly protest and so I gave in. But I could not help noticing, as I went with my guides to Saxony and the Baltic Sea, that neither of them spoke any English: so that the pretence that they were necessary to me as interpreters seemed to me a trifle thin.

Anyway, all was arranged, and I went. And what an experience it was! It seemed incredible to me, as I went through that oriental, Balkan country, that it had once been part of Europe. Nothing in it now recalls that distant time. It is an extension of Bulgaria or Rumania. The hotels are squalid and decayed, or new and shoddy (as in Russia); the servants slovenly; the plumbing does not work; out of the bathroom taps come only gurgling noises and spiders. The food is uniform and disgusting; the wine is not hock or moselle but the refuse of Hungary or Rumania. And yet behind this material squalor one could sense everywhere a new power far more formidable, because far more ruthless and disciplined, than anything in West Germany. It is guns not butter: far more so than in Nazi Germany. And the propaganda reminded me of Nazi Germany too, only it is rather more sophisticated: whereas Nazi propaganda appealed to shopkeepers, communist propaganda is directed to intellectuals, and to workers through intellectuals. And among the intellectuals it is clearly successful: my two guides, and everyone else I met at the Humboldt university, were complete *croyants*, even *dévots*: I got to know them well, and liked them very much, but argument, even discussion, was clearly quite out of the question. My impression was that the propaganda is now beginning to work with the workers too. In the last two years material conditions have clearly improved, and now the new way of life, at first resented, is being accepted: a generation is growing up that knows no other – after all, it has already lasted longer than Hitler – and, in its way, it works. It even has a certain puritan appeal: certainly it is less gross and soft than the petit-bourgeois materialism of West Germany.

So you see, altogether I returned depressed from the East. I was depressed by the squalor, depressed by the unceasing propaganda – even the Goethe-Haus in Weimar, which might be a monument to the Enlightenment, even the concentration-camp at Buchenwald, which might be a monument to humanity, are museums of propaganda – depressed by the evidence of systematic purpose, the building up of monstrous, inhuman power. For East Germany is being converted into a formidable industrial state, the Black Country of the Balkans: no wonder Khrushchev doesn't want to see

it reunited – incompatibly reunited – with the Ruhr (except, of course, as a new all-communist Germany). At times I felt as I had felt in 1938.

But enough of Germany: let me return to England, or rather to Scotland. Xandra and I are very excited because at last, after long search, we have discovered and have bought a new house in the Borders.[5] We have looked at dozens, and either turned them down or lost them; and now we are glad if we lost them, for the new house, which came on the market, and to our notice, by the merest fluke, is far more charming than anything we have ever seen; and it is in the right place, just outside Melrose. It is a little Regency house – the only Regency house in the Borders, built in 1820 by Sir Walter Scott for his daughter Sophia when she married Lockhart. Scott wrote *The Pirate* in it, and Disraeli stayed twice in it, in 1825. It was part of

---

[5] Chiefswood, near Melrose, Roxburghshire. The T-Rs sold the house in 1987 after the erection of the Borders General Hospital on adjoining land made the place intolerable.

the Abbotsford estate but was sold off from it ten years ago. It has a wonderful situation, at the end of my (and Sir Walter Scott's) favourite walk; and a charming garden with a stream running through it, through woods and flowers. Also it is no further from Bemersyde than we are at present. So altogether we are delighted, and now I expect to spend far more time in Scotland than I have done hitherto. My only fear is that the example of Sir Walter Scott may prove too ominous, and that I shall spend the rest of my life writing against time to pay the debts thus incurred!

And now what else can I tell you? I have been in the courts, which has been a great nuisance – as the result of a trivial motor-accident which I had at the height of Xandra's illness when I was taking James back to Eton in January – but have emerged triumphantly acquitted. I have been involved in a great battle with Lord Beaverbrook, who tried to cheat me, but (I am glad to say) I ended by cheating him.[6] (When I say Lord Beaverbrook, I am merely giving a convenient name: what I mean is his Press empire.) And I am now writing, writing, writing – or rather re-writing, re-writing, re-writing. I shall go on doing so till the end of July, and then we shall go to our Vallombrosa in Scotland. [...]

PS. You asked about my letters to BB. I don't know what to answer. I think if they came back to me I would destroy them: but I should not like to think of them getting into the wrong hands! Perhaps the safest thing would be for them to come ultimately to me and I can let Xandra decide whether they are safest in the Bank or in the fire. After all, they are written for you and BB, and for no one else. I shudder to think of some of the things I sometimes say! [...]

Nicky Mariano replied on 14 July 1959:

'I am sitting by BB's bed, "baby-watching" as usual over his sleep and enjoying your letter for the third time. I read it once to him and a second time to him and his old friend Countess Serristori. Your account of Eastern Germany "n'est pas réjouissant" and yet enjoyable because it is so beautifully done, so clear, so convincing, as one of our Neapolitan friends used to say "dolorosamente esatto". [...] your letter has made me think of the fascinating collection of your epistles to BB and if you say that you want to destroy them then I shall only let you have copies of them! Of course, should they appear in print in your life-time they would have to

---

[6] The *Sunday Express* had tried to avoid paying fees to T-R after publishing opportunistic articles based on Hitler documents recently acquired by François Genoud and originally printed under T-R's supervision in *Figaro*: see p. 260.

be judiciously expurgated. [...] BB has just waked up and asks me who I am writing to. He sends you and Xandra his most affectionate messages.'

Berenson died on 6 October 1959, as the result of a virulent infection spreading from a small cut in his mouth; and after obsequies at his local Catholic church was interred in the small private chapel at I Tatti. The author Iris Origo, who had known Berenson for half a century, described him 'as he lay on that last day – wrapped, like a figure in one of his own Renaissance pictures, in a winding-sheet made of his soft white cashmere shawl – on the great central table in the library which was, for all who had sat with him there, the very core of his house [...] The body that lay there was so small, so frail, the exquisite long hands were worn to so thin a transparency, the face bore a look of such withdrawn serenity, that it seemed easy to believe that there had been "no self left to die".

1960

After a week in Rome in March 1960, the Trevor-Ropers made a detour to I Tatti, where on 21 March they lunched with Nicky Mariano. This letter is the sequel.

31 March 1960   8 St Aldate's, Oxford

My dear Nicky,

We did enjoy seeing you on our brief visit to Florence. It made I Tatti seem almost the same in spite of being without its tutelary spirit. I hope you will have a restful summer, and we shall see you again soon. And thank you very much for the two books – *The Passionate Sightseer* has arrived here,[1] and we are taking them both up to Scotland with us on Saturday. Burns will sit there appropriately on our still rather empty shelves (what a problem it is, splitting one's books),[2] and we shall read *The Passionate Sightseer*.

I suppose you have seen the *Times Literary Supplement*, and Harold Nicolson in the *Observer*, on Sylvia's book. I'm afraid she will not be pleased with the Nicolson family, father or son, now, and I suppose she is now feeling sorry for Vita too![3] I don't know who wrote the article in the *TLS*, which I thought excellent: I suspect it was John Pope-Hennessy.[4] I thought the phrase about the sculptor Macdonald who came to Abbotsford in 1831 a happy touch! I'm afraid I feel pretty flinty-hearted about poor old Sylvia now. That letter to you about K. Clark's lecture was really too smug for words: 'all those fashionable people in the front: what did *they* know or feel about BB? Whereas I, who really understood, sat modestly and inconspicuously behind!'

---

[1] BB's travel jottings, *The Passionate Sightseer: From the Diaries 1947 to 1956*, were published by Thames & Hudson in March 1960.
[2] *The Poetical Works* of Robert Burns, published at Lepizig in 1845, and bearing two inscriptions ('Bernhard Berenson Nov. 1884'; 'To Hugh and Xandra a souvenir from B.B.'s library with Nicky's love. I Tatti. March 21st 1960'), was sold by Heywood Hill's bookshop for £150 in 2004.
[3] Ben Nicolson ('B.B. in the Flat', *New Statesman*, 19 March 1960, pp, 420–1), combined a hostile review of Sprigge's *Berenson: A Biography* with an appreciative reference to *The Passionate Sightseer*. Harold Nicolson's review, 'The Berenson Story', *Observer*, 27 March 1960, p. 22, was gentler to Sprigge. Vita Sackville-West was Harold's wife and Ben's mother.
[4] Pope-Hennessy's 'Portrait of an Art Historian', *TLS*, 25 March 1960, pp. 185–7, was unsparing to Sprigge.

I wanted to write an article on a certain kind of biographer. The idea came to me after reading first about Sylvia's book, then Cyril Connolly's review of that book on Logan's family.[5] The basic idea is this. In the Middle Ages there were saints, and their saintliness was recognised. Ordinary people knew that (say) St Francis or St John of the Cross were extraordinary people. But *how* they were extraordinary, wherein their extraordinary quality, their saintliness, lay, they simply could not understand because their own faculties were too ordinary. Consequently, in their attempt to share or describe this quality they clutched desperately at mere peripheral, accidental things. Unable to define the true quality, which is intangible, they clutched at tangible material, and utterly unimportant details. They snipped off hair or toenails from the corpses of their saints, exposed their eyes, teeth, bones in golden reliquaries, grovelled at the sight of alleged fragments of their underclothes. And now (I go on), in this our enlightened 20th century, we have intellectuals. Real intellectuals are a kind of lay saint. The vast, semi-literate mass of pulp-reading, strap-hanging ordinary men and women recognise, they feel instinctively, that a BB, a Logan, a Bertrand Russell was (or is) someone extraordinary: that his gifts were (or are) rare and genuine; but how are they ever to understand or share those gifts, to give body & expression to that feeling? Alas, they cannot. And so, just as in the Middle Ages there arose an indispensable tribe of friars and pardoners going round with rag-bags full of haberdashery and pig's bones, saying 'this is the curative toe of St Bumbulus', or 'this is a fragment of the True Knickers of Blessed Virgin St Jezebel', so now we have a tribe of eager journalists and busy hack-biographers going round (for the public demand must be satisfied) hawking the collected and spurious relics and irrelevancies of a BB, a Logan, a Bertie Russell, and thinking, poor things, that they have explained their greatness, communicated their quality.

I developed this parallel at some length to Xandra, trying to get her to agree that I should publish it, fully elaborated, in some appropriate journal. But alas, she has vetoed it, saying that it will only raise up a host of enemies. What did it avail Erasmus to poke fun at monks and friars? For a quiet life one must gape with the crowd ... or at least pretend to do so. Such are the prudent counsels of my dear wife, to which, of course, I always yield. [...]

---

[5] Cyril Connolly, 'Biography Reduced to Caricature', *Sunday Times*, 27 March 1960, was a withering review of Robert Allerton Parker's *A Family of Friends: The Story of the Transatlantic Smiths* (1960).

APPENDIX

TWO LETTERS TO
WALLACE NOTESTEIN

22 January 1951   236 Edwards St, New Haven, Conn.

Dear Trevor-Roper:

My wife and I have enjoyed your letter a great deal. What a born letter-writer you are, if you will allow me to say it. This is not to answer your letter, but is merely a note to say how much I am interested in the Lawrence Stone business. As you may know, John Cooper has been exceedingly critical of Stone's conclusions, and Cooper is a careful scholar. [...]

I shall hardly live to see the letters of the late Warden of — Hugh Trevor-Roper, in eight volumes, edited by — but they will be worth publishing, and will be a great deal better than most of the sets of letters I have read [...] Someone someday will do to Tawney – whom I honor – what you are doing to Lawrence Stone. No, not that. Tawney's work is imaginative and penetrating, but not based on sufficient data. [...]

If the gods are kind and there is no war, we sail April 13 for Italy and expect to arrive at 16 Old Bldgs., Lincoln's Inn early in June and spend four months there. Any chance that we might see you in Italy? [...]

Tell me any news of historians at Oxford, and comments upon said news. Any changes taking place?

      Hurriedly yours,
      Wallace Notestein

28 January 1951   Christ Church, Oxford

Dear Notestein,

I was delighted to hear from you and to know that you are to be in this hemisphere soon. I hope to be in Italy sometime in the spring, but can't be sure yet. I am now Senior Censor of this college, – which means in practice and at present (the Dean being Vice-Chancellor) that I have most of the duties which in another college are imposed on the Head of the College and the Senior Tutor. Some of my predecessors in this office have instituted a practice, and sought to establish a tradition, whereby a Censor is a kind of universal nurse-maid following undergraduates around with a nappy or diaper, wiping up after them. I intend to end this tradition sharply and replace it with one of ruthless, mechanical, automatic efficiency which will leave opportunities to the Censor for the more important pursuit of Truth and Pleasure. As a first step in this direction I have ordered a rubber stamp of my signature and (all being well) will give this instrument to my secretary and leave these shores for Italy and Greece in the middle of March. It may be that I will be in Italy, staying with Berenson at Settignano, when you arrive; but if not I hope I shall certainly see you later when you are in England.

Meanwhile you asked for learned news from Oxford. You should know that at present all research, learning, teaching, writing, lecturing, administration, is utterly and indefinitely suspended owing to one of those important and all-absorbing *saturnalia* in English life, – an election. It is the election to the Chair of Poetry. For there are in this university two chairs (and only two) to which the incumbent is elected not by a narrow and statutorily predetermined *junto* of elderly office-holders but by popular academic suffrage: the Lady Margaret Chair of Divinity (the last election to which, in 1945, was accompanied by heroic controversies and gigantic scandals) and the chair of Poetry, – a distinguished and comfortable chair founded in the first instance to accommodate the fastidious bottom of Matthew Arnold,[1] but since, by the notorious tendency to decay of human institutions, become – with brief intervals – a pocket-borough of Magdalen College. But in order fully to explain the complex politics involved in this election, I must first give a short historical *résumé*.

Magdalen's long monopoly of this chair began with that most famous academic snob, the late Sir Herbert Warren, President, for some forty years, of Magdalen College, – the man who put Magdalen on the social map by nabbing, as an undergaduate – during the temporary social eclipse of Christ Church after the great Blenheim row of 1894 – the afterwards ungrateful (see his *Memoirs*) Prince of Wales.[2] For Warren had some claims as a poet: i.e. he had published a slim volume of poems which Lord Alfred Douglas (then an undergraduate of Magdalen) had hailed, in a published review, as showing that the President was 'the worst English poetaster since Pye'.[3] Warren's successor as President of Magdalen, George Gordon, was also a literary man, and also obtained the Chair of Poetry;[4] but in 1938, when

---

[1] Matthew Arnold (1822–1888), Professor of Poetry at Oxford 1857–67.
[2] The great Blenheim row – actually in 1876 – was a complicated affair of adultery and pomposity involving Lady Aylesford, Lord Blandford and the then Prince of Wales. The Duke of Windsor (previously King Edward VIII) had been an undergraduate at Magdalen in 1912–14. His memoirs, *A King's Story* (1951), depicted Sir Herbert Warren (1853–1930), President of Magdalen College 1885–1928, as a crashing snob and implacable bore on the subject of poetry.
[3] Lord Alfred Douglas (1870–1945), sonneteer, vituperative journalist and Oscar Wilde's catastrophic Ganymede, was referring to Henry Pye (1745–1813), a much-despised Poet Laureate.
[4] George Gordon (1881–1942), Merton Professor of English Literature at Oxford 1922–8, Professor of Poetry 1933–8, President of Magdalen from 1928 until his death, and Vice-Chancellor 1938–41.

Gordon's tenure of the chair came to an end, a serious attempt was made
to break the Magdalen monopoly. This seemed at the time to be at last
possible, because (1) owing to Warren's policy of peopling the college
exclusively with illiterate lords, who were always sent down long before
competing for degrees, the necessity of literacy among Magdalen dons had
disappeared and not one of them had written a line in either prose or verse,
and (2) the chair, as I have said, is elective, the electors being all such MAs
of the University who, on the day of election, choose (or can be persuaded)
to vote in person. In these propitious circumstances two distinguished
candidates were proposed, neither of them from Magdalen: Sir E.K.
Chambers, the great Panjandrum of Shakespearean scholarship,[5] and the
arbiter elegantiarum of the modern literary world, Lord David Cecil.[6] The
English Faculty could be relied upon to march solid to the poll in support
of Chambers; David Cecil of course commanded the united votes of Christ
Church and New College (his own colleges); and the university duly prepared to choose between them.

But was Magdalen College prepared thus tamely to resign its monopoly?
Not at all. They determined to find among their number a third candidate
and vote solid behind him. The difficulty of course was to find a candidate
who could command any other support, but after some research they
discovered, as the likeliest figure, their own chaplain, the Revd Adam Fox.[7]
Fox was a worldly clergyman of epicurean tastes, lavish hospitality, and (in
consequence of his hospitality) many friends. As a pastor of souls he may
indeed have been somewhat defective, – indeed, my colleague Robert Blake,
who was then an undergraduate of Magdalen College, tells me that the
religious undergraduates of the college held a special prayer-meeting in the
cloisters to pray for the conversion of their chaplain to Christianity, –
but as a vote-catcher he had certain undoubted possibilities, and these
possibilities his colleagues determined to exploit. First, to qualify for the
post it was thought that the chaplain ought perhaps to write either some
poetry or some literary criticism. As the latter alternative seemed to entail
the preliminary fatigue of reading, he chose the former, and sitting up late
one night with a sequence of bottles he dashed off several pages of barbarous
doggerel which were immediately printed in a slim volume with the title

Despite being one of Oxford's most brilliant talkers, his only substantial book was a collection of
broadcast talks, although he left a desk filled with unfinished manuscripts.
[5] Sir Edmund Chambers (1866–1954), civil servant, historian of medieval drama and Elizabethan
literature.
[6] Lord David Cecil (1902–1986), essayist and biographer, was a Fellow of New College, Oxford,
1939–69 and Goldsmiths' Professor of English Literature 1948–69.
[7] Adam Fox (1883–1977), Fellow of Magdalen 1929–42, Professor of Poetry at Oxford 1938–43.

Old King Cole. Having thus qualified for the race, he was duly entered. But how were the Fellows of Magdalen to secure backers for this somewhat ridiculous outsider whom they had so strangely entered against one tried and regular gold-cup-winner (aged indeed, but of enormous staying-power) and one fancied thoroughbred from an aristocratic stable? After all, having defeated King James II in 1688, they have never ceased to pique themselves on their political acumen; and they now prepared a masterly manoeuvre.

Magdalen College is the lay-patron of some thirty livings in twelve counties. All these livings are naturally held by old Magdalen men who, being MAs of Oxford University, would of course be entitled to vote, provided – and only provided, – that they happened to be in Oxford on the day of election. But how can country clergymen be persuaded to abandon their cosy rural vicarages in Leicestershire and Lincolnshire, Warwickshire and Wiltshire, and make the tedious journey to Oxford, – which, being known as a place of learning, naturally has singularly little attraction for them? On such a question the Fellows naturally addressed themselves to their own chaplain, now – since his nomination – doubly interested in the success of the college policy; and he as naturally, from his own experience, assured them that only two temptations were strong enough to overcome the habitual sloth of his order, cash and food. There-upon the fellows sent for the bursar, and finding that cash was plentiful in the coffers of the college (it is the richest college in Oxford and even then had a gross annual revenue of well over £100,000) they decided to declare a dividend to be paid to all the incumbents of college livings – provided that the said incumbents attended in person to draw it on the day of issue: which day was conveniently fixed to be the day of election to the chair of Poetry. As a gesture of civility the clergymen were of course informed that they could rely on lavish entertainment in the college during this remunerative visit.

What need of further words? On the appointed day all roads leading to Magdalen College were black with travel-stained clergymen converging on their dividends. Arrived at the college, they ate, they drank, they voted. It is even maintained by some that they voted unawares, signing the voting-papers for the Revd Adam Fox in the mistaken belief that they were signing receipts for their dividends. And meanwhile from Radley School, four miles out of Oxford, – a school of which Adam Fox had formerly been Warden – specially chartered buses brought the loyal undermasters to the polling booth. This sudden mass-invasion of the Magdalen interest turned the scales: the devotees of literature found their votes divided between the other candidates; and the Revd Adam Fox, as Professor of Poetry in Oxford, saved the Magdalen monopoly for another five years. He did not, of course, write any more poetry: *Old King Cole* remains his only achievement in that line.

The next challenge came in 1946 (having been deferred by the war from 1943). Now it happened that in 1946 Magdalen College was caught up in a revolutionary crisis. A policy of ruinous financial extravagance had not only split the Governing Body from top to bottom between radicals who wished to economise by abolishing the choir and choir school and turning the chapel into a public swimming-bath, and conservatives who wished to economise by abolishing the radicals, – thus making corporate action impossible; but also had entirely emptied that party chest upon whose copious contents the successful policy of the past had (as I have shown) been based. Meanwhile the Revd Adam Fox, foreseeing that the college cellar might have to be sold to reduce the deficit, had prudently moved on to become a canon of Westminster Abbey and dining chaplain to a rich and self-indulgent City Company. It thus happened that in 1946 Magdalen College was caught unprepared, and in this brief interval of its power the Warden of Wadham College, by an astute mobilisation of interest in certain decisive quarters, carried an unopposed victory. But we are now in 1951, and the interval of weakness in Magdalen College is over. By a ruthless policy of wage-cutting, depopulation and enclosure – dismissing the servants, starving the undergraduates, and keeping vast herds of more profitable pigs on the college lawns, – Magdalen has now recovered from its financial crisis; with opulence has returned some measure of political solidarity; and a united Governing Body is now preparing to recover the monopoly which (they now maintain) they had merely leased out, not lost, for the past five years. To recover it they need, of course, a candidate. Their candidate is C.S. Lewis.[8]

Do you know C.S. Lewis? In case you don't, let me offer a brief character-sketch. Envisage (if you can) a man who combines the face and figure of a hog-reeve or earth-stopper with the mind and thought of a Desert Father of the fifth century, preoccupied with meditations of inelegant theological obscenity: a powerful mind warped by erudite philistinism, blackened by systematic bigotry, and directed by a positive detestation of such profane frivolities as art, literature and (of course) poetry: a purple-faced bachelor and misogynist, living alone in rooms of inconceivable hideousness, secretly consuming vast quantities of his favourite dish – beefsteak-and-kidney-pudding; periodically trembling at the mere apprehension of a

[8] Clive Staples Lewis (1898–1963), Fellow of Magdalen and English tutor there 1925–54; Professor of Medieval and Renaissance English at Cambridge 1954–63.

feminine footfall; and all the while distilling his morbid and illiberal thoughts into volumes of best-selling prurient religiosity and such reactionary nihilism as is indicated by the gleeful title, *The Abolition of Man*. Such is C.S. Lewis, whom Magdalen College have now put up to recapture their lost monopoly of the chair of Poetry.

They are wise in their generation. For behind Lewis they can mobilise not only the Magdalen interest but also that of the English faculty in the University (eager to recapture the chair for one of its own members as against outsiders or members of other faculties) and of course the clerical interest, which sees in him the champion of religion against infidelity. Now the clerical interest, as you know, is omnipresent in Oxford. It has been computed that there are in the University more priests per head of population than in any other community in the British Empire, with the possible exception of Malta. But this interest, in spite of its numerical strength, is driven hither and thither by a panic fear of infidelity. Like the Spanish monks in the age of Erasmus, they see that in spite of all their force and numbers, the intellectual *élite* consistently escape them; and so they are prepared, on such occasions and on such an issue, to suspend all sectarian interests and vote solid for religion without disputing the exact meaning of that abstract term. Therefore although Lewis, as an Ulster bigot, is violently anti-popish and regularly, in his monastic bath, intones the old Belfast litany, *To Hell with the Pope!*, nevertheless, on this occasion, the name of Fr Corbishley SJ, Master of Campion Hall, is to be found in the list of his sponsors, and he will doubtless, on the day of election, lead to the poll a unanimous crocodile of obedient Jesuits.[9]

What is the anti-Magdalen party to do? Alas, the odds are against it. Enid Starkie – the Joan of Arc of the Resistance – has worn herself to a string organising opposition.[10] She has persuaded Cecil Day Lewis to stand against his namesake and has collected sponsors of varying degrees of gravity to support him.[11] Then, last Friday, a well-intended intervention caused all her devoted labours to dissolve in barren sand. That afternoon I was telephoned by the Provost of Worcester,[12] who, after cautious manoeuvring, crept gingerly out in the open and revealed that he, his colleague Cyril

[9] Thomas Corbishley (1903–1976), Master of Campion Hall 1945–58, entered the Society of Jesus in 1919.
[10] Enid Starkie (1897–1970), Fellow of Somerville College, Oxford 1934–65 and Reader in French Literature at Oxford University.
[11] Cecil Day Lewis (1904–1972), poet, critic, translator, broadcaster and committee-man, held the chair of poetry at Oxford from 1951 until 1956, when he was succeeded, after another sharp contest, by W.H. Auden.
[12] J.C. Masterman: see T-R's letters of 24 October 1954 and 22 March 1957.

Wilkinson,[13] and the Warden of Merton,[14] fired by a laudable opposition to C.S. Lewis, but ignorant – such is the watertight compartmentalisation of our lives – of the very existence of another anti-Lewis lobby, had, with commendable but misapplied ingenuity, prevailed upon Edmund Blunden to stand for the chair, thus at the crucial moment fatally splitting the forces of Light.[15] I of course urged him to conjure down this inconvenient spectre, but he explained (a) that it had taken three days of unremitting pressure from all sides, and the use of absolutely irreversible arguments, to persuade Blunden to be a candidate and it would be quite impossible now to sound the retreat, and (b) that Cyril Wilkinson had already left to attend the funeral of the late Reader in English Literature, H.B. Brett-Smith,[16] for the sole purpose of lobbying all the mourners in the Blunden interest, and no instructions to the contrary could possibly now be conveyed to him. Thus, unless (as we all hope) a timely withdrawal, preferably by Blunden, can be arranged, our cause is doomed, and through this fatal division in our front the forces of Magdalen College, the English Faculty, and clerical reaction will indubitably carry their holy totem victorious into the chair.[17]

At this point I must leave the story which I merely intended, in the first instance, to introduce as a casual explanation why no other news could conceivably be expected from Oxford. I find I have dealt with the subject at some length. But I should like to end with one observation arising from your letter. You suggest that one day someone will do to Tawney what I am doing to Stone.[18] Allow me to demur. I am critical of Tawney, whom I also greatly admire, and I have contested him on one point in my article. You will see whether you agree with him or with me on that. But I don't believe anyone will be able to do to him what I am doing to Stone: i.e. proving (as I submit) that he is neither honest nor a scholar.

Let me know your movements when they are definite, and if you are in

---

[13] Colonel C.H. Wilkinson (1888–1960), Fellow of Worcester 1918–58 (sometime Vice-Provost and Dean), was a man of whimsical opinions and magnificent martial aspect who commanded the Oxford Officers' Training Corps and was Delegate of Military Instruction for the University Police. As a lecturer in English literature 'he scarcely held the attention of young hearers for his love of English literature was not confined to any particular purpose' (*The Times*, 21 January 1960).

[14] Geoffrey Mure (1893–1979), a philosopher, was elected as Fellow of Merton in 1922 and as Warden in 1947.

[15] Edmund Blunden (1896–1974), poet, teacher and scholar, was finally elected to the chair of poetry at Oxford in 1966.

[16] Herbert Brett-Smith (1884–1951), formerly Goldsmiths' Reader in English at Oxford University, bibliophile and editor of Peacock's collected works, had died on 14 January.

[17] Blunden withdrew from the contest after learning that Day Lewis was already a candidate. On 8 February 194 votes (including Blunden's) were cast for Day Lewis, and 173 for C.S. Lewis.

[18] See T-R's letter of 8 November 1953 (pp. 130–132).

Florence, ring the Villa Berenson (60764) and see if I am there. I look forward to seeing you both again.

> yours ever,
> Hugh Trevor-Roper

PS. You know that Woodward is leaving his Worcester chair – if indeed he can ever be said to have occupied it, or indeed any of the other chairs to which, in indecent succession, he has been elected? How long do you give him at Princeton?[19]

23 March 1960   History Faculty Library, Merton Street, Oxford

My dear Notestein

I was delighted to hear from you: I always am; and of course, in the mood of delight thus generated, I shall gladly send you an account of the great battle, now happily terminated, of the Oxford Chancellorship. Let me then plunge straight into the vortex. What a vortex academic politics are, you do not need to be told, although now, like the Epicurean sage, you sit outside it, only seeing the occasional blood-stained froth which a shift in the wind carries past your eyes, or hearing, muted by intervening distance, the elaborate, learned, archaic squeals of the temporary victims. I say 'temporary' because, of course, as you know, our academic politics never *determine* anything of significance. Those who are suppressed today bob up tomorrow. Those who today crow in triumph tomorrow bleat in anguish, and on the next day crow again – again prematurely. As after the Last Judgement, the particular postures may vary from time to time, but the general pattern remains eternal. Therefore, what I am describing is simply a brief *section* of the eternal struggle, in which no one ever wins a final victory, between academic Light (represented by me and my friends) and Darkness (represented by them). This brief section occupies the time between the death, just before Christmas 1959, of Lord Halifax, and the election, on 5th March 1960, of Harold Macmillan.[1]

But why, you might ask, is the election of any importance at all? What, in fact, does the Chancellor do? What indeed? The answer is, nothing. He sits, infinitely grand, infinitely remote, in purple or ermine-tinted clouds, from which on rare occasions he descends, in solemn and stately fashion, wearing a golden robe valued in current prices at £1,000, in order to utter

---

[19] E.L. Woodward's resignation as Professor of Modern History at Oxford is mentioned in T-R's letter of 6 July 1951.
[1] Lord Halifax had been installed as Chancellor of the University of Oxford in 1933 following the death of Lord Grey of Fallodon.

a few unintelligible blessings at purely ceremonial functions. Otherwise ...
well, it is said that there are occasions when the Chancellor's position *might*
be important, when his intervention, coming from such a height, *could* be
effective. And, in fact, one cannot altogether deny this. Did not Lord Halifax
once, by waving his magical cancellarial wand, move a gas-works from
Oxford to Reading? Who can say whether Lord Curzon,[2] if that stately
nobleman had ever lowered his mind to such base mechanical affairs, might
not equally have moved Mr Morris, now Lord Nuffield, and all his banausic
belching motor-works from Oxford to – well, say Cambridge?[3] And then,
supposing Sir Maurice Bowra were to achieve the desire of his temporarily
frustrated heart and to find himself placed, by Prime Minister Gaitskell, in
charge of a Royal Commission to reform the university by razing All Souls
College, with its cloud-capped towers and airy pinnacles, even to the
ground, would not it then be useful to the Warden of that threatened
institution to have a Chancellor who, by intervening as *Deus ex Machina*,
could reverse the threatened doom? So one cannot altogether dismiss the
suggestion that the Chancellor matters. In fact, one must (I think) conclude
that the Chancellorship, like so many English institutions, though theoretically useless and only historically defensible, has acquired, by successive adaptations, a curious and indeed almost scientific utility. He is
like Newton's God, whose subordinate universe has long since become
independent of him, leaving him in a purely decorative position of great
eminence and respect, but who cannot altogether be dispensed with, since
who knows that he might not be required, on some extraordinary occasion,
to interpose a divine finger, to rectify a cometary disturbance, to wind up
again the suddenly failing machine?

   This being so, it is patently clear to any rational being like you or me that
the Chancellor must be, as he always has been, a great political figure: a
man who is fortunately too busy to intervene in our day-to-day politics,
but who, on the rare occasions when we need his intervention, can intervene
effectively, from a very great height: and that means, in effect, from a
political height: for it is from the political level alone that effective intervention can come when the ordinary administrative machinery becomes,
as it sometimes does, stuck. For this reason the Wisdom of our Ancestors –
that blind, unthinking wisdom which so often, in retrospect, thanks to

---

[2] George Curzon, 1st Marquess Curzon of Kedleston (1859–1925), Viceroy of India 1898–1904,
Foreign Secretary 1919–24, Chancellor of Oxford University 1907–25.
[3] William Morris, 1st Viscount Nuffield (1877–1963), began manufacturing motor-cars at Cowley
on the outskirts of Oxford in 1919. His factory swiftly became the dominant industrial presence
in Oxford.

silent transformation and adaptation in practice, seems so logical and calculated – has seen to it that for centuries our Chancellor has always been in one or other house of parliament. In fact, he has nearly always been in the Other House, i.e. the Lords. I think that the last Commoner to be Chancellor was Oliver Cromwell, and he, of course, was an unfortunate exception in our history. Still, even he was in the house of commons, and no one could deny that he was – however unfortunately – in politics.

So much by way of introduction: now I shall proceed to narrative: narrative which will often be interrupted by necessary digressions. I'm afraid this is going to be a *huge* letter; but ... *tu l'as voulu, Georges Dandin* ...

Animated by the general views which I have described, when Lord Halifax died, I naturally exercised my mind about the succession; and at first, surrounded as I then was by the ancient, deeply conservative hills and valleys, landlords and peasants, of Scotland, I naturally thought of that greatest, most conservative, and almost most ancient of political peers, Lord Salisbury.[4] Is he not an Oxford man? Is he not a man of fine intellectual outlook? Is he not an Honorary Student of Christ Church (and such a position naturally arouses all my atavistic, tribal loyalty)? And is he not, above all things, that rarest, most refined, most aristocratic, in fact unique, type of aristocrat: a Cecil? So, as I listened to the melodious bleating of sheep and the convivial gossip of dukes and duchesses along the curling valley of the Tweed, I almost made up my mind that Salisbury was our man, and that no other man was possible. Then, in January, I returned to Oxford, and found, of course, that my colleagues, scattered abroad as they had been, in Naples or Málaga, in Birmingham or London, or even – far worse, sitting congregated in those dens of conspiracy (never more conspiratorial than in the depths of vacation, when their more mobile colleagues are away, and the dank miasma of the river Thames mixes most dangerously with the fumes of port and clouds of snuff), Oxford colleges, – had also been thinking of the same general problem and had come to other and far different conclusions. Most of these conclusions I easily dismissed; but one could not be dismissed, because it had been reached by that most determined, most active, most radical, most ruthless, most skilful of all academic politicians, Sir Maurice Bowra. Moreover, Maurice's decision was not in favour of Lord Salisbury, or of any other peer, or even of a member of the House of Commons: he had decided on that dullest of dogs, that 'bum-faced purveyor of last year's platitudes' (as my Liberal colleague Sir

[4] Robert Cecil, 5th Marquess of Salisbury (1893–1972), Conservative statesman and Chancellor of Liverpool University 1951–71.

Roy Harrod has described him),[5] that 'Martin Tupper of our times' (as my Socialist colleague A.J.P. Taylor has described him), Sir Oliver Franks. In fact, on Friday 22nd January, before any public step had been taken, before the university had even said its official farewell to the corpse of Lord Halifax, Maurice confidently announced to his entourage – so well had he already prepared the ground, so sure was he of success – 'Franks is in!'

When I learned that Maurice had resolved on Franks, I hastily made what your late Secretary of State Mr Dulles[6] used to call an 'agonising reappraisal'. I don't say there was much agony in it but then perhaps there wasn't for him either. But however that may be, I reappraised the situation, and, on reflexion, decided to drop Lord Salisbury. There were various reasons for this, but the essential reason, which I regarded as decisive, was simply this. It seemed to me that the Chancellor of Oxford University ought to be not only an Oxford man, devoted to Oxford, distinguished in politics, in the Lords or Commons: he ought also, since this is a university, to be a man of intellectual distinction, or at least a man who genuinely respected intellectual matters. Lord Halifax, after all, had a first-class honours degree and a fellowship of All Souls. Now undoubtedly Lord Salisbury has intellectual interests, but the fact is that he read for a pass degree only and did not in fact take the examination; and since there was, in British politics, at that time, a man equally qualified in all other respects and superior in this, having taken first class honours in classics and distinguished himself in the 1914 war by being discovered by an ambulance-party, after being wounded, reading Aeschylus in Greek in a shell-hole, it seemed to me logical and natural that we should prefer him even to Lord Salisbury. Besides, as Xandra acutely pointed out, there is Lady Salisbury ... [here a providential gap occurs in my manuscript].[7] It is true, as some of my friends pointed out, this better qualified candidate may be rejected by some on the grounds that, as Prime Minister, he is too busy; but that, it seemed to me, was for him to judge. And I further argued that if Macmillan were to be considered suitable if he had not won the 1959 election, it was unreasonable to penalise him simply because he had won that election.

Thus, by the time Maurice Bowra had decided on Franks, I had decided on Macmillan. Unfortunately, from my point of view, I, as a mere professor (or rather, for university purposes, as a mere Fellow of Oriel), had no status from which to advance my view, while Maurice could advance his from the

---

[5] Sir Roy Harrod (1900–1978), Student in modern history and economics at Christ Church 1924–67, and Macmillan's trusted friend and economic adviser.
[6] John Foster Dulles (1888–1959), US Secretary of State 1953–9.
[7] Elizabeth Cavendish (1897–1982) had married Lord Salisbury at the age of eighteen.

most powerful position in the whole university. For he was by now, during the illness of Tom Boase, Acting Vice-Chancellor; and as such he was due to preside, on Saturday 23 January, over a meeting of 'heads of houses' which was to start the electoral ball rolling. Therefore, if my views were to be heard at all, it was necessary for me to obtain the support of a powerful and influential head of a house. In such a position I naturally turned to my old tutor, Sir John Masterman, Provost of Worcester College, and – apart from Maurice Bowra – the only ex-Vice-Chancellor still active in the university.

You know J.C. Masterman as well as I do. You know that he is a skilful operator, a man of great, not to say excessive prudence, a man widely respected and much followed, who, however, prefers to lead his followers down paths of guaranteed safety, at a gentle pace, towards attainable ends. It would be wrong, and in me very unjust (for he fought to the death for me in the great battle for the Chair of History long ago), to say that J.C. *never* fights; but I think it would be fair to say that he never fights unless he judges victory to be already so clearly attainable that his belligerency can turn the balance and secure it. In general, he prefers not to fight: he likes great issues to be solved in the *coulisses*, not on the battlefield; and his own *rôle* is more often that of reconciling the minority to an inevitable decision than that of singing its protestations. Still, the fact remains that J.C.'s *views* are generally sound (i.e. they coincide with mine), and that *if* his support can be obtained, he is an influential supporter: when he raises his flag (and he raises it only when victory seems at least likely) an army of prudent and respectable men will note the signs and wheel in behind him, as they would never wheel in behind me, whom they regard (alas, perhaps rightly) as an incorrigible rattle-pate, an enthusiast unballasted by that solid, sober gravity and circumspection so necessary to those who would tread the narrow, labyrinthine and funambulatory track of worldly success. Happily, in this particular case it seemed as if the Provost of Worcester was going to bring his forces in with me; for when I wrote to him, in tones of such gravity as even I can sometimes assume, he wrote back to say that the arguments of myself and my friend and ally the Senior Proctor (Robert Blake) had 'converted' him. This, on 22 January, the eve of the Heads of Houses meeting, seemed an important conversion.

Then, next day, came the meeting. Scarcely had the last pious organ-notes of the memorial-service for Lord Halifax died away in the university church when the 'heads of houses' gathered in the Delegates' Room, a hundred yards away, under the brisk and ruthless chairmanship of Sir Maurice Bowra. At this point you may well ask, what is the constitutional position of the heads of houses in such a matter? The answer is, None:

none at all. In fact, since the Reforms of 1850, the heads of houses, as a body, are quite unrecognised by the university, all power having then been transferred from them to the Hebdomadal Council, on which some of them indeed sit but of which the majority of members are elected. Nevertheless, there is of course no reason why the heads of houses should not meet informally, just as the college bursars or college chefs or any other persons in this home of liberty may meet together for informal discussion, – provided that it is realised that they have no power to conclude anything, or to represent the university, or to act in its name. In this particular case, no one objected to the heads of houses starting the ball rolling. Someone had to start it; so why not they? The normal procedure would then be for the Vice-Chancellor to summon a general meeting of the university to his college hall and try to find the sense of such a meeting in the matter. To such a general meeting the meeting of heads of houses would be considered as an informal preparation.

Thus the heads of houses came to the meeting, for the most part, quite unprepared. They came not to conclude – they had no power to conclude – but to deliberate, to think aloud. As Sir William Hayter,[8] the Warden of New College, afterwards admitted to me, 'not one of us went into that building expecting to vote for Franks'. But in fact one man did. Maurice Bowra, from the start, was decided and prepared; and the skill and rapidity with which he contrived the result cannot but extort, even from his adversaries, a reluctant admiration. How he did it, – how he shouted the Prime Minister's name down, swept Lord Salisbury aside as 'no friend to the University', secured a voice here in favour of a non-political nomination, a murmur there in favour of a 'working chancellor', and then, by ventriloquial use of his own massive vocal powers, created the illusion of general consent to such propositions as he had himself indirectly started – I have not time to describe. Suffice it that, at a given moment, astutely chosen by him, he called for a vote on certain names, the only names which he had allowed to go forward, names which, it was observed, did *not* include that of the Prime Minister. When the votes were counted, it was found that Sir Oliver Franks, with 18 votes, had a majority over his next rival, Lord Bridges. Lord Salisbury was third, with 5 votes.

And now, as it seems to me, Maurice made his great error. And yet, can one say that? For in fact he very nearly pulled it off. Like Hitler in 1941, he saw before him victory so large and decisive that, at that moment, the risks seemed trivial; and after victory, who would have challenged him on petty

---

[8] Sir William Hayter (1906–1995), Ambassador in Moscow 1953–7, Warden of New College 1958–76.

points of procedure? Of course he should have said, 'Well, it seems that the heads of houses prefer Franks; let us now disperse, sound our colleges, or have a general meeting, and return to this building a week hence to nominate a candidate.' But in fact he did not do this. In fact, he said: 'Franks has it!' and at once, on the spot, he circulated a paper asking for the signatures of all those who would now agree to nominate the agreed candidate, Sir Oliver Franks. When the paper returned to him, he was gratified to notice that whereas only 18 persons had voted for Franks, 27 had now signed for him: another nine, having seen the way the wind was blowing, had adhered to the majority. Thereupon Maurice proposed to send a telegram to Franks (then in India), in the name of 27 out of the 33 heads of houses, inviting him to accept their nomination. And he would have done so had not the registrar protested and obliged him to wait, not indeed for a general meeting (as past custom required), but at least till after the meeting of Hebdomadal Council on Tuesday, three days later.

Meanwhile, what of J.C. Masterman, in whom I had put my trust? Alas, when J.C. saw the way the wind was blowing, he too bowed before it. He did not indeed vote for Franks, or sign for him. Indeed, he made a short speech, naming no one, coming out on no side, but explicitly reserving his own freedom of action for the future, until he should see upon which side a prudent man could with safety and dignity come out. Next day, after I had both called on him and written to him, begging him to resist, he wrote me a letter saying that, on mature reflexion, he had decided that Franks was an excellent choice, and that he hoped he would be unopposed. Afterwards – six weeks afterwards, when he had at last emerged from his long and dignified neutrality (and emerged on the winning side, just in time to be carried forward as its leader, or at least its totem-pole), he confessed to me that he had thought the landslide had gone too far: that it was irreversible.

At this point two questions naturally arise. First, why did Maurice plump for Franks? Secondly, why did the Heads of Houses fall in so readily with his plans? Of course it may be said that Franks is a very able man. Undoubtedly he is. But he is also a very dull man. He is completely without intellectual distinction. His success has been entirely as an administrator, not as an intellectual; and no one wants a Chancellor who administers, least of all one who, like Franks, lives in Oxford and gets in the way, or can be dragged into the way, all the time. The more I ask myself the first of these two questions, the more perplexing I find it. I have asked Maurice himself, but am entirely unconvinced by the retrospective answers with which he has now perhaps convinced himself. Moreover, the personal and intellectual differences between Maurice and Franks are such that they cannot conceivably be sympathetic to each other. Where Franks is intellectually ordinary and of dull, puritan, not to say sanctimonious virtue, Maurice is brilliant, gay, convivial, and intolerant of all forms of puritanism. In the end, I am forced to conclude that Maurice was simply determined, in general, to keep out a conservative politician (recently he has become more and more anti-conservative and, I think, genuinely wants to become dictator of the university under a Labour government), and, particularly, to keep out Lord Salisbury, whom he seems to hate; and that he decided that the only way to do this (since no socialist politician had a chance) was to run a non-political candidate behind whom he could rally both the anti-conservative voters and the university establishment. If this was his reason, he certainly reasoned well. Franks – who owed his appointment in OEEC[9] and as ambassador to the USA to the Labour government – has been supported throughout by many of the Left and all the 'successful' people in the university. As Chairman of Oxford Hospitals, as Visitor of St Hugh's College, as former Provost of Queen's, as Trustee of Rhodes House, etc. etc., he has links, interest, support everywhere, and his colleagues on this or that board or committee have, at the very least, been afraid of coming out openly against him. If Maurice was determined to have a non-political administrator, whose election would incidentally have changed the whole character of the office, he could not have chosen a more likely candidate than Franks.

The second question, why the heads of houses so readily supported him, is more easily answered. As you no doubt know, our heads of houses are, on the whole, men (as Curzon described Stanley Baldwin) 'of the utmost insignificance'. They are elected to their positions – positions of outward grandeur – by their colleagues, and are generally 'compromise candidates' – i.e. persons elected not because of their positive qualities but because, thanks to the lack of such qualities, they have, for the past twenty years, divided their colleagues the least. Having reached eminence in this way, these men are eager to preserve it by the same technique, *viz:* by preventing any issue from arising which can ever divide the world around or beneath them and by ensuring that whenever a post is to be filled, it be filled, as theirs have been, by compromise, not election. For like all administrators – from Mr Khrushchev to Dr Salazar[10] – there is nothing our university establishment dislikes so much as a real election; and no election is in danger of being so real, of enlisting so much of the outside, untimid,

---

[9] Organisation for European Economic Cooperation.
[10] Antonio Salazar (1889–1970), the despotic Prime Minister of Portugal 1932–68, had a longer political ascendancy than any other twentieth-century European leader.

non-academic electorate, the disorderly, lay, genial Country Party, impatient of professionals, 'courtiers', academic civil servants, etc., as an election to the Chancellorship, where every MA can vote provided only that he comes up to vote in person. In the meeting of heads of houses this argument was freely and effectively used. 'Above everything,' one head said after another, 'we must avoid an election!' and at that word they all shuddered, and drew together under the dull, protective name of Franks, which, it was thought, was a talisman against any such calamity. Unfortunately, from their own point of view, they drew *too* closely together. By making Franks, in effect, the nominee of the heads of houses only, they sought to confine the election not merely to the resident teaching and administering members of the university at the expense of the 'Country Party' but also to the little caucus of 'heads of houses' at the expense of the rest of the resident teaching and administering members of the university. That, as it proved, was an error. Even the academic body, though not bold, is not quite so timid as the caucus of its heads.

For a long time we have been becalmed at 23 January, and unless we move faster, I fear we may never reach the actual election; so let us now take a bold leap forward, to Tuesday 26 January, when the Hebdomadal Council was to meet. Here Maurice Bowra, presiding over it too as Vice-Chancellor, announced that the heads of houses – 27 of them – had agreed to nominate Franks. When this was announced, members of Council were pretty restive, and the Senior Proctor, at my request, firmly stated, as a matter of fact, that the Prime Minister would be asked to stand, and that it would be quite wrong to suppose, or to let Sir Oliver Franks suppose, that his nomination would be uncontested. At this point it would have been possible and proper for Maurice to say that, in that case, we should agree to a moratorium: that neither party would nominate anyone until some agreement had been reached within the university; but in fact he did not do so. In fact, so confident was he in the support of his 27 heads of houses and his lead in point of time, that he thought he could plunge forward and secure an uncontested victory before we could even mobilise to resist him. He therefore prudently did *not* call for a vote in council but dissolved the meeting without any record of its views and immediately thereafter sent the invitation to Franks in India. In deference to the views of Council, he stated, in the invitation, that an uncontested election could not be guaranteed, but he did not say who the rival might be, and he no doubt reckoned that Franks, seeing himself invited by 27 heads of colleges, and assuming that these heads represented their colleges, would suppose himself invited by almost the whole university, and would accept nomination before the Prime Minister (then in Africa) could even be approached by us. And then, he reckoned, the Prime Minister would never agree to enter the lists. Why should he, when the university had already declared itself, when its candidate was already in the field, and when, by entering, he would merely risk defeat as the candidate of an insignificant minority party? In thinking thus, as I am sure he did think, Maurice made a great mistake: he misunderstood the character of the Prime Minister.

For now the scene changes and we must switch from Maurice Bowra and his party to me and mine (if I may, for convenience, use such egotistical terms). For when Maurice swept ahead, as it seemed to him, and indeed to J.C. and almost everyone else, to a certain victory, we did not despair. I know the PM personally (he has been my publisher for twenty years) and think that I know his character. I know him as a gay, cavalier figure, ready for battle, fond of life and an occasional skirmish, and, above all, a rebel: a rebel against the Establishment. He was a rebel in the Tory party in the 1930s, and, in a sense, he is a rebel still. In this sense he is very like Winston Churchill, whom he greatly admires. Throughout his career, as throughout Winston's, the official Tory party has been against him, or at least (even when, ultimately, accepting him as its leader) has distrusted him. This is one reason why I admire him. He is in the great tradition of Disraeli and Winston as opposed to that other tradition of Bonar Law and Baldwin – men who, by their mediocrity, really represented instead of commanding the dull, impersonal, conventional, respectable forces of the Establishment.

I have used the word Establishment often, and am ashamed of doing so, for it is a hackneyed word without any agreed meaning.[11] But I use it for convenience to represent a force which, I think, does exist. By it I mean *not* the English ruling class, which is far more original, interesting and various, but that essentially dull, conventional, respectable and, above all, successful world which, in an entirely impersonal, anonymous way, dominates the established institutions of England. (Being married to a Scot, I always, in self-defence, say England, not Britain; perhaps, in writing to *you*, the blood of whose ancestors has so often dyed the Bannock Burn red, I should, in civility, say Britain; but it is hard to change.) To this concept of the Establishment I shall have to return when I describe the election itself – if, in this snail-paced letter I ever get so far – but meanwhile it is enough to define it and to say that just as the University Establishment consists not of the men whose *names* one knows (i.e. of men of some *personal* distinction)

---

[11] The earliest known use of the phrase 'the Establishment' was by Hugh Thomas in a taxi passing the Royal Academy in August 1954. It gained conversational currency among thoughtful young men, and was first used in print by Henry Fairlie in an article discussing the Burgess–Maclean revelations in 1955. See T-R, 'The Establishment', *Spectator*, 21 October 1955, pp. 530–31.

but of the nameless, faceless Wardens of This, Provosts of That, Rectors of the Other, so the national establishment consists not of known men but of the anonymous (generally Wykehamist) heads of government departments, presidents of companies, editors of 'national' papers, chairmen of banks, etc.; and that the interesting thing is that both these 'establishments', thus defined, though predominantly tory in politics, *opposed* the PM's candidature at Oxford, supported Franks against him, and agreed that to have an election was in itself positively deplorable: a deplorable event which would have been avoided if only the PM had done what they all wanted, and sometimes advised him to do, – kept out. And I may add that the PM himself, as he remarked incidentally in parliament a few days after it, regards his victory as a victory over the Establishment, even over the Tory establishment, and enjoys it the more for that reason.

This being my judgement of the PM, I always, even in the face of Maurice's successive, lightning victories and the defection of our only ally among the college-heads, now united against us, believed that he would fight. I believed it not merely because he is a man of spirit, but also because he is a real intellectual in his outlook and, I thought, would love the position. But how was one to mobilise him? This was a real difficulty, because while Maurice was proceeding triumphantly through a vacant field, easily collecting nominators for an uncontested candidate, the PM was in darkest Africa, moving from place to place with hectic rapidity, being pelted with brickbats by black men in Nairobi and by white men in Cape Town. If we were to invite him, it was essential not to deceive him into thinking that the position was any easier than in fact it was. We had to admit that almost the whole university establishment had committed itself to Franks. But if we admitted that, might we not frighten the PM off? Of course we could explain it away, but would he, on such a whistle-stop tour, and between the brickbats, have time to read our explanations? On the whole, we thought not. So what were we to do? In our difficulty we consulted his friends. We asked his personal assistant David Stephens,[12] who thought it best to prepare for battle but not to sound the PM at all till he returned from Africa – which was not for three weeks. But good God, I thought, how can we keep our forces in being and indeed, as we must, augment them, for three weeks of absolute silence? We asked the Lord Chancellor, Lord Kilmuir.[13] He thought the PM would be very ill-advised to stand: from a political point of view he had very little to gain by victory

---

[12] (Sir) David Stephens (1910–1990), Secretary for prime ministerial appointments 1955–61.
[13] David Maxwell Fyfe, 1st Earl of Kilmuir (1900–1967), Home Secretary 1951–4 and Lord Chancellor 1954–62.

and everything to lose by defeat. Why then should he risk his political neck? Altogether, at this point, the prospects even of communicating with the PM seemed pretty dim.

And then something happened. In any section of life it seems to me that by the ordinary laws of chance one has a right to expect a limited number of favourable flukes. In this history, to compensate for our quota of misfortunes, we had two such favourable flukes. The first was that I had long ago accepted an invitation – an invitation which had long preceded any of these incidents – to luncheon with the PM's son Maurice Macmillan.[14] This invitation had completely disappeared out of my conscious memory until the day came for its fulfilment, and this day happened to fall just at the juncture which I have now reached in my narrative. Of course after luncheon we discussed the problem. Maurice was at once enthusiastic: told me he *knew* his father would like nothing so much in the world; and offered (since he was in daily private communication with him about his uncle, the PM's brother, who was dangerously ill) so to put the matter that a favourable or non-committal answer could be obtained at once, while a refusal could be absolutely ruled out at least until the PM was back and could consider the facts. We arranged that all the documents (including, I'm afraid, some very indiscreet letters of mine) should be sent out to his personal assistant in South Africa, with instructions not to put them before the PM until he had been two full days at sea on his way from Cape Town to the Canary Islands. In this way we reckoned that the PM would see them when he had rested from politics and was revived by the rest, when he was undistracted, *incommunicado*, and at leisure to read and consider and savour the details, and when he still had opportunities for reflexion ahead. And so indeed it was. A few days later Maurice Macmillan rang me up with a radio message from his father. The PM said that there was nothing he would like more than to be chancellor of Oxford; that he 'would not shrink from a contest'; that much would depend on the attitude of the head of his own college, Balliol;[15] and that he himself must judge, on his return, whether the support we had mustered would warrant his standing. Meanwhile nothing was to be said or done to commit him before his own decision.

Of course when I heard that he 'would not shrink from a contest' I was delighted; but I decided not to publish this as it might seem to commit him. The essential thing now was to mobilise Balliol College and to muster such a show of support as might convince the PM, on his return, that it

---

[14] Maurice Macmillan, Viscount Macmillan of Ovenden (1921–1984), publisher and Tory politician.
[15] Sir David Keir (1895–1973), constitutional historian, Master of Balliol 1949–65.

was worth his while to stand. In respect of Balliol College we were favoured by the second of our two flukes. The Master of Balliol was abroad and had missed the famous meeting of heads of houses on 23 January. Had he been there, I have no doubt that he would have drifted with the majority and ended up as a nominator of Franks. But he had not been there, and so he was still uncommitted: his political virginity had been preserved by the artificial chastity-belt of the intervening Mediterranean Sea. I therefore quickly organised the Balliol vote, and the vice-master obtained the support of the Master by telegram to Africa. In this way the first of the PM's conditions was fulfilled. The fulfilment of the second was more arduous: it entailed securing the signatures of at least 150 men of substance in the university in order to overtop the 149 signatories whom Maurice Bowra had easily recruited, in an empty field, for Franks.

I must admit it was not easy. For although I always believed that we could get the PM in, it was difficult to get the timid academic world to publish their names as opponents of their friend, their neighbour, their colleague, their banker, their fellow-trustee of this or that, Sir Oliver Franks. It was in collecting my fellow-nominators that I discovered how solid the Establishment, the world of the middle-aged successful mediocrities, was for Franks. However we persevered and, I must also admit, enjoyed it. What efforts we made in that fortnight before the PM's return! What funerals I attended for the sole purpose of lobbying my fellow-mourners! What committees I attended, what long-lapsed friendships I revived, what obscure colleges I suddenly honoured by my visits to their high-tables and common-rooms! Of course all scholarship, all lectures, all pupils went by the board: for undergraduates have no votes. And in the end I was able to send the PM a list of 200 nominators. If we were short of heads of houses (though we had seduced one of theirs, just in time before Maurice Bowra stopped the rot by publishing his list), we had 33 professors against their 8; and if the women – that conformist sex – were solid for Franks, ... well, the college bursars were solid for Macmillan: why, I can't think: possibly simply because bursars always oppose heads: I simply don't know: it is an electoral mystery, like the Liberalism of the Celtic fringe in Scotland and Wales.

It was on 15th February that the PM arrived in London. That night he saw my last report, and we awaited his reply. I have been told how the matter was discussed with the '1922 committee', the committee of Tory MPs. As so often, the political objections were stated, just as Kilmuir had stated them to me: 'you have nothing to gain and everything to lose'; 'you risk your neck for something you don't really need'. The PM's answer was summary: 'you might say the same about fox-hunting.' To that answer the solid ranks of fox-hunting Tory MPs could say nothing. Disraeli might have said the same to his followers, and been as unanswerable to them. A day later the PM decided. 'I'll take a chance on it,' he said; and at once I published my list.

What a splendid moment it was when the PM accepted! What astonishment, even mortification, it caused among the Establishment! *The Times*, which had tried to prevent Macmillan becoming PM in 1957; the *Daily Telegraph*, which had already published a positive statement that Franks would be elected unopposed and that the PM would never stand; in fact all the 'respectable' press, except the *Sunday Times*, were extremely stuffy about it. But by now it was a fact, and had to be faced. So a new set of problems was posed. The first problem was, would Franks stand down?; the second, if Franks would not stand down, how could we organise the Country Party to ensure victory?

Maurice Bowra, having failed to get Franks in unopposed, now panicked and wanted him to stand down. He even telephoned him in India in the hope of persuading him. But Franks was firm. He followed the precedent (you know how, in England, we always keep to precedent) of the Duke of Wellington in 1833.[16] Certain gentlemen, he said, had put him up and published their names: he would not now let them down. Many of the gentlemen concerned were by now only too anxious to be let down, but it was now too late: they had been trapped; their own weakness had trapped them; and now there was no means of escape. If their original leader failed them, a more radical leader (as in all revolution) stepped into his place. This more radical leader was the Master of Pembroke College, R.B. McCallum, who, only a year or so ago, had published an article in the *Contemporary Review* urging that the PM and most of his colleagues be impeached, and who now had no wish to see the same man, as Chancellor of the University, becoming *ex officio* Visitor of Pembroke College.[17] Under McCallum therefore the Franks party prepared to fight to the end; and we also prepared to fight. For of course, having persuaded the PM to stand, we could not possibly now afford to let him be beaten.

So a new period of desperate activity began. Hitherto we had been organising nominators only, and these, we considered, must be resident members of the university. But now we must organise voters, and here we

---

[16] Arthur Wellesley, 1st Duke of Wellington (1769–1852), Field Marshal and twice Prime Minister, was installed as Chancellor of Oxford University in 1834.

[17] Ronald McCallum (1898–1973), Master of Pembroke College, Oxford 1955–67 and university member of Oxford City Council 1958–67, gave incisive tutorials in both modern history and PPE and was an astute monitor of public opinion.

must organise not the Court but the Country. We considered that whereas the election within the university might go against us (though we hoped it would not), the country vote would be overwhelmingly for us: we could not see the country party stumping up to Oxford to vote for so colourless a figure as Franks. In this, I must now admit, we were wrong: we underestimated not indeed the popularity of Franks, but the tenacity of the Establishment even in the country. But I shall come to that.

What hundreds of letters I wrote in those last three weeks before the election! My hand is still feeble in consequence (perhaps you doubt this as I approach page 30 of this letter). To every schoolmaster, every parson, every bishop, every convivial city business-man, every backwoods peer whom I thought reliable I wrote personally, in my own hand, using arguments *ad hoc* or *ad hominem*. I soon found that one could tell a Franksite a mile off. Once again it was the anonymous 'Establishment' that was unsound. Bankers – after being rebuffed by Lord Brand[18] – I realised were rotten, root and branch (Franks is chairman of Lloyds Bank). Headmasters were generally unsafe: to them a vote for the PM was a vote against educational authority. My bishops I picked with care, having failed with the Bishop of Winchester (a Wykehamist and a former headmaster): I should have realised he was no good, but I wrote to him before I had got the pattern clear in my own head.[19] The newspaper world was unreliable, except for the editor of the *Sunday Times*, a former fellow of All Souls (All Souls in general was reliable: afraid of abolition by the tyrant Bowra). Rural peers on the whole were reliable; so was clubland, especially convivial clubland (Franks disapproves of all forms of pleasure). Parsons were very unpredictable: I had hoped that the cry *The Church in Danger!* might rally them (Franks being the son of a dissenting minister), or else the natural opposition of backwoods parsons to Franksite bishops – for surely the spirit of Dr Sacheverell is not dead in our loyal and orthodox rectories and parsonage-houses! But I am not sure that this was a safe calculation: Franks has become a conformist – it is part of his deadly respectability – and anyway the parsons think that, as a banker, he might somehow whack up their equity shares in the Mammon of the Established Church. As a general rule the steady, successful middle-aged men were the most dangerous: the giddy-pated young and the rakish old were far better. An old gentleman of

[18] Robert Brand, 1st Baron Brand (1878–1963), merchant banker and Fellow of All Souls 1901–32, 1937–63.
[19] Alwyn Williams (1888–1968), Headmaster of Winchester College 1924–34, Dean of Christ Church, Oxford 1934–9, consecrated 87th Bishop of Durham 1939 and translated 92nd Bishop of Winchester 1952.

85 came specially up from Colchester to vote for the PM, and Sir John Miles, rising 90, was one of my nominators.[20] Unfortunately I knew I could never get him to the poll, but he skilfully contrived to pair with an active head of a college who had nominated Franks. The Dissenting Colleges – Mansfield and Regent's Park – were of course solid for Franks. So, I'm afraid, were the women, who were dragooned by the heads of their colleges. I soon realised that our only hope lay in the married women, and I urged my few agents in the women's colleges to write only to their married ex-pupils, inculcating on those who had married sound Macmillanite husbands the Christian duty of obedience to their husbands, and on those who had married unsound Franksite husbands the modern duty of ostentatious feminine independence. I also persuaded several sound Macmillanite husbands to enfranchise their wives by paying up their back dues in time for the poll. But I must admit that on polling day the women gave us a lot of trouble. They are an unreliable sex (see the ancient philosophers, *passim*). I fear that Franks' moral uplift disguised as philosophy knocks them all off balance. There was even a moment when one of my allies, noting the large number of men holding children while women went to vote, cried out, We are lost (or rather, since all proceedings are in Latin, *Actum est de nobis!*)[21]

However, let me look rather on the bright side of the picture. Christ Church and Balliol of course were solid throughout, keeping firmly to our gentlemen's agreement that we each support our joint monopoly of the Chancellorship. All my ex-pupils turned up, and of course I also wrote to every parent whose son I had ever jobbed into Christ Church. One of them was a baronet whose son located him for me in Paris: I found he was coming over for Cheltenham races, so I made him come over a day early and break his journey at the poll. Another wrote to me from wildest North Wales, 'since you put my candidate in at the tail of the university, the least I can do is to help to put yours in at the head'; and he duly came, voted, and deposited a crate of champagne at my house *en route*. Sir Gladwyn Jebb, our ambassador in Paris, sent a blank cheque in order to pay his own and his son's back dues and so qualify both of them to fly over from Paris on polling day and vote for the PM. The last degree day before polling day was a splendid occasion: a marquis, three barons and (I am told, but it sounds excessive) fifty knights took degrees in absence in order to vote; so did several cabinet ministers, who were not going to miss promotion at the next cabinet-reshuffle for a trifle like this. The Registry tell me that they

---

[20] Sir John Miles (1870–1963), law tutor (1899–1930) and Warden (1936–47) of Merton College, Oxford.
[21] 'We are done for.'

made £2,000 in composition for dues on that day. On polling day my brother-in-law came down from Scotland, the bishop of Exeter from his diocese, a French marquis from Paris, a Scottish professor and his wife from Glasgow, an English squire from Westmoreland, and a Canadian businessman made a special trip by air from Montreal. I must admit I was rather cross with the bishop of Exeter, who had arranged a meeting of the governors of Macmillan's old private school in Oxford on the day *between* polling-days, so that many governors, unable to spare two days in Oxford, missed the poll. I instructed the headmaster to lay on a rich banquet and inebriate them all beyond the possibility of movement, so that they would all have to spend the night in Oxford, and could be wheeled up to the poll early next morning in barrows; but I'm afraid that even so some of them got away.

The election itself was a splendid occasion. Balliol – not usually a convivial college – laid on luncheon for 150 people. Christ Church kept open house for voters all day: the whole college seemed to groan under hams and bottles from dawn to dusk. So did our house. Queen's no doubt administered suitably frugal refreshment to the Franksites. But there were some troglodyte colleges which seemed to take no interest at all. Magdalen, for instance, sat buried in its hole, its fellows refused to come out on either side, and old Magdalen men who came to vote were given no food at all. (My stepson is in for a scholarship at Magdalen; we have now decided that even if he gets one, we shall refuse it and send him as a commoner to Christ Church.) St John's similarly remained sunk in grubby neutrality.

But I rush on too fast: I must steady my pace, for there are two incidents still to be described, which took place before the polling had begun. First there was the interesting case of Sir A.P. Herbert, formerly parliamentary burgess for the university.[22] In the early days of the battle, before the PM had been nominated, Herbert had been nobbled as a nominator for Franks; but later, when the PM was nominated, he was thrown into agonies of conscience, and went to my friend Lord Birkenhead to ask if there was any way of changing sides without dishonour.[23] I looked into the precedents and found that at our last contested election, in 1925, the then Lord Salisbury had found himself in an exactly similar predicament and had solved it by firmly and openly changing sides and publishing his reasons in a letter to *The Times*.[24] Herbert was duly informed and duly followed the precedent.

---

[22] Sir Alan Herbert (1890–1971), humorist, legal reformer and MP for Oxford University 1935–50.
[23] Frederick ('Freddy') Smith, 2nd Earl of Birkenhead (1907–1975), biographer, lived in north Oxfordshire and was a close friend of T-R.
[24] James Cecil, 4th Marquess of Salisbury (1861–1947), whose own name had been canvassed for the Oxford Chancellorship, initially upheld the candidature of the former Liberal Prime Minister,

But this time *The Times*, which had been growing perceptibly stuffier every day, refused to publish his letter. Fortunately Freddy Birkenhead's brother-in-law owns the *Daily Telegraph*, and although that organ was pretty stuffy too, a little pressure there ensured that the letter was published, not a moment too soon, in it. Xandra was particularly cross because *her* brother-in-law owns *The Times*, which had behaved so badly; but there is worse to come.

Herbert's letter was published in the *Telegraph* on Tuesday 1st March, and at once caused a sensation: it opened a way for all the jellies to wobble over into our camp. But we had more to come. For by now at last our ancient but unadventurous ally J.C. Masterman had been hotted up and had decided to come out openly on the side of the PM. As an ex-Vice-Chancellor, entitled to be heard, he wrote a letter of stupendous gravity and sent it to *The Times*, timing it to be published on the very eve of the election, which began on Thursday 3rd March. I myself, in view of *The Times'* general attitude, doubted whether it would be published; but my faithful ally Charles Stuart was, as usual, right.[25] He said, 'yes, they will publish it, but on Thursday morning, I will bet any money you like, they will come out with a leader in favour of Franks.' And so, sure enough, they did. In tones of such pomp and sanctimony as only *The Times* can use, its editor, Sir William Haley,[26] gravely adjured all Oxford MAs to vote against the PM, whose indecent candidature, he said, had forced upon the university this unedifying contest.

Haley's leader was a godsend to us, and to the Franksites the kiss of death. As Randolph Churchill hastened to point out, Haley himself had received his education in the island of Jersey, and the only degree which he holds is an honorary LLD, Cambridge. That he should presume to instruct Oxford MAs how to vote in a matter exclusively concerning themselves was generally regarded as outrageous impertinence, and caused many a floating voter to descend finally on our side. And then, while Haley blasted the hopes of our adversaries, God himself declared for us: both polling days were beautiful sunny days, such as might tempt any old Oxford man to revisit the place, – especially when the election had made the whole place as social and convivial as at a Gaudy or at Encaenia. On such a day, I thought, as I stood in the Bodleian quadrangle watching the queue of voters grow, surely we must *win*.

Lord Oxford, but, in a letter to *The Times* (22 June 1925), transferred his support to Lord Cave, a Tory lawyer-politician. Cave was duly elected.
[25] Charles Stuart (1920–1991), historian, T-R's wartime subordinate in the Radio Intelligence Section, Student of Christ Church 1948–87, Censor of Christ Church 1953–8.
[26] Sir William Haley (1901–1987), director-general of the BBC 1944–52 and editor of *The Times* 1952–66.

And yet, as I have hinted, we were wrong in one respect. We had calculated that the internal vote would be pretty equally divided, but that the
country vote would be overwhelmingly for the PM. In fact – as far as we
can judge by simple tests – our first calculation was correct but our second
was not. We assume that most resident voters voted on the Thursday, most
outside voters on the Saturday. Of course there are exceptions to this rule,
but by and large I imagine it to be true. Now in fact the PM was leading
slightly on Thursday night and only slightly increased his lead on Saturday.
His total lead, at the end, was 279, which, in a total poll of 3,500, was less
than we had expected. This conclusion seems obvious: the country vote
was much more evenly divided than we had expected.

Why was this? Was it that the name of Franks drew voters from West-
morland and Devonshire, Scotland and France and Montreal? I cannot
think so. Rather I think it was the genuine solidarity of the Establishment
as I have defined it, even in the country. This was confirmed by some of
my friends in the country. Lady Harrod,[27] who was in Norfolk at the time,
planned to organise a bus to bring Norfolk Macmillanites up to the poll,
but reported that she found 'so many unsound solicitors, doctors, even
parsons and country gents' that she thought it less risky to leave it to private
enterprise. The Macmillanites could be trusted to find their way up, but
any organisation might well be exploited by the Franksites too. And this
pattern was repeated elsewhere. In general my impression was that whereas
only the Macmillanites would make heroic efforts, the anti-Macmillanites
would take any convenient opportunity to come up and vote, not indeed
for Franks, but for the 'establishment' at which Macmillan's candidature
was in itself a blow. For in the end the supporters of Franks against Macmillan were *not* the supporters of the Left against the Right. It is true that
Maurice Bowra is on the Left and that Gaitskell came up to vote for Franks;[28]
and it is true that the respectable *dull* Left voted for Franks – but so, in fact,
did the respectable dull Right. But several socialist MPs who came specially
up from London to vote did so to vote for Macmillan. These included
R.H.S. Crossman[29] and Marcus Lipton.[30] The radical socialist Balogh[31] voted

---

[27] Wilhelmine ('Billa') Cresswell (1911-2005) lived at Holt in Norfolk, and had married T-R's Christ
Church colleague, Roy Harrod. The calm, pleasant character of Fanny Logan in Nancy Mitford's
novels *The Pursuit of Love* and *Love in a Cold Climate* is based on her.
[28] Hugh Gaitskell (1906–1963), Leader of the Labour party 1955–63.
[29] Richard Crossman (1907–1974), Fellow of New College 1930–7 and tutor there in philosophy,
leader of the Labour group on Oxford Council 1934–40, Labour MP 1945–74, Cabinet Minister
1964–70, editor of the *New Statesman* 1970–2.
[30] Marcus Lipton (1900–1978), Labour MP and relentless self-publicist.
[31] Thomas Balogh (1905–1985), an unpopular and even reviled Fellow of Balliol 1945–73, confidential economic adviser to the Labour party and to Harold Wilson, who rewarded him with a

for Macmillan. Altogether, I am convinced that the real division, as it worked out was not political: it was a battle between the Establishment and the Rebels, between, on one hand, the solemn, pompous, dreary, respectable *Times*-reading world which hates elections (indeed, hates life) and thinks that everything should be left to the experts, the professionals, themselves and, on the other hand, the gay, irreverent, genial, unpompous world which holds exactly opposite views, the world of the educated laity who do not see why they should be excluded from politics because they are not politicians, nor from intellectual matters because they are not scholars, nor from the university because they are not academics.

And now, praise be to God, this party, the party of the laity and the gaiety, has won. The solemn professionals have been defeated. It is a glorious victory. The PM himself is delighted. So am I. Oh frabjous day! Calloo, callay! Of course, as I began by saying, 36 pages ago, it will not, in all probability, make twopence worth of difference in the end. But still, a blow had been struck for liberty, threatened, as it generally is, not from without but from within, by the encroachment of professional administrators: a blow against the creeping paralysis of drabness disguised as efficiency, reaction disguised as expertise, moral uplift disguised as Scots philosophy. And, of course, the battle itself was so enjoyable. *They* didn't enjoy it at all, and wouldn't have enjoyed it even if they had won. Like *The Times*, they regarded it all as an unedifying contest (they would regard Magna Carta, the reformation, the Glorious Revolution, etc. as 'unedifying contests'). But *we* enjoyed every minute of it. And besides, we won, and 'twas a glorious victory ...

Of course I have only given the briefest and most sketchy outline of it. I am sorry I have had to omit, for brevity's sake, my happy comparison of Maurice Bowra with Long John Silver, the pirate captain, and the heads of houses with his captives, battened in the hold of his private ship; as also my eloquent description of the defection of Maurice Platnauer, the Principal of Brasenose,[32] from him to us, and various other details, some of which (I shudder to think) are now preserved in the PM's files – I have begged them back, but in vain: I receive promises, but they do not come. Still, if you are as insatiable as all that, I will fill in the picture when we meet, which I hope will be soon, and meanwhile, we both send you all our love. Come and visit us again in Scotland.

     yours ever
       Hugh Trevor-Roper

---

life peerage in 1968.
[32] Maurice Platnauer (1897–1974), classicist, Principal of Brasenose 1956–60.

Index

Canterbury, Geoffrey Fisher, Archbishop of, **245**-6
Canterbury, William Laud, Archbishop of, xviii
Caravaggio, Michelangelo Amerighi da, 33, 60, 61
Carcopino, Jérôme, **14**-15, 16
Carlisle, George Howard, 9th Earl of, 145
Carlisle, Charles Howard, 10th Earl of, 145
Carlisle, Rosalind, Countess of, 145
Carlyle, Thomas, 87
Carrière, Moritz, xxxviii
Carritt, David, **206**-7
Carroll, Lewis, 101
Carswell, John, 76n
Carthusian, The, 26
Casa al Dono, Vallombrosa, xx, 4, 38n, 47, 49, 257
Casandi, Signora, 116
Catholicism: T-R's animosity towards, xx, xxxv, 111, 197; BB received into Catholic Church, xxii, 14n; Catholic Church denounced by BB, xxxv; T-R on the Vatican's Index of Prohibited Books, xxxv, 197; English converts to, 48–9, 165–6, 180n, 181, 201; T-R's study of the Roman Catholic revival in England, 115, 121; and the Scottish aristocracy, 140, 180–81; the English Catholic *élite*, 159–60; and the English Right, 243; *see also* Jesuits
Cecil, Lord David, 283
Cecil, Robert (*later* 1st Earl of Salisbury), 115
Cellini, Benvenuto, 186
Cervantes, Miguel de, *Don Quixote*, 122
Chadwick, John, 255
Chamberlain, Dame Ivy, 19n
Chamberlain, Neville, 19, 20n, 22, 28n, 61, 209, 213
Chambers, Sir Edmund, 283
Champollion, Jean-François, 255
Charnwood, John Benson, 2nd Baron, 75
Charterhouse (school), xiii, 26
Chartwell, Kent, 26n
Cherwell, Frederick Lindemann, 1st Viscount, **26**, 28
Chiefswood, Melrose, 272–3
Chilver, Guy, xiii, xxxixn
Christ Church, Oxford: its Meadow, xiii, xvi, 178–80, 203–4, 222; T-R and Robert Blake at, xx; T-R as mentor to undergraduates, xxxiii; Princess Margaret visits, xxxvii; its pictures, 17, 33,

89, 95–6, 101–2, 192–3; T-R as Censor, 58; death of the Visitor and illness of the Dean, 87; redecoration of, 128; undergraduate behaviour, 145n; T-R leaves, 183n; and Moses Finley, 199; and Lord David Cecil, 283; and the Chancellorship election, 303, 304
Christina, Queen of Sweden, **90**, 108
Churchill, Randolph, **172**, 305
Churchill, (Sir) Winston: his memoirs, 24, 26n, 28; his paintings, 25, 26, 28; and Roosevelt, 33; suffers strokes, 118; as a rebel, 297
Ciano, Galeazzo, **19**-20, 27
Cicero, **14**–15
Cicogna, Contessa Anna-Maria, xiv, **168n**, 169, 203n
Cicogna Mozzoni, Count Cesare, 168n
Cipolla, Carlo, 74
Cippico, Monsignor Edoardo Prettner-, 15
Clarendon, Edward Hyde, 1st Earl of, xxxii, **65**
Claridges (hotel), 199n, 200
Clark, Alan, **9**, 11, 22
Clark, Jane, Lady, 11, 22, 159, 196, 267
Clark, Sir Kenneth (*later* Lord Clark): on William James's influence on BB, xxi; and Mary Berenson, xxiii; on Nicky Mariano, xxvii; at I Tatti, 22, 49, 267; T-R's views on, **52**; and Sebastian Isepp, 89n; his lectures, 99, 196, 277; and Alda von Anrep, 116n; and BB's 90th birthday, 157; and Kent society, 159; proposes BB for honorary doctorate, 169
Clarke, Sir (Henry) Ashley, **129**, 185
Clarke, Lady (*later* Virginia Surtees), 129, 149, 150, 165, 185
Clary Aldringen, Prince Alphonse, 258, 259
Clauzel, Comte Ghislain, **195–6**
Clementis, Vladimír, 259
Clephane, John, 251
climate change, 182
Cole, Mary, 53n
Colefax, Sybil, Lady, 49–50, 101, 113, 196; as correspondent with BB, xxxi, **16**, 84
Colenso, John, Bishop of Natal, 166
Collins Magazine, 219
Colnaghi, P. & D. (art dealers), xxiv
Colville, (Sir) John, 243
Colville, Lady Margaret, 243
Comenius, Johann, 10
Cominform, 10, 12, 20n

155–6; distanced from T-R, 198; rupture
with T-R, 244
Hamilton, Yvonne: introduced to BB's
circle, xxxvi; BB's description of, xxxvii;
brings news of BB, 72, 99, 241; and
Signora Casandi, 116; on T-R's love affair
with Lady Alexandra Howard-Johnston,
143, 149; in society, 148; at T-R's wedding,
155–6; distanced from T-R, 198; rupture
with T-R, 244n
Hammond, John, xvii
Hampshire, Stuart, xv
Hancock, Sir Keith, 131
Hand, Learned, xxxvi, **101**
Harcourt-Smith, Simon, 117
Harrod, Sir Roy, 156n, **290**-91, 306n
Harrod, Wilhelmine, Lady, 306
Hart, H.A.L., xviii
Harvard University, xxi, xxvii, 34, 38n,
76
Haslip, Joan, 117
Hassell, Ilse von, **9**, 25
Hassell, Ulrich von, **9n**, 25
Hayter, Sir William, 293
Hayward, Max, 252
Hegel, G.W.F., 251
Helen, Queen of Romania, 185
Helleu, Paul-César, 173
Helsinki, 20, 236, 238–9
Henderson, Sir Hubert, **70**-71, 86
Henry VIII, King, 87n
Henson, Herbert Hensley, Bishop of
Durham, xv
Herbert, Sir Alan, **304**-5
Herbert, George, 62
Herodotus, 15n
Hesketh, Christian, Baroness, 181
Hess, Rudolf, 93n
Heuss, Theodor, 259
Hexter, J.H., 130n
Hichens, Phoebe, **117**-18
Hill, Christopher, xxxiv, **17n**
Hill, Derek: at I Tatti, **28**, 84, 123n; and
Desmond Guinness, 88; his gossiping,
120; visits Balmoral, 127; in Armenia, 153;
and T-R's wedding, 156; his social agony,
172; in Donegal, 181, 182, 198, 202
Hillary, Richard, *The Last Enemy*, xvii
Himmler, Heinrich, 51, 59, 60n, 97
Hindenburg, Field-Marshal Paul von, 18
Hiss, Alger, **52**, 73
History Today, 171

Hitler, Adolf, 167, 206, 235, 259, 293; and
Mussolini, 34n; and Czechoslovakia, 61;
Hitler's Tabletalk, 74, 93–4, 113–14, 115, 124,
260; *Mein Kampf*, 74; his last days, xvii–
xviii, 183–4; death, xvii, 193, 200
Hoare, Sir Samuel (*later* Viscount
Templewood), 213
Hodson, Henry, **144**, 149, 150–51, 158, 253–4,
302
Hoffman, Heinrich, 211
Hofmannstahl, Lady Elizabeth von, 153
Hofmannstahl, Hugo von, 153n
Hofmannsthal, Raimund von, xxxiv, **153**
Hölderlin, Friedrich, xxix
Holland *see* Netherlands, The
Hollar, Wenceslaus, 10
Holloran, Father Patrick, **5**-6
Holmes, Oliver Wendell, 115n
Holstein, Friedrich von, 75
Homer, xiii, xvi, 24n, 95
homosexuality, 132–3, 211
Honour, Hugh, 181n
Hopkins, David, xxx, xxxiii, **35**, 38
Hopkins, Harry L., 33–4
Horace, 19n, 177n
Horowitz, Bela, 23n, 166, **168**
Horstmann, Lali, *Nothing for Tears*, 129
Howard-Johnston, Lady Alexandra *see*
Trevor-Roper, Lady Alexandra
Howard-Johnston, Rear Admiral Clarence:
resigns staff appointment, **102**; his
character and appearance, 119–20;
divorce, 129, 137–9, 142, 143–4, 147, 150,
151, 154; intercepts T-R's letters, 148–9; his
later legal manoeuvres, 157, 163–4, 167,
169, 170, 173, 194; third marriage, 173–4
Howard-Johnston, James, **139**, 225, 255n;
education, 167, 170, 173, 273, 304
Howard-Johnston, Paulette (*née* Helleu),
173, 260
Howard-Johnston, Peter, 139
Howard-Johnston, Xenia, **139**, 167, 170
Hudson, Geoffrey, 201
Hudson, George, 194
Hughes, Emrys, 63
Humboldt University, Berlin, 270, 271
Hume, David, 179, 250–**51**, 252

I Tatti: cypress avenue, xix–xx, 45; BB buys
and improves, xxiii; as place of
pilgrimage, xxvi–xxvii, xxx–xxxi, 44;
bequest to Harvard University, xxvii,

CHRIST CHURCH
OXFORD

6th July 1951

My dear B B

I must apologise for my long silence, or
at least explain it. As Sir Walter Scott observed, when
explaining the sudden intermission of Lord Ravensworth's
vast building programme, 'elections have intervened'; and
indeed, as you doubtless know, Oxford and Cambridge
are now the only places where elections are still conducted
in the old 18th century manner: with that elaborate attention
to the individual weaknesses, cupidities, ambitions etc. of
a small and personally-manipulated electorate. This Term
there have been three elections: consequently all research,
teaching, administration have been suspended, and such
~~has~~ social life # as has been allowed to continue has
been solely governed by the design to win over, by
appropriate attentions, that elusive abstraction: the
Floating Vote. But I shall descend from the general
to the particular.

Of the election in University College, from which your
distinguished compatriot. Professor Goodhart has emerged
triumphant as Master in apostolic _{if indirect} succession ~~from~~ ^{to} the
alleged founder of that institution, King Alfred, there
is little to say. Contrary to all Oxford tradition, the